The "Last Days" Timeline

Do You Know the EXACT Events of the Last Days in Their SPECIFIC Order According to the Scriptures?

- For Latter-Day Saints -

By James T. Prout

ISBN-13: 978-0-9985443-0-4

The Last Days Tin

www.LastDaysTimeline.com

Gentile Roman Empire BC-450AD

Middle Ages

Church of God Established Personally by Christ 30AD

Great and Abominable Whore Church Rises 300AD

Nephite K
Lamanites Rule America an

DOWNLOAD THE WHOLE TIMELINE IN COLOR FOR FREE AT
WWW.LASTDAYSTIMELINE.COM

neline

1. Brittish Empire 1540-1940AD

2. Rus Empire

American Revolutionary War with the Brittish 1775-1783

USA Formed w/ Constitution 1789AD

USA Mo

Church of God Re-established Personally by Christ 1830AD

Indian Wars 1730 - 1900AD

ingdom Falls
d Fall into Unbelief 400-1890AD

Lost 10 Tribes of

DOWNLOAD THE WHOLE TIMELINE IN COLOR FOR FREE AT
WWW.LASTDAYSTIMELINE.COM

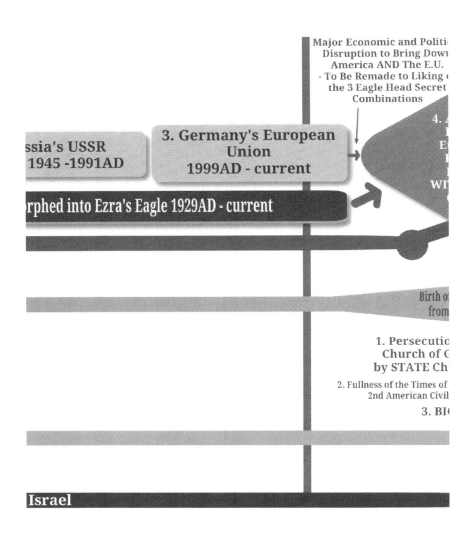

Major Economic and Politi
Disruption to Bring Dow
America AND The E.U.
- To Be Remade to Liking
the 3 Eagle Head Secret
Combinations

4.

E
WI

ssia's USSR
1945 -1991AD

3. Germany's European Union
1999AD - current

rphed into Ezra's Eagle 1929AD - current

Birth o
from

1. Persecutio
Church of C
by STATE Ch

2. Fullness of the Times of
2nd American Civil

3. BIC

Israel

DOWNLOAD THE WHOLE TIMELINE IN COLOR FOR FREE AT
WWW.LASTDAYSTIMELINE.COM

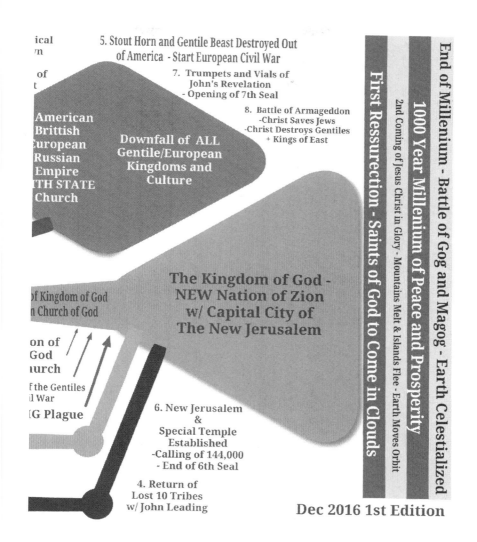

ical
ɪn

of
t

American
Brittish
European
Russian
Empire
TH STATE
Church

5. Stout Horn and Gentile Beast Destroyed Out
of America - Start European Civil War

7. Trumpets and Vials of
John's Revelation
- Opening of 7th Seal

8. Battle of Armageddon
-Christ Saves Jews
-Christ Destroys Gentiles
+ Kings of East

Downfall of ALL
Gentile/European
Kingdoms and
Culture

of Kingdom of God
n Church of God

on of
God
ιurch

f the Gentiles
il War

IG Plague

The Kingdom of God -
NEW Nation of Zion
w/ Capital City of
The New Jerusalem

6. New Jerusalem
&
Special Temple
Established
-Calling of 144,000
- End of 6th Seal

4. Return of
Lost 10 Tribes
w/ John Leading

First Ressurection - Saints of God to Come in Clouds

2nd Coming of Jesus Christ in Glory - Mountains Melt & Islands Flee - Earth Moves Orbit

1000 Year Millenium of Peace and Prosperity

End of Millenium - Battle of Gog and Magog - Earth Celestialized

Dec 2016 1st Edition

DOWNLOAD THE WHOLE TIMELINE IN COLOR FOR FREE AT
WWW.LASTDAYSTIMELINE.COM

THE PRIMARY PURPOSE OF THIS WORK

The primary purpose of this work is to demonstrate with precision, what the future holds using the scriptures themselves. Not dreams, not visions, and not extra-curricular prophecies. Ranging from next week - to the Second Coming of the Lord Jesus Christ.

So, you may know how to prepare your family physically and spiritually for the exact events directly ahead.

This timeline of the *last-day* events in prophecy will focus on the: Who, What, Where, When, Why, and sometimes How. For a Timeline to be CONCISE, we must focus most on What, Where, and When or ... **What happens, When does it happen, and Where does it happen.** The Who, Why, and How, will be addressed in the Appendices. This will include much of the identification of the symbolism. Remember, we are focused on a timeline in this work.

This is a "living work". This is a book to keep on your shelf <u>for the rest of your life</u>. Refer to it often as a reference. Share it with your friends. Stay connected with me through the website www.LastDaysTimeline.com. As new material becomes available, I will update you and continue the struggle for **truth**.

I want the truth of a good timeline. That is all.

Nothing more than the truth, and nothing less than the truth.

Table of Contents

FOREWARD
By
Author Val Brinkerhoff

Why should you read another book on the last-days? There are three reasons I suggest you invest time into this work. First, there is new, worthwhile material on the timeline of our Lord's return. Most unique are insights into Ezra's Eagle, a forgotten vision of the ancient Prophet Ezra, where he saw a great last-days bird with differing feathers of note. James provides good evidence showing that the bird is a clear representation of the United States of America, and that its feathers are symbols for this nation's presidents, including one potentially tied to President-Elect Donald Trump.

Secondly, there is a solid overview of Daniel's four beasts, the nation's they represent, and the emergence of the last, fourth beast, a composite beast of America and other nations of the coming global goverment. Tied to them and other prophecy is a very useful, neatly organized and summarized timeline. It synchronizes all major prophets addressing our day, including the seven viles and trumpets of John's Revelation. James then summarizes this detailed timeline into an easy to use graphic for quick reference.

Of special note is the author's complete reliance upon the word of God for foundational support of his interpretation of symbols and the all-important prophetic timeline. Instead of dreams, near-death experiences, and opinions; there is the power, clarity, and the Spirit in God's word and the chosen prophets He called to inform the wise virgins among us, those placing their faith and trust in the Rock, Jesus Christ. Those founded upon Him and His word will not be washed away when the wind and rains come.

I recommend you add the insights of this work to those you've already gleaned from God's informative word.

Val Brinkerhoff

ACKNOWLEDGEMENTS

No work of substantial importance is accomplished by one person. It is always a team effort. This is a big THANK YOU to those that helped with image artwork creation, editing, and with doctrine correctness.

I express deep gratitude toward my wife and my Heavenly Father. Without the support of both, this work would not have taken place.

How to Read this Book

This book is written in several segments. It was not written to be a novel to be read from front to back. This book was written to be more of a resource of all available material and prophecy on the subject of "The Last Days".

This book was also written to be very precise, without a lot of fluff. Your author has tried to keep the words to a minimum. That is very strange in the world of book writing. But, in the world of understanding and knowledge, if an idea can be stated simply, then that is usually best.

Prophecy is defined as information from God about the future, given to man.

There is no one man that has a corner on the market of prophecy, except our Father in Heaven. The living prophet of God has the right to prophesy officially for the whole church. This book is the assembly of all things and topics surrounding the future as stated by the prophets and apostles.

This work is unique in that it is a lifelong work. Once deciding to write a book on revelation and prophecy of the future, I came to the sudden knowledge that it is a never ending work. The topic keeps expanding as new insights into old scriptures come into view; also the events of the last days keep getting fulfilled. So, I have dedicated the remainder of my life to updating this book and this project with the most up-to-date information for the reader.

As a lifelong research project directed by the Spirit of the Almighty, I request your prayers to gain power over Satan and the darkness of mind that fills the natural man. For when this work is underway, I desire that the light of truth will wash over your mind that you may prepare physically and spiritually for the trials of fire for the Saints ahead.

This book is written to be read like an internet blog post. The main **Last Days Timeline** will have several appendices in the back of the book and the website www.LastDaysTimeline.com. Use these notes and links to discover more on the topics mentioned in the timeline. For the Timeline will not discuss in depth the subtopics. A precise timeline is what we want. The rest will be in the Appendixes.

Format and Printing

This book is <u>written in web format style</u>, to be easy to read in chunks, and easy to scan.

The book is meant to be printed inexpensively, to get the information out to the most people possible. It is not in color. The website reference link www.LastDaysTimeline.com will be placed on important images, so that you can see the **full size** versions in color for your study. <u>This book resource is to be used with the website www.LastDaysTimeline.com together.</u>

About Your Author and The Dilemma

Your Author for this book is James T Prout.

I am a veteran of marketing and business leadership and the use of the written word has been with me during my whole career. I have built and sold several businesses and love doing that. My mind works well in that field.

The #1 skill I have developed that has influenced me the most in writing this book has been the reading of 10-15 pages of a good book every day. I have been reading like that since 1997. When the total number of good books, good documentaries and audio books are added to the mix, I regularly cover 120-160 books, documentaries, and audio books each year. That is a lot of digested materials on a lot of different subjects. I am a good student and I take notes on what I study under the direction of the Spirit.

There was no plan to write a book at all. I like reading them, not writing them.

Recently, there was a prophecy last-days book written that I gleaned much good information and I felt edified. The next book I read was a "dreams and visions" book. It claimed many things that were against the scriptures. Yet, the author claimed their vision was "the truth" and that the scriptures were "misunderstood". I was shocked at how far off the vision's timeline was from the scriptures. This should not be.

I wanted a timeline that was straight-forward and answered the question of "What is the reliable last-days timeline from scripture?" A timeline that is good enough for my own family and friends to know what to prepare for *next*.

This work surely has my opinion woven into the fabric of the pages. However, I will do my best to state what is my opinion and theory and to keep the reader on solid footing with the research, rather than project the research to fit my own theories.

<u>Elder Packer</u> of the Quorum of the 12 Apostles said this about the hidden treasures of the scriptures:

> (<u>The Mystery of Life</u> Nov 1983)
> "For His own reasons, <u>the Lord provides answers to some questions, with pieces placed here and there throughout the scriptures. We are to find them; we are to **earn** them. In that way sacred things are hidden from the insincere.</u>"

I want truth and **only truth** will do for me…and I feel that many Latter-Day Saints want truth as well.

> (D&C 93:24)
> "24 And truth is knowledge of things **as they are**, and **as they were**, and **as they are to come**:"

Truth of the present, the past, and the future.

Sources and Emphasis Fonts

I will use *all* the sources that are known to me at this time. They are rated from very authentic down to less believable. However, we will include them *all* and then research under the direction of the Spirit to find the answers…..as to what sources should be added to the Timeline of Future Last Days Events.

This is an ongoing work and will be updated on a regular basis. When new sources or materials become available to me, this work will be expanded.

In the scriptural quotes and other quotes, I have added emphasis in **bold** and with **bold underline** for extra important emphasis. And any author explanatory additions to the scriptures are put in [brackets].

Authority for Conclusions

I have authority only for my own words and family. I have no authority for The Church of Jesus Christ of Latter-Day Saints in general. If there is a statement by one who has authority from The Church that is opposite or contrary to what I have stated, their statement should supersede.

What is the Purpose of Good Research?

Good research should get to the nitty-gritty of the topic and to paint the topic in a simplistic light, so that all readers can understand the topic.

If one reads the books written by Albert Einstein, his expansive ideas and concepts of atomic energy and waves are distilled into simple concepts that are easily understood by the common man. Simplicity was one of his greatest gifts.

The sequence of last days events will get better as time passes. There will be frequent updates to this book and the website www.LastDaysTimeline.com will hold much of the new information before it goes into the next edition of this work.

Identifying Prophecy is Like "Hitting an Archery Target"

Much of what is written in the scriptures and recorded in the written Word of God is interpreted through our own frame of reference. We all have a frame of reference. Our minds insert it, **before** we draw conclusions on the information we have collected with our 5 senses.

This means that our Frame of Reference prevents us from interpreting ideas and concepts the way that our perfected God interprets the same ideas and concepts.

(Isaiah 55:9)
"For as the heavens are higher than the earth, **so are my ways higher than your ways, and my thoughts than your thoughts.**"

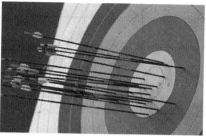

Reading prophecy of the future is always subjective. It can be no other way. It's like hitting around the center on this archery target. However, real history is like hitting the bulls-eye. When the events of the last days come to pass, it becomes history, not prophecy any longer. We will all have the opportunity of seeing how history is played out.

I Do Not Believe in a Truncated Short Timeline – This Stuff Takes Years

After looking at the compilation of knowledge on the subject of future prophecy and the events on the Timeline, it is quite clear that many of these things take years and decades to happen. Rome wasn't built in a day.

I do not believe in a truncated short timeline. As you will discover from the research, many of these things take years to come to pass. Christ's second coming is not going to happen tomorrow. But it will happen…as the events on the Timeline come to pass one-by-one.

Always Include the Spirit

Every church book and author I have ever read has always said to "pray for inspiration of the spirit as you read my book."

Yet, all of these books on last-days events have conflicting material and author interpretations that are going to be wrong.

THE PROBLEM: Literally, they all say their conclusions have been sought by the spirit and are correct. However, the authors of "prophecy last-days books" are coming to different conclusions as to what the symbol images mean and the timeline of how they fit together.

I do not believe that God the Father is the author of confusion. I do not believe that all the Christian churches in the world, with all their varying understandings of doctrine, to all be correct. The problem is the same with prophecy last-days book writers.

I do not claim any special "hidden knowledge" or dream nor vision. I simply have all the same material available to me that you the reader have.

Please pray for the Holy Spirit as you read this book, *and* also pray for me that the work of recording prophecy of last days events may be correct and *tightly aligned with real history of the future events* as they unfold as have been revealed.

I do *not* claim to have it right the first time. This is an ongoing work and will be added upon as new information comes into view. That new information *will* change my opinions over time. However, I am committed to this work of recording the Prophesies of the Last Days from all authoritative and semi-authoritative sources and presenting them to you, the reader, for a lifetime.

This is a collaborative work. I am asking **directly** for you, the reader, to participate in the ideas surrounding The Last Days Timeline. After you read this work and read additional work that is on this book's website www.LastDaysTimeline.com, please contact me and share your ideas… thus expanding this work. Thank you.

When This Book Was Written

The time of this writing is November 2016 through January 2017. This will be one of the only sections that discusses current events. The book speaks of prophetic timeline items that take place far into the future. Yet, some of the seeds of prophetic fulfillment are happening right now.

I want you that are reading this book long after 2016-2017 to know that this book was written directly for you. Also, for you to know the backdrop of history that the Last Days Timeline was written.

Donald John Trump was just elected 10 days before this book was started on November 18, 2016. The election was won because the battleground states had more people in the country rural areas show up to vote, as compared to the people in the cities. (Ohio, Wisconsin, North Carolina, Florida, Pennsylvania, and Michigan)

The non-peaceful riots of liberals against the democratic process that elected Trump happened during the writing of the main section of the book. They erupted biggest in the liberal voting states of California and New York; plus dozens of big cities across the nation generally starting November 9th 2016, the day after the election. They lasted strong for 10 days, with small bursts into Feb 2017. The liberal protesters blocked freeways, burned offices, looted, sprayed grafitti, and burned flags. Liberal funders were busing people into the protest areas, to stoke the fire for several more days.

Blocks of buses in Chigago transporting protestors. Who paid for the buses?

Some Trump supporters were physically attacked. There was even a kidnapping of a Trump supporter. (For more pictures and videos, see www.LastDaysTimeline.com/donald-trump-riots)

These people were rioting by the 10s of thousands, simply because they lost a democraticly held election. **This is not normal**.

The main timeline section of the book was finished on December 9th, 2016. The Appendices and images were done over Christmas and New Years 2016. The final tuning of the message and test-reader mark-ups were added during Jan 20, 2017; Donald J. Trump's Inauguration Day as President.

He lived to be inaugurated. That was a concern of many that it might not happen. Even the "dreams and visions" crowd had predicted that Barack Obama was the last US President before America goes down.

The death threats against Trump on social media were huge. Several social media hashtags concerning "#KillTrump" appeared. All of that was coming from the liberal protesters that simply lost an election.

The Establishment was not happy that an outsider who had never held public office before, was elected to the highest public office in the land. Newt Gingrich in March 2016, long before the election, said during an interview with Fox News concerning the Republican Leadership…

> "And now they're faced with a very real prospect of Donald Trump becoming the leader of the party, and it absolutely drives them crazy." …
> "Because he's **an outsider**, he's not them, he's not part of the club. He's uncontrollable. Uh, you know, he hasn't been through the **initiation rites**; he didn't belong to **the secret society**."

This is the historical backdrop upon which the words of this book were penned. After dissecting Ezra's Eagle and the other prophecies of Daniel, Ezekiel, John the Revelator, Isaiah, Joseph Smith and many more; the more I see American political discord building unto a crescendo to fulfill prophecy of the future.

Time is in consistent motion. God's word moves through time to fulfill His prophecies and His purposes; to bring eternal life to man.

SECTION 1: Early America – and the Formation of the Great and Abominable Church (300AD to 1900AD)

YOU ARE
HERE

The Last Days Tir
www.LastDaysTimeline.com

Gentile
Roman Empire
BC-450AD

Middle Ages

Great and
Abominable
Whore Church
Rises 300AD

Church of God
Established
Personally by
Christ 30AD

Nephite
Lamanites Rule America a

1: *Before America and the Formation of America and the Great and Abominable Church*

Let us Start at the Beginning

The beginning we are starting with is the beginning of America and Europe. Before we can look at prophecy of the *current time period,* **which is most important to us,** we must first look earlier to get our bearings on the Timeline.

Nephi, son of Lehi, as recorded in The Book of Mormon, shows an angel of the Lord giving a communication of the beginning of a Great and Abominable Church in Europe by the Gentiles (See Appendix 1: Gentiles). This is important to yet future prophetic events.

> (1 Nephi 12:1-3)
> "1 And it came to pass that the angel spake unto me, saying: Look! And I looked and beheld **many nations and kingdoms**.
> 2 And the angel said unto me: What beholdest thou? And I said: I behold many nations and kingdoms.
> 3 And he said unto me: These are the **nations and kingdoms of the Gentiles**."

Learning Points:

A. The Gentiles live in an area of the world with a lot of smaller nations grouped together. The kingdoms are smaller and the nations are larger. (See Appendix 1: Gentiles)

B. This part of the Angel's vision to Nephi was not part of the last Chapter 11 vision. This is something (or somewhere new).

> (1 Nephi 12:4-5)
> "4 And it came to pass that I saw **among the nations of the Gentiles** the formation of **a great church**.
> 5 And the angel said unto me: Behold the formation of **a church** which is most **abominable above all other churches**, which **slayeth the saints of God**, yea, and **tortureth them** and bindeth them down, and yoketh them with a yoke of iron, and bringeth them down into **captivity**."

Learning Points:

A. It is among the Gentile nations that this great church forms. Where are the Gentile Nations? (See Appendix 1: Gentiles)

B. It is a "great church" or large church. The angel of the Lord said this was a "church" - not a secret combination organization, not a Jewish synagogue, not a Muslim mosque, not a general group of wickedness. We must admit that the word "church" was used. Let us not overlay our own frame of reference on top of this. Remember, this is the angel's language in heaven, not even Nephi's language.

C. THIS church is most abominable above all other churches.

D. It has the power to kill people, and has done it. Also to tortureth them and bind them down in captivity or a form of slavery.
   a. (**Author's Analysis**):This is no ordinary church of today 2017. What Christian church could get away with that in today's modern world? **Answer**: there isn't any. The governments of most Gentile nations now have Freedom of Religion. We are looking at a **time period** that pre-dates the modern world. Back in a time when **the church** was **a state religion**. And the **state** had those powers of death over its people. So, the real question is "*when* and *where*?".....and we are about to receive our answer.

See Appendix 1 for a good working definition of "The Gentiles" as used in the Book of Mormon. (See Appendix 1: Gentiles)

(1 Nephi 12:6 and 12:9-10)
"6 And it came to pass that I beheld this great and abominable church; and I saw the devil that he was the founder of it." (1st Nephi 12:6)

(skip 7 thru 8)

"9 And also for the praise of the world do **they destroy the saints** of God, and bring them down into captivity.
10 And it came to pass that I looked and beheld **many waters**; and they divided the Gentiles from the seed of my brethren [Lamanites]."

Learning Points:
A. The devil had personal business in founding this Great and Abominable Church
B. (v9 – **"When"**) Also the implication from "they destroy the Saints of God," is that there must be Saints of God for this evil church to destroy. So, the logic follows, that this is a **time period** when the Christian gospel was on the Earth.
C. (v10 – "*where*") Lots of ocean water was between the nations of the Gentiles and the Americas, where the Lamanite seed was dwindling in unbelief.

We will see in the remainder of this Section that the **location data** for the foundation of the Great and Abominable Church is Europe. As the Gentile Church held the Bible in their control and altered it and took away many plain and precious ordinances of the Lamb. The Great and Abominable Church was not formed in North Africa, The Middle East, or Palestine. It was Gentile Europe.

Author's Analysis:
I believe that **the time** of the formation of the Great and Abominable Church of the Devil that Nephi saw in vision, was after the late persecutions of the Saints of God by the Roman Empire about 300-380 AD. After it had absorbed the Christianity-of-the-day and made it a **state** Church by Constantine the Great.

The Great Apostasy from the true gospel of Jesus Christ had happened much earlier. The bondage effects of a **state** religion upon the fundamentalist Christians of the day were devastating.

(See Appendix 1: The Whore – Babylon the Great – Mother of Harlots – The Great and Abominable Church of the Devil)

This "Whore of all the Earth" **symbol** is very important to John the Beloved/Revelator's last-days message.

The Gentiles Come Across the Ocean to the Americas

Let us continue with what happens in *time* to the Great and Abominable Church and the Gentile nations where it was established.

(1 Nephi 13:12-14)
"12 And I looked and beheld **a man among the Gentiles**, who was separated from the seed of my brethren [Lamanites in the Americas] by the many waters; and I beheld the Spirit of God, that it came down and wrought upon the man; and he went forth upon the many waters, **even unto the seed of my brethren**, who **were in the promised land.**
13 And it came to pass that I beheld the Spirit of God, that it wrought upon **other Gentiles**; and they went forth out of captivity, upon the many waters.
14 And it came to pass that I beheld **many multitudes of the Gentiles** upon the land of promise; and I beheld the wrath of God, that it was upon the seed of my brethren; and they were scattered before the Gentiles and were smitten."

Learning Points:
A. The man who was separated from the Lamanites in the Americas that went forth upon the big waters with the Spirit of God appears to be Christopher Columbus. Columbus' first voyage in 1492 landed in the Bahamas just south of Florida on a small island he named *San Salvador*. He also sailed 3 more times and visited the Greater and Lesser Antilles. Also, the islands and coasts of Venezuela and Central America. (See https://en.wikipedia.org/wiki/Christopher_Columbus)
B. More Gentiles from Europe came after Columbus: the Spanish, French, English, Portuguese and more.

Christopher Columbus wrote a short book that detailed his journeys and how he was impressed directly by the Holy Spirit to accomplish his work. Below is a quote from this book in Christopher Columbus' own words:

(Book of Prophecies, Christopher Columbus, Introduction)
"At a very early age I began to sail upon the ocean. For more than forty years, I have sailed everywhere that people go.

I prayed to the most merciful Lord about my heart's great desire, and He gave me the spirit and the intelligence for the task: seafaring, astronomy, geometry, arithmetic, skill in drafting spherical maps and placing correctly the cities, rivers, mountains and ports. I also studied cosmology, history, chronology and philosophy.

It was the Lord who put into my mind (I could feel His hand upon me) the fact that it would be possible to sail from there to the Indies. All who heard of my project rejected it with laughter, ridiculing me.

There is no question that the inspiration was from the Holy Spirit, because he comforted me with rays of marvelous illumination from the Holy Scriptures … encouraging me to continually to press forward and without ceasing for a moment they now encourage me make haste.

Our Lord Jesus desired to perform a very obvious miracle in the voyage to the Indies, to comfort me and the whole people of God. I spent seven years in the royal court, discussing the matter with many persons of great reputation and wisdom in all the arts; and in the end they concluded that it was all foolishness, so they gave it up. …

It is possible that those who see this book will accuse me of being unlearned in literature, of being a layman and a sailor. I reply with the words of Matt. 11:25, "Lord, because thou has hid these things from the wise and prudent, and hath revealed them unto babes. …

For the execution of the journey to the Indies I did not make use of intelligence, mathematics or maps. It is simply the fulfillment of what Isaiah had prophesied. All this is what I desire to write down for you in this book. No one should fear to undertake any task in the name of our Savior, if it is just and if the intention is purely for His holy service. The working out of all things has been assigned to each person by our Lord, but it all happens according to His sovereign will even though He gives advice. He lacks nothing that it is in the power of men to give him. Oh what a gracious Lord, who desires that people should perform for Him those things for which He holds Himself responsible! Day and night moment by moment, everyone should express to Him their most devoted gratitude. …"

(Get this short autobiographical work of Christopher Columbus by FREE download at www.LastDaysTimeline.com/christopher-columbus)

As the Book of Mormon says, the Spirit of the Lord wrought upon this Gentile man to sail across of the Atlantic Ocean. As we know from history, Christopher Columbus was not the only European to come to the Americas. Many European Gentiles came seeking religious freedom from the **state** Churches. These settled in North America. We will focus our attention on these Gentiles.

(1 Nephi 13:15-16)
"15 And I beheld the Spirit of the Lord, that it was upon the Gentiles, and they did prosper and obtain the land for their inheritance; and I beheld that they were **white, and exceedingly fair** and beautiful, like unto my people before they were slain.
16 And it came to pass that I, Nephi, beheld that the Gentiles **who had gone forth out of captivity** did humble themselves before the Lord; and the power of the Lord was with them."

Learning Points:

A. These new white Gentiles were fair skinned. At least whiter skinned than the current Lamanites dwindling in unbelief. Nephi was familiar with the skin tone.

B. The Gentiles prospered over time and they were a humble people before the Lord. The Lord was with them.

We shall see next that these Gentiles were escaping religious persecution from the **state** Religions of Europe. They had the Bible with them. In other words, these Gentiles were seeking religious freedom. They were *not* connected to or part of the **state** Religions of Europe.

This precludes the stance of Spain and Portugal (which were highly Catholic at the time, and were literally forcing Christianity upon the natives in South and Central America.) Thus, we are looking at another group of European Gentiles other than Spain and Portugal... that Nephi is describing here.

The Humble Gentiles Receive THE Great Blessing of Independence

(1 Nephi 13:17-19)

"17 And I beheld that **their mother Gentiles** were gathered together upon the waters, and upon the land also, **to battle against them**.

18 And I beheld that the power of God was with them, and also that the wrath of God was upon all those that were gathered together against them to battle.

19 And I, Nephi, beheld that the **Gentiles that had gone out of captivity were delivered** by the power of God out of the hands of all other nations."

Learning Points:

A. Now we know **who** these European Gentiles are that were escaping bondage from the **state** Religions. The only nation that had a big war in the Americas (North and South) and lost badly was Great Britain (mother Gentiles) and the 13 Colonies of North America later to become the United States of America. These Gentiles seeking religious liberty were the Pilgrims that landed on Plymouth Rock and that had the first Thanksgiving feast with the natives after their first successful harvest season. Also, these Gentiles that were seeking religious liberty would include the Puritans coming out of Great Britain. A few hundred years later, these Gentiles from Europe would fight the War of Independence starting around 1776 A.D.

    a. (v17) Great Britain had hundreds of navy ships against the Americans which had no navy and only some merchant ships. So "upon the waters, and upon the land also" holds very true.

B. These Gentiles of the 13 Colonies soon were delivered from spiritual captivity (and physical captivity) of the European **state** Churches...in the home countries of the early pilgrims.

    a. (**Author's Analysis**): These **state** religions with power of death and torture were very real threats to the early pilgrims and settlers in America. The pilgrims on the Mayflower were moving around Europe for years and had their property stolen and their lives in danger for their fundamentalist Christian religion. They would rather risk-it-all in a new wilderness, than endure the **state** Religions of Europe.

      i. Just ask William Tyndale the translator of 95% of the Latin Bible into English. He was burned at the stake by the English King Henry the VIII for translating the Bible from Latin into English. Tyndale gave the English people an English Bible and was executed by the **state**. This happened just 6 months before King Henry separated his nation from the Roman Catholic Church and started the Church of England. *Both* churches were **state** religions with power of death and torture. Both churches maintained their power upon the principles of using force to control the beliefs of everyone within their reach.

C. The Gentiles in the 13 Colonies were indeed delivered by God out of the hands of all other nations.

D. As referenced in verse 18, "all those" gathered against the Americans to battle, were not just the Red Coats of Great Britain. The English used Hessian mercenaries from Germany as a large component of their ground troops against their own colony subjects.

(See the book "The Making of America" by W. Cleon Skousen for details)
(See the 3 episodes of "The Fire of Faith" by BYU TV for FREE on www.LastDaysTimeline.com/fires-of-faith. See how the King James Bible was really translated into English and the Martyrs that died at the hands of a state church to accomplish it.)

A Choice Land of Free Men that Scatters the Natives

We are now between 1776-1785 in Nephi's Timeline. And the official United States of America is being born as 13 Colonies and then we see more of what these Gentiles do and WHY they came.

(1st Nephi 13:30-31)
"30 Nevertheless, thou beholdest that **the Gentiles who have gone forth out of captivity**, and have been lifted up by the power of God above all other nations, upon the face of **the land which is choice above all other lands**, which is **the land** that the Lord God hath covenanted with **thy father [Lehi] that his seed should have for <u>the land of their inheritance</u>**; wherefore, thou seest that the Lord God will **not suffer that the Gentiles will utterly destroy the mixture of thy seed [Nephites], which are among thy brethren [Lamanites]**.
31 Neither will he suffer that the Gentiles shall destroy the seed of thy brethren."

Learning Points:
A. These English Gentiles in the 13 Colonies (United States of America) live in a choice land above all other lands on Earth and it is *the covenant land* for the children of Lehi, who is of Manasseh, who is of the Joseph who was sold by his brethren into Egypt, who is of Jacob/Israel.

B. The Gentiles start expanding into Native Indian "frontier" territory during the Manifest Destiny period of America in the 1800s and the Indian Wars.

a. (**Author's Analysis**): The Eagle of America is soaring and growing. America won the War of 1812 against the British. This time was on much firmer terms. America won the Mexican-American War in 1846. The Union won the Civil war in 1860's and stayed in one piece. America won the Spanish-American War of 1898. And through all of this... the Native Americans of Nephite/Lamanite blood fought the Indian Wars which ended in the 1890s. They weren't utterly destroyed. They lived on. Prophecy was fulfilled. These sons of Lehi will have a big part to play in the future of America.

The Manifest Destiny Doctrine was pushed to the extreme against the American Indians by John Wesley Powell of the United States Smithsonian in the 1860s-1900s. This was the time period when all the natives were rounded up and put in camps or reservations. The Native American Geronimo documented this time period. He was an Apache Chief in the American Southwest and Northern Mexico that eluded capture for decades. He even tells of how he converted to the Christian God. (Get the FREE audiobook of *The Life of Geronimo* by Geronimo at www.LastDaysTimeline.com/geronimo)

The Manifest Destiny Doctrine is directly related to The Indian Wars and the deep smiting of the Natives by the hand of the Gentiles. Yet, the Native Americans live-on today. The 1830 Book of Mormon spelled this out approximately 40 years before it happened. Prophecy Fulfilled

See FREE video clips demonstrating this at www.LastDaysTimeline.com/manifest-destiny

Focusing on the timeline, the Gentiles are in North America 1860-1900 and are smiting the Native Americans who are the seed of Lehi. But, the Gentiles themselves stumble in Christian religious matters.

(1 Nephi 13:34)
"34 And it came to pass that the angel of the Lord spake unto me, saying: Behold, saith the Lamb of God, **after** I have visited the remnant of the house of Israel—and this remnant of whom I speak **is the seed of thy father** [Lehi]—wherefore, **after** I have visited them **in judgment**, and **smitten them by the hand of the Gentiles** [Manifest Destiny and Indian Wars], and after the Gentiles do **stumble exceedingly**, because of the most plain and precious parts of the gospel of the Lamb which **have been kept back by that abominable church**, which is **the mother of harlots**, saith the Lamb— I will be merciful unto the Gentiles in that day, insomuch that **I will bring forth unto them, in mine own power, much of my gospel, which shall be plain and precious**, saith the Lamb."

Learning Points:
A. The Angel says that Jesus says that *after* Lehi's children in America are smitten with judgments of God by the hand of the Gentiles, that the Gospel will come forth in plainness unto the Gentiles. This is the Restoration of the Gospel through Joseph Smith Jr in the 1830s and 1840s.

B.   (Note there are many other learning points in this section about the **identity** of the Great and Abominable Church. See Appendix 1 for details)

More Books of Scripture than Just the Bible and Book of Mormon to Come Forth From the Believing Gentiles

We are now up to the year 1830, at least. The location is firmly the continental United States of America.

> (1 Nephi 13:39-40)
> "39 And **after it** had come forth unto them I beheld **other books**, which came forth by the power of the Lamb, **from the Gentiles unto them**, unto the convincing of the Gentiles and the remnant of the seed of my brethren, and also the Jews who were scattered upon all the face of the earth, that **the records of the prophets <u>and</u> of the twelve apostles of the Lamb** are true. 40 And the angel spake unto me, saying: These **last records**, which thou hast seen among the Gentiles, shall establish the truth of **the first**, which are of **the twelve apostles of the Lamb**, and shall make known the plain and precious things **which have been taken away from them**; and shall make known to all kindreds, tongues, and people, that the Lamb of God is the Son of the Eternal Father, and the Savior of the world; and that all men must come unto him, or they cannot be saved."

Learning Points:
A.   After the Book of Mormon comes forth of the Gentiles, unto the Seed of Lehi (Native Americans), more scriptural books come out. These other books establish the New Testament and Old Testament of the Bible as being true. This is the first mention of the New Testament. We now have the Old Testament "the records of the prophets" and the New Testament "records….of the twelve apostles of the lamb" mentioned in the Book of Mormon by the Angel instructing Nephi.
B.   Nephi uses the term "books". The angel uses the term "records". So, we can assume that both the angel and Nephi are referring to the same documents.
C.   After the Book of Mormon comes forth, there are multiple books/records to come forth. This is plural…more than one. So, this would list: The Bible (both Old and New Testaments), The Book of Mormon, plus 2 other books/records minimum. This is the 1830 prophecy.
D.   What could these other records be?
   a.   The Doctrine and Covenants of the Church of Jesus Christ of Latter-Day Saints. This group of records re-establishes all the doctrine that was taken out of the New Testament by the leaders of the Whore Church, and its harlots. The Doctrine and Covenants are direct revelations from Jesus Christ through his Prophet to his Church: full ordinances, church government, and temple administration is all inclusive. These things are hinted at in the New Testament, but are not complete as a record because of the removing of material by the Great and Abominable Church.
   b.   The other record is the Pearl of Great Price. It gives much greater light on a variety of very ancient topics.

c. We have multiple "records"/"books" mentioned in the Book of Mormon published in March 1830 before the Church was organized and **before** the Doctrine and Covenants and Pearl of Great Price were organized as books. Prophecy fulfilled.

The very next verses of 1st Nephi chapter 13, establish the Church of God on the earth among the repentant believing Gentiles. We are to the years at the *end* of the Indian Wars in America, about 1900 A.D.

The years in this revelation to Nephi get blended right here with yet future years for us in the modern age 2017. I will continue with Nephi's Vision of what happens next after a look into Daniel's First 3 Beasts of Chapter 7 and Ezra's Eagle in Section 2. NOTE: These 2 scriptural visions happen in the **gap** between 1900 A.D. and 2017.

SECTION 2: Gentile Europe`s Rise and America`s Rise (1540 AD to 2017 AD)

YOU ARE
HERE

neline

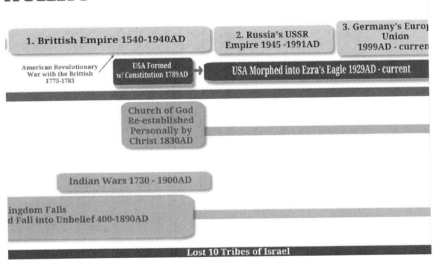

1. Brittish Empire 1540-1940AD

2. Russia's USSR Empire 1945 -1991AD

3. Germany's Euroj Union 1999AD - curren

American Revolutionary War with the Brittish 1775-1783

USA Formed w/ Constitution 1789AD

USA Morphed into Ezra's Eagle 1929AD - current

Church of God Re-established Personally by Christ 1830AD

Indian Wars 1730 - 1900AD

ingdom Falls
d Fall into Unbelief 400-1890AD

Lost 10 Tribes of Israel

2: Daniel`s Beasts 1-3 and The 4<sup>th</sup> Beast is Ezra`s Eagle Empire

This chapter will go back just a bit, in the timeline so that we can get a clear vision of Daniel's 4th Beast. This is important to set the stage for this evil entity that the Saints of God will be dealing with in the future to 2017.

There has been much speculation over the millennia as to which kingdoms represent these 4 Beast Kingdoms in Daniel Chapter 7. See (**Appendix 1**) to discover the evidence within the scriptures themselves, as to *when* these 4 Beasts would present themselves to the world.

Note: From Daniel's 4-Beast Vision, each beast does not "reign" at the same time. They come in consecutive order; one-after-another in a time sequence.

Let us now examine the timeline from the 4 Beasts in Daniel Chapter 7.

> (Daniel 7:2-3)
> "2 Daniel spake and said, I saw in my vision by night, and, behold, the four winds of the heaven strove upon **the great sea**.
> 3 And four great beasts came up from the sea, diverse one from another."

Learning Points:

A. Four "great" or large beasts came up from the "great sea". They all look different.

(Daniel 7:4)

"4 The first *was* like **a lion, and had eagle's wings**: I beheld **till** the wings thereof were **plucked**, and it was **lifted up** from the earth, and made **stand upon the feet** as a man, and a **man's heart** was given to it."

Original Artwork

Learning Points:

A. The first beast was a lion with big wings....but had its feathers plucked as Daniel watched. This lion was made to stand **up** on its two rear feet. This flying lion's wings were plucked.

    a. (**Author's Analysis**): We can *assume* that at one point it was a flying lion with great power. But, at this *time* in the timeline the wings were plucked and had no feathers, and it could not fly....and it was made to "dance" on its rear feet. Definitely *not as powerful* as it once was. It is more tame.

B. The feathers were pulled out.

C. Plus it was given a human heart, instead of "the heart of a lion"... as the saying goes. At one *time* it had a lion's heart. But, now in *time*, it has a man's heart.

    a. (**Author's Analysis**): I think this means that as a man's heart is full of problems in the sight of God, that this Lion's inner-self is now full of all the sin and problems of a Man's Heart.

Remember in old Biblical English "Beasts" are translated as "Animals". Thus, we are simply looking at 4 odd looking animals.

Author's Analysis:
<u>This awesome flying lion sounds a lot like the transformation of Great Britain in modern times.</u> At one time, Great Britain was the most powerful country in the world. It had the largest navy. The largest holdings of land and territory spread out all over the globe, in all seas. From 1540s through 1920s, the British Empire was in expansion mode.

"The sun never sets on the British Empire" (Christopher North of Great Britain 1829)

In 1919, the British Empire reached a territorial size that was larger than any other empire in the history of the world. They occupied land in every inhabited continent of the world. They held sway over one-fifth of the world's population (including 458 million people). This is a powerful "last-days" flying lion.

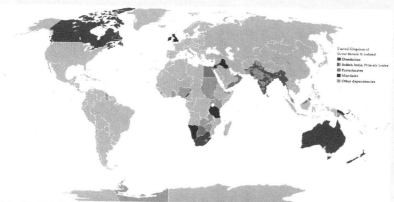

Every continent is inhabited by a British colony or presence in 1919-1922.
(public domain image) See full color image at www.LastDaysTimeline.com/british-empire

Yet, after World War 2 in 1947 Britain had had its feathers/colonies "plucked out" and was withdrawing from India because of Mahatma Gandhi's peaceful protests. Britain eventually released the Caribbean Islands to be free; also to withdraw from Hong Kong's 100 year lease later on. Canada, Australia, New Zealand, and South Africa were all released from major taxation to Great Britain and are now self governing countries with only small ties to Great Britain. This also goes for the holdings in Africa of Kenya and Rhodesia. And the death blow to Great Britain's former power, was the 1957 Suez Canal Crisis in the Middle East where they lost the

Suez Canal; the most strategic oil shipping lane in the world. This sounds like the plucked lion that has been made to "dance".

See the BBC documentary on Britain's downfall at www.LastDaysTimeline.com/british-empire

See also "Gandhi" the movie to understand the pressures the people of India were under when in the British Empire. www.LastDaysTimeline.com/gandhi

This prophecy of the Plucked Dancing Lion Kingdom is over 2600 years old. Yet, nations of modern times "self selected" their own animal mascots. England selected the Lion.

The "3 Lions" of England has been their Coat of Arms for a very long time. In 2010, English archaeologists discovered an 800 year old "3 Lions Badge". It dates back to the 1200s AD.

(See article here: www.LastDaysTimeline.com/british-empire)

The Royal Crest of England has an "upraised" Lion on it's 2 rear feet. This official symbol is everywhere in England. It also has the 3 Lions in the middle.

The Royal Crest of England on the Gate of Buckingham Palace

The Royal Crest of England in Stained Glass in a Church

Stylized Royal Crest of England on 2015 1 Troy OZ Gold Coin by the Royal Mint

The British Empire crumbled financially in the 1930s and 1940s under the weight of huge debt. The finances of the empire never fully recovered. Today, in 2017 England controls a much smaller realm than it once did.

It is my opinion after looking at the evidence, including more below, that the British Empire from the 1540s to 1940s is Daniel's 1st Beast – the plucked dancing lion.

The 2nd Beast of Daniel's Vision – Who is it?

(Daniel 7:5)

"5 And behold another beast, a **second**, like to **a bear**, and it raised up **itself on one side**, and *it had* three ribs in the mouth of it between the teeth of it: and **they** said thus unto it, Arise, devour much flesh."

Original Artwork

Learning Points:
A. The second animal is a bear that was "laying down" on one side.
B. It raised **itself**, not being made to rise as the Lion was.
C. The bear had 3 ribs of another animal in its mouth, between its teeth.
D. The ribs said to the bear to "get up" and eat much flesh. This "arise" or "get up" means the bear was previously lying down with the 3 ribs in its teeth.

Author's Analysis:

If the 1st Beast Kingdom of the British Empire declined in the 1940s, the next empire that rose up **after** 1940 would be the "bear" empire of Russia's USSR.

Notice these empires appear to be Gentile Kingdoms in Europe. Also, that they have the animal's image in their national identity. There is a trend developing here.

Russia has been a country for hundreds of years under the Czars before the Communists came to power under Vladimir Ulyanov "Lenin" by armed insurrection against the Czar and the royal family in the Bolshevik "Red October" Revolution of 1917. Joseph Stalin was a military general during the instigated civil wars brought on by Communist Russia itself and in the neighboring states. The Communists won each time.

When Lenin died in 1924, a power struggle to claim leadership of the Communist Central Committee ensued and Joseph Stalin murdered his way to the top; executing a massive purge of all those that stood against him.

Between 1926 and World War 2, Stalin and his government policies murdered approximately 10,000,000 people in Russia and its newly controlled territories including: direct executions, multiple famines caused by government policy, civil wars, political prisoner gulag camps, religious murders, etc... (See https://en.wikipedia.org/wiki/Joseph_Stalin)

By the time World War 2 started, Joseph Stalin was seated firmly in power in his own country of Russia, but Russia was in expansion mode. Russia fought off Germany's advance toward Moscow during the winter, and reversed them. The fighting continued on the Russian Front on the East, while the Americans advanced on the Western Front. All were moving toward Berlin, Germany.

Joseph Stalin, Lenin, and Kalinin 1919

After World War 2 was over, America gave back the territory to the people of those countries. However, Russia became the Communist USSR Empire. Russia kept it's territories that it conquered and put up the Berlin Wall separating East and West Berlin in Germany. Thus, the Cold War began. Russia's USSR Empire had "arisen and eaten much flesh".

The Bear Empire of the Russian USSR ranges from the 1940s after WW2 to 1991. Russia has self-selected the symbol of its national identity as the bear.

Dozens of Large Cities in Russia have Coats of Arms that Contain Bears	The 1980 Olympic Games in Moscow- Symbol was the Misha Teddy Bear During the Cold War	1980 Olympic Stadium in Moscow. Apparently the USSR in 1980 wanted to project a "welcoming friendly" Misha bear image to the world.	1987 USSR Minted Silver Bear Coin. A more "cuddly" rendition of the polar bear.

The "3-ribs" come under much debate. Online websites are buzzing with all sorts of ideas as to what the 3-ribs are. The scripture says these 3 ribs **themselves** encourage the bear to arise and devour much flesh. It's the rib's own voice that says this phrase.

If the "much flesh" that the USSR devoured was in the land grab of Eastern Europe under Joseph Stalin on their way to Berlin Germany during WW2; then the 3-ribs would be 3 kingdoms that were devoured BEFORE WW2.

During 1922, the Communist Bolsheviks were victorious under Lenin's leadership and Joseph Stalin's military strategy in creating the Soviet Union (U.S.S.R.) with the unification of the Russian Republic (Bear), Transcaucasian Republic (Rib 1), Ukrainian Republic (Rib 2), and Byelorussian Republic (Rib 3). All this happened before World War 2, where the Bear did arise to eat much flesh.
(See https://en.wikipedia.org/wiki/Soviet_Union)

The USSR crumbled financially as well. Mounting debt spending on it's military in the 1980s crippled the USSR as it tried to keep up with the USA in military tech spending. In 1989, the Berlin Wall in Germany was abandoned by the USSR military and the people broke it down. A few years later in 1991 the job of financial destruction was complete and the USSR defaulted on it's government bonds. The USSR Empire was over and the individual countries in Eastern Europe retook their own sovereignty.

It is my opinion that the Bear Empire in Daniel Chapter 7 is the Russian USSR Empire from the 1940s through 1991.

(Daniel 7:6)

6 After this I beheld, and lo another, like **a leopard**, which had upon the back of it **four wings of a fowl**; the beast had also **four heads**; and **dominion was given to it**.

Original Artwork

Learning Points:
A. This third beast/animal was a leopard. Leopards have spots and are jungle creatures that hunt prey. Leopards are a type of panther or jaguar. They are the same "large cat" animal just with different pigmentation. Also, they are prolific around the world and are called by different names. (See https://en.wikipedia.org/wiki/Black_panther) (The leopard is **not** to be confused with the Cheetah)
B. This leopard had 4 bird wings. Which means it can fly.
C. This leopard has 4 heads
D. And power was **given** unto it. Why would the scripture mention "power/dominion?" Don't all of these first 3 beasts have power of some sort? Yes. But why mention it with this one?

Author's Analysis:

If the 2nd Beast Kingdom of Russia's USSR Empire declined in 1991, the next empire that rose up **after** 1991 would be the "leopard/panther/bird" empire of Germany and France's European Union.

The 3rd Gentile Empire in Europe

Germany is the lead member (or body) of the 2017 European Union "empire". In the 2015 Greek Financial Crisis, it was **German Banks** that bailed out Greece and put the Greek people upon the austerity measures to limit government spending that were so unpopular. (See https://en.wikipedia.org/wiki/Greek_government-debt_crisis)

At the time, there was talk of Greece exiting the European Union "Grexit". The German loan modifications toward Greece were done to "hold the EU together".

Germany has **self-selected** its national identity with the symbol of the leopard/panther.

The 3 Panthers Coat of Arms of Baden-Wurttemberg is on the 1992 German Post office Stamps	The 3 Modern Tanks of Germany have been: - The Panzer Tanks 1937 - The Panther Tanks 1942 - The Leopard Tanks 1965	Silver Coin Minted 1317AD in Bavaria Germany Under Ludwig IV. Depicting a Panther

The 4 Wings of a Foul

Germany's official national symbol is the Eagle with 2 wings. The German Coat of Arms of the Eagle has lasted through the Prussian Empire, the Weimar Republic,

Nazi Germany, and the current modern age. The black Eagle on the German Coat of Arms was borrowed specifically from the Holy Roman Empire's Coat of Arms.

Current 2017 German Coat of Arms is the Eagle with 2 wings	1860 German Silver Coin Showing the Eagle of Germany with 2 Wings	1180AD Holy Roman Empire Coat of Arms

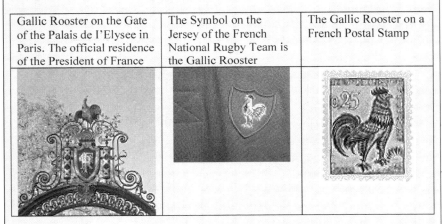

The second lead member in the 2017 European Union "empire" is France.

Germany and France have been the 2 largest influences in the EU for decades. France's unofficial national symbol is the Gallic rooster. It was an important symbol during the French Revolution and beyond.

Gallic Rooster on the Gate of the Palais de l'Elysee in Paris. The official residence of the President of France	The Symbol on the Jersey of the French National Rugby Team is the Gallic Rooster	The Gallic Rooster on a French Postal Stamp

Since there are no birds with only one wing, bird wings always come in pairs. These 2 fouls of Germany's Eagle and France's Gallic Rooster are the 2 dominant forces of the European Union.

FOUR Power Centers in The EU

Most Americans and people of the world do not know how the European Union was established or how it functions. There are 4 power centers. Below is a simplistic view of the separation of powers within the European Union.

1. **Brussels, Belgium** – European Commission – is a cabinet of officials from each member state. It proposes legislation and enforces law. One member is elected President by the European Parliament, not the people.
2. **Strasbourg, France** – European Parliament – is a legislative body. They vote on laws to be implemented across all member nations. They do not create the laws. The European Commission with President has the power to propose new legislation.
3. **Luxembourg City, Luxembourg** – European Court of Justice – The supreme court of law in the EU. One judge per member nation.
4. **Frankfurt, Germany** – European Central Bank – Prints the currency called "The Euro". The ownership stock is owned by each of the member state's private central banks.
5. Note: there are other branches of the European Union's governmental powers located in these same 4 cities.

(See https://en.wikipedia.org/wiki/Institutional_seats_of_the_European_Union)

There are 4 primary heads of power in the European Union. "The beast had also four heads". Heads are decision making centers of power.

The entire European Union was setup using **treaties**. The member states **voluntarily** gave their governing power to the European Union. "Dominion was given unto it" by treaty.

It started in the 1950s, after World War 2, but ramped up the power in the late 1990s and early 2000s when the whole of the Eurozone adopted the common currency of *the Euro*. One central bank has power to print the currency of all member nations. This is the source of the financial problems of the European Union, as shown below.

How Will the European Union Eventually Go Down?

The first two Gentile Beast Empires of Britain and the USSR broke up because of financial issues…too much government debt. It looks to be about the same with the 3rd Beast Empire.

Think of this: All the debt of the whole European Union is riding on Germany to hold it up. Britain just exited the EU ("Brexit" in Summer 2016), so Germany is left holding the debt bag for the whole EU. France can't help much with this problem.

The EU member states all hold the same currency banknote *the Euro*. It is issued by the European Central Bank. However, member states are still allowed to issue their own BONDS = Government Debt. Thus, it is advantageous for small member states to issue as much government debt as they can and have that debt paid off with Euros issued by the EU Central Bank. This provides a pseudo "free-ride" that the big member states (Germany and France) will bail out the smaller member states (Greece, Italy, etc).

This is what melted down Greece 2010-2015. There was too much debt and no freedom to print their own currency into oblivion (hyper- inflation). To hyper-inflate the currency to pay off the debt that Greece owed would have been par-for-the-course in the last 100 years. But, without the freedom to do that, because they were in the EU and couldn't print their own currency, Greece imploded by defaulting on their debt by 50% instead. (See https://en.wikipedia.org/wiki/Greek_government-debt_crisis   also see www.LastDaysTimeline.com/greek-debt-crisis)

Conclusion

The 3rd Beast of Daniel Chapter 7 is Germany and France's European Union with 4 power centers. The 4 wings of a fowl represent the 2 birds of Germany and France. Power was "given" by treaty of the member nations voluntarily.

Very Important: In 2017, we are living during the time period of the 3rd Beast. We now have our "bearings" on the Last Days Timeline.

Worldwide View

For those readers in Europe, this 3rd Beast of Daniel is a very real empire to you. Watch over time as it gains in power. Be prepared for when it will go down. It must go down *before* the 4th Beast of Daniel will rise. Remember, generally the British empire fell in the 1940s with too much debt. The Russian USSR empire fell in 1991 with too much debt. Odds are high that the European Union "empire" will fall because of too much debt.

For those readers in South America, Africa, and Australia/Asia; watch the 3rd Beast develop and be ready for a worldwide financial collapse of Europe and America that will bring the need for a 4th Beast Kingdom to rise. Distant goods and services won't be available for a time, between when the 3rd Beast falls and the 4th Beast rises.

The Unknown 4th Beast of Daniel Chapter 7, is Now Known.

The full Daniel Chapter 7 Forth Beast account will be given hereafter in a future chapter. We must fill-in the gap in the Last Days Timeline as **how** the 4th Beast rises to power after the 3rd Beast goes down. For that information was not recorded by Daniel, but was recorded by Ezra (Daniel's contemporary) in 2nd Esdras in the old King James Apocrypha of the Bible.

Daniel received the main vision of the 4th Beast and Ezra received the full detailed vision of how the 4th Beast Kingdom of the Gentiles rises to power in the last days. Let us see what the 4th Beast really looks like.

3: America`s Rise to Full Influence in the World— Ezra`s Eagle (1929-2017 Plus)

We were to the point of about 1900AD, toward the end of the Indian Wars, at the middle of 1st Nephi chapter 14. We will fill in the holes with Ezra's Eagle which picks up in the early 1900s… and takes us into **our near future to 2017**.

This material on Ezra's Eagle will be very new to most people. I first discovered it in the book _A Remnant Shall Return_ by Michael Rush (See book review www.LastDaysTimeline.com/remnant-shall-return). Rush did a great job identifying the feathers of the Eagle in the Ezra's Eagle Prophecy; however the work you are now reading, has additional symbolic identifications and comes to a much different conclusion as to the outcome of the final feathers of the prophecy. This book is being first written just after the election on November 8, 2016. This is important timing because of what happens with Ezra's Eagle and President Elect Donald J. Trump. Let us begin.

The Apocrypha – What is It?

Ezra's Eagle is recorded in the book of 2nd Esdras in the Apocrypha. 2nd Esdras was written by Ezra, a contemporary to Daniel, helper to King Nebuchadnezzar of Babylon when the Jews were taken away. This was just a few years *after* Lehi's family and Ishmael's family left Jerusalem.

The Apocrypha was included in the original 1611 King James Version of the Bible and was removed from the Non-Catholic King James Bibles in 1885. The Apocrypha was included in the Bible for a long time, and just **recently** in the last 130 years taken out. (see https://en.wikipedia.org/wiki/Apocrypha)

Joseph Smith was engaged in the work of translating the King James Bible in the late 1830s and early 1840s. He got to the Apocrypha in his King James Bible and received the revelation as recorded in Section 91 of the Doctrine and Covenants:

> (D&C 91:1-6)
> "1 Verily, thus saith the Lord unto you concerning the Apocrypha—There are **many things contained therein that are true, and it is mostly translated correctly**;
> 2 There are many things contained therein that are **not true**, which are **interpolations by the hands of men.**
> 3 Verily, I say unto you, that it is not needful that the Apocrypha should be translated.
> 4 Therefore, whoso readeth it, let him understand, for the Spirit manifesteth truth;
> 5 **And whoso is enlightened by the Spirit shall obtain benefit therefrom**;
> 6 And whoso receiveth not by the Spirit, cannot be benefited. Therefore it is not needful that it should be translated. Amen."

Learning Points:
A. The Apocrypha contains **many things that are true** along with many interpolations by man. Read it with the Holy Spirit in prayer to gain the **true material.** For it can be gained.

Note: I am not going to propose that the entire Apocrypha is true. The Lord told us that is not the case. However, Ezra's Eagle takes place in only 2 chapters. These 2 chapters fall within a piece of the Apocrypha 2nd Esdras (4 Ezra) that has been argued for centuries about being incorporated into the actual cannon. 2nd Esdras (Chapters 3-14) was so important of a work, that the Christian Church translated it from Hebrew and Greek to Latin by Jerome in 382AD…and **Jerome didn't like the Apocrypha**. **Jerome was overruled** and 2nd Esdras became an appendix item of the official cannon in Latin. Many Christian Churches of today in Europe and other places, still have this one book of the Apocrypha "The Apocalypse of Ezra" included in their official cannon of scripture.

(See https://en.wikipedia.org/wiki/2_Esdras and also https://en.wikipedia.org/wiki/Vulgate)

Currently the Church of Jesus Christ of Latter-Day Saints uses the 1769 edition of the King James Bible without the Apocrypha. This is why many church members have never heard of Ezra's Eagle, because we don't have common access to the Apocrypha.

You can read the Apocrypha online for FREE here:
http://www.kingjamesbibleonline.org/2-Esdras-Chapter-11/

Hugh Nibley wrote highly of the whole Apocrypha in his book *Since Cumorah*.

> ("A New Age of Discovery," *CWHN* 7:29)
> "What are the Apocrypha?
> They are a large body of writings, Jewish and Christian, existing alongside the Bible, each of which has at some time or other been accepted as true revealed scriptures by some Christian or Jewish group.
>
> Where do they come from?
> The actual manuscripts are as old as our Bible manuscripts and are sometimes written by the same hands, but their contents betray widely scattered sources, some of which are orthodox and some of which are not.
>
> Then why bother about them?
> Because writers of the Bible respect them and sometimes quote them, thus including excerpts of the Apocrypha in our Bible, while the fathers of the church in the first three centuries accept many of them as genuine and quote them as scripture."

So, as a source rating, the Apocrypha is right up there, just under scripture, because it was scripture for 1000s of years. However, the Lord did say that not all of it was correct. Read it with the Holy Spirit and pray for guidance.

The specific "part" we are going to read is 2nd Esdras. This book of 2nd Esdras written by the prophet Ezra in our Bible cannon was found written in Hebrew in the Dead Sea Scrolls. Thus it is older than the Bible's Greek or Latin translations. It's old. This one book *may be* higher than "interpolations of men"… because it may be part of the **absolutely true parts** that the Lord has affirmed.

I choose to believe these **2 chapters** whole heartedly… based on the researched evidence below…and upon seeking God the Father in prayer and asking if it be true. The Father confirmed that it was true to me. I encourage you as the reader to research this out, then seek Him and ask. He will tell you.

> **Important Interjection**: If you have a problem feeling the Spirit and getting answers to your prayers, simply read and follow D&C 9:7-9. Repent first and exhibit your faith by praying in the manner described. Research the subject in question. Pray and phrase your questions with "Yes/No" answers at first. Then wait and *feel* how you feel. It's that simple.

Ezra's Eagle Empire Rises in 1929 to Develop into The 4th Beast of Daniel

Ezra's vision of the Eagle was recorded in 2nd Esdras Chapters 11 and 12. Let us go through it verse by verse.

Author's Analysis:

Many scholars believe that this Ezra's Eagle Prophecy is speaking of Rome as the Eagle, because Rome used the Eagle as its national symbol. I have read material saying that Hitler's Nazi Germany is the Eagle, because the Nazis used the symbol of the Eagle. However, America also uses the Eagle as its national symbol. It's clear that everyone that knows of this prophecy is trying to match up the Eagle, but careful consideration must be paid to **the full prophecy** of Ezra's Eagle in both chapters 11 and 12. Not just "looking for a convenient Eagle", as the scholars have done.

This is the same situation the scholars were doing with the 4 beast kingdoms of Daniel Chapter 7. (See Appendix 1: concerning the beasts of Daniel Chapter 7)

(2nd Esdras 11:1-6)
"1 Then saw I a dream, and, behold, there **came up from the sea an eagle**, which had twelve feathered wings, and **three heads**.
2 And I saw, and, behold, she **spread her wings over all the earth**, and all the winds of the air blew on her, and were gathered together.
3 And I beheld, and out of her feathers there grew **other contrary feathers**; and they became **little feathers and small**.
4 But her **heads were at rest**: the **head in the midst was greater** than the other, yet rested it with the residue.
5 Moreover I beheld, and, lo, **the eagle flew with her feathers, and reigned upon earth, and over them that dwelt therein.**
6 And I saw that **all things under heaven were subject unto her, and no man spake against her, no, not one creature upon earth.**"

Learning Points:
A. The dream shows Ezra an Eagle coming out of the sea or water. One definition of "water" in the scriptures, means "many peoples". (See Rev 17:15 water=people. Many of the Beasts in Daniel and Revelations rose out of the water.) So, this Eagle kingdom is "rising out of the people", is one way of defining this verse.
B. The eagle has lots of feathers on 2 wings. Later on in the vision we see that the wing count is 2 (not 12). Also that there are 12 **long** feathers.
C. The eagle has some **short** (small) feathers. We shall see later a total of 8 short feathers. For a total of 20 feathers.
D. This eagle has 3 heads. The middle head is larger than the other 2.
E. This eagle apparently is "at rest" or sleeping. Even while it is soaring and exerting great influence over all the nations of the earth. The 3 heads are all sleeping.
   a. (**Author's Analysis**): My opinion is that the 3 heads sleeping means that the people working in the "background", not in the open. When they wake up, they will be working in the "open". As we shall see.

(2nd Esdras 11:7-10)
"7 And I beheld, and, lo, the eagle **rose upon her talons, and spake to her feathers**, saying,
8 Watch **not all at once**: sleep every one in his own place, and **watch by course**:
9 But let the **heads be preserved for the last**.

10 And I beheld, and, lo, **the voice went not out of her heads, but from the midst of her body."**

Learning Points:

A. The eagle comes down from the flight and sits upon her talons to continue sleeping. This seems to be quite a lazy eagle. It sleeps while flying and sleeps while sitting.

B. The voice to the feathers is not from the Heads, but from the Body.

    a. (**Author's Analysis**): My opinion is that the body is "the people" of this kingdom or nation.

C. The voice tells the feathers to "be alert and watch" in a consecutive fashion. Not all at once.

D. The heads are preserved for the end times of this Eagle Kingdom. (we shall see the explanation of this in Chapter 12 of 2nd Esdras)

God's Interpretation

Let us match up God's own Interpretation from Esdras Chapter 12

(2nd Esdras 12:13-16)

"13 Behold, **the days will come**, that there **shall rise up a kingdom** upon earth, and it shall be **feared above all the kingdoms** that were before it.

14 In the same shall **twelve kings** reign, **one after another**:

15 Whereof the **second** shall begin to reign, and shall have **more time than any of the twelve**.

16 And this do the twelve wings [feathers] signify, which thou sawest."

Learning Points:

A. There will be a "last-days" kingdom that shall be feared (or respected) above all kingdoms before it. (The "last-days" part shall be demonstrated shortly.)

B. There shall be 12 kings/feathers/Presidents/rulers, that come in order. Not all at once.

C. The **second** feather/king/President will rule twice as long as all the other feathers/Presidents. This, second feather, and some other feathers in the middle, are used in identification of the kingdom itself. So we in the latter-days could see it.

Long and Short Feathers

Continuing with the last days timeline narrative in 2nd Esdras Chap 11:

(2nd Esdras 11:11-12)

"11 And I numbered her **contrary feathers**, and, behold, there were **eight of them**.

12 And I looked, and, behold, on the **right side** there arose **one feather**, and reigned over all the earth;"

Learning Points:

A. There were 8 total **short** feathers.
B. On the **left** wing of the eagle (Ezra's right) the 1st feather/President rose up and reigned with great influence.

Author's Analysis:
This **right / left** thing had me pondering for 2 weeks. Either the few good feathers are on the Eagle's **left**, which is opposite to God keeping his good sheep on the **right**, and the goats on the left. Or, ... Ezra is simply looking at the Eagle and recording this vision on **his** right and left.

Either way though, it doesn't matter; just realize that the majority (14) of these initial 20 feathers are all following the 3 sleeping Eagle heads. The only feathers that give the Eagle heads problems, they will **eliminate**. Thus, the few good feathers are all short and attacked by the 3 Eagle Heads... as we shall discover.

For the purpose of the scripture below, we will **assume** that the Eagle's **left** is Ezra's **right** and vice versa.

God's Interpretation
Let us discover what God's Interpretation about these 8 short feathers are from 2nd Esdras Chap 12:

> (2nd Esdras 12:19-21)
> "19 And whereas thou sawest the **eight small** under feathers sticking to her wings, this is the interpretation:
> 20 That in him there shall arise **eight kings**, whose **times shall be but small, and their years swift.**
> 21 And **two** of them shall perish, the **middle time approaching**: **four** shall be kept until their **end begin to approach**: but **two** shall be kept unto **the end.**"

Learning Points:
A. There were 8 total **short** feathers/kings/Presidents that will have short terms of office.
B. Two short feathers of the 8 total will be "used up" during the **middle** of the time of the feathers/Presidents. Meaning, look for 2 short feathers during the middle of all the **Presidents**/rulers.
C. Four more short feathers will be toward the end. Then the last two short feathers are at **The End** of all the feathers/presidents/rulers.

The Extra Long 2nd Feather

> (2nd Esdras 11:13-17)
> "13 And so it was, that when it reigned, **the end of it came, and the place thereof appeared no more**: so the next following stood up, and reigned, and had **a great time**;
> 14 And it happened, that when it reigned, the end of it came also, **like as the**

first, so that it appeared no more.

15 Then came there **a voice** unto it, and said,

16 Hear thou that hast borne rule over the earth so long: this I say unto thee, **before thou beginnest to appear no more,**

17 **There shall none after thee attain unto thy time, neither unto the half thereof.**"

Learning Points:

A. The first feather/President had an end come and it faded off the scene of history.
   a. (**Author's Analysis**): Just like when the term limits of a President come and they go off the world stage.

B. The second feather/President starts to rule and it rules for a "great" or long time. It rules twice as long as any following feather/President.

C. Notice the "voice" may be from God, or the "voice" may come from the body/people of the Eagle. The text doesn't say. The "voice" tells the 2nd feather that none of the other feathers that come after it shall be even ½ as long as the 2nd feather.
   a. (**Author's Analysis**): Franklin Roosevelt died just months into his 4th term of office. He was elected for 4 terms and died in office in April 1945. Republicans in congress passed the 22nd Amendment to the Constitution limiting Presidents to 2 Terms in 1947; and was ratified by the States in 1951. There has not been any President elected to more than 2 terms after the 22nd Amendment was passed. Thus, "none after thee" has been fulfilled. So, to get our bearings on the Timeline, if the 2nd feather/President is Franklin Roosevelt, we have our year on the Last-Days Timeline set to about 1945. (See https://constitutioncenter.org/interactive-constitution/amendments/amendment-xxii)

The Feathers/Kings/Presidents Continued Their Rule…Consecutively

(2nd Esdras 11:18-19)

"18 Then arose the third, and reigned as the other before, and appeared no more also.

19 So went it with all the residue one after another, as that every one reigned, and then appeared no more."

Learning Points:

A. The third feather/President stands up to rule and does like normal and exits office at the end of their time. Then all the rest of the feathers/Presidents do likewise.
   a. Remember, there are **long** and **short** feathers/Presidents in this initial 14 feather mix. (more on this in Chapter 12 of 2nd Esdras)

(2nd Esdras 11:20-21)

"20 Then I beheld, and, lo, **in process of time** the feathers that followed stood up upon the **right side**, that they might rule also; and some of them ruled, but within a while **they appeared no more**:

21 For some of them were set up, but ruled not."

Learning Points:

A. "In process of time" means "after a while" or "a length of time goes by".

B. All the rest of the feathers/Presidents on the Eagle's **left** (Ezra's **right**) side ruled for a time and then were out of office.

C. Some feathers/Presidents were set up, "but ruled not." I do not know what this part means. If you have information on this part, please contact me and if it makes sense, we'll add it to the book.

    a. (**Author's Analysis**): My hunch is that a feather/President would be elected but would not take office at the Inauguration Day. This is just a hunch, *but* at this point we have not seen this concept happen.

No More Feather's on the Eagle's LEFT Wing

(2nd Esdras 11:22)

"22 After this I looked, and, behold, the **twelve feathers** appeared no more, **nor the two little feathers:**"

Learning Points:

A. Up to this point in Ezra's Eagle Prophecy, we now have 12 **long** feathers/Presidents + 2 **short** feathers/Presidents = 14 Presidents. These 14 feathers/Presidents are on the Eagle's left wing. These are all the feathers up to this point in the history of this Eagle Kingdom.

Remember, we have 20 total feathers/Presidents from the start of this Prophecy. Later (in Chap 12 of 2nd Esdras) we see that the Eagle's **left** Wing holds the 14 bad feathers (12+2).

Author's Analysis:

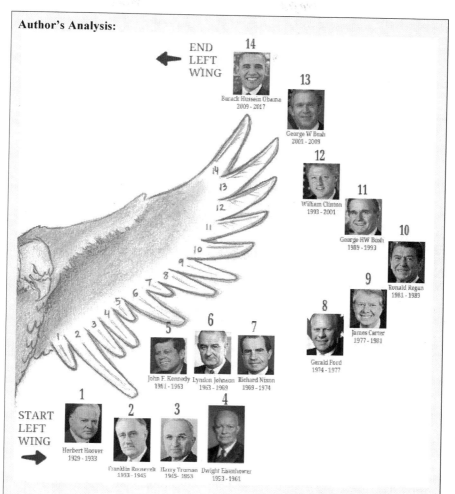

END
LEFT
WING

14
Barack Hussein Obama
2009 - 2017

13
George W Bush
2001 - 2009

12
William Clinton
1993 - 2001

11
George HW Bush
1989 - 1993

10
Ronald Regan
1981 - 1989

9
James Carter
1977 - 1981

8
Gerald Ford
1974 - 1977

5
John F. Kennedy
1961 - 1963

6
Lyndon Johnson
1963 - 1969

7
Richard Nixon
1969 - 1974

1
START
LEFT
WING
Herbert Hoover
1929 - 1933

2
Franklin Roosevelt
1933 - 1945

3
Harry Truman
1945 - 1953

4
Dwight Eisenhower
1953 - 1961

For Ezra or anyone else, to have guessed the precise Presidential sequence of the last 14 Presidents in last-days United States of America, the probability odds would be miniscule. In Rush's work, he calculated the odds at a number with 35 zeros. I don't think it's quite that that bad, but it's certainly small.

The statistics calculation: Taking a possible long feather or a possible short feather is a ½ or 0.5 possibility. Then calculating that over a 14 President sequence.

The probability = 0.5^{14} = .000061
That probability statistic has a near zero chance of occurring in real life.

You can calculate the even smaller probability of that 14 President sequence:

- Happening within an "Eagle" Kingdom.
- Occurring within the last days of the world.
- Being recorded by Ezra as a slave in Babylon 2600 years ago.
- Having the 2nd feather being twice as long as the other normal long feathers.

I see the foreknowledge of God is at work here. Ezra recorded the vision from God. God saw the future of the last-days Eagle Kingdom of the United States of America.

The Great Seal of the United States has been used since 1782. It is an Eagle.	Not only is America's official seal an Eagle, but the Presidential Seal itself is an Eagle, as well.

(See https://en.wikipedia.org/wiki/Great_Seal_of_the_United_States)

These 14 Presidents are the end of the "bad" feathers on the Eagle's **left** (Ezra's **right**) wing. The next section is where America elects a good ruler that will take "rule unto himself" away from the 3 "evil" Eagle Heads. *Then* the whole vision tumbles...into dark problems. Before the ultimate LIGHT breaks forth.

Before we go there….Let us stick to the **timeline of this study** and cover Daniel's 4 Beasts up to the present, about 2017.

NOTE: 1928 was the last time America had a **firm** Republican controlled House, Senate and President. Karl Rove says here that the 1920s and 1930s was the last time "a populist candidate" was in control. (See www.LastDaysTimeline.com/karl-rove)

We know that the beginning of the George W. Bush administration, January 2001 had slight Republican control of the House and Senate. In June of that year one Republican switched parties to become a Democrat and the control was lost. The Calvin Coolidge Whitehouse in 1928 was the last time that *firm* control was had by the Republican Party. The very next year, 1929 is the beginning of the Ezra's Eagle vision with Herbert Hoover as the 1st long feather.

Why Herbert Hoover? To understand this topic, we must understand the modern Prophet Ezra Taft Benson. Ezra Taft Benson served for 8 years as Secretary of Agriculture to President Eisenhower. This is a cabinet level position that is in-line for the Presidency under the chain of succession.

Elder Benson as an Apostle, served for a while in **both posts at the same time**. He had more first hand knowledge than anyone else in church leadership about the inner-workings of government.

In the April 1972 General Conference of the Church, then Apostle Benson gave a talk from the pulpit called *Civic Standards for the Faithful Saints*.

> (Civic Standards for the Faithful Saints, Apr 1972 General Conference, Ezra Taft Benson)
>
> "... Moroni could have pointed out many factors that led to the destruction of the people, but notice how he singled out the secret combinations, just as the Church today could point out many threats to peace, prosperity, and the spread of God's work, but it has singled out the greatest threat as the godless conspiracy. There is no conspiracy theory in the Book of Mormon —it is a conspiracy fact.
>
> (Space with nothing there in the text dictation of the speech...)
>
> Then Moroni speaks to us in this day and says, "Wherefore, the Lord commandeth you, when ye shall see these things come among you that ye shall awake to a sense of your awful situation, because of this secret combination which shall be among you" (Ether 8:14.)"

Video: https://www.lds.org/general-conference/1972/04/civic-standards-for-the-faithful-saints?lang=eng
Text: https://www.lds.org/ensign/1972/07/civic-standards-for-the-faithful-saints.p9?lang=eng

The text transcript of the conference talk on the Church website leaves out a small "blurb" at the 12min 30sec mark of video, where Elder Benson recommends that the whole church read the book *None Dare Call it Conspiracy* by Gary Allen written in 1972. The book contains:

- A forward essay written by a congressman.
- The Secretary of Agriculture (Elder Benson) wrote a snippet on the back cover.
- A former assistant to FBI Director J. Edgar Hoover wrote a snippet on the back cover.
- A Government Investigator on the Reece Committee wrote a snippet on the back cover.
- A Former Chief of Security for the Atom Bomb Project wrote a snippet on the back cover.

I have read the book *None Dare Call it Conspiracy* based upon the recommendation from Elder Benson and it says the Counsel on Foreign Relations (C.F.R) was founded in 1921. (See Appendix 1: Secret Combinations)

President Herbert Hoover was elected as US President in November 1929 and was an early member of the C.F.R..

(See – This URL lists President Herbert Hoover (31st President of the United States) on the list of early CFR membership: https://en.wikipedia.org/wiki/Members_of_the_Council_on_Foreign_Relations)

This would mean that Hoover was the first US President to start the control of the C.F.R. on the Whitehouse. Over the next 14 Presidents all of them have been C.F.R. members directly, or have loaded their cabinets and staff with CFR members.

(Get the None Dare Call It Conspiracy book here – www.LastDaysTimeline.com/none-dare-call-it-conspiracy)

This means, in my opinion, that the **current** 2017 C.F.R. organizational lead members and their corresponding international groups would represent *a part* of the 3 sleeping Eagle Heads that are about to awake and take an **active role** in governance of the United States of America.

> (None Dare Call It Conspiracy – by Gary Allen, page 87)
> "Today [1972] the C.F.R. remains active in working toward its final goal of a government over all the world – a government which their INSIDERS and their allies will control. The goal of the C.F.R. is simply to abolish the United States with its Constitutional guarantees of liberty."

This idea of "global government" and "internationalism" becomes very important as the 3 Eagle Heads wake up and take power in the world, as shown in the 2nd half of Ezra's Eagle.

Think of it: November 8, 2016 is the first time since 1928 that the American people have elected and given the Republican Party (usually the more Constitutionally conservative party between the 2 main political parties) the total reins of government: the Presidency, the House, the Senate, the important outstanding Supreme Court nominations, the bulk of the new state governorships, and the local county and city officials as well.

That has *got* to make those 3 sleeping Eagle Heads very upset. They like to stay behind the scenes and pull the strings of the feathers/Presidents. But, they are about to take a more active role and "waking up" after eliminating the next 4 short feathers.

Newt Gingrich said in March 2016, during an interview with Fox News concerning the Republican Leadership…

> "And now they're faced with a very real prospect of Donald Trump becoming the leader of the party, and it absolutely drives them crazy." … "Because he's **an outsider**, he's not them, he's not part of the club. He's uncontrollable. Uh, you know, he hasn't been through the **initiation rites**; he didn't belong to **the secret society**."

Many members of the LDS Church are familiar with the topic of secret combinations since it is taught in the Book of Mormon. Study it for yourself. If you are not familiar or are new to the subject, these are your best resources on the subject. (See Appendix 1: Secret Combinations) (See also Book Reviews in Appendix 3)

1. The Book of Mormon – by God
2. None Dare Call it Conspiracy – by Gary Allen
3. The Naked Communist – by W. Cleon Skousen
4. The Naked Capitalist – by W. Cleon Skousen
5. Strategic Relocation – by Joel Skousen
6. Foundations of Betrayal – by Phil Kent
7. Other People's Money – by Brandeis – Written in 1914. A detailed expose' on the power of the Money Trust. The data in the book comes from **before** the Money Trust was codified into law in December 1913. Available in audiobook for FREE Download at www.LastDaysTimeline.com/other-peoples-money

We have covered the feathers/Presidents right up to current with President Barack Obama. The future is in front of us.

SECTION 3: America Morphs into The Gentile 4th Beast Kingdom - Grows Rich - Oppresses the Saints with STATE Religion of The Whore Church. (2017 – future)

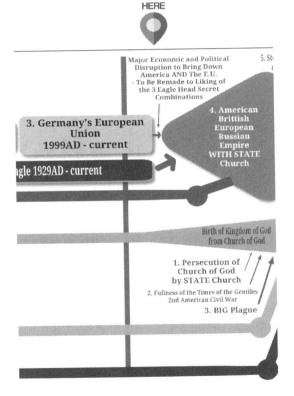

4: *America's Last 6 Short Feathers and the "Awakening" of the 3 Eagle Head Secret Combinations*

This is in the future to 2017. In this book I will try to paint it in very clear concise terms. I want the truth, and believe that the reader wants the same. We will continue to review all the relevant information that I have found on the subject and give ratings to the information as to its reliability.

Up until now, we have been dealing with the past. Now the heat is turned up a notch and some clarity is coming into view.

Note: that this prophecy of Ezra's Eagle couldn't have been fully known until about this time in history (2017) ….when the last long feather President Barack Hussein Obama ends office.

Onto the 2nd half of Ezra's Eagle (2nd Esdras chapter 11 and 12)

> (2nd Esdras 11:23)
> "23 And there was **no more** upon the eagle's body, but **three heads that rested, and six little wings [feathers].**"

Learning Points:
A. All the feathers/Presidents on the Eagle's **left** (Ezra's **right**) "bad side" have been used up.
    a. (**Author's Analysis**): These would represent 14 Presidents from Herbert Hoover through Barack Obama. All 14 of these Presidents have dismantled our Constitution heavily and have generally not been the people's friend. They have generally been agents or **"front men"** for the 3 conspiring Eagle Heads. Much damage has been done. (See FREE video www.LastDaysTimeline.com/oligarchies-republics-democracies about Oligarchies VS Republics VS Democracies. Oligarchies always put one of their own members out in front.)
B. At this moment in the history of the Eagle Kingdom, only 6 short feathers/Presidents remain plus the 3 Eagle Heads which were to wait until the end-times of the Eagle Kingdom to reign.
    a. (**Author's Analysis**): The six short feathers/Presidents that remain in our future from 2016, going forward, start with Donald John Trump. He is the 1st feather on the Eagle's right wing.
C. The 3 Eagle Heads are still sleeping

> (2nd Esdras 11:24)
> "24 Then saw I also that **two little feathers divided themselves from the six**, and remained under the head, that was upon the **right side**: for the four (feathers) continued in their place" (on Eagle's Right side).

Learning Points:

A. CRITICAL PART WITH SPECIAL ATTENTION: Ezra saw 2 of the last 6 short feathers on the "good side" (Eagle's **right**=Ezra's **left**) move over to the "bad side".

a. Later on, we will see in God's interpretation that these last 2 little feathers that moved from the "good side" to the "bad side" will reappear at the end of the whole saga….**after** the 3 bad Eagle Heads take over.

God's Interpretation

Let us match up God's Interpretation from Esdras Chapter 12

(2nd Esdras 12:29-30)
"29 And whereas thou sawest **two feathers** under the wings **passing over** [to] the head that is on the right side;
30 It signifieth that these are they, **whom the Highest hath kept unto their end**: this is the **small kingdom and full of trouble**, as thou sawest."

Learning Points:
A. These 2 "moving" feathers from Ezra's **left** to Ezra's **right** (vice versa for the Eagle) would be 2 feathers/Presidents that God has kept back for **The End** of the Feathers/Presidents of this Eagle Nation.
B. And when these 2 short feathers rule at the end, the kingdom is **smaller** than it had once been. And it's full of problems and trouble. So, if modern America is the Eagle, then these last 2 feathers/Presidents are presiding over a smaller America. I won't speculate as to how America is smaller at this point in the future.
C. Note: these 2 last short feathers come *after* the 3 Eagle Heads. However, when these last 2 official feathers/Presidents are in office, they serve under the "bad" side and *with* the last remaining Eagle Head.

When these last 2 feathers/Presidents serve, the whole kingdom is full of trouble and has great problems. The whole Eagle kingdom goes down…and is "restored again" (as shown in later verses).

"They Thought to Set Up Themselves, And to Have the Rule"

Continuing with the Timeline Narrative of 2nd Esdras Chapter 11:

(2nd Esdras 11:25-27)
"25 And I beheld, & lo, the [short] feathers that were under the [Eagle's Right] wing, **thought to set up themselves, and to have the rule**.
26 And I beheld, & lo, there was one set up, but shortly it appeared no more.
27 And the second was sooner away then the first."

6

5

4

3

2 — Mike Pence

1 — Donald J. Trump 2017 -

Learning Points MIXED with **Author's Analysis:**

A. **MISSION CRITICAL TO 2017 ALERT:** The defining characteristic of feathers/Presidents under the Eagle's "good" **right** wing is that they "take rule unto themselves." At first I thought that was a bad thing, as it seemed against the Constitution…. However, when the standard rule-of-the-day is what the 3 conspiring Eagle Heads are dictating, then this is a *very good thing*. We haven't had a feather/President stand up from the Eagle's Right Wing **ever** in this Eagle's history since 1929. We haven't had a President elected from a populist movement in America since before 1929. All the previous 14 feathers/Presidents have come from *The Establishment*. The 2600 year old prophecy of Ezra's Eagle is lining up with **real life** right now, in 2016.

a. This 2600 year old Prophecy by Ezra just said that the 15th feather/President who we **now know** is President Elect Donald J. Trump **would be a "short feather**," and that he would be set up, but *shortly* appear no more. In other words "be taken out".

b. The last 2 feathers that were "short" in the past were John F. Kennedy and Richard Nixon. They were on the Eagle's **left** side. (We will discover more about these 2 short feathers in God's interpretation of the dream.)

    i. John F. Kennedy – President Kennedy (1961-1963) was elected to 1 term and was cut down while in office by assassins. **So, a short feather may be created by assassination.** There is much controversy as to who, what, and how President John F. Kennedy was murdered. (See Jessie Ventura, former Governor of Minnesota, give evidence on our website www.LastDaysTimeline.com/kennedy). The facts remain that the man who was placed on the Warren Commission to investigate the murder of the President and who *invented* the "Magic Bullet Theory" to explain away that there was only **one** Gunman but *lots of holes*…was none other than Gerald Ford. The man that was *replaced* into the Vice President's chair, just before Richard Nixon resigned. Ford became the first non-elected President in US history… with a Rockefeller as an *appointed* Vice President. (See book "The Making of America" by W. Cleon Skousen on www.LastDaysTimeline.com/making-of-america)

    ii. Richard M. Nixon – President Nixon (1969-1974) was elected to 2 terms and resigned from office over the *Watergate Scandal*. So, a short feather may be created by resigning office.

B. The 2nd short feather from the Eagle's **right** side would then come to power through the authorized Line of Succession only to be "cut down" even quicker. This next eliminated, or short feather/President would be current Vice President Mike Pence.

NOTE: From the observation of the last 2 short feathers Kennedy and Nixon, it is possible that a short feather could get all the way to the 2nd term of office before being "taken out". So, we are looking at a maximum 7 year timeframe of December 2016, to a possible 2023, for Donald J Trump to be a short feather.

However remember, "shortly it appeared no more." I have no deeper information on this subject, until it happens.

You can read the Apocrypha for yourself at http://www.kingjamesbibleonline.org/2-Esdras-Chapter-11/

The Good Wing Feathers VS The 3 Eagle Heads – Who Wins?

Now we have seen that this 2600 year old Prophecy of Ezra shows what happens to these 2 "good side" feathers. Let us see what happens next.

(2nd Esdras 11:28-31)

"28 And I beheld, and lo, the **two** [feathers on the Eagle's **right**] that remained, **thought also in themselves to reign.**

29 And **when they so thought**, behold, there **awaked one of the heads** that were **at rest**, namely it that was in the **midst, for that was greater** then the two other heads.

30 And then I saw, that the **two other heads were joined with it.**

31 And behold, the head was turned with them that were with it, and **did eat up the two feathers** under the wing that **would have reigned.**"

Learning Points:
A. The next 2 feathers/Presidents also "think" in themselves to reign/rule against what the party-line Eagle Heads dictate.
   a. The next 2 feathers "think" to reign. Meaning, they didn't even have a chance to *do* anything against the wicked 3 Eagle Head's agenda, before they are cut down.
B. The next 2 feathers/Presidents die *at the same time*, because the 3 conspiring Eagle Heads "awake from their sleeping" from behind the scenes and eat them.
C. The next 2 feathers might not make it to office, because of the "would have reigned" clause.

Author's Analysis:
In the Line of Succession in the United States of America authorized by The Constitution, when one President goes down, there is *always* another man to fill the shoes in the line of elected offices.

If President Donald J. Trump is taken out and Vice President Mike Pence is quickly taken out, the next in line is the Speaker of the House, currently Paul Ryan. Also the next in line is President Pro Tempore of the Senate = Senator Orrin Hatch of Utah. Senator Hatch has said he would not run for office in 2018. So, keep that in mind.

Remember, all must stay the same in the line-up to get this outcome. If too much time passes after the removal of Donald Trump from office, then Mike Pence, as President, will choose a new Vice President. So, keep that in mind.
(See https://en.wikipedia.org/wiki/United_States_presidential_line_of_succession)

The 3 Eagle Heads Start to Rule Oppressively, While Setting-up a Multi-National Order of Global Governance - Daniel's 4th Beast Kingdom

(2nd Esdras 11:32-33)

"32 But **this head** put the **whole earth in fear**, and **bare rule in it** over all those that dwelt upon the earth, with **much oppression**, and it had **the governance of the world more then all the wings [feathers] that had been**.

33 And after this I beheld, and lo the **head that was in the midst, suddenly appeared no more, like as the wings [feathers]**."

Learning Points:

A. Apparently this **big** middle conspiratorial head takes the power of government unto itself. It has woken up and the feathers/Presidents aren't in charge any longer.
B. The whole earth is put into fear with much oppression.
C. It has the **governance of the world** more than all the feathers/Presidents before it.
    a. (**Author's Analysis**): This "governance of the world" phrase is something NEW. Up to this point the feathers/Presidents have had much influence, over the world. But, this apocryphal scripture uses this particular phrase "governance of the world"….a few times in this sequence of verses. Thus, the 3 wicked conspiring Eagle Heads have *this* **as their main mission, to "govern the world"**.
D. The big middle head suddenly is gone…" like as the [feathers]".
    a. (**Author's Analysis**): This phrase means that this wicked Eagle Head goes "out" like the feathers/Presidents. This Eagle Head may go out of Presidential office and be gone. Another idea is that in God's Interpretation of this Eagle Head (shown below) says he will die by the sword in his bed. So, either way, after a time of switching the United States of America *over* to a more powerful global government, he is dead.

Author's Analysis:
Now to the pure speculation: For a bad power broker to interfere with the Constitutional Line of Succession, there must be <u>*an interrupt*</u>. A perfect solution to the 3 wicked Eagle Head problem of "national leaders taking rule unto themselves and not following the Eagle Head *establishment* party line" is to take out the whole top level of government at one time. As in "eating" the 2 next feathers (after Trump and Pence) at *the same time*.

This would likely cause great confusion in government, a condition which is ripe for a strong leader to come in and clean things up by remaking them to his own liking. (Reminder: just like Hitler did with the Reichstag Fire)

If there is to be an elimination of the next 2 "good" feathers at the same time. Then the place would **most likely** have to be at a time when they are both together. I too feel as Rush does…that there is no bigger event to do this than the State of the Union Address. A big bomb would do the job to eliminate not only the next 2 feathers/Presidents in the Line of Succession, *but* would put **one single man** in sole charge of the federal government, with no checks and balances. The very thing our founding fathers tried to avoid; placing all power in one man.

During each of the large Joint Sessions of Congress where many heads of the federal government departments are in one place at one time, it is a common practice to callout one man as the "Designated Survivor" to guarantee continuity of government. It is usually a low level presidential cabinet member or a congressman, but it could be anyone they decide. The decision usually comes from the Office of the President.

Note that the "Designated Survivor" is a calling in government when the State of the Union or other Joint Sessions of Congress takes place. The January 12, 2016 State of the Union Address was the first time in history when **two** Designated Survivors were called. One was Orrin Hatch of Utah. The other was the Secretary of Homeland Security. * (See https://en.wikipedia.org/wiki/Designated_survivor)

THINK ABOUT THIS: all of these people at the head of our federal government are all in the same room at the same time.

The President, Vice President, and Speaker of the House

The House and The Senate

The President's Cabinet

The Supreme Court

Top Military Generals and Navy Admirals

If a conspiring Eagle Head wanted to take over government, all they would have to do would be to make sure their man would be selected as The Designated Survivor, and then blow up the State of the Union.

I put this forth as a speculation. Only time will tell the real story. *But* we do know that the 3 Eagle heads eat the 2 last "good" feathers/Presidents, at the same time.

The Problem of the Eagle Head Identification:

There are a few different ideas concerning "who" these 3 Eagle Heads controlling the Eagle Kingdom are:
1.   3 important leaders within 3 of the United States secret combinations. (IE. Leader of C.F.R. plus others)

2. 3 important leaders within 1 of the United States secret combinations. (IE. 3 Leaders of just the C.F.R.)
3. 3 different secret combinations within the United States (IE. C.F.R. plus 2 more)
4. 3 different secret combinations that influence the United States at home or abroad (IE. C.F.R. plus other foreign secret combinations that are tied to the C.F.R.)

We can positively tie the C.F.R. into this mix because of Herbert Hoover's involvement and the rest of the US President's involvement at different levels.

I was shocked to think about such a thing. However in the interpretation by God of Ezra's Eagle (shown below) it says that one head kills off the Big Head. Then that Head is killed off by the other head. They take each other down. The wicked destroy the wicked.

I tend to lien toward the 3 Eagle Heads as secret combinations connecting at home and in foreign lands (#4). In God's Interpretation of Ezra's Eagle in Chapter 12, these Eagle Heads are called "Kingdoms," not "kings." Also, as seen already, the 3 Eagle Heads are going to setup a global government AND blend it with the European Gentile nations (as demonstrated below).

I won't take a stance on positive identification of the 3 Eagle Heads until more evidence becomes clear. The possible identifications above seem plausible, based upon existing evidence.

Also note: that identification may not be clear on the Eagle Heads yet, but we *know* what they **do** and what they *stand for*. They stand for global government under their control. We know that their way of doing things is by being extra secretive, controlling world leaders (US Presidents – Leaders of the "free world"), and that they do commit murder if a person stands in their way. These combinations have done it before; they will do it again.

From Daniel's vision this new 4th Beast (Daniel 7), which these 3 Eagle Heads setup, additionally stands for: combining with other governments to form a large 10 nation beast, cajoling nations to be eaten up (to join it), grinding and crushing nations that don't join, going to war with the Saints, speaking great things against God publicly, and allowing a Stout Horn to take over their group and become the Anti-Christ as seen in John's Revelation. That is what these evil secret combinations of men stand for.

This evil organization will continue to "wake up" and reveal itself *over time*. This study has a long range "lifetime" timeframe. Keep watching and pondering deeply and praying.

Power Corrupts – Absolute Power Corrupts Absolutely

(2nd Esdras 11:34-35)
"34 But there **remained the two heads**, which also **in like sort** ruled upon the earth, and over those that dwelt therein.

35 And I beheld, and lo, the head upon **the right side, devoured it, that was upon the left** side."

Learning Points:
A. The big head in the middle is gone, and the 2 smaller heads remain.
B. They *each* take rule on the earth in the same *manner* as the big middle head did. Building the new world government and mashing nations into it.
C. The head on the Eagle's **left** (Ezra's **right**) killed the other head. Now, there is only one head left…and that last Eagle head dies by the sword of a 3rd party.

God's Interpretation:
Let us match up God's Interpretation from Esdras Chapter 12

(2nd Esdras 12:22-28)
"22 And whereas thou sawest **three heads resting**, this is the interpretation:
23 In his **last days** shall the **most High** raise up **three kingdoms**, and **renew many things** therein, and they shall have **the dominion** of the earth,
24 And of those that dwell therein, **with much oppression, above all those that were before them**: therefore are they called **the heads of the eagle**.
25 For these are they that **shall accomplish his wickedness**, and that **shall finish his last end**.
26 And whereas thou sawest that the **great head appeared no more, it signifieth that one of them shall die upon his bed, and yet with pain.**
27 For the **two that remain shall be slain with the sword.**
28 For the **sword of the one shall devour the other: but at the last shall he fall through the sword himself.**"

Learning Points:
A. The 3 sleeping Eagle Heads are placed there by **God** to "renew many things" in the **last days**.
   a. (**Author's Analysis**): I do not see how God would want these evil secret combinations to "renew many things". If you have thoughts upon this topic, please contact me through the website www.LastDaysTimeline.com.
   b. (**Author's Analysis**): The **last days** note is very important to realize that this is **not Rome**, but Ezra's Eagle is a specific last-days kingdom. Rome was not in the last days. The United States of America with its exact feather/president line-up *is* a last-days kingdom. NOTE: "his last days" still is "the last days" because this Eagle Kingdom is tied to Daniel's 4th Beast, which comes after Daniel's 3rd Beast of the European Union (as shown above).
B. Notice the terms that God used was "three kingdoms" to describe the 3 Eagle Heads - not "kings".
   a. (**Author's Analysis**): This is where the ambiguity as to the "who" and "what" these 3 Eagle Heads represent specifically. But remember, it doesn't matter the exact interpretation, because we know specifically what they will *do* and what they *think like*. Also, we know that the C.F.R. secret combination is tied into the mix through Herbert Hoover (as shown above).

C. These 3 Eagle heads rule with great oppression above all the former feathers/Presidents that came before them.

D. These 3 Eagle heads will "accomplish his wickedness" and bring about the "end" thereof.

    a. (**Author's Analysis**): I think that "his" is Satan. For it seems unlikely that God would want his children to behave in this evil way. But, God would allow Satan to build this evil 4th Beast of Daniel "global government" up, so that God's mighty arm can save his loving children through his *strange dividing act*. (More to come on this topic).

E. The middle eagle head dies "upon his bed, with pain"…at the hands of one of the other Eagle Heads. Then the 2 remaining eagle heads get killed by the sword. At the hands of each other.

    a. (**Author's Analysis**): The last head is killed by a 3rd party. Who is this 3rd party? (speculation: this 3rd party very well may be Daniel's evil Stout Horn. Remember this Stout horn takes out 3 of the horns as he rises. Just a hunch). God allows the wicked to slay the wicked.

    b. These apocryphal scriptures seem to indicate these 3 Eagle Heads are "men" who die in their beds, or by the sword etc. But, above seems to indicate these 3 Eagle Heads are "kingdoms." So the jury is still out on this topic. But remember, we know what they **do** and what they **stand for**. Time will reveal them to us. Most likely right after the 2 short feathers get "eaten" by these 3 Eagle Heads….the clues will become clearer.

Author's Analysis:

It does seem correct that the 3 Eagle Heads have **time** to create and setup this **new** "American-European World Government" riding on the coat-tails of American power and wealth. The new entity that appears at the end of Ezra's Eagle and Daniel's 4th Beast is the same **type** of entity that those **real live** conspiring men have been trying to setup for a very long time… a multi-national order of global government.

W. Cleon Skousen in the 1972 book *The Naked Capitalist*, does a book-review of Carroll Quigley's *Tragedy & Hope*. It appears that within this secret combination, *all* the conspirators talk about is this upcoming global government entity.

President George H.W. Bush talked about this global government entity openly during the State of the Union and on TV to the nation several times. You may not be aware that he mentioned it so often. This was George H.W. Bush's main objective, even directly after the 1991 Desert Storm war. (see the videos at www.LastDaysTimeline.com/george-hw-bush)

This is not a Republican or Democrat thing….This was always about **Globalists VS Nationalists** with solid Constitutions and guaranteed freedoms. This is why George H.W. Bush voted for Hillary Clinton in the 2016 Presidential Election, which would seem rather odd at first glance. (See www.LastDaysTimeline.com/george-hw-bush)

I did not watch or listen to many of the 2016 campaign speeches of Donald Trump or Hillary Clinton this election cycle. However, this author found some surprising information.

Have a look at what Donald Trump said about these same "behind the curtains" sleeping Eagle Heads in late October 2016, just before the Nov 8 elections... (See www.LastDaysTimeline.com/donald-trump)

See the 1961 Dwight D. Eisenhower presidential address on TV warning Americans against allowing the concentration of power in the hands of just a few people. These 3 Eagle Heads have been working behind the scenes for a long time. (See www.LastDaysTimeline.com/military-industrial-complex)

We should bolster our efforts around this topic, because:
- The richest and most powerful people in the world care about this topic and are in the act of creating a more globalist government to concentrate power.
- The Book of Mormon specifically warns the Saints in Ether Chapter 8 to not let these Secret Combinations of powerful people get above us.
- These secret combinations are Satan's tools for his kingdom. God expects us to do whatever is in our power to resist Lucifer, the common enemy of all.

(See Appendix 1: Secret Combinations)

In our future to 2017, after the next 4 short feathers/Presidents, we will discover these 3 Eagle Heads and what they want to build.

Worldwide View

For those readers in Europe, these 3 Eagle Heads in America will want to join with the ruins of what is left of the European Union 3rd Beast of Daniel. Fight against it for as long as possible in practical ways. Make sure you have your food storage for the bumpy ride period between the two kingdoms.

For those readers in South America, Africa, and Australia/Asia...the 4th Beast of the Gentiles will be aggressive. Mostly toward the Middle East at first (see Appendix 1: The Ram and the He Goat). Over time, I expect that aggression to be pointed in many directions. Stay out of it's way. Follow the prophet of the Lord.

The Roaring Lion Running Out of the Woods to Take Down the Evil Eagle

After the oppression of the world by these 3 Eagle Heads, comes **the roaring lion** upon the Eagle. This Lion takes down the evil Eagle and rescues the Saints of God.

But first... let's have a look back at Daniel's 4th Beast/Ezra's Eagle and the perspective of the Stars of the Heavens that are God's faithful witnesses, as to *when* in the timeline these things will happen in our future. This is recorded by John the Beloved/Revelator.

5: Birth of the Kingdom of God from the Church of God, THEN John`s Scarlet Beast Rises...IN THAT ORDER.

The Description of this 4th Beast of Daniel 7 as given by John the Revelator

We could start in many places in The Book of John's Revelation. There is much to discuss in last-days prophecy here. I desire succinctness in this work.

There are generally 3 parts to the Book of John's Revelation:
1. **Part 1** – (Chapters 1-3) The description of the 7 Churches with symbolic candlesticks and other problems happening inside the Church of God itself. I have read that these same problems in the ancient church exist inside the different wards and branches of today. However, this is beyond the scope of this work.
2. **Part 2** – (Chapters 4-11) The description of the Last-Day events from the perspective of the Jews in Jerusalem and Israel– we will touch on a few points from this section of the work.
3. **Part 3** – (Chapters 12-22) The description of the *same* Last-Day events from the perspective of the rest of the world including the rest of the Gentiles and Heathen. This we will focus on for our understanding of the Scarlet Beast, The False Prophet, and the Whore "Babylon the Great", as these are Gentile 4th Beast establishments.

The parts of the timeline we are currently looking at is The rise of the 4th Beast 10 nation conglomerate also seen in John the Revelator's vision known as the Scarlet Beast. Plus, the Whore-Babylon the Great, that is riding the Beast.

Let us start with Chapter 12 available here:
https://www.lds.org/scriptures/nt/rev/12?lang=eng
The important footnotes are easily available in the printed LDS scriptures themselves (in the back after the Bible Dictionary)

Let us jump to the Joseph Smith Translation of the entire Chapter 12. This is the last big piece of translation work that Joseph Smith Jr. did in the Bible. And it is very important to our timeline.

> (JST Revelation 12:1-3)
> "1 And there appeared **a great sign in heaven**, in the **likeness of things** on **the earth**; a **woman** clothed with the **sun**, and the **moon** under her feet, and upon **her head a crown of twelve stars**.
> 2 And the **woman being with child**, cried, **travailing in birth, and pained to be delivered**.
> 3 And she brought forth a **man child**, who was **to rule** all nations with a **rod of iron**; and her **child was caught up** unto God and his throne."

Learning Points:

A. A sign in the stars, moon, and sun will *be like* what is going to happen on the Earth. The stars are to be used for "signs and for seasons." People in 2017 are very familiar with using these celestial bodies for seasons, but much less so for signs. *But*, through the prophet Joseph Smith Jr. we now have one of the biggest signs in all of scripture returned to its purity. Watch what it shows.
B. A specific star pattern that involves multiple stars, the sun, the moon, and other constellations.
C. A woman that is pregnant and in a heavy painful labor. The baby is a **big** baby.
D. The baby is born and it's a man child. This man child is to rule the nations with the "iron rod" which is commonly known to be the word of God. The child will eventually be caught up to God's throne.

God's Interpretation:

And the Angel speaking with John the Revelator gives the interpretation of this section of the vision as follows…in the same chapter:

(JST Rev 12:7)
"7 And the dragon prevailed not against Michael, neither **the child**, nor the **woman which was the church of God**, who had been delivered of her pains, and **brought forth the kingdom of our God** and his Christ."

Learning Points:
A. The woman is The Church of God.
B. The **big** baby man-child is The Kingdom of God. The Kingdom of God is different than the Church of God. The Kingdom of God is the **political** kingdom of Christ.

In the early LDS Church in Nauvoo March 1844 Joseph Smith formed *the Council of Fifty* when the Prophet Joseph was running for President of the United States. The *Council of Fifty* was the political Kingdom of God or "Living Constitution" for the Latter-Day Saints as they moved West and established Utah. This was the government of the land. It was an elected representative based Republican Theocracy.

The full name of the Council of Fifty is "**The Kingdom of God and His Laws with the Keys and Power thereof, and Judgment in the Hands of His Servants, Ahman Christ**". Joseph Smith taught there was a distinction between the Church of God and the Kingdom of God. The Church was designed to teach the commandments that would affect the hereafter. The Kingdom was designed to govern people during mortality only.

The *Council of Fifty* folded in 1884 as the need for it ceased. However, when the need for the *Council of Fifty* political Kingdom of God rises again, it will be reinstituted.

See these multiple resources:
- Wikipedia.org https://en.wikipedia.org/wiki/Council_of_Fifty
- BYU Harold B. Lee Library http://eom.byu.edu/index.php/Council_of_Fifty
- The Joseph Smith Papers Project http://www.josephsmithpapers.org/topic/council-of-fifty
- LDS.org Church Website https://history.lds.org/article/council-of-fifty-minutes-

joseph-smith-papers?lang=eng

Author's Analysis:
During this time of the Revelation Chapter 12 star pattern in the sky, or close to it, the Church of God will birth the political Kingdom of God. In 2017, we don't have the full expanded political Kingdom of God *yet*, it hasn't been born yet. We have the Church of God… which is The Church of Jesus Christ of Latter-Day Saints. However, the Kingdom of God resides as a seed inside the Church of God's priesthood leadership.

The Stars as God's Faithful Witnesses – Just Look UP

In regards to this subject of the Revelation Chapter 12 star pattern of the woman with the sun, moon, and 12 stars in correct placement on the "Last Days" Timeline; the very best work on this subject is the book *Seven Heavenly Witnesses of the Coming of Jesus Christ* – by Val Brinkerhoff. Available on www.LastDaysTimeline.com/seven-heavenly-witnesses

In the Seven Heavenly Witnesses book, several important points are made:

A. The heavens are God's faithful witnesses. Man cannot ever change them. Thus, they are direct truth.
B. The star patterns have been used in the scriptures for special events: Christ's birth, Christ's death, the Revelation of John the Beloved.
C. *The Revelation 12 Sign* of the woman with 12 stars over her head giving birth will take place on September 23, 2017.

These signs in scripture have been known for 1000s of years. This is a church in Belgium showing the image of the woman and the man child standing on the moon and crushing the Beast.

The Revelation 12 Sign of the Church of God birthing the Kingdom of God is coming September 23, 2017. This is happening over the Jewish holiday of Rosh Hashanah. It involves the constellation Virgo, with the Sun in her belly and the moon at her feet. Plus 12 Stars are over her head.

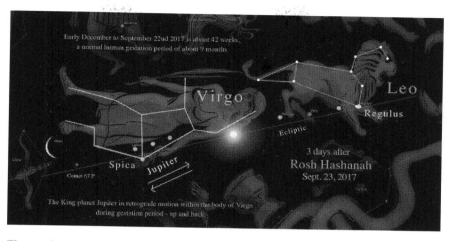

The maximum information you can get on this entire topic is in the book *Seven Heavenly Witnesses of the Coming of Jesus Christ* by Val Brinkerhoff. Note: I do not endorse *all* of the ideas and concepts printed in the book, but for this one topic of the *Revelation 12 Sign* coming on Sept 23, 2017, it goes deep. You can get it on the website www.LastDaysTimeline.com/seven-heavenly-witnesses.

Author's Analysis:
The important points here are that the heavens are showing that the Church of God will birth the Kingdom of God close to Sept 23, 2017 and it will be a painful delivery when it happens. I feel that if the actual events happen within a year or two of the sign in the heavens we are still on track. If more than 3-5 years go by after the Rev 12 sign in the heavens, then it will not be legitimate evidence. So, time will tell. But, be prepared for it, just in case. That's a good motto, "be prepared."

The Beast with 7 Heads with Crowns and 10 Horns Appears AFTER the Kingdom of God

And onto the rest of the Joseph Smith Translation of Revelation 12…

(Revelation 12:4-5)
"4 And there appeared **another sign in heaven**; and behold, a **great red dragon, having seven heads and ten horns, and seven crowns upon his heads**. And **his tail drew the third part of the stars of heaven**, and did cast them to the earth. And **the dragon stood before the woman** which was delivered, **ready to devour her child after** it was born.

5 And the woman fled into the wilderness, where she had **a place prepared** of God, that they should **feed her there a thousand two hundred and threescore years**."

Learning Points:
A. Now we see another star constellation in the heavens. This time a red dragon with 7 heads with crowns and 10 horns.
    a. (**Author's Analysis**): We can **assume** by the 1ˢᵗ sign in heaven of the woman that this red dragon sign is to also be shown in the stars and then take place physically on the earth too.
B. Notice the order. The Church of God births the political Kingdom of God *First*. Then this new Dragon with 7 crowned heads and 10 horns stands by to eat the Kingdom of God *after* it was born. So, the birth sign happens first. Then the dragon sign happens second. The Red Dragon then goes after the new Kingdom of God to destroy it. What is the Red Dragon with 7 crowned Heads and 10 Horns? The answer is in the next few chapters of John's Revelation.
C. This piece of scripture mentions a "great red dragon" with 7 heads and 10 horns. In the very next chapter, we see a "beast kingdom" is born with 7 heads and 10 horns.
    a. (**Author's Analysis**): It appears to me that this "dragon" in chapter 12 in the stars is synonymous with the "Beast Kingdom" in chapter 13, because of the linking of the 7 heads with crowns and 10 horns, and the color scarlet/**red**. Also, this Red Beast Kingdom is Satan's earthly political kingdom, so they are natively synonymous, as it is. If you, the reader, have a different understanding that has a good basis, please contact me at the website www.LastDaysTimeline.com. Understanding of this Beast Kingdom is vitally important to the "last days" timeline. The only symbol more important is The Whore, which rides the Red Beast Kingdom.
D. Remember: in King James English a "beast" is an "animal". Modern English portrays the word "beast" differently than the word "animal".
E. The woman/church flees into the wilderness to a place where God has pre-ordained. *Away* from the Red Dragon, so it cannot touch her.
F. The woman is fed in the wilderness 1,260 years. I do not know the specific meaning the 1,260 years. (My pure estimate: Joseph Smith did translate this as "years". However, if it was "days", then that would be 3.46 years or about 3.5 years. Which is a common time frame for the end times Prophecy of 3.5 years of Tribulation.)

The Dragon/Beast Kingdom with 7 Heads and 10 Horns Attacks the Church of God

We shall skip verses 6-12 for brevity. In them, the dragon is identified as Satan himself.

    (Revelation 12:13-14)
    "13 For when the dragon saw that he was cast unto the earth, he **persecuted the woman** which brought forth **the man-child**.

14 Therefore, **to the woman were given two wings** of a great eagle, that **she might flee into the wilderness, into her place,** where **she is nourished** for a **time, and times, and half a time, from the face of the serpent.**"

Learning Points:

A. The dragon (Satan) comes upon the earth and goes after the Church of God with great persecutions. Remember, above the dragon had 7 crowned Heads and 10 Horns. This vision is now saying that this dragon is Satan and a Serpent. The language is changing to morph them all together.

    a. (**Author's Analysis**): A more familiar way of saying it may be... The Red Dragon with 7 crowned Heads and 10 Horns is the serpent Satan's long desired kingdom on the earth.

B. The political Kingdom of God has already been born.

C. The Church of God was given 2 wings of large eagle and she *flew* into the wilderness to the place.

D. The Church of God was fed, away from the Dragon's Kingdom for 3.5 years. "Time, and times, and half a time" is generally understood by most writers to be 3.5 years. Notice this 3.5 years in this part of the prophecy *doesn't* match the 1,260 years in the earlier part of this same prophecy by Joseph Smith. *But, if* one thinks of this 1,260 number as *days* (3.5 years), then everything lines up perfectly. If you, the reader, have a different explanation as to why this is days or years, contact me at the website www.LastDaysTimeline.com.

Author's Analysis:

There has been much said by early church leaders about a "wall" that will take place when the rest of America is going down. The "wall" is between the rest of America and the area of Utah. There is a certain extra curricular prophecy by Joseph Smith that states the exact manner the "wall" will take place. (See Appendix 4)

Note: Utah is a wilderness. Compared with the rest of the United States, Salt Lake City is a very isolated major city. Simply look at a map. It is not close to any other big city.

I have read many ideas concerning "the wilderness" of where the Church of God will go away from the Beast Dragon Kingdom with 7 crowned Heads and 10 Horns. However, I have low evidence supporting any of the ideas.

(Revelation 12:15-17)

"15 And the **serpent casteth out of his mouth water as a flood after the woman,** that he might cause her to be carried away of the flood.

16 And **the earth helpeth the woman,** and **the earth openeth her mouth,** and **swalloweth up the flood** which the dragon casteth out of his mouth.

17 Therefore, the **dragon was wroth with the woman, and went to make war** with the **remnant of her seed,** which **keep the commandments of God, and have the testimony of Jesus Christ.**"

Learning Points:

A. After the Church of God is secured in the wilderness, the Satanic Beast/Dragon Kingdom uses its mouth to cast a flood into the protected area that the Church of God is residing.
B. The Earth (Earth is a woman), helps the Church of God by swallowing up the Flood.
C. Then the Dragon (we are back to "dragon kingdom" again) makes war with the Saints of God.
D. The "remnant of the Church of God's seed" is slightly perplexing to me. I am *assuming* that means "the Saints of God" based upon them "keeping the commandments" and "have the testimony of Jesus Christ."

Author's Analysis:

This is interesting. The Dragon with 7 crowned Heads and 10 Horns tries to flood the Church of God out of the protected wilderness area. I know that in other places in John's Revelation that "water" means "peoples". So, this could mean that the Beast/Dragon Kingdom uses its mouth to convince other people to flood into the protected area around the Church of God.

(Pure speculation) The famed "White Horse Prophesy" by Joseph Smith claims that the "heathen Chinese" will invade the West Coast of the United States. If any nation on earth has enough people to be considered a "flood" it would be China. (See Appendix 4)

The Earth herself will swallow the flood before they reach the Church of God's protected area. This is not the first time that the Earth has swallowed evil men. The earthquakes swallowed up the evil backsliding Israelites that wanted to go back to Egypt against Moses' and the Lord's will.

At this point we have seen the rise of Satan's Dragon/Scarlet "red" Beast Kingdom with 7 crowned Heads and 10 Horns. We have seen it projected in the star constellations themselves. Now, it's on the Earth in reality. Let us discover some more about it in the in *very next chapter* John's Revelation, chapter 13. We will get there.

Yet, we have at least one more person to investigate about the formational period of the 4th Beast Kingdom of the Gentiles. That is Daniel himself in Chapter 7. Remember, we are holding tight to our "last days" timeline...and we are in the early formation period of the Beast Kingdom.

6: Daniel`s 4ᵗʰ Beast rises as the 3ʳᵈ Beast Goes Down

On to the main event: Daniel's 4ᵗʰ Beast = Ezra's Eagle under the 3 Eagle Heads = The transformed United States of America into a conglomerate 10 nation global government entity Beast Kingdom of the Gentiles.

> (Daniel 7:7-8)
> "7 After this I saw in the night visions, and behold a **fourth beast, dreadful and terrible, and strong exceedingly**; and it had **great iron teeth**: it **devoured and brake in pieces**, and **stamped the residue** with the **feet** of it: and it *was* diverse from all the beasts that *were* **before** it; and it had **ten horns**.
> 8 I considered **the horns**, and, behold, there came up among them **another little horn**, before whom there **were three of the first horns plucked up by the roots**: and, behold, in this horn *were* **eyes like the eyes of man**, and **a mouth speaking great things**."

Learning Points:
A. This fourth beast is a kingdom that is very strong and hard to get along with.
B. It has large iron teeth for eating and with those teeth it eats and breaks nations up.
C. It crushes the remainder of nations that it doesn't swallow, with its heavy feet.
D. This beast is very different than the last 3 beasts that were **before** it: the plucked dancing lion, the laying down rib eating bear, and the flying leopard with 4 heads.
   a. (Author's Analysis): These 4 latter-day kingdoms do come in a series. Britain's Empire comes first. Second is Russia's Communist USSR. Third is Germany and France's European Union. And Fourth is this ferocious creature being described now. Notice that all 3 animals before it, came and went….Which means the EU **goes down too**…while the next 4ᵗʰ Beast Kingdom comes onto the stage.
E. It has 10 *horns*.
   a. (**Author's Analysis**): Wait a minute. Eagles don't have 10 horns….well, this Eagle will morph into a kingdom with 10 horns. Now this sounds like John the Revelator's Scarlet Beast with 7 Heads and 10 Horns that are kings. We will get there in just a bit.
F. A "little horn" came up *after* the first 10 horns were established. The "little horn" plucks up 3 of the first horns and supplants them. Kicks them out.
G. The "little horn" had eyes of a man, and a mouth that spoke large things. Many interpretations of these 2 special features of the 'little horn' could be made. I will not yet venture.

Author's Analysis:
This 4ᵗʰ beast, looking this way and doing these things, looks like America, but not quite. Some of these things make sense for the current *time*. But, I believe this 4ᵗʰ beast is *yet future* to 2017…because of what is contained in the 2ⁿᵈ half of Ezra's Eagle vision (demonstrated below).

This **last** Beast of Daniel Chap 7 is special. It doesn't have a strong animal descriptive

---

quality that the first 3 had. (ie. Lion, Bear, Leopard), However the Lord says that this 4th Beast starts out as an Eagle in 2nd Esdras Chapter 11, as seen below.

In Ezra's Eagle vision 2nd Esdras Chapter 12, Ezra receives the interpretation of the dream itself....and God gives **the link** to Daniel's 4th Beast.

> (2nd Esdras 12:11-12)
> "11 The eagle, whom thou sawest come up from the sea, is the kingdom **which was seen in the vision of thy brother Daniel.**
> 12 But it was **not expounded unto him, therefore now I declare it unto thee.**"

> (also 2nd Esdras chapter 11:38-40)
> "38 Hear thou, I will talk with thee, and the highest shall say unto thee,
> 39 Art not thou it **that remainest of the four beasts**, whom I made to reign in my world, that the **end of their times might come through them**?
> 40 And **the fourth came and overcame all the beasts that were past**, and had power over the world with great fearfulness, and over the whole compass of the earth with much wicked oppression, and so long time dwelt he upon the earth with deceit."

Learning Points:
A. (v11-12) The Eagle shown to Ezra was the same **beast/animal** as the 4th Beast in Daniel Chapter 7....and **Ezra** received and recorded the interpretation, not Daniel.
B. (v38-40) God is saying that Daniel's 4th beast is the last beast of the 4 that is on earth *in the last days* during the end of their times. That 4th Beast was bigger and overcame the other 3 Beasts/animals that were also from Daniel's dream. Those other 3 beasts **came before the 4th**. The empires do not present their strength at the same time. They are sequential. (keep this in mind as we read Daniel 7 and Ezra's Eagle)

God said that this 10 horned ferocious animal, the 4th Beast Kingdom of Daniel's dream was the same animal as Ezra's Eagle. However, this 4th animal doesn't look anything like the Eagle described by Ezra. Not in the feathered/Presidential era, anyway.

The "3 Eagle Head" era that comes after the "18 feathers/Presidents" era; looks very much like this ferocious global government creature with 10 horns. Daniel's 4th Beast with 10 horns also lines up very nicely with John the Revelator's Scarlet Beast with 7 heads and 10 horns.

Follow along in the scriptures yourself here:
https://www.lds.org/scriptures/ot/dan/7?lang=eng

(Daniel 7:11)

"11 I beheld then because of **the voice of the great words which the horn spake: I beheld** *even* **till the beast was slain, and his body destroyed, and** given to the **burning flame**."

Learning Points:
A. IMPORTANT: - I skipped a few verses of Daniel Chapter 7 speaking of "The Ancient of Days" casting down the thrones of the 7+1 remaining horns of this 4th Beast.
B. Daniel watched as the Little Horn spoke his bad words.
C. Daniel watched until the 4th beast/animal was burned by fire. Important note: the end of this 4th Beast is to **be burned**. Ezra's Eagle vision says the same thing. There are many "hard links" between these 2 prophesies. Read them together as one.

(Daniel 7:12)
"12 As concerning the **rest of the beasts**, they had **their dominion taken away**: yet **their lives were prolonged** for a season and time."

Learning Points:
A. The other 3 earlier beast/animals/gentile nations **lived** for a time…yet their power was taken away from them….by what? The answer is in King Nebuchadnezzar's dream that Daniel interpreted (See Appendix 1) **and** in the 2nd half of Ezra's Eagle….which is yet in our future of 2017.

NOTE: God's interpretation of Daniel's 4 Beast Vision is Verse 17 through the end of the chapter 7. Remember, most of this material is yet future to 2017.

(Daniel 7:17-18)
"17 **These great beasts**, which are four, are **four kings**, which shall arise out of the earth.
18 But the **saints of the most High shall take the kingdom**, and possess the kingdom for ever, even for ever and ever."

Learning Points:
A. After the 4th Beast is slain, and judgment comes from "The Ancient of Days," then the Saints shall have their kingdom. Meaning the Zion society in Jackson County, Missouri can then begin… *after* this 4th Beast goes down in America and is no longer oppressive to the Saints of God, and is cleared out.

Daniel is Told the Truth of this 4th Beast Kingdom of the Gentiles

(Daniel 7:19-20)
"19 Then I would know the truth of the fourth beast, which was diverse from all the others, exceeding dreadful, whose teeth were of iron, and his **nails of brass**; which devoured, brake in pieces, and stamped the residue with his feet;
20 And of **the ten horns that were in his head**, and of **the other [stout horn]** which came up, and before whom three fell; even of that horn that had

eyes, and a mouth that spake very great things, whose look was more stout than his fellows."

Learning Points:
A. Daniel is rehashing what he saw. We now know that his nails were made of brass. This part was missing from the initial recording of the dream.

> (Daniel 7:21-22)
> "21 I beheld, and, **the same horn made war with the saints, and prevailed** against them;
> 22, **Until the Ancient of days came**, and judgment was given to the **saints** of the most High; and the time came that the saints possessed the kingdom."

Learning Points:
A. Daniel saw that the "little horn" made warfare against the saints and **won** for a time….until the "Ancient of Days" comes and takes away the little horn's kingdom and gives it to the Saints.

Author's Analysis:
I have read many theories from prophecy book authors concerning the man called The Ancient of Days. They have stated at least 3 different meanings:
1. **Jesus Christ** – I don't think so, because we see in a later verse, the Son and The Ancient of Days are mentioned together. (See Dan 7:13-14)
2. **Adam** – Joseph Smith said this is the traditional LDS understanding of the Ancient of Days. Adam will collect all the Keys of the Priesthood at Adam-ondi-Ahman from the previous Prophets and return all keys back to Jesus Christ. So, this verse in Daniel may be referring to this event. I agree with this view.
3. **John the Beloved/Revelator** – This theory is newer. It does hold a little merit. Yet this idea does go against scripture. I do not subscribe to it.

The Ancient of Days judges the oppression of the evil Stout Horn ruler and gives the Saints the kingdom.

I think the Ancient of Days is Adam as Joseph Smith Jr. and Joseph F. Smith stated.

> (D&C 27:11)
> "11 And also with **Michael, or Adam, the father of all**, the prince of all, the **ancient of days**;"
>
> (D&C 116:1)
> "1 Spring Hill is named by the Lord Adam-ondi-Ahman, because, said he, it is the place where **Adam** shall come to visit his people, or the **Ancient of Days** shall sit, as **spoken of by Daniel the prophet**."
>
> (D&C 138:38)
> "38 Among the great and mighty ones who were assembled in this vast congregation of the righteous were **Father Adam**, the **Ancient of Days** and father of all,"

The translated John the Beloved/Revelator also plays a big part in freeing the Saints of God from the 4th Beast Kingdom. Then, the grand council at Adam-ondi-ahman with Adam receiving the keys and giving them to Christ takes place. Most likely, in that order.

The Beast Kingdom Lead By the Little Stout Horn Persecute the Saints of God

(Daniel 7:23-25)

"23 Thus he said, The fourth beast shall be the fourth kingdom upon earth, which shall be diverse from all kingdoms, and shall devour the whole earth, and shall tread it down, and break it in pieces.

24 And the ten horns out of this kingdom *are* **ten kings** *that* shall arise: and another [stout horn] shall rise **after** them; and he **shall be diverse from the first** [10 horns], and he shall **subdue three kings**.

25 And he shall speak *great* **words against the most High**, and shall **wear out the saints** of the most High, and think to **change times and laws**: and **they shall be given into his hand** until a **time and times and the dividing of time**."

Learning Points:

A. The first 10 kings of the 10 kingdoms will arise and collude to combine their power and will be doing a good job of that. *Then* a "little horn" rises up and takes out 3 of the previous kings and kingdoms of the 10 kingdom conglomerate.

B. This "little horn" is *the* bad guy. He speaks against the most High God. He makes war and wins over the Saints of God. He changes times and changes laws (as seen later). And the saints are put in bondage for a time. What type of bondage?

C. The "time and times and dividing of time" is typically understood by most scholars to be 3.5 years. This is a guestimate by the scholars and I happen to believe it.

(Daniel 7:26-28)

"26 But **the judgment** shall sit, and they shall **take away his dominion**, to **consume** and to destroy *it* **unto the end**.

27 And the kingdom and dominion, and the greatness of the kingdom under the whole heaven, **shall be given to the people of the saints** of the most High, whose kingdom *is* an everlasting kingdom, and all dominions shall serve and obey him.

28 Hitherto *is* **the end of the matter**. As for me Daniel, my cogitations much troubled me, and my countenance changed in me: but I kept the matter in my heart."

Learning Points:

A. When "the Judgment shall sit"…the man who is to come and rescue the Saints of God from the oppression of the 10 nation 4th Beast……that beast will be destroyed **by fire and consumed**. That will be the *end* of the 10 nation conglomerate 4th Beast.

   a. Note: all 3 accounts of Daniel, Ezra, and John say this 4th Beast will be finally consumed by fire.

B. The Saints of God shall be given the kingdom after this Beast Kingdom is removed.

So if the 4th Beast of Daniel's vision is still in our future, we must also have a look at Nebuchadnezzar's Dream (Daniel Chapter 2) of the Kingdoms of the Earth from ancient to modern. The dream by Nebuchadnezzar King of Babylon relates directly with the latter-days and **the end** of this big ferocious kingdom in Daniel chapter 7. (See Appendix 1)

This full vision of Daniel's 4th Beast was left intact, however the part where the Ancient of Days comes and Judges the Beast and gives the Kingdom to the Saints of God is a bit further in our Timeline. However, this Author wanted to leave it in this section, of "the Rising Beast" so that you, the reader, will know that there is a very good happy ending for the Saints of God in America. Now, let's look at the *rise* of the Gentile Beast Kingdom in America from a few more perspectives.

7: Rev Chap 13, John`s Scarlet Beast Becomes a Reality, Not Just in the Stars

As with Daniel, John the Beloved/Revelator saw the rise of the Gentile Beast Kingdom. It was not limited to the vision of the stars that John received in Chapter 12. Because in the very next Chapter 13, John sees the earthly creation of the figurative Beast he saw in the star constellation.

Remember: **important timeline point**..in Chapter 12, we saw the Kingdom of God being born *before* the full creation of the Scarlet Beast Kingdom's sign in the constellations.

There is a lessor known dragon constellation in the heavens named *Draco*. *Draco* does indeed fit the description of the Revelation 12 Dragon Constellation. It hugs and surrounds Polaris, the North Star. It's tail swings out over 1/3 of the stars in the sky as the world turns upon it's axis.

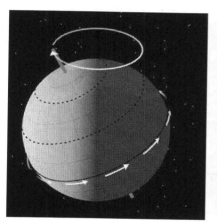 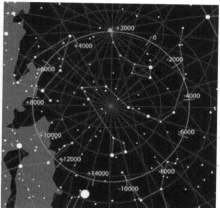

I do not have any specific timely events happening with Draco after the September 23, 2017 date. I'll be researching this topic for a future edition of this work. If there is anything happening with Draco that you, the reader are aware of, please contact me at www.LastDaysTimeline.com.

And now the Scarlet Beast with 7 Heads with Crowns and 10 Horns is born into physical reality…in John's Revelation Chapter 13.

> (Revelation 13:1-2)
> "1 And I stood upon the sand of the sea, and saw **a beast rise up out of the sea**, having **seven heads and ten horns**, and upon his **horns ten crowns**, and **upon his heads the name of blasphemy.**
> 2 And the beast which I saw was **like unto a leopard**, and his feet were as the **feet of a bear**, and his mouth as the **mouth of a lion**: and **the dragon gave him his power**, and **his seat**, and **great authority.**"

Learning Points:

A. This 7 crowned Head and 10 Horned Beast rose up from the sea. Sea or "water" is usually people. This is very similar to how Ezra's Eagle rose up from the sea. However, most of these visionary beasts rise up from the sea. Only a few rise up from land.

B. On the heads was the "name of blasphemy". I do not venture to estimate what that name is.

C. This Beast looks to have the **body of a leopard, the feet of a bear, the mouth of a lion**. These are the same 3 animals as in Daniel's 3 Beasts that came before the 4th Beast. However, it appears from the evidence that we are describing the 4th Beast. Thus, the 4th Beast is an amalgam of Daniel's **first three beasts**. This is a direct link from Daniel's Vision to John's Vision. Make a note of it.

D. The Dragon Satan loves this Beast. He gives it *power*, his *seat*, and great authority in the Earth. This is Satan's mission. This Beast Kingdom is what he wants.

This Scarlet "red" Beast with 7 crowned Heads and 10 Horns looks like an *amalgam* of the 3 last-day Gentile kingdoms of England, Russia's USSR, and Germany's European Union. However, this time, there are even more clues.

The **body** of the beast is the leopard. Thus, the bulk of the body is the old European Union.

The **feet** of the beast is the bear. Thus, the moving force of this beast is Russia's USSR.

The **mouth** of the beast is the lion. Thus, the rhetoric and oratory of this beast is England and it's speaking English.

The Deadly Wound Comes to ONE of the Heads of the Beast Kingdom

(Revelation 13:3-4)
"3 And I saw **one of his heads** as it were **wounded** to death; and his **deadly wound was healed**: and all **the world wondered after the beast**.
4 And they **worshipped the dragon** which gave **power unto the beast**: and they **worshipped the beast**, saying, Who is like unto the beast? Who is able to make war with him?"

Learning Points:

A. One of the 7 crowned heads of this beast was almost taken down. Remember, this beast is a multi-state kingdom of multiple nations and kings. So, **after** the Beast is formed....one of the Heads goes down. But, then comes alive again after being healed.
   a. This piece of scripture has been interpreted to mean at least 20 different things by the prophecy writers. **However**, only *after* the Beast Kingdom is formed can this come to pass.

B. The world in general, goes toward the Beast.

C. The world in general, worships the dragon/serpent/Satan. This may be a reference to a **state** religion under the 10 Beast nations.

a. We have seen in Daniel chapter 7, that great persecutions come under this Beast upon the Saints of God. History tells us that the absolute worst persecutions upon religion comes directly from the **state**, which has power over life and death. (See *Foxes Book of the Martyrs* – by John Fox. Also *History of the Christian Church* – by Cheetham. Free audiobook downloads on www.LastDaysTimeline.com)

D. The world also worships this great 10 Nation Beast…mostly because of its great power of war in the world.

Author's Analysis:

We have not seen the "deadly wound" happen yet in 2017 because the Beast hasn't been formed, and the signs in the star constellations haven't come to pass yet. Remember, this Beast is Daniel's 4th big "empire" type kingdom that is initially formed by the 3 Eagle Heads in Ezra's Eagle.

Therefore, this whole "Beast" saga in John's Revelation takes place *after* the star constellation *signs* in the heavens of the birth of the Kingdom of God….and the Sign of the Dragon Beast in Heaven….*and* after Germany and France's European Union (Daniel's 3rd Beast) goes down.

(Revelation 13:5-8)

"5 And there was **given** unto him **a mouth** speaking **great things and blasphemies**; and power was given unto him to continue **forty and two months**.

6 And he opened his mouth **in blasphemy against God**, to **blaspheme his name**, and his **tabernacle**, and them that **dwell in heaven**.

7 And it was given unto him to **make war with the saints**, and **to overcome them**: and power was given him **over all kindreds, and tongues, and nations**.

8 And **all that dwell upon the earth shall worship him**, whose names are **not written** in the book of life of the Lamb slain from the foundation of the world."

Learning Points:

A. This 7 crowned Head 10 Horned Beast was "given" a mouth. Remember, the mouth of this Beast was as a Lion's mouth. The plucked dancing lion in Daniel 7 most likely is latter-day Gentile England. Remember, this beast has the "mouth of the lion". So, at this point the Lion shows up to speak.

B. "The Mouth" speaks of very bad things against God, his name, his temple, and his angels. So, this Beast Kingdom who now has an English mouth speaks against all Christian religions. *Yet*, as shown in the previous verses, will have a **state** religion of its' own. Remember, the Whore, Babylon-The Great will mount and ride this Beast Kingdom.

C. This Beast Kingdom made war with the Saints of God and **won**….for a time.

D. This Beast has great power over **all** of Earth's peoples. Remember this Beast is a 10 Nation Government, *but* it is only 10 nations. All the nations of the world aren't on the team. However, all nations are within the influence of this Beast…

E. 42 months = 3.5 years – That is all the time that this Beast will be around… *in America*, before the Roaring Lion comes to take down the Beast. (Ezra's Eagle).

For the yet future Battle of Armageddon, the remnant of this Beast remains intact, because "the Anti-Christ" (Stout Horn leader of the Beast) is killed by Jesus in that final battle. But, America is freed *early* to restore the Constitution, and build the New Jerusalem (as shown in a few more chapters).

Author's Analysis:

Talk about "going backwards" in the world. American God-given liberties and civil liberties have been an institution in the world for 100s of years now. However, a return to a **state** religion under this 4th Beast would be really problematic for the Saints of God and all Christians that would rather die than worship something or someone who is false, to their understanding. Remember, freedom of religion was the very reason and basis the Pilgrims chose to leave their mother lands. To worship God according to the dictates of their own conscience….as recorded in the Holy Scriptures.

It would make sense that the new **state** religion of this Beast would cut-down the other Christian religions. As this new **state** religion would need to be promoted and made "the standard"… by official legal decree, then all the other Christian religions or otherwise would have to be degraded and demagogued. *And*, as we shall see, this new leader of The 4th Beast Kingdom will be an "Anti-Christ" that will have great super-natural power to show the world the dark-arts of Satan *openly*. Combine that material, with false religion and they will have what they need to make the masses bow down to their new **state** religion of The Beast.

The main influence in which America has on the world is through money, debt/finance, and commerce. There are plenty of other influencing factors, but these are the top 3. It most likely will be much the same with other nations that are not in the 10 nations within this new 4th Beast….We can estimate this, because of *who* is going to start it up and run it. It is the same people (3 evil Eagle Heads) that are running America's systems from behind-the-curtain right now.

The next set of verses in Revelations Chap 13: 9-10, deal with *principles* of the patience for the Saints of God living through this time period. The wicked will kill the wicked. Let it happen.

Rev 13: 11-18 deals with *another* beast that looks like a goat with 2 horns. This *new* Beast raises an image to the *old* Beast and starts an economic system based upon the Mark of the Beast. (See Appendix 2)

Now that John and Daniel's Beast with 7 Heads and 10 Horns has been raised up. …and it has gotten rich and powerful. It took some *time* to do that. Let us see what this 4th Beast Kingdom of the Gentiles' ultimate goal is to do.

SECTION 4: The 4th Beast Kingdom of the Gentiles Goes Down in America and Continues to Grow in Europe - The Lost 10 Tribes Return with Power to Save the Saints of God

YOU ARE
HERE

Political
; Down
: E.U.
iking of
iecret
s

5. Stout Horn and Gentile Beast Destroyed Out
of America - Start European Civil War

7. Trumpets and Vials of
John's Revelation
· Opening of 7th Seal

8. Battle of A
-Christ Sa·
-Christ Destr(
+ Kings (

4. American
Brittish
European
Russian
Empire
WITH STATE
Church

Downfall of ALL
Gentile/European
Kingdoms and
Culture

The Kingdom of (
NEW Nation of Z
w/ Capital City
The New Jerusal

·Birth of Kingdom of God
from Church of God

·cution of
h of God
'E Church

mes of the Gentiles
m Civil War

3. BIG Plague

6. New Jerusalem
&
Special Temple
Established
-Calling of 144,000
· End of 6th Seal

4. Return of
Lost 10 Tribes
w/ John Leading

8: _The Persecution, Oppression, and Martyrdom of the Saints by the Beast Kingdom in Nephi, Daniel, and John_

Of all things that the Saints of God have to focus on preparing for; this is it. This oppression of the Saints by the Beast Government will happen. It's inserted into the visions of many end-days seers: Nephi, Daniel, Ezra and John, plus others including Ezekiel and Isaiah.

Remember, where this oppression comes from....The Whore Church that is riding the Beast Kingdom with 7 Heads and 10 Horns. This is the **state** Religion of the Beast Kingdom._ The State has power over life and death of its citizens, which at this point will include the citizens of the United States of America under the awakened 3 Eagle Heads and the last 2 wicked short feathers/Presidents that moved from Right to Left.

This is all happening **during the end of the 6th Seal**, because the New Jerusalem hasn't been built yet, and the 144,000 haven't been sent forth to preach. This is **before** the absolute downfall of the secret combination Beast in America and the restoration of the United States Constitution.

President J. Reuben Clark taught this in General Conference in 1944.

> (Clark, Conference Report, April 1944, p 116.)
> "We of this Church will...have more sacrifices to make and more persecutions to endure **than we have yet known,** heavy as our sacrifices and grievous as our persecutions of the past have been."

Why must the Saints of God endure persecution for Christ's sake? Elder McConkie wrote:

> (McConkie, Doctrinal New Testament Commentary, 2:530)
> "When the saints suffer persecution for righteousness' sake, **they stand in the place and stead of Christ** and are receiving what the ungodly would heap upon the Son of God were he personally present."

The world, led by Satan using the power over death of the Government, crucified and murdered the Son of God. And so it goes with His Saints of God. We must prepare spiritually and physically for this.

We have already handled this Beast in Daniel Chapter 7 with its oppression of the Saints of God and the deliverance by "The Ancient of Days" which sits in Judgment upon the Beast and tears it down and burns it. Let us start off this section with Nephi.

Picking back up in the Timeline at the point of America has been "morphed" to part of the 10 Nation Beast Kingdom and is being oppressive to the Saints. Remember the Whore Church is riding the Beast... The persecutions and oppression of the Saints of God begins. (Returning to Nephi)

(1st Nephi 14:3-6)

"3 And that **great pit, which hath been digged for them by that great and abominable church, which was founded by the devil and his children,** that he might lead away the souls of men down to hell—yea, that great pit which hath been digged for the destruction of **men shall be filled by those who digged it, unto their utter destruction,** saith the Lamb of God; not the destruction of the soul, save it be the casting of it into that hell which hath no end.

4 For behold, this is according **to the captivity of the devil,** and also according to the justice of God, upon all those who will work wickedness and abomination before him.

5 And it came to pass that the angel spake unto me, Nephi, saying: Thou hast beheld that if the **Gentiles** repent it shall be well with them; and thou also knowest concerning the covenants of the Lord unto the house of Israel; and thou also hast heard that whoso repenteth not must perish.

6 Therefore, wo be unto the Gentiles if it so be that they harden their hearts against the Lamb of God."

Learning Points:

A. The oppression of the Saints of God by the Great and Abominable Church – Babylon the Great – The Whore and Mother of Abominations (she has a lot of names) will become great.

B. The Church Babylon the Great sets a trap for the Saints of God by putting a State Religion into the Beast Kingdom, which America is a part. (Shown in John the Revelator's section below)

C. The devil just wants to destroy people, even those that do his bidding. The captivity of the devil is always such.

The Lord's Divisive Act That Will Make The Unbelieving Gentiles Choose His Church of God or the Church of the Devil – The Lord Will Make Bare His Holy Arm in the Eyes of All the Nations

(1st Nephi 14:7)

"7 **For the time cometh,** saith the Lamb of God, that **I will work a great and a marvelous work** among the children of men; a work which **shall be everlasting, either on the one hand or on the other—either** to the **convincing of them unto peace** and life eternal, or unto the **deliverance of them to the hardness of their hearts** and the blindness of their minds unto their being brought down into captivity, and also into destruction, **both temporally and spiritually,** according to the captivity of the devil, of which I have spoken."

Learning Points:

A. Jesus will do a *divisive* act, at this point in the "last days" timeline. It will work on the minds and spirits of men for them to *make a choice.* 1. The Savior's Gospel or 2. Deliverance unto captivity and destruction *temporally* and *spiritually*....to fall into the **pit/trap** dug by the Great and Abominable Church for the Saints of God.

a. (**Author's Analysis**): In other words…will the people choose The Beast Kingdom with the **state** religion of the Whore Church **OR** will they choose the Kingdom of God with freedom of religion including the Church of God?

Author's Analysis:
At this period in the timeline….the Church of the Devil/Babylon the Great who is riding the 4th Beast Kingdom is on the run. They are going down in America. They planned war upon the Saints, they are going to get war upon themselves; both abroad in America, and at home in Europe via civil war.

The **divisive act**, or the Lord's strange act is **only an estimate**. For we can't know for sure….However, we know that around this time the Lost 10 Tribes of Israel start to make their way from the North to the boundaries of the Everlasting Hills (See Appendix 1-Everlasting Hills). Then they take down the evil secret combinations in the government of America, and kick the Beast Kingdom out of America. John the Beloved/Revelator is leading them (as demonstrated below). (See Appendix 1-Location of Lost 10 Tribes of Israel)

Only 2 Churches? – It Will Be True in The Future

This phrase in 1st Nephi of "save two churches only" has perplexed prophecy writers for a very long time. It was not true in Nephi's time of 600BC. It still is not true in our time of 2017. Yet, it will be true in the future...as our years catch-up to **when** Nephi is seeing this vision happen.

> (1st Nephi 14:8-11)
> "8 And it came to pass that when the angel had spoken these words, he said unto me: Rememberest thou **the covenants of the Father unto the house of Israel**? I said unto him, Yea.
> 9 And it came to pass that he said unto me: Look, and **behold that great and abominable church**, which is **the mother of abominations**, whose **founder is the devil**.
> 10 And he said unto me: Behold **there are save two churches only**; the **one is the church of the Lamb of God, and the other is the church of the devil**; wherefore, whoso belongeth not to the church of the Lamb of God belongeth to that great church, which is the **mother of abominations**; and **she is the whore** of all the earth.
> 11 And it came to pass that I looked and beheld **the whore** of all the earth, and she **sat upon many waters**; and she had dominion over all the earth, among all nations, kindreds, tongues, and people."

Learning Points:
A. This passage of scripture has stumped many people for a very long time. Remember, during the time period Nephi is seeing, there is a **state** Religion under the Beast Kingdom. So, in reality, there are only 2 **big** churches at that time. The Church of God rising higher in America to new heights of influence for good. And the Whore **state** religion of the 10 nation Beast Kingdom.

B. (v9-11) This is one of the scriptures to direct link "The Great and Abominable Church" in Nephi's vision to "The Whore – Babylon the Great – The Mother of Harlots and Abominations" in John's vision.

The next few verses in 1st Nephi 14 talk of the Church of God being small numbers, yet spread all over the Earth.

(1st Nephi 14:13-15)
"13 And it came to pass that I beheld that **the great mother of abominations** did **gather together multitudes** upon the face of all the earth, among **all the nations of the Gentiles, to fight** against the Lamb of God.
14 And it came to pass that I, Nephi, beheld the **power of the Lamb** of God, that it **descended upon the saints of the church of the Lamb,** and upon the covenant people of the Lord, who were scattered upon all the face of the earth; and they were armed with righteousness and with the power of God in great glory.
15 And it came to pass that I beheld that **the wrath of God was poured out upon that great and abominable church,** insomuch that there **were wars and rumors of wars among all the nations and kindreds of the earth.**"

Learning Points:
A. The Whore Church now brings armies up to America and other countries within reach, to attack the Church of God with men from the 10 Nation Beast Kingdom of Gentile Europe. This says the attacks are focused in the Nations of the Gentiles, that belong to the Beast Kingdom. (See Appendix 1: Gentiles)
B. The Saints of God hold their own with priesthood power, all over the globe.
C. Apparently the attack doesn't last very long, because the civil wars start **at home,** in Gentile Europe and America. Remember, it's all one big combined Beast Kingdom Empire.
D. (v15) Nephi's was shown that this is a bigger civil war than just America. This is evidence that the 2nd American Civil War may be the start of a much larger civil war in Gentile Europe and beyond.

When The Civil War Breaks Out in America and in Europe – The Promised Lands are About to Be Returned to Israel

(1st Nephi 14:16-17)
"16 And **as there began** to be wars and rumors of wars among **all the nations which belonged to the mother of abominations [Gentile Europe],** the angel spake unto me, saying: Behold, the wrath of God is **upon the mother of harlots;** and behold, thou seest all these things—
17 And **when the day cometh** that the wrath of God is poured out upon **the mother of harlots,** which is **the great and abominable church** of all the earth, whose founder is the devil, then, at that day, **the work of the Father shall commence, in preparing the way** for the fulfilling of his covenants, which he hath made to his people who are of the house of Israel."

Learning Points:

A. As there **began** to be civil wars among the Gentile Beast nations of America and Europe….this is nearing the time of the Lost 10 Tribes come back from the Lands of the North. (see below)
B. Another important direct link scripture from Nephi's "Great and Abominable Church" to John's "The Whore – Babylon the Great – The Mother of Harlots". This is very important. Make sure you, the reader, note that this exists.
C. This Civil War, **after** the Great Persecution of the Saints, is the start of the *work of God* to fulfill his covenants with Israel about *their lands being restored*, plus other covenants. The **clearing out** of the Promised Land of Joseph to prepare "a place" for Ephraim and Manasseh and the other Tribes of Israel to build the new Nation of Zion is to now commence.

Author's Analysis:

At this point in the timeline the Great and Abominable Church/The Whore-Babylon the Great is amassing armies from those European Gentile Nations of the 4th Beast Kingdom that the Whore Church is riding. The armies come up upon the Saints of God. (See 1st Nephi 14:13 from above)

The Saints of God have most likely already had massive oppression. Or else, why would "headquarters" send such a large army? It's because the oppression has been real for a very long time and the Saints of God are still not succumbing to it and giving-in to the *new* **state** Church. Remember, under **state** religions, the state has the power over life and death. There will be death for not following the new **state** religion of the Whore Church that is riding the 4th Beast Kingdom.

This same setup has been enacted by **state** religions upon those that were more *fundamental* in their belief systems. Some common examples are:

1. The new Church of Christ in the Jewish territories. The abuses of the new Christians by the Jews, with the power of the **state**, is even spoken of inside the New Testament. Saul/Paul was a lead Jewish persecutor. (Download FREE audiobook *The Great Apostasy* by James Talmadge at www.LastDaysTimeline.com/great-apostasy)
2. The new Church of Christ in the Roman territories. These abuses of the Roman **state** are famous. They roasted Christians and fed them to lions. The **state** religion of the day among the Romans was the worship of paganism with multiple gods. (Download FREE audiobook *Foxes Book of Martyrs* by John Fox at www.LastDaysTimeline.com/foxes-book-of-martyrs)
3. The Inquisitions. Any speaker of *heresy*, would be systematically persecuted by the **state**. (see https://en.wikipedia.org/wiki/Inquisition)
4. The Waldenses (also known as the Vaudois) of the French Alps. They suffered at the hands of the Roman Church for their believe that there was a Great Apostasy and that they were called by God to restore the Church of Christ. (Download FREE audiobook *Foxes Book of Martyrs* by John Fox on www.LastDaysTimeline.com/foxes-book-of-martyrs)
5. The Hugonauts in France. They suffered at the hands of the Roman Church.
6. The Roman Catholics in England. They suffered at the hands of King Henry VIII as he officially transitioned the country to the new **state** Church of England.
7. The Church of England in England. They suffered at the hands of Bloody Mary, Queen of England as she transitioned the **state** back to the Roman Church.

8. The Thirty Years War 1618-1648. The Protestants suffered at the hands of the invading Roman Church troops. It involved most of Europe with 8,000,000 dead. (see https://en.wikipedia.org/wiki/Thirty_Years%27_War)

9. The USSR anti-religious campaign to implement Atheism among the Russian population starting in 1921 under Lenin, then Stalin. The Protestants, Muslims, Jews, Russian Orthodox Church leadership were all murdered. Tens of thousands of religious clergy members, plus others. All in the name of **state** Atheism. (See https://en.wikipedia.org/wiki/USSR_anti-religious_campaign_(1921%E2%80%9328))

10. The Jewish Holocaust. The Jews in Germany, Austria, France, Poland, and more in the 1940s suffered at the hands of Adolf Hitler because their religion and body-type were not accepted by the 3rd Reich. There were other religions and body types that were persecuted including: black people, Romani, Slavs, and Jehovah's Witnesses. The **state** put them to death in mass work camps.

11. The current Muslim persecution of Christians in Saudi Arabia, Jordan, Iran, and more. The **state** religion is Islam. The use of Sharia Law enthroned by the **state** to enforce religious practices is still alive on the Earth today. These Islamic nations have **religious police** looking to enforce their official brand of Islam. (see https://en.wikipedia.org/wiki/Islamic_religious_police)

12. Communist China and the persecution of lots of religions. In China 2017, there are only 5 government sanctioned religions. The Protestant Christian brands are not any of them. The Communist federal government actively persecutes and murders many fundamental religious men and women. (see https://en.wikipedia.org/wiki/Freedom_of_religion_in_China)

The playbook is pretty much always the same in these situations. As the new persecutions upon the Saints of God get ramped up, it would *look and feel* like this:

1) The government declares a law that there is a ***new* state** Religion.
2) All other religions or Christian fundamentalist religions are commanded to join the new **state** religion.
3) There will be dissenters all over the place. These are people of high moral character with principals. Just the type of people that an aggressive State would not want to have around.
4) The Inquisition begins with the sending of "Agents of the State" into the areas with the dissenters. These agents have *authority* from the State to put down dissent and make people "recant and repent" and help them join the new **state** Religion.
   a. The main "agents of the State" hire more unscrupulous people to put in force the actions needed.
   b. This is the time of torture and death to get the dissenters to "recant and repent".
5) For the most part, the Inquisition is successful at quelling the small towns and villages. However, where there are large blocks of dissenters who hold on to their religion, the Inquisitor Agents of the State lose their battle with the local people.
   a. The local people get very angry that these Inquisitor Agents of the State are making people "disappear". The people fight back.
6) The Inquisitor Agents of the State make the call to "headquarters" to send more men to *force* this large block of people who are holding on to their religion to

submit or destroy them.

7) The Army Troops of the State roll-in and surround the large block of people just trying to worship God to the dictates of their own conscience.

    a. Or the families in the town/city see the troops coming and "take to the hills" and remain up there while the Army Troops take possession of the town and hold it.

8) There are battles between the two groups…and eventually the Army with its supply chain wins, because the citizens don't have supplies, neither in-bound to the city nor up in the mountains.

    a. Most of the time, the war becomes desperate for the citizens and they have a final stand and the Lead Inquisitor Agent of the State has been made to "look bad" for so long that he wants them all dead. And he orders "no quarter given" and a massacre happens. Just like that. It's over.

This same sequence happened in France, Spain, Austria, England and Germany…under the Inquisition of the **state** religion of the Roman State Church against those religious sects that sprang up in the Middle Ages and Renaissance.

Remember, the history of Europe is completely intertwined with the history of the Roman Church. They are the same history.

If you haven't heard of the Inquisitions of Rome before now, I highly recommend reading the books below:

Download FREE audiobooks from the website www.LastDaysTimeline.com:
- Foxes Book of the Martyrs - by John Fox
- History of the Christian Church - by Cheetham

The Edict of Thessalonica issued by the fractured Roman Empire on February 27, 380AD was the edict that made The Roman Church with the Nicene Creed the official religion of the state. Thus, a new **state** religion was born. Here is an excerpt:

(See https://en.wikipedia.org/wiki/Edict_of_Thessalonica)
"It is our desire that all the various nations which are subject to our Clemency and Moderation, should continue to profess that religion which was delivered to the Romans by the divine Apostle Peter, as it has been preserved by faithful tradition, and which is now professed by the Pontiff Damasus and by Peter, Bishop of Alexandria, **a man of apostolic holiness**. According to the apostolic teaching and the doctrine of the Gospel, **let us believe in the one deity of the Father, the Son and the Holy Spirit, in equal majesty and in a holy Trinity**. We authorize the followers of this law to assume **the title of Catholic Christians**; but as for the others, since, in our judgment **they are foolish madmen**, we decree that they shall be branded with the ignominious name of **heretics**, and **shall not presume to give to their conventicles the name of churches**. They will suffer in the first place **the chastisement** of the divine condemnation and in the second **the punishment of our authority** which in accordance with the will of Heaven **we shall decide to inflict**."

Notice that the *new* **state** Religion is *good*. Notice also, that the people who worship God in another way are made fun of as "foolish madmen." They are **branded** "heretics." Their churches are not to be legally sanctioned as "churches" by the government. Also, notice that the **state** will punish those heretics.

Just one week before this decree, those subjects who worshiped God in *another way* were tolerated and were on relatively equal footing under the **law** of the **state**. But, at this moment February 27, 380 A.D., that legal footing to be a church was stripped away by the stroke of a pen of the men who were in charge.

This began the massive persecutions upon the fundamentalist Christian religions in the Roman Empire. All the religions that were "not official" or that believed different doctrines than the official Nicene Creed were persecuted with torture and death. Much bloodshed was committed **by the state** to get people to "convert" and join the club of the new **state** Religion.

Much of the same playbook will be used in the future under The 4th Beast conglomerate kingdom with The State Whore Church–Babylon the Great riding the Beast.

This playbook will be rolled-out upon the Saints of God.

Remember, it's Satan's playbook. He *loves* **state** Religions that have power over life and death. I encourage you, the reader, to be ready for this playbook. Nephi saw it in America's future (See 1 Nephi 14:13 from above). It certainly has been done in the past. We are living in the middle-time. Prepare for the Inquisitor Agents of the State.

The modern prophets have also been preaching about the dangers to the Freedom of Religion.

Supporting what Nephi has seen in vision, the modern prophets and apostles have stated the same themes. From 2011-2016 there has been several General Conference talks that had topics surrounding protecting the God given right of *the freedom of religion*. This is a relatively new topic in 2016 for the Brethren to be talking about on a regular basis. Remember, the "attack on the family" topic started in the mid 1990s. By 2010, we could see the damage.

> (Apr 2015 General Conference, Robert D. Hales, Preserving Agency, Protecting Religious Freedom)
> "As we walk the path of spiritual liberty in these last days, we must understand that **the faithful use of our agency depends upon our having religious freedom.** We already know that **Satan does not want this freedom to be ours.** He attempted to destroy moral agency in heaven, and now on earth he is fiercely undermining, opposing, and spreading confusion about religious freedom—what it is and why it is essential to our spiritual life and our very salvation."

(Dec 16, 2011 BYU Commencement, Quentin L. Cook, Restoring Morality

and Religious Freedom)
"We share with many others a love and appreciation for the Constitution and **a concern about efforts to diminish the Bill of Rights' guarantee of freedom of religion... Religious freedom all over the world is also under attack.** It is important for us to become well educated on this issue and assume responsibility for ensuring that the religious freedom we have inherited is passed on to future generations. We must work together to both protect religious freedom and restore morality."

Currently, there are whole sections of the www.lds.org website dedicated to the topic of protecting *the freedom of religion*. The modern prophets of the Lord can see the trends of global society degradation. Follow the Prophet.

If you, the reader, combine Nephi's vision of our yet future, with the **new** topic of protecting *the freedom of religion*, and the past quotes of the prophets of God enduring massive persecution in the future; the reader can see where all of this is leading.

(Heber C. Kimball - Deseret News, May 23, 1931)
"After a while the gentiles will gather by the thousands to this place, and Salt Lake City will be classed among the wicked cities of the world. A spirit of speculation and extravagance will take possession of the Saints, and the results will be financial bondage. **Persecution comes next and all true Latter-day Saints will be tested to the limit.**" (See Appendix 4 for the full talk)

(Brigham Young 1857, Journal of Discourses, 5:339)
"We need not think that we are always going to be unmolested by the efforts of mobs.... If we live, **we shall see the nations of the earth arrayed against this people**; for that time must come, in fulfillment of prophecy"

(President J. Reuben Clark, Conference Report April 1944, page 116)
"We of this Church will...have more sacrifices to make and **more persecutions to endure than we have yet known**, heavy as our sacrifices and grievous as our persecutions of the past have been."

Good news: In Nephi's vision, it appears that the Army arrives to inflict its damage on the Saints of God, but that it doesn't get very far and the civil war starts, so they pull back. From Ezra's Eagle, we will soon see that the Saints of God are rescued by the Lion that puts down the 4th Beast Kingdom and kicks them out of America. So, we know that the Saints of God won't be wiped out like so many other groups have been in the past by the **state** religion.

Look at Who We Encounter NEXT in Nephi's Vision, AFTER the Civil War around the time of the DIVISIVE ACT by GOD........The Very Person Who is to Come and Fulfill His Last-Days Mission

(1st Nephi 14:18-27)

"18 And it came to pass that the angel spake unto me, saying: Look!
19 And I looked and **beheld a man**, and he was dressed in a white robe.
20 And the angel said unto me: Behold one of the **twelve apostles** of the Lamb.
21 Behold, **he shall see and write the remainder of these things**; yea, and also many things which have been.
22 And he shall **also** write concerning **the end of the world**.
23 Wherefore, the things which **he shall write are just and true**; and behold they are written in **the book which thou beheld proceeding out of the mouth of the Jew** (Bible) ; and at the time they proceeded out of the mouth of the Jew, or, **at the time** the book proceeded out of the mouth of the Jew, the things which were written **were plain and pure**, and most precious and easy to the understanding of all men (The Great and Abominable Church twisted it up).
24 And behold, the things which this **apostle** of the Lamb shall write are many things which thou hast seen; and behold, the remainder shalt thou see.
25 But the things which thou shalt see hereafter thou shalt not write; for the Lord God hath ordained the **apostle of the Lamb** of God that he should write them.
26 And also **others who have been** (Brother of Jared in sealed Book of Mormon Plates), to them hath he shown **all things**, and they have written them; and **they are sealed up** to come forth in their purity, according to the truth which is in the Lamb, **in the own due time of the Lord, unto the house of Israel**.
27 And I, Nephi, heard and bear record, that the **name of the apostle** of the Lamb was **John**, according to the word of the angel."

Learning Points:

A. Nephi sees the apostle John the Beloved/Revelator. Nephi is not allowed to write the remainder of John's Vision.
B. John was ordained to write the main last-days vision we call The Book of Revelation in the New Testament of the Bible.
   a. Another reference to the New Testament, not just the Old Testament is mentioned in the Book of Mormon. Both are mentioned at least twice.
C. When the Book of Revelation of St. John was first given and recorded, it was plain and pure. However, this reference by the angel of God in the Book of Mormon 2,600 years ago **knew** that the Book of Revelation would be twisted up and hard to understand. This intentional "twisting" problem was caused by the Whore – Babylon the Great – The Great and Abominable Church founded by the Devil.
   a. This Author has taken a deep look at this problem and has untwisted the riddle of the Seals, Trumpets, and Vials. Also matching up the Doctrine and Covenants Trumpets to the timeline. (Download it FREE at www.LastDaysTimeline.com/seals-trumpets-vials)
D. Nephi's Vision ends long before the start of the Millennium. For John alone was given the vision through the "end of the world".
   a. Nephi's vision ends at the start of the civil war among the nations of the Beast Kingdom of the Gentiles.

E. **IMPORTANT**: Nephi's vision ends inside the 6th Seal of John's 7 Seals. The New Jerusalem is not built yet, nor are the 144,000 sent forth to preach from Jesus in the New Jerusalem temple. These acts are at the end of the 6th Seal. *But,* Nephi did come right up to the approximate point when the Lost 10 Tribes come from the land of the North, who will be led by John himself...and the point is that Nephi ran into the apostle John the Beloved/Revelator at the **exact moment** in the vision, that he would have made his appearance with the Lost 10 Tribes from the North. I am amused by that.

    a. **Author's Note:** the material on John the Beloved/Revelator leading the Lost 10 Tribes is in a future chapter. This is just a foreshadow of what is to come.

    b. Remember, the Great and Abominable Church gets in a civil war with the Beast Kingdom back home in Europe, while America is still part of the Beast's 10 Nation Kingdom. The Lost 10 Tribes that come to push it out of America.

The Promised Land of America is to Be Cleared to Prepare a Place for Israel

This next piece is important. After Nephi's vision is complete, he is overwhelmed and tired. He gains his strength again and then speaks with his brethren Laman and Lemuel and tells them of the olive tree; and grafting-in of the **natural branches** of all Israel, including the 10 Lost Tribes from the North.

> (1st Nephi 15:12-18)
> "12 Behold, I say unto you, that **the house of Israel** was compared unto an olive tree, by the Spirit of the Lord which was in our father; and behold are we not broken off from the house of Israel, and are **we** not a branch of the house of Israel?
> 13 And now, the thing which our father meaneth concerning **the grafting in of the natural branches through the fulness of the Gentiles**, is, that in the latter days, when our seed shall have dwindled in unbelief, yea, for the space of many years, and many generations after the Messiah shall be manifested in body unto the children of men, then **shall the fulness of the gospel of the Messiah come unto the Gentiles**, and **from the Gentiles unto the remnant of our seed**—
> 14 And **at that day** shall the remnant of **our seed** know that they are of the house of Israel, and that they are the covenant people of the Lord; and then shall they know and come to the knowledge of their forefathers, and also to the knowledge of the gospel of their Redeemer, which was ministered unto their fathers by him; wherefore, they shall come to the knowledge of their Redeemer and **the very points of his doctrine**, that they may know **how** to come unto him and be saved.
> 15 And then **at that day** will they not rejoice and give praise unto their everlasting God, their rock and their salvation? Yea, at that day, will they not receive the strength and nourishment from **the true vine**? Yea, will they not come unto **the true fold of God**?
> 16 Behold, I say unto you, Yea; they shall be remembered again among the house of Israel; they shall be grafted in, **being a natural branch of the olive tree**, into the true olive tree.

17 And this is what our father meaneth; and he meaneth that it will not come to pass until **after** they are scattered by the Gentiles; and **he meaneth that it shall come by way of the Gentiles, that the Lord may show his power unto the Gentiles** [The Church of Jesus Christ of Latter-Day Saints], for the very cause that he shall be rejected of the Jews, or of the house of Israel. 18 Wherefore, our father hath not spoken of our seed alone, but also of **all the house of Israel [including Lost 10 Tribes]**, pointing to **the covenant which should be fulfilled in the latter days [remember, this is how Nephi's vision ended....looking toward the fulfilling of the covenant]**; which covenant the Lord made to our father Abraham, saying: In thy seed shall all the kindreds of the earth be blessed."

Learning Points:

A. The vision that Nephi just saw involved this very event. That Lehi's children, who are of the tribe of Manasseh+Ephraim of Joseph who was sold into Egypt, shall *receive* the gospel from the believing *gentiles* (of Ephraim)... just like **all Israel will**... including the 10 Lost Tribes from the North. (Exception of the Jews only, they will receive His gospel directly from Jesus on the Mt of Olives at the end of the Battle of Armageddon.)

   a. (**Author's Analysis**): Lehi was of Manasseh, however there were other families blended into the current Natives of the Americas. Ishmael's family was of Ephraim. Also, the Mulekites/People of Zarahemla were of Judah.

B. This scripture from Nephi, comes just **after** the vision he received. This fact tells us that the next thing in the vision is that the natural branches of the Tribes of Israel (the Lost 10 Tribes + Lehi's seed of Manasseh) are to be graphed into the tree which is being maintained by the Gentile/Ephraim Church of God (The Church of Jesus Christ of Latter-Day Saints). The true points of The Christ's doctrine will then be taught to all Israel... (Except the Jews, who will come last).

To lead off, Nephi realizes that Isaiah saw the same vision that he just saw... Remember Nephi was forbidden to write what *he* saw, but he wasn't forbidden to transcribe the very next events in the vision that *another prophet* saw and wrote.

So, Nephi wrote the words of Isaiah (Isaiah 48 and 49) at the exact chapters that left off of his vision.

More will be written about these Isaiah chapters in future editions of this work. However, here are the highlights to fill in the Timeline. 1st Nephi 19:23... Remember Nephi mainly saw America and the European Gentiles in his vision.

(1st Nephi 19:23)
"23 And I did read many things unto them which were written in the books of Moses; but that I might more fully persuade them to believe in the Lord their Redeemer **I did read unto them that which was written by the prophet Isaiah;** for I did liken all scriptures unto us, that it might be for our profit and learning."

Author's Analysis:

To save space in this book, please refer directly to the scriptures themselves concerning these 2 Isaiah chapters. Have a look for your yourself here https://www.lds.org/scriptures/ot/isa/48?lang=eng

1st Nephi 20 = Isaiah 48 – This chapter Isaiah 48 is the **lead-in** to Isaiah 49 which talks of (v15) "I have called him to declare, I have brought him, and he shall make his way prosperous." (v16) "The Lord God, and his Spirit, hath sent me." This is speaking of the man who declares the Lord's Word in the next chapter of Isaiah 49.

1st Nephi 21 = Isaiah 49 – This is John the Beloved/Revelator at the front of the Lost 10 Tribes speaking of what he will do in the Last Days.

Isaiah 49 says John will do FOR Israel:
- The gathering
- To restore all things
- To be a light to the Gentiles
- To save the Saints of God on isles of the sea (America)
- To rebuild the desolate cities or heritages
- Liberate the prisoners of the State Religion of the Beast.

Isaiah 49 says John will do AGAINST Babylon-The Whore Church that rides the Beast Kingdom:
- Israel shall take down the "destroyers"
- Deliver the captives away from the mighty Beast Kingdom
- Feed the Beast Kingdom with their own **flesh** (civil war amongst themselves. Beast vs. Whore).

Then Nephi backs out of Isaiah and doesn't write more of Isaiah for a while. Nephi actually starts **to explain what Isaiah wrote**; still keeping the commandment of the Lord to not write the remainder of the vision.

In Nephi's explanation of Isaiah we can catch these snippets…

> (1st Nephi 22:4)
> "4 And behold, **there are many [tribes] who are already lost** from the knowledge of those who are at Jerusalem. Yea, **the more part of all the tribes** [the Lost 10 Tribes from the North] have been **led away**; and they are scattered to and fro **upon the isles of the sea**; and whither they are **none of us knoweth**, save that we know that they have been **led away**."

Learning Points:
A. Nephi says the Tribes of Israel have already been led away. Especially the *bulk* of the tribes, the Lost 10 Tribes are already gone.
>   (skipping vs 5)

> (1st Nephi 22:6)
> "6 Nevertheless, **after they shall be nursed by the Gentiles** [believing Gentile Church of God], and the Lord has **lifted up his hand upon the**

Gentiles and set them up for a standard, and their children have been carried in their arms, and their daughters have been carried upon their shoulders, behold these things of which are spoken are temporal; for thus are the covenants of the Lord with our fathers; and it meaneth us in the days to come, and also all our brethren who are of the house of Israel.

7 And it meaneth that the time cometh that **after** all the house of Israel have been scattered and confounded, that the Lord God will raise up **a mighty nation among the Gentiles** [United States of America], yea, even upon the face of **this land**; and **by them** shall **our seed [Nephites/Lamanites]** be scattered."

Learning Points:
A. The Gentile Church of God, The Church of Jesus Christ of Latter-Day Saints, shall be lifted up in 1830 and shall be the standard to which all Israel shall flow, even the Lost 10 Tribes when they return from the North. That Church of God shall be in the land of America.
B. The USA should scatter the Native Americans (Nephite+Lamanite blood of Israel).

The Lord Makes Bare His Holy Arm by Completing His Covenants with Israel AND Bringing The Gospel Through the Believing Gentiles

(1st Nephi 22:8-12)

"8 And **after our seed is scattered** the Lord God will **proceed to do a marvelous work among the Gentiles**, which shall be of great worth unto our seed; wherefore, it is **likened unto their being nourished by the Gentiles** and being carried in their arms and upon their shoulders.

9 And it shall **also be of worth unto the Gentiles**; and not only unto the Gentiles **but unto all the house of Israel**, unto the **making known of the covenants of the Father** of heaven unto Abraham, saying: In thy seed shall all the kindreds of the earth be blessed.

10 And I would, my brethren, that ye should know that all the kindreds of the earth cannot be blessed **unless he shall make bare his arm in the eyes of the nations**.

11 Wherefore, the Lord God will proceed to make bare his arm in the eyes of all the nations, **in bringing about his covenants and his gospel unto those who are of the house of Israel**.

12 Wherefore, **he will bring them again out of captivity, and they shall be gathered together to the lands of their inheritance;** and they shall be brought out of obscurity and out of darkness; and they shall know that the Lord is their Savior and their Redeemer, the Mighty One of Israel."

Learning Points:
A. This scripture has a double meaning. The Book of Mormon is the marvelous work. But, the Gentile/Ephraim LDS Church cannot nurse *all* the Tribes of Israel until they return... including the Lost 10 Tribes from the North.

B. And the Church can't *gather them to the lands of their inheritance*, if the Lost 10 Tribes haven't returned yet. So, the marvelous work is still yet future (to 2017) for the Gentiles and the Lost 10 Tribes of Israel.
C. The term "make bare His arm in the eyes of the nations." is usually referring to the **large** miracle of the ice bridge in the land of the North that the Lost 10 Tribes will use to return to the North American Continent on their way to the Everlasting Hills. (See Appendix 1: Everlasting Hills)

It is important to note here that the Lost 10 Tribes of Israel are generally in one body. There is evidence on both sides of the issue as to whether they are in one body or if they are completely scattered and blended into the societies of the world. (Please see Appendix 1: The Lost 10 Tribes)

The Multiple Nations of the Great and Abominable Church Have a Civil War

(1st Nephi 22:13-14)
"13 And the blood of that **great and abominable church, which is the whore of all the earth,** shall turn **upon their own heads; for they shall war among themselves** [civil war], and the **sword of their own hands shall fall upon their own heads,** and they shall be drunken with **their own blood.** 14 And every nation which shall war against thee, **O house of Israel, shall be turned one against another,** and they shall fall into **the pit which they digged to ensnare the people of the Lord.** And all that fight against **Zion** shall be destroyed, and **that great whore,** who hath **perverted the right ways of the Lord,** yea, that **great and abominable church, shall tumble** to the dust and great shall be the fall of it."

Learning Points:
A. (v13-14) Another great scripture to direct link the "Great and Abominable Church" of Nephi's vision to the "Whore – Babylon the Great" of John's vision. They were viewing the same vision of the last-days.
B. Civil war among the Great and Abominable Church of the Devil and *who*? Who is fighting the Whore?
   a. Answer: it's the Beast Kingdom of Gentile Europe. In John's Revelation it says (paraphrased) "The Beast shall hate the Whore and shall make her desolate, and eat her flesh, and burn her with fire" (Rev 17:6). So, the Beast's Anti-Christ leader, who works "dark art" miracles will win the civil war and beat the Whore church – Babylon the Great.
   b. (v13) Also shows that this is a civil war, and not a normal war between 2 nations. This is a war of nations that are inside the 4th Beast Conglomerate Kingdom of the Gentiles.
C. All those that assemble to fight against the new Zion Nation will also be destroyed.
D. Notice that this Civil War amongst them will be the tipping point that shall bring the **fall** of the Great and Abominable Whore Church.

(1st Nephi 22:15-17)
"15 For behold, saith the prophet, the time cometh speedily that **Satan** shall

have no more power over the hearts of the children of men; for the day soon cometh that all the proud and they who do wickedly shall be as stubble; and the day cometh that **they must be burned**.

16 For the time soon cometh that the fulness of the wrath of God shall be poured out upon all the children of men; for **he will not suffer that the wicked shall destroy the righteous**.

17 Wherefore, he will preserve the righteous by his power, even if it so be that the fulness of his wrath must come, and the righteous be preserved, even unto the destruction of their enemies by **fire**. Wherefore, **the righteous need not fear**; for thus saith the prophet, they shall be saved, even if it so be as **by fire**."

Learning Points:

A. Speaking of the Whore – The Great and Abominable Church, Satan shall have no more power to operate that false State Religion of the Beast Kingdom.

B. The Whore must be burned – because that is what John and Nephi saw. This Whore entity is **burned**. There are lots of references to fire here.

C. The Whore tried to destroy the Gentile Saints of God in America. And God would not allow that. So, He caused a civil war on the Whore Church by the Beast, *and* The Lost 10 Tribes were strong to save the Saints of God and kick out the Beast Kingdom from America. (See Ezra's Eagle and the Lion)

D. The Saints of God shall be saved by the Great Jehovah and his strong arm, which will be made bare in the eyes of the nations…with his 'wonders'.

(1st Nephi 22:18)

"18 Behold, my brethren, I say unto you, that these things must shortly come; yea, even **blood, and fire, and vapor of smoke** must come; and it must needs be upon the face of this earth; and it cometh unto men according to the flesh if it so be that they will harden their hearts against the Holy One of Israel."

Learning Points:

A. Nephi makes another allusion to Blood (civil war), Fire (the Great Whore Church goes down by Fire), and Vapor of Smoke. This 'Vapor of Smoke' is the exact language used by John to describe the way the Whore's City on 7 mountains, near the sea, gets destroyed.

   a. **(Author's Analysis):** That looks like a nuclear bomb is used by The Beast Kingdom against the **seat** of the Whore Church (See John's Revelation vision below).

The Lord God is to Be The ONLY King in America

In the last verses of 1st Nephi 22, Nephi talks of the Millennium, just a bit. And we have to wait till we get to 2nd Nephi Chapter 10 before Jacob again explains the writings of Isaiah in clear terms.

(2nd Nephi 10:7-14)

"7 But behold, thus saith the Lord God: When **the day cometh** that **they** [all 12 Tribes of Israel] shall believe in me, that I am Christ, then have I covenanted with their fathers that they shall be restored **in the flesh**, upon the earth, **unto the lands of their inheritance.**

8 And it shall come to pass that **they shall be gathered in from their long dispersion,** from the **isles of the sea**, and from **the four parts of the earth;** and the **nations of the Gentiles shall be great in the eyes of me, saith God, in carrying them forth to the lands of their inheritance.**

9 Yea, the kings of the Gentiles shall be nursing fathers unto them, and their queens shall become nursing mothers; wherefore, the promises of the Lord are great unto **the Gentiles**, for he hath spoken it, and who can dispute?

10 But behold, this land, said God, shall be a land **of thine inheritance**, and **the Gentiles** shall be blessed upon the land.

11 And this land shall be a **land of liberty unto the Gentiles**, and there shall be **no kings** upon the land, who shall raise up unto the Gentiles.

12 And I will **fortify this land** against all other nations.

13 And he that fighteth against Zion shall perish, saith God.

14 For he that **raiseth up a king against me shall perish,** for I, the Lord, the king of heaven, will be their king, and I will be a light unto them forever, that hear my words."

Learning Points:

A. The 12 Tribes of Israel shall be restored in the flesh to the lands of their inheritance. To the land of Israel for most tribes and to America for the Seed of Lehi (Manasseh) and the believing Gentiles (of Ephraim). Ephraim and Manasseh are both children of Joseph who was sold into Egypt. America is the covenant land of Joseph.

B. America shall be a land of liberty for the Gentiles and no kings will be raised up here, unless they are destroyed. For the King of Heaven will be the King of America.

C. The phrase "from the four parts of the earth" and "from the four quarters of the earth" has reference to the place where the Lost 10 Tribes are currently residing. This phrase is found all over Nephi's writings and John's writings.

That material from the end of Nephi's vision was pretty graphic as to the oppression of the saints and **the war armies** that will be assembled against the Church of God by the Beast Kingdom with the Whore Church riding it.

Now, let's see John's martyrs standing at the throne in heaven that overcame The Beast, The Mark of the Beast and the Number of his Name.

9: *The Martyrs in the Church of God that Overcame the Beast and the Mark of the Beast and the Number of His Name*

In Chapter 15 of John's Revelation, there are a few brief verses that share that there were Saints of God that were among the dead in the Celestial Kingdom (apparently), that had overcame the 4th Beast Kingdom and the Mark of the Beast and the Number of his Name.

This comes *before* the 7 Angels with the 7 Trumpets and 7 Vials are delivered upon the nations of the Gentile Beast Kingdom.

> (Rev 15:1-4)
> "1 And I saw another sign in heaven, great and marvellous, **seven angels having the seven last plagues**; for in them **is filled up the wrath of God**.
> 2 And I saw as it were **a sea of glass mingled with fire**: and **them** that had **gotten the victory over the beast, and over his image, and over his mark, and over the number of his name, stand on the sea of glass, having the harps of God**.
> 3 And **they sing** the song of Moses the servant of God, and the song of the Lamb, saying, Great and marvellous are thy works, Lord God Almighty; just and true are thy ways, thou King of saints.
> 4 Who shall not fear thee, O Lord, and glorify thy name? for thou only art holy: for all nations shall come and worship before thee; for thy judgments are made manifest."

Learning Points:

A. **Before** the 7 Angels are loosed to pour the 7 Vials of plagues upon the Beast Kingdom in Europe, John sees dead martyrs standing in a Celestial Sphere. These martyrs lived and fought the Beast Kingdom and were killed and martyred for the cause of Christ. These are *not* ancient martyrs. **These are modern martyrs** who stood against the Whore Church and would not relent and join it. They held their faith.

B. These martyrs sang a new song; which is displayed above.

And more evidence from a future chapter of Revelation about those Saints that will be martyred by the 4th Beast Kingdom for their religion.

> (Revelation 20:4)
> "4 And I saw thrones, and they sat upon them, and judgment was given unto them: and **I saw the souls of them that were <u>beheaded</u> for the witness of Jesus**, and for **the word of God**, and which **had not worshipped the beast, neither his image, neither had received his mark upon their foreheads, or in their hands**; and they lived and reigned with Christ a thousand years."

Learning Points:

A. Same as before; John saw the souls of the people who didn't worship the Beast, neither received his mark, nor worshiped his image.
B. An additional point, is that apparently many of these people had been **beheaded** in their manner of death. (See Appendix 1: United Nations of Churches.)

Author's Analysis:
These dead Saints of God who would not relent to the *new* **state** Religion but held their faith, were modern Saints of God. They lived during the time of the 4th Beast Kingdom of the Gentiles (yet future to 2017). They fought it. They would not change their faith. And they were killed for it. Thus, the Beast and the Whore-Babylon the Great do have the blood of the Saints of God on their hands. And if they oppressed and murdered the leadership of the Church of God today, they would have the blood of Prophets on their hands.

Even Jesus Said It, in His Mortal Ministry in Jerusalem

Let us take a snippet from Luke 21 and examine it in light of what we have seen with the persecutions on the Saints of God by the Beast Kingdom which is ridden by The Whore Church. This is Jesus answering the question from his 12 Apostles asking, "When shall all these be that you have spoken?"

(Luke 21:9-16)
"9 But when ye shall hear of wars and commotions, be not terrified: for these things must first come to pass; but **the end is not [yet] by and by**.
10 Then said he unto them, **Nation shall rise against nation, and kingdom against kingdom**:
11 And great **earthquakes** shall be in divers places, and **famines**, and **pestilences**; and fearful sights and **great signs shall there be from heaven**.
12 But **before** all these, **they shall lay their hands on you**, and **persecute you**, **delivering you up** to the synagogues, and **into prisons**, being **brought before kings and rulers for my name's sake**.
13 **And it shall turn to you for a testimony**.
14 Settle it therefore in your hearts, not to meditate before what ye shall answer:
15 For **I will give you a mouth and wisdom**, which all your adversaries shall not be able to gainsay nor resist.
16 And ye shall be betrayed both by parents, and brethren, and kinsfolks, and friends; and **some of you shall they cause to be put to death**."

Learning Points:
A. Looking at this scripture in this "Persecution and Oppression Chapter" is to make a clear point; that the oppression of the Saints of God by the Beast which is ridden by The Whore-Babylon the Great happens *before* the Trumpets and Vials in the 7th Seal of John's vision.
B. The persecutions will cause some Saints of God to be put to death, apparently by beheading (See Rev 20:4 above).
C. This is Jesus saying these things at about 33-34 AD. He saw that the Gentile Saints of God toward the end days would suffer at the hands of the Gentile Beast and Whore.

D. Also that "great signs shall there be from heaven."
   a. (**Author's Analysis**): John the Revelator saw 2 big signs in the constellations of the stars. They are the Church of God give birth to the Kingdom of God. And the Sign of the birth of the Beast Kingdom with 7 Heads and 10 Horns, as already discussed. There may be even more "signs in the heavens" than these two.

This is a short chapter to specifically call to the reader's attention that this Beast Kingdom of the Gentiles with its **state** Church will be oppressive unto death. John saw the dead on a Celestial Sphere. They achieved "the victory" of Christ.

What else happens during this period of oppression of the Saints and the start of the Civil War in the 4th Beast's Kingdom of the Gentiles? It's the BIG Plague.

10: Jackson County Missouri and Much of the East Coast is Cleared Out by The 2nd American Civil War, Earthquake, and the BIG Plague while America is YET Inside the 4th Beast Kingdom of the Gentiles. The Times of the Gentiles are Now Fulfilled.

The visions of the oppressed Saints of God are now completed. Nephi's vision turns to a civil war that starts in America while it is inside the time of the 4th Beast Kingdom. Then Nephi's vision now wraps the timeline into some other visions by prophets and apostles of the future.

This is the point when there is a civil war in the 10 Nation Beast kingdom, including the United States *and* a Big Plague. Nephi saw the civil war start, just **after** the attack on the Church of God.

WHEN: The last 2 "bad" short feathers/Presidents of Ezra's Eagle are presiding over a smaller kingdom of troubles. They are ruling from under the last evil secret combination Eagle Head.

The vision of the 2nd American Civil War and the BIG Plague is seen by President John Taylor and Joseph Smith Jr. …and some others. (see Appendix 4)

The Times of the Gentiles are Fulfilled

The Lord gives ample warning about this period. The Times of the Gentiles are fulfilled when they actively sin against the Lord's gospel, or fight against the Church of God.

> (3 Nephi 16:10)
> " 10 And thus commandeth the Father that I should say unto you: **At that day when the Gentiles shall sin against my gospel**, and shall reject the fulness of my gospel, and shall be lifted up in the pride of their hearts above all nations, and above all the people of the whole earth, and shall be filled with all manner of lyings, and of deceits, and of mischiefs, and all manner of hypocrisy, and murders, and priestcrafts, and whoredoms, and of **secret abominations**; and if they shall do all those things, and shall reject the fulness of my gospel, behold, saith the Father, **I will bring the fulness of my gospel from among them.**"

The Lords missionaries will be pulled away from the Gentile nations when their time is fulfilled. The Prophet Joseph Smith Jr. received this:

> (D&C 88:88-90)
> "88 And **after your testimony** cometh wrath and indignation upon the people.

89 For **after your testimony** cometh the testimony of earthquakes, that shall cause groanings in the midst of her, and men shall fall upon the ground and shall not be able to stand.

90 And also cometh the testimony of the voice of thunderings, and the voice of lightnings, and the voice of tempests, and the voice of the waves of the sea heaving themselves beyond their bounds."

Additionally, there will be more light and knowledge that breaks forth at the **end** of the Times of the Gentiles; which is yet future to 2017.

(D&C 45:28-33)

"28 And **when the times of the Gentiles is come in**, a **light** shall break forth among them that sit in darkness, and it shall be **the fulness** of my gospel;

29 But they receive it not; for they perceive not the light, and they turn their hearts from me because of the precepts of men.

30 And in that generation shall the **times of the Gentiles be fulfilled**.

31 And there shall be men standing in that generation, that shall not pass until they shall see **an overflowing scourge; for a desolating sickness** shall cover the land.

32 But **my disciples shall stand in holy places**, and shall not be moved; but among the wicked, men shall lift up their voices and curse God and die.

33 And there shall be **earthquakes** also in divers places, and many desolations; yet men will harden their hearts against me, and they will take up the **sword, one against another, and they will kill one another**. [civil war]"

The 2ND American Civil War

This civil war starts in America. It is said by multiple sources to start because of political parties. Let us see the sources…

Brigham Young said this about the state to state civil wars:

(Journal of Discourses: Brigham Young 8:30)
"When the testimony of the Elders ceases to be given, and the Lord says to them, "Come home; I will now preach my own sermons to the nations of the earth," all you now know can scarcely be called a preface to the sermon that will be preached with **fire and sword, tempests, earthquakes, hail, rain, thunders and lightnings, and fearful destruction**….

…You will hear of magnificent cities, now idolized by the people, sinking in the earth, entombing the inhabitants, The sea will heave itself beyond its bounds, engulfing mighty cities, Famine will spread over the nations, and nation will rise up against nation, kingdom against kingdom, and **states against states, in our own country and in foreign lands**; and they will destroy each other, caring not for the blood and **lives of their neighbors, of their families**, or for their own lives."

Learning Points:

A. There is a lot here, but the point is that there will be State to State fighting in the USA and people won't have compassion upon their own neighbors or their own families.
   a. (**Author's Analysis**): This seems to be the same type of fighting that occurred when the Jaredites went down in the book of Ether in the Book of Mormon. Then too, it was because of secret combinations.

Orson Pratt gets even deeper and calls this fighting city vs. city and neighborhood vs. neighborhood.

(Journal of Discourses; Orson Pratt 20:18)
"But what about the American nation? That war that destroyed the lives of some fifteen or sixteen hundred thousand people was nothing, compared to that which will eventually devastate that country.

The time is not very far distant in the future, when the Lord God will lay his hand heavily upon that nation. ... It will be **a war of neighborhood against neighborhood, city against city, town against town, county against county, state against state**, and they will go forth destroying and being destroyed and manufacturing will, in a great measure, cease, for a time, among the American nation. Why? Because in these terrible wars, they will not be privileged to manufacture, there will be too much bloodshed-too much mobocracy-too much going forth in bands and destroying and pillaging the land to suffer people to pursue any local vocation with any degree of safety.

What will become of millions of the farmers upon that land? They will leave their farms and they will remain uncultivated, and they will flee before the ravaging armies from place to place; and thus will **they go forth burning and pillaging the whole country**; and that great and powerful nation, now consisting of some forty millions of people, will be wasted away, unless they repent."

Learning Points:
A. This civil war in America is a *localized* civil war taking place very locally to where the people live… even down to the neighborhood. What could make one neighborhood/county rise up against another neighborhood/county?

Politics!

As we shall see, John Taylor, the 3rd President of the Church saw it.

(Journal of Discourses, John Taylor 25:41)
"[I]t looks very much like as though the time was drawing near when this country will tumble to pieces; for if the people of this nation are **so blind** and in fatuated as **to trample under foot the Constitution and other safeguards provided for the liberties of man**, we do not propose to assist them in **their suicidal and traitorous enterprises**; for we have been **told by Joseph Smith** that **when** the people of this nation would **trample upon the**

Constitution, the Elders of this Church would rally round the flag and defend it.

And it may come to that; we may be nearer to it than some of us think, for the people are not very zealous in the protection of human rights. And **when legislators, governors and judges unite in seeking to tear down the temple of liberty and destroy the bulwarks of human freedom**, it will be seen by all lovers of liberty, that they are playing a hazardous game and endangering the perpetuity of human rights.

For it will not take long for the unthinking to follow their lead, and **they may let loose an element that they never can bind again.** We seem to be standing on a precipice and the tumultuous passions of men are agitated **by political and party strife**; the elements of discord are **seething and raging** as if portending a coming storm; and no man seems competent to take the helm and guide the ship of State through the fearful breakers that threaten on every hand. These are dangerous things, but it becomes our duty as good citizens to obey the law as far as practicable, and be governed by correct principles."

Learning Points:
A. President John Taylor saw that the **ripping-power** behind the future civil war was the power of the two political parties.
B. This **ripping-power** comes to the fore when the legislators and judges trample the U.S. Constitution.
   a. (**Author's Analysis**): In late 2016, after the Nov 8,16 election of Donald J. Trump, there was massive medium-level rioting involving 1000s of people in many cities in the United States, simply because one party lost an election. This is the first time in recent history that America had mass rioting after an election. The transition of power was less smooth than normal. (See www.LastDaysTimeline.com/donald-trump-riots)

Author's Analysis:

It appears that the 2nd American Civil War starts just at the time when the Armies of The 4th Beast Kingdom in the USA start to roll toward the Saints of God to put down the rebellion "of worshipping God" in a different way than the Whore Church prescribes… who is riding the 4th Beast Kingdom of the Gentiles.

It also appears that *this is the* **"sin against my gospel"** that the Gentiles will do, which will mark the end of the Times of the Gentiles. So, God turns them to fight amongst themselves in a civil war. And this happens at the fall of the Eagle during the last 2 short feathers/Presidents under the last remaining Eagle Head.

When America goes down to civil war + BIG Plague + The Lost 10 Tribes returning from the North… that is the start of the time the Beast Kingdom of 7 heads and 10 horns will eventually fall apart and lead to the Battle of Armageddon. (Note: the BIG Plague is seen below)

Think of that! Most countries or alliances between countries would topple over and

---

go through major reform at any one of these things. But this alliance of 10 nations will still keep going, even through the Trumpets and Vials of John's Revelation. They still show up with a very strong host to attack Israel at the Battle of Armageddon. That is how powerful this 10 Nation Beast Kingdom of the Gentiles is.

NOTE: **It appears**... that over time... there is another civil war that starts in the Beast Kingdom's homeland itself...Europe. It is unclear to me if these 2 civil wars are connected; or if they start at slightly different times. It appears the 2nd American Civil War starts because of politics. But, the civil war inside the Beast's Kingdom of Europe **appears to be** a religious civil war between the **new** Stout Horn "miracle man" who worships Satan directly, and the **state** religion Whore Church of the Beast Kingdom. (There will be more on this topic in a coming chapter, as it is yet future to the timeline.)

The BIG Plague

This BIG Plague has been seen by many prophets. It is also seen in Doctrine and Covenants Section 45.

> (D&C 45:30-32)
> "30 And in that generation **shall the times of the Gentiles be fulfilled**.
> 31 And there shall be men standing in that generation, that shall not pass until they shall see **an overflowing scourge**; for a **desolating sickness shall cover the land**.
> 32 But **my disciples shall stand in holy places, and shall not be moved**; but **among the wicked**, men shall lift up their voices and curse God and die."

Learning Points:
A. Right **at the start** of when the Times of the Gentiles is completed... this overflowing scourge/desolating sickness shall begin. This is one of the clues that the Gentiles have "had their day". And that the unbelieving of the Gentiles are about to be wiped out... in preparation for the return to Jackson County to build the New Jerusalem. And also to prepare a place for the Lost 10 Tribes to inhabit, temporarily.
B. The Saints of God will be better-off where they are located near "holy places". The Lord declares this fact.

Again in D&C 84, the same point is made:

> (D&C 84:96-97)
> "96 For I, the Almighty, have laid my hands upon the nations, to **scourge** them for their wickedness.
> 97 And **plagues shall go forth**, and they shall not be taken from the earth until I have completed my work, which **shall be cut short in righteousness**—"

Learning Points:

A. The BIG Plague is a scourging upon the earth because of wickedness.

B. These plagues (plural) shall be cut short to preserve the righteous.

Yet all the righteous will not be spared, because of the weakness of the flesh. **Assumingly**, some will have lowered immune systems.

> (Joseph Smith Jr., Teachings of Joseph Smith, Chapter 21)
> "[I] explained concerning the coming of the Son of Man; also that it is a false idea that the Saints will escape all the judgments, whilst the wicked suffer; for all flesh is subject to suffer, and 'the righteous shall hardly escape' [see D&C 63:34]; still many of the Saints will escape, for the just shall live by faith [see Habakkuk 2:4]; **yet many of the righteous shall fall a prey to disease, to pestilence, etc., by reason of the weakness of the flesh,** and yet be saved in the Kingdom of God."

The Bubonic Plague transmitted by rat fleas, in the 1300s in Europe, Asia, and Africa killed roughly 50% of those infected.
(See https://en.wikipedia.org/wiki/Bubonic_plague)

The 1918 Spanish Flu Pandemic infected 500 Million people. It killed 50-100 Million people worldwide in just a few months. That was 3-5% of overall world population. This flu virus killed predominantly healthy young adults, instead of a normal flu virus that kills the old and the young. It was spread by sneezing and coughing with people in tight quarters. (see https://en.wikipedia.org/wiki/1918_flu_pandemic)

The 2014 Ebola outbreak in Western Africa killed 40% of it's 28,616 cases, or 11,310 deaths. Ebola is a weaponized biological warfare agent. Ebola only spreads by blood or direct body fluid contact. (see https://en.wikipedia.org/wiki/Ebola_virus_disease)

However, this future BIG Plague seems to be worst. This BIG Plague is *new* compared to what humans have seen in the past.

Zion Shall Escape IF The People Follow God and His Commandments

> (D&C 92:22-26)
> "22 For behold, and lo, vengeance cometh speedily upon the ungodly as the whirlwind; and who shall escape it?
> 23 **The Lord's scourge** shall pass over by night and by day, and **the report thereof shall vex all people**, yea, it shall not be stayed until the Lord come;
> 24 For the indignation of the Lord is kindled against **their abominations** and all their wicked works.
> 25 Nevertheless, **Zion shall escape** *if* she observe to do all things whatsoever I have commanded her.
> 26 But if she observe not to do whatsoever I have commanded her, **I will visit her according to all her works, with sore affliction, with pestilence, with plague, with sword, with vengeance, with devouring fire.**"

Learning Points:

A. The scourging sickness, which I'm calling the "BIG Plague" shall pass over the land and the report of what it has done and how many it has killed will **vex** all people.
B. Zion shall escape *if* she follows the Lord's command with exactness. However, *if* Zion doesn't follow well, then it appears that much more than the BIG Plague would come upon her: sore affliction, pestilence, plague, war, fire.

It's in Isaiah too, in Chapter 28. Almost the same language

(Isaiah 28:18-22)
"18 And **your covenant with death shall be disannulled**, and your **agreement with hell** shall not stand; when **the overflowing scourge shall pass through**, then ye shall be trodden down by it.
19 From the time that it goeth forth it shall take you: **for morning by morning shall it pass over, by day and by night: and it shall be a vexation only to understand the report.**
20 For the bed is shorter than that a man can stretch himself on it: and the covering narrower than that he can wrap himself in it.
21 For the Lord shall rise up as in mount Perazim, he shall be wroth as in the valley of Gibeon, that he may do **his work**, his **strange work**; and bring to pass **his act**, his **strange act**.
22 Now therefore be ye not mockers, lest your bands be made strong: for I have heard from the Lord God of hosts **a consumption, even determined upon the whole earth.**"

Learning Points:
A. There is much more here, in these verses than just the BIG Plague. But, let's concentrate on that for a moment. Those evil men that are wicked on the earth during this plague shall have made a covenant with death and an agreement with hell. That sounds just like a secret combination's oath. (See Appendix 1: Secret Combinations)
B. Again, the overflowing scourge or BIG Plague will pass over the lands. And just the report of what it has done to the population will VEX the people. It will be a "consumption."
C. This verse in the middle (v21) between talking about the BIG Plague...that speaks of the strange work and the Lord's strange act. This is just like what Nephi says....just at the **same time** as the civil war starts in America and in Europe under those last 2 "bad" feathers/Presidents under the last Eagle Head in Ezra's Eagle. That is the kingdom of troubles *and* right before the "anointed Lion" (see below) shows up with a prophet of God at its lead to take down the Eagle. This strange act of God comes right at the point of the Big Plague.

Author's Analysis:
In the extra curricular visions (in Appendix 4), often there is found a passage about the Gentiles walking from East to West on the highways with small bags on their backs *during* the BIG Plague period. And that those walking are women and children, with very few men among them. This would make sense then that the civil war comes first; then the BIG Plague, as nothing clears out men alone from the population faster than war.

IMPORTANT NOTE: I am not basing my analysis upon what the extra-curricular visions say, but rather upon what the scriptures say and using those extra-curricular visions to fill in some missing timeline gaps. And preferably *only* those extra-curricular visions by prophets and apostles. The others would be of low grade value.

High grade data points first, medium grade data second, and low grade data last, if at all. This is the way proper research should be done.

These Clear Out Jackson County Missouri Too – Just in Time for the New Arrivals

Jackson County Missouri will be wiped out by the BIG Plague in America and neighborhood to neighborhood civil war. This is the plague that "begins upon my house" saith the Lord. Not a lot of super detail is known about how it starts. God has said this in the Doctrine and Covenants.

> (D&C 112:24-26)
> "24 Behold, vengeance cometh speedily upon the inhabitants of the earth, a day of wrath, a day of burning, a day of **desolation**, of weeping, of mourning, and of lamentation; and as a whirlwind it shall come upon all the face of the earth, saith the Lord.
> 25 And **upon my house shall it begin, and from my house shall it go forth**, saith the Lord;
> 26 First among those among you, saith the Lord, **who have professed to know my name and have not known me, and have blasphemed against me in the midst of my house**, saith the Lord."

Learning Points:
A. This scripture talks of many types of judgments, not only a plague but other judgments too. However, we know that they start with the members of the Church of God that have said, they know Jesus but have entered into the Temples of God unworthily. They will be hit first with these judgments.
   a. Note: this passage of scripture is usually interpreted by prophecy writers to mean "the plague" saw in John Taylor's vision. However, this scripture doesn't limit the meaning to just a plague disease. So, I choose to *not* limit God's word to a single definition.

The prophet Joseph Smith Jr. also saw the main reason that the civil war and plague took place…To clear out the land from the unbelieving Gentiles to prepare it for the Lost 10 Tribes of Israel with their millions to return.

> (History of the Church; Joseph Smith 1:315)
> "And now I am prepared to say by the authority of Jesus Christ, that not many years shall pass away before the United States shall present such a **scene of bloodshed** as has not a parallel in the history of our nation; **pestilence, hail, famine, and earthquake** will sweep the wicked of this generation from off the face of the land, **to open and prepare the way for the return of the lost tribes of Israel from the north country**."

Learning Points:
A. A "pestilence" is a contagious disease that spreads out of control. (See https://en.wikipedia.org/wiki/Pestilence)
B. The 10 Lost Tribes of Israel come back AFTER this sweeping of America by The 2nd American Civil War and the BIG Plague in the timeline.
C. Joseph *did* mention not only pestilence/plague and famine, but also **hail** and **earthquake**.
   a. (**Author's Analysis**): This earthquake mentioned *may* be the division needed to stop the Gentile East Coast USA from running over to the Mountain West.

Large Earthquake in America

There is to be a large earthquake in America before Lost 10 Tribes return from the North. The problem is that there is no location information with this quake. It could be anywhere officially. Since, we are talking about clearing out the middle section of the country to prepare for the new Nation of Zion, then the New Madrid Fault in Missouri and Arkansas would be the obvious choice. However, that is just one scenario. There could be many earthquakes in all of the faults. I leave this topic open for further research in a future edition of this work.

If we look at the New Madrid Fault Line in the center of America, the last time this fault erupted was during December 1811 thru February 1812. Right before the War of 1812. (See https://en.wikipedia.org/wiki/New_Madrid_Seismic_Zone)
The quaking in Missouri and Arkansas was so large it:
   • hit 7.9 magnitude
   • made the church bells ring in New York City and Boston 1000 miles away
   • turned the Mississippi River upstream for hours creating multiple new lakes.

On a more modern note, the reader can get very acquainted with what happens in American civilized society after a large earthquake by studying the 1906 San Francisco Earthquake. It struck at 5:12am while everyone was asleep, on April 18, 1906 with estimated magnitude of 7.8. 80% of San Francisco was destroyed. The city had electricity, water pipes, gas lines, railroads, brick buildings, steel skyscrapers, and cars (mixed with horse & buggies).

Download the FREE audiobook of "The San Francisco Calamity by Earthquake and Fire" by Charles Morris 1906 Edition with original first-hand accounts at www.LastDaysTimeline.com/san-francisco-earthquake

(San Francisco Earthquake - public domain) Notice 80% of the buildings are demolished. This was from the quake not the fire, which came through afterward.

(San Francisco Earthquake – public domain) Looking down a street with people wading through the rubble. The city-wide fire is in the distance.

(San Francisco Earthquake – public domain) This is the fire that swept through the city within hours after the quake. Firefighters didn't have access to water, so they used dynamite to make a firebreak line. It was ineffective. People were setting fire to their own houses because they had fire insurance and not earthquake insurance.

No Yellow Dog Will Be Left to Wag It's Tail

The famous "no yellow dog will be left to wag its tail" quote from Brigham Young comes in at this time. The whole area of Missouri and adjoining States will be swept clean. There are varying schools of thought on this "no yellow dog" idea. And therefore, I have left the quote out. But, nonetheless the non-believing Gentiles in America must be cut down before the land can be given to the Children of Joseph; Ephraim and Manasseh, and the new Nation of Zion as the Kingdom of God can be built.

The Special Plague Disease of God Using "Flies and Maggots"

We know that God has a "special" plague that is poured out from time to time upon the wicked that has flies that lay maggot larvae into live people and the victims are eaten from the inside out. (See Appendix 1)

This BIG Plague that takes down America doesn't quite look like that. It was seen by President John Taylor and others in the extra-curricular visions in Appendix 4. It appears to start off with a purple dot. Also flies and maggots are never mentioned in the BIG Plague in America, which would be a critical factor, *if* they were actually present.

However, I do *not* rule the "special fly/maggot plague" of God out. Evidence is fairly weak as to the exact nature of the BIG Plague to hit America and much of the rest of the world. We know what it will do for God's purposes. We don't know if it's bacterial, viral, parasite based (flies/maggots), etc…

The Extra-Curricular Visions Take Place Right Here in the Timeline

A great bulk of the extra-curricular visions of Prophets, Apostles, and members of the LDS church happen in this period of the timeline right here. The collapse of America, yet *before* the building of the New Jerusalem Temple and the start of the new Nation of Zion. (See Appendix 4)

I have noticed that many of these extra-curricular visions say nothing of the condition the world is in as it relates to Nephi's vision, Ezra's vision, Daniel's vision or even John the Revelator's vision.

These extra-curricular visions speak nothing concerning:

- The 10 nation Beast Kingdom of the Gentiles in America and Europe.
- The persecution of the Saints of God very aptly described and seen by Nephi.
- The specific order of the Seals, Trumpets, and Vials as seen by John (mostly because they haven't happened yet, in their visions).
- The Lost 10 Tribes returning to rescue the Saints of God from the oppression of the Whore Church as seen by Daniel, Ezra, and Isaiah.
- The civil war in Gentile Europe among the 10 Nations of the Beast Kingdom which ultimately takes down the Whore Church riding the Beast Kingdom as seen by Nephi and John.

Nonetheless, these extra-curricular visions are believed to be true by the people who recorded them. So, if we take them at their word, they deserve to be analyzed for *this* period of the timeline. (See Appendix 4)

In most of the extra-curricular visions, it is seen that mass amounts of the unbelieving Gentiles, mostly women and children are walking from *east to west* to get to the Intermountain West. This is the time when those that are purer in heart, who don't want to fight their neighbors, are repenting as they are walking to the West. The Saints of God welcome these new people and help them.

The Gulf Between the UN-Believing Gentiles and the Believing Gentiles

These new un-believing Gentile people might have some pretty large chasms to cross on their walk West. The Prophet Joseph Smith spoke of **Earthquakes** to assist in the take-down of the unbelieving Gentiles in America. Brigham Young spoke of a "gulf" that would prevent the intercourse one with another.

> (Journal of Discourses, 12:284)
> "By and by there will be **a gulf** between the righteous and the wicked **so that they cannot trade with each other and national intercourse will cease**."

> (Journal of Discourses, 5:10)
> "The time will come when we will be obliged **to depend upon our own resources**; for the time is not far distant when **the curtain will be dropped between us and the United States**. When the time comes, brethren and sisters, you will wish you had commenced sooner to make your own clothing. I tell you, God requires us to go into home manufacture; and, prolong it as much as you like, you have got to do it."

Learning Points:

A. Some sort of barrier or "curtain" will block off traffic and intercourse from the USA and the Intermountain West.
B. No goods will be moving, so the Saints of God will need to produce their own supplies.

Author's Analysis:
This "curtain" or "gulf" could be any number of different barriers to prevent commerce and transportation of goods. Here are a few that have been mentioned, as a summary:

1. A large earthquake with some pretty deep and wide cracks for several hundred miles **north to south**, would do it.
2. The elimination of powered transportation, that would be a great distance to travel over the rocky mountains. This seems logical, as many people were seen "walking West" rather than driving West.
3. A barrier of commerce problems, because the Saints and the wicked will not trade with each other because the Saints will not carry the Mark of the Beast. I do not think this is the reason for the barrier as some other prophecy writers propose.
4. A barrier of "men" preventing the travel West by light armored vehicles. In Joseph Smith's famous White Horse Prophecy (Appendix 4) he saw that the Native American Indians were providing a "band" around the mountains to stop evil-doers from going West.

So, any one of these methods to stop transportation would be a major problem for travelers, good or bad, to the West.

The 2nd civil war and BIG Plague have now wiped out most of the un-believing Gentiles from America. The semblance of the national government of America, under the 4th Beast Kingdom of the Gentiles may still be operating, a little. Or they may be trying to gain control of the territory of America once again. But, either way, that military from the Stout Horn is much weaker than it once was. Now it's time to witness the salvation that the Lord has promised to rescue the Saints of God and restore the Constitution to its original form and principals.

There is **now** open space prepared for the Lost 10 Tribes of Israel to return from the North countries and the **need** has arrived to provide water in the desert for the millions of people walking to the Intermountain West to cultivate crops to feed themselves.

Next, let's see the finale of Ezra's Eagle and how the Lion finally takes down the Gentile 4th Beast in America.

11: _The Saints of God are Saved by the Lion in Ezra's Eagle. The Eagle is Burned. The Constitution is Restored._

We left off from Ezra's Eagle when the 3 conspiring Eagle Heads were leading the show actively and openly, but that they started killing each other off. Now, with the last Head still alive and the last 2 short feathers/Presidents of the United States that switched from the Eagle's **right** to the Eagle's **left**,.....now we pick up the story of how it goes down.

Let us continue with the timeline of the destruction of the Eagle by the Lion and the Man leading the Lion. Read along at: http://www.kingjamesbibleonline.org/2-Esdras-Chapter-11/

> (2nd Esdras 11:36-37)
> "36 Then I heard **a voice**, which said unto me, **Look** before thee, and **consider** the thing that thou seest.
> 37 And I beheld, and lo, as it were **a roaring lion chased out of the wood**: and I saw that **he sent out a man's voice unto the eagle**, and said,..."

Learning Points:
A. At this point in Ezra's Eagle, we have a **change** in the nature of the vision by the words, "Look" and "consider." The Angel is going to show Ezra something different.
B. An image of a ferocious **Lion** that is running fast is coming upon the Eagle.
C. Note: This is a new lion. Not to be confused with the proposed Daniel Chapter 7 British Empire plucked dancing lion.
D. "Chased out of the wood" or [the woods] is where this lion comes from. He was previously hidden in the wood, but now storms out. The word "chased" means that something else was pushing him, out into the open.
E. This Lion's mission is to destroy this morphed Eagle by the command of God (as we will read in a few verses). To start, the Lion sends out an "ambassador-ish" type man unto the Eagle to talk and reprimand that evil kingdom. (Remember at this time, there is only 1 of the Bad Heads Left (or maybe none, depending upon how fast those 3 Eagle Heads get killed) _and_ the **last** two short feathers/Presidents, who are now on the **bad side**.)

> (2nd Esdras 11:38-40)
> "38 Hear thou, I will talk with thee, and **the Highest** shall say unto thee,
> 39 Art not thou it **that remainest of <u>the four beasts</u>**, whom **I made to reign** in my world, that the **end of their times might come through them**?
> 40 And the **<u>fourth</u>** came, and **<u>overcame all the beasts that were past</u>**, and had **power over the world** with **great fearfulness**, and over the **whole compass of the earth** with much wicked **oppression**; and so **long time** dwelt he upon the earth with **deceit**."

Learning Points:

A. This is the start of what the man's voice says to this morphed global government 10 Nation Beast Eagle.
B. This Man at the front of the Lion is sent from "the Highest" or God. And these words are the words of God given through the Man to the Eagle, which means that this man is a Prophet of God by definition.
C. This Lion is led by a Prophet of God.
D. The Lord's rebuke begins upon the morphed Eagle through a Prophet.
E. This Eagle Beast is the same as Daniel's 4th Beast. God made all 4 Beasts to have power in the world. That the last-days will be allowed to happen through these last 4 big kingdoms of Daniel.
F. This 4th Beast Eagle is the **last,** and it overcame or swallowed up the other 3 kingdoms that were past.
G. This 4th Beast had greater power in the nations than all the other 3 Beasts before it. And it wielded that power badly... with "oppression" of the people... and with "deceit".
H. This 4th Beast was on the earth a "long time." This is one of the first clues that this is *not* a short term endeavor, for us in 2017, before Christ returns.
    a. The "long time" might also be alluding to the *whole* time that America as the Eagle with feathers/Presidents was among the nations... which did stretch a good while in the last-days.

This 4th Beast needs time to grow. This 4th Beast must run through 3 big-time evil leaders (3 Eagle heads) and the rise to power of the Stout Horn leader. *Also,* this 4th Beast must build itself up so that John's Revelation can come true about this Beast, which just happens to be a *composite* of the first 3 Beasts of Daniel Chap 7 (Lion, Bear, Leopard - Rev 13:2).

Remember, the "Great Whore – Babylon the Great" must *mount* this 4th Beast Kingdom. And that Great Whore must have time to build-up an awesome city of riches, while riding the 4th Beast (Rev 18:11-19). We are not talking about a short timeline here.

Author's Analysis:
We know a few things about Daniel's 4th Beast as it relates to Ezra's Eagle:
1. Ezra's Eagle is Daniel's 4th Beast. The Lord just told us this directly in 2nd Esdras 11:38-39 and 2nd Esdras 12:11-12.
2. We know that Ezra's Eagle is talking about America in the Last Days. Approximately 1929 through 2017+. The feathers/Presidents line up perfectly and it's an Eagle kingdom with much power in the Earth in the last-days.

Logical Deduction: If Ezra's Eagle is America, and the Eagle is the symbol of America. Then it stands to reason that as Ezra's contemporary... Daniel and his vision may use similar symbolism with the animals as well.

These 4 Beasts/Animals *could* be the 4 most influential Gentile "empires" in the latter-days, in the *exact* Time order that they appeared.
- Lion = Brittan's Empire 1540s-1940s
- Bear = Russia's Empire (USSR) 1940s-1992
- Leopard = Germany and France's European Union Nov 1, 1993-2017+

- Eagle =America + global government conglomerate (this is known from the Lord sharing the interpretation of Ezra's Eagle.)

Much evidence has been given for this conclusion in an earlier chapter.

It is currently my analysis that these 4 beast/animals of Daniel's dream represent the biggest 4 latter day kingdoms of the Gentiles, in time order… and as we have learned from Nephi, the big Gentile nations are in Europe. It makes sense that all 4 beast/animals will involve Europe, including the 4th and biggest of them all.

This is my opinion. It seems to line up nicely. And because we *know* that the Lord showed Ezra the 4th Beast of Daniel as the Eagle 2600 years ago….At that point, there was no **Eagle Empire**. However, today the clue is quite obvious. Thus, if the Lord showed Ezra an **Eagle Empire** and seems quite obvious, *then* why not follow the same pattern and show a last-days **Lion Empire**, **Bear Empire**, and **Leopard Empire**.

The 4th beast rises when the 3rd beast is going down. Just like all the others have.

The "overcame" part may mean that this morphed 10 nation Eagle kingdom may have swallowed up these first 3 kingdoms. Which means England, Germany and France's EU, and Russia are all part of this 10 nation morphed Eagle. John's Revelation supports this same concept for The Scarlet Beast with the body of leopard, feet of a bear, and mouth of a lion.

If the Eagle is America…..it means that the westernized secret combination does indeed get Russia into the mix.

The Russian country may come with the Stout Horn/Anti Christ that was seen by John the Revelator.

Remember, first there were 10 horns/nations/kingdoms/kings that join this 4th Beast. But, then **one more** Stout Horn rises *late* and knocks out 3 established horns. That 11th little Stout Horn bringing his 11th Nation, may be Russia….and they may "stab" 3 nations or 3 kings in the back…to then take over rule of the whole 4th Beast.

The Lord Gives This 4th Beast Eagle Some More "Ripping" Through the Roaring Lion's Prophet

(2nd Esdras 11:41-46)
"41 For the earth hast thou **not judged with truth**.
42 For thou hast **afflicted the meek**, thou hast **hurt the peaceable**, thou hast **loved liars, and destroyed the dwellings of them that brought forth fruit**, and hast **cast down the walls of such as did thee no harm**.
43 Therefore is thy wrongful dealing come up unto **the Highest**, and **thy pride unto the Mighty**.
44 **The Highest** also hath looked upon **the proud times**, and, behold, **they are ended**, and **his abominations are fulfilled**.
45 And therefore **appear no more**, thou eagle, nor thy horrible **wings**, nor

thy **wicked feathers** nor thy **malicious heads**, nor thy **hurtful claws**, nor all thy **vain body**:

46 That all the **earth may be refreshed, and may return**, being delivered from **thy violence**, and that **she** may hope for the **judgment and mercy of him that made her**."

Learning Points:

A. This 4th Beast Eagle has been a **bad judge**. Remember judges preside in a court of law and have great power over people's lives. This morphed Eagle didn't appear to love truth in a court of law. It loved lies in a court of law.

B. This 4th Beast did many evil things that were uncalled for: 1. Afflicting the meek (God's Saints are the meek – by definition) 2. Hurt the peaceable (God's Saints are the peace makers) 3. Loved liars (God's Saints are commanded to tell the truth) 4. Destroyed the houses of people who brought forth fruit (the "bringing forth of fruit meet for repentance" is part of the Baptism covenant of the Saints). Apparently this Beast is destroying the houses, or families, of the Saints of God. 5. Cast down the walls of people that didn't attack the Beast Kingdom.

    a. It appears that this Lion has come to save the Saints of God against this oppressive 4th Beast of 10 Nations. These descriptions of the people that the 4th Beast has oppressed, does not sound like the rest of the world in general. It sounds like the qualities of the Saints of the Most High God.

    b. Remember, the affliction and oppression on the Saints of God and all Christians gets really heated *after* the Stout Horn takes over the Beast from the other 10 earlier Nations/Kings.

C. This 4th Beast has "pride" and "proud times"....but **they are over**. And "his", Satan's, abominations using this 4th Beast are done, as decided by God.

D. The whole Eagle with all its parts are to be cast into the fire. (from the interpretation)

    a. Notice the "claws" are hurtful. The rest of the earlier scripture barely mentioned the claws. This is the first time they really come into play. This is a hidden link to Daniel's 4th Beast vision that said the beast tramples and crushes those nations under its "claws" that do not join with the Beast.

E. (v46) This 4th Beast makes great violence upon the woman called "Earth". The Earth doesn't like it. (See Moses 7:48-49, the Earth is female.)

F. This is the wrap-up of the rebuke of the Almighty upon the 4th Beast Eagle. And the end of the **words** or talking that the Roaring Lion's Prophet will do. Next comes action.

Author's Analysis:
It is my opinion, that this Lion represents the Lost 10 Tribes of Israel returning from the land of the North. They will first come to the children of Ephraim in the Everlasting Hills (shown below). Then they will do battle to free God's Saints from the oppression of the Stout Horn/Anti-Christ that rules this 4th Last-Days Beast.

While the Last 2 Feathers/Presidents Reign, There is UPROAR

The Ezra's Eagle vision continues into the next chapter. (2nd Esdras Chapter 12)

(2nd Esdras 12:1-3)

"1 And it came to pass, while **the lion spake these words unto the eagle**, I saw,

2 And, behold, **the head that remained** and the **four wings [feathers] appeared no more**, and the **two [feathers] went unto it** and **set themselves up to reign**, and their **kingdom was small**, and **full of uproar**.

3 And I saw, and, behold, **they appeared no more**, and the whole body of the **eagle was burnt** so that **the earth was in great fear**: then awaked I out of the trouble and trance of my mind, and from great fear, and said unto my spirit,…."

Learning Points:

A. The Roaring Lion, or the Roaring Lion's leader prophet (as described above), ended speaking…but even while he was speaking, there was some movement in the vision of the 4th Beast Eagle kingdom.

B. There was *one head* that remained. The 4 "good" **right** wing feathers/Presidents were already gone.

C. The 2 very last short feathers/Presidents have a short reign. The kingdom is changed from big to small during these last years of this kingdom of the Eagle. And apparently it's **not** a peaceful kingdom. It is full of uproar and problems.

    a. Apparently these last 2 short feathers/Presidents reign at the same time as the **last** "awake" eagle head, meaning, that a different power structure in the Eagle has already emerged.

    b.   The "uproar" portion seems to be when America finally goes down. This comes just prior or just after, to when the Roaring Lion emerges and is talking to the Eagle kingdom.

          i.   (**Author's Analysis**): The "uproar and problems" of this kingdom was the beginning of the **2nd American Civil War** among the Beast Kingdom's internal struggle *and* the **BIG Plague**. These hit at *this* moment in the timeline.

D.   The very next thing that happens after the 2 last short feathers/Presidents rule…is that the morphed 4th Beast Eagle kingdom appears no more...and is burned. (The same as in Daniel 7). This "burning of the 4th Beast" puts the rest of the earth in "great fear." This is an interesting statement. The **manner and method** that the 4th Beast goes down puts the rest of the world's nations in "fear." Why would the destruction of such a bad Beast in America cause fear in the rest of the nations of the world?

Author's Analysis:
Remember Nephi says the internal civil war happens when the Saints of God are oppressed to the max. And the BIG Plague will go through about this time as well.

But, it is none other than the Lion itself and the Lion's "anointed" prophet that takes the 4th Beast Eagle out in America…and rescues the Saints of God from oppression in the process. Remember, the BIG Plague is what clears room for the large host of the Lost 10 Tribes plus the other Tribes of Ephraim and Manasseh to return and rebuild the cities. Including the New Jerusalem in Jackson County Missouri.

The Eagle Nation Gets a 2nd Chance and is Restored as at First

---

God's Interpretation:
Let us see what God's interpretation has to say about the end of this kingdom and how it goes down:

> (2nd Esdras 12:17-18)
> "17 As for **the voice** which thou heardest speak, and that thou sawest **not to go out from the heads but from the midst of the body** thereof, this is the interpretation:
> 18 That **after the time** of that kingdom there **shall arise great strivings**, and it shall **stand in peril of failing: nevertheless it shall not then fall, but shall be restored again to his beginning.**"

Learning Points:
A.   This part of the interpretation doesn't seem to line up with the story line. The only voice that was heard coming from the body was near the beginning of the feathers/Presidents. But, if we discount the misalignment, we can learn much about what it says. I make no interpretation as for an apparent misalignment. If you, the reader, know more about this voice, please contact me at www.LastDaysTimeline.com
B.   IMPORTANT: When this 4th Beast Eagle Kingdom *starts* to go down, great "strivings" happen that will have the kingdom stand in "peril of failing." But, it shall not fall but "shall be restored again to his beginning."

a. Remember, this Eagle kingdom is a big part of a much bigger 10 nation 4th Beast of Daniel. It has morphed. The 3 Heads of the Eagle started this 10 Nation 4th Beast. But, apparently while inside this 10 nation Beast, this Eagle kingdom will go **down**, *but* shall be restored again to its beginning.

Author's Analysis:
Wow, this important statement about the nation being "restored," makes the whole picture very clear.

What an odd thing to say. That after the destruction of this Eagle, that it will be restored…after all the damage that this morphed 4th Beast has done with its 3 wicked Eagle Heads and 10+1 Nation **state** oppression upon the Saints of God. I know of no other place in any scripture that has said "the nation will be restored" after it has been brought down and been judged by God. This is an odd thing to happen in history. Usually nations that go down don't come back.

Remember that Joseph Smith Jr said (paraphrased) that the United States of America would be in danger of failing and that the Constitution would hang as it were, by a thread. And that the Saints would reinstate it and restore the Constitution in this land of America.

Many early brethren wrote that the Prophet Joseph said these words…always a little different, but that was the main concept as stated in the 1840-1842 Navoo period, recorded by: The Joseph Smith Papers, Parley P. Pratt, James Burgess, Orson Hyde, Eliza R. Snow, Jedediah M. Grant, Brigham Young, John Taylor, and J. Reuben Clark Jr. Plus many modern prophets have mentioned it.

(See https://www.lds.org/ensign/1976/06/i-have-a-question?lang=eng)

The point is, that *both* of these 2,600 year old prophesies by Ezra and Daniel appear to **link directly** to what the Prophet Joseph Smith Jr. said would happen to America in the end. *And*, this is from a section of the apocrypha that was not read much by the early brethren because Joseph Smith was not commanded to translate it. Our God is a Great All-Knowing and Everlasting God. Only He could make such great connections. I give all praise to our Father in Heaven.

These "great strivings" that produce the result of the Eagle kingdom going down, would represent the 2nd Civil War of neighborhood VS neighborhood that has been spoken of by the extra curricular prophetic visions of John Taylor and others (See Appendix 4). If these extra-curricular visions are correct, ***this* is the *time*** when they will come to pass… after the first 2 Eagle Heads go down and these last 2 "bad" feathers/Presidents are in office.

The Lion Delivers The Saints of God with Mercy and Shall Make Them Joyful

God's Interpretation:
Onto God's Interpretation of the Lion and what the Lion **Does**:

(2nd Esdras 12:31-36)

"31 And **the lion**, whom thou sawest **rising up out of the wood**, and **roaring**, and **speaking to the eagle, and rebuking her** for her unrighteousness with all the words which thou hast heard;

32 This is **the anointed**, which **the Highest hath kept for them** and for their wickedness **unto the end**: **he** shall **reprove them**, and **shall upbraid them** with their cruelty.

33 For **he** shall **set them before him alive in judgment**, and **shall rebuke them**, and **correct them**.

34 For **the rest of my people <u>shall he deliver</u> with mercy, those that have been pressed** upon my borders, and **he shall make them joyful** until the coming of **the day of judgment**, whereof I have spoken unto thee from the beginning.

35 This is the dream that thou sawest, and these are the interpretations.

36 **Thou only hast been meet to know this secret** of the **Highest.**"

Learning Points:
A. The Roaring Lion shall rebuke the morphed 4th Beast Eagle kingdom and take it down by fire (shown below).
B. This Lion is "the anointed" of the Lord. This Lion has been kept hidden in the woods by the Lord, for this very purpose to bring down this 4th Beast 10+1 nation conglomerate. <u>This Lion will **_judge_** and carry out the **judgments** of God upon this 4th Beast.</u>
C. *However*, <u>this Lion will also **deliver** God's people</u>, the Saints, that have been oppressed by the 4th Beast.
    a. (**Author's Analysis**) This sounds exactly what the Lost 10 Tribes of Israel will do when they return from the Land of the North where God has led them (more on this subject to come).
D. This is the end of the dream and the end of God's interpretation of the dream. Ezra was the only prophet that was shown **this** *part* of the grand vision of the last-days history of this Earth.
    b. (**Author's Analysis**) This seems to be why Daniel, John the Revelator, Isaiah, and others have not spoken much of the early history of this Eagle 4th Beast. Many have spoken of the 4th Beast and what happens to it, but not any have recorded the "early history" of how this 4th Beast rose up in the world. **Now** we have our answers....and we, in 2017 are right in the middle of it. We are living during the time of Daniel's 3rd Beast Kingdom, the Leopard Germany and France's European Union.

Author's INTERJECTION Estimate:
On verse 45 of Chapter 12 of Ezra's Eagle – the whole of Ezra's Eagle vision didn't mention anything about "claws" except that the eagle sat upon them. Yet in the Interpretation in Chapter 12 "thy hurtful claws" is mentioned by God through the Lion's messenger.

Also in Daniel's Vision of the 4th Beast (Daniel chap 7:19)... *Only* in the interpretation do we see "nails of brass." The main vision of Daniel didn't mention "nails" at all.

If "nails and claws" are the same, this additional clue allows us to integrate Daniel's vision and Ezra's vision a bit more.

A Word on World War 3

Ezra's Eagle vision of the feathers/Presidents of America does not mention World War 2 or any other major wars that America has faced. Ezra's Eagle would also be silent upon any World War 3 that may erupt as well.

There are many prophecy writers that this Author has read, that say that World War 3 with Russia/China is right around the corner from 2017 in the timeline. Joel Skousen's work on *Strategic Relocation* is highly recommended. As is Duane Crowther's work *Prophecy – Key to the Future*. I see the timeline differently than these two authors, but both books were good starting points and have much material that is *very* useful. Pick them up on our website www.LastDaysTimeline.com

Many authors are predicting World War 3 with Russian/China. I see the world "leaning" that way too. Yet, I do *not* take a direct stance on *when* such a war would happen. I do reserve the right to change my mind in the future.

(pure estimation) I see a possibility that the Stout Horn is the leader of Russia. If The evil Stout Horn leader comes from Russia, this Stout Horn will then take-out 3 earlier horns/kings/kingdoms. That take-down may include a nuclear exchange. ----- Again, I reserve the right to change my mind and include further evidence on this topic in the future.

The Stout Horn = The Anti-Christ/False Prophet of John's Revelation, could also be from Turkey or Europe. This could be demonstrated from Daniel's Dream of the Ram and He Goat (see Appendix 1).

This Lion that is sent by God with a prophet at the lead, to take down the Eagle Nation that is part of the new 10 Nation 4th Beast... *appears to be*, the same Lion that the Savior spoke to the Nephites about in his address following their destruction (see next chapter).

Wouldn't that be something? That Jesus uses the same figurative animal to describe the same event, yet talks about the same animal more than 600 years apart to two different groups of people; Ezra and the Nephites.

God is all wise. He knows the end from the beginning.

Let us look at the features of both of these Lions and get to the bottom of the story.

12: The Unbelieving of the Gentiles Will Get Tread Down by the House of Israel as a Lion

This chapter is here to determine if "the Lion that goes through the Gentiles that none can deliver," is the same Lion as recorded in Ezra's Eagle that takes down the secret combination that is ruling the Eagle Nation.

Quick Bullet Points on the Lion in Ezra's Eagle:

- The Lion has a prophet leader that is "anointed" at the lead (2nd Esdras 11:37-38 and 11:32).
- The Lion comes "out of the wood" or has been hidden in the wood and comes out into the open.
- The Lion comes quickly upon the Eagle. He is running fast.
- The Lion's leader "the anointed" rips into the Eagle and calls it to repentance in a big way.
- The Lion's leader delivers a message to the Eagle directly from the Lord.
- The Lords message to the Eagle is that it is Daniel's 4th Beast. And Daniel's 4th Beast is a Gentile Kingdom, just like the 3 kingdoms before it. The 4th Beast is a combination of first 3 Beasts of the (Dancing plucked Lion, laying Bear with 3 ribs in teeth, the 4 winged 4 headed Leopard).
- The Lion saves the people who are meek and non-destructive *from* the Eagle
- In the end, the Eagle is burned. The scripture doesn't say if the Lion did it, or if the Lord did it. For the sake of this work, we "may" say that the Lion did the burning and the destruction of the Eagle. However, it is not perfectly conclusive.

Now, onto Jesus speaking with the Nephites of the Lion that will go through the Gentiles.

Summary for brevity: In 3rd Nephi Chapter 16, Jesus is speaking with the gathered Nephites at the Temple in Bountiful **about the other 10 Lost Tribes of Israel from the North countries.** Jesus will be going to them soon to declare his Word unto them directly. Also that in the latter-days "the truth" shall come unto the believing Gentiles. And the Gentiles will bring it to the House of Israel.

But, the **unbelieving** of the Gentiles, **when they shall "sin" against Jesus' gospel**, the fullness of the gospel shall be withdrawn from them. Then Israel will be remembered and the covenant of their lands (plus other parts of the covenant) will start to come to pass. And it starts in verse 13…

> (3 Nephi 16:13-20)
> "13 But if the Gentiles will repent and return unto me, saith the Father, behold they shall be numbered among my people, O house of Israel.
> 14 And **I will not suffer my people, who are of the house of Israel, to go through among them, and tread them down,** saith the Father.
> 15 But if they will not turn unto me, and hearken unto my voice, I

will suffer them, yea, **I will suffer my people, O house of Israel, that they shall go through among them, and shall tread them down, and they shall be as salt that hath lost its savor, which is thenceforth good for nothing but to be cast out, and to be trodden under foot of my people, O house of Israel.**

16 Verily, verily, I say unto you, thus hath the Father commanded me—that I should give unto <u>this people this land</u> for their inheritance.

17 And then the words of the prophet Isaiah shall be fulfilled, which say:

18 Thy watchmen shall lift up the voice; with the voice together shall they sing, for they shall see eye to eye when the **Lord shall bring again Zion.**

19 Break forth into joy, sing together, ye waste places of Jerusalem; for the Lord hath comforted his people, he hath redeemed Jerusalem.

20 The <u>**Lord hath made bare his holy arm in the eyes of all the nations**</u>; and <u>**all the ends of the earth shall see the salvation of God**</u>."

Learning Points:
A. If the non-believing Gentiles **in America** (or the America's) where Lehi's children are, don't repent, then the House of Israel will tread them down. And the House of Israel shall do it. The question then comes in… which Tribes?
   a. Remember earlier in this same Chapter 16, Jesus was speaking of the Lost 10 Tribes that the Father had led away from the knowledge of everyone, both Jew and Gentile.
B. This land of America (or the America's) shall be a Promised Land unto Lehi's children (of Manasseh - Nephites and Lamanites). Also, to all the seed of Joseph, including Ephraim.
   a. Remember, it was by Manasseh that the Book of Mormon was written, compiled, and buried. And it was by the Ephraimite Gentiles that bring the Book of Mormon forth to the world as the latter-day Church of God. The House of Joseph will inherit this land of America, as it is covenanted by the Lord to them.
C. This Isaiah passage is drenched in meaning. Jesus, in Isaiah's language, is saying that the unbelieving of the Gentiles *must be* cut down, out of the land of America, so that the House of Joseph will start the foundations of the new Zion Nation.
D. Then, the last statement is very cryptic about what the Lord will do to "make bare his holy arm in the eyes of all the nations."

Author's Analysis:
My current opinion is that the way the Lord will make bare his holy arm in the sight of all the nations so that they will **see** the salvation of God is with the grand miracle at the time of the Lost 10 Tribes return from the lands of the North. This huge miracle is very important and will be discussed in a chapter by itself, because it is of **great importance** to the timeline of last-days events.

Jesus Split This Message From the Father About "The Restoration of Israel" into 2 Separate Days – WHY?

Look at this transition that Jesus does in Chapter 20. The 2nd Day of His visitation to the children of Lehi...The people have been taking the sacrament that Jesus miraculously provided to them. Then, they transition to speaking of the words of Isaiah and the House of Israel running through the un-believing Gentiles in the land of America.

(3 Nephi 20:9-22)
"9 Now, when the multitude had all eaten and drunk, behold, they were filled with the Spirit; and they did cry out with one voice, and gave glory to Jesus, whom they both saw and heard.

10 And it came to pass that when they had all given glory unto Jesus, he said unto them: Behold now I finish the commandment which the Father hath commanded me concerning this people, who are a remnant of the house of Israel.

11 Ye remember that I spake unto you, and said that when the words of Isaiah should be fulfilled [at Jesus' visit from the day before]—behold they are written, ye have them before you, therefore search them—

12 And verily, verily, I say unto you, that **when** they shall be fulfilled **then** is the fulfilling of the covenant which the Father hath made unto his people, O house of Israel. [about the **land**]

13 And **then** shall **the remnants**, which shall be scattered abroad upon the face of the earth, be gathered in from the east and from the west, and from the south and from the north; and they shall be brought to the knowledge of the Lord their God, who hath redeemed them.

14 And the Father hath commanded me that **I should give unto you [children of Lehi] this land** [of America], for **your** inheritance.

15 And I say unto you, that if **the Gentiles** do not repent after the blessing which they shall receive, **after** they have scattered my people [the Indian Wars]—

16 **Then** shall **ye**, who are **a remnant of the house of Jacob**, go forth among them; and **ye shall be in the midst of them [Gentiles] who shall be many**; and **ye** shall be among them as **a lion** among the beasts of the forest, and as **a young lion among the flocks of sheep**, who, if he goeth through both treadeth down and teareth in pieces, and none can deliver.

17 **Thy hand** shall be lifted up upon **thine adversaries** [the unbelieving Gentiles], and all thine enemies shall be cut off.

18 And I will **gather my people** together as a man gathereth his sheaves into the floor.

19 For I will make **my people** with whom the Father hath covenanted, yea, I will make **thy horn iron**, and I will make **thy hoofs brass**. And thou shalt **beat in pieces many people [unbelieving Gentiles]**; and I will consecrate their gain unto the Lord, and their substance unto the Lord of the whole earth. And behold, I am he who doeth it.

20 And it shall come to pass, saith the Father, that the sword of my justice shall **hang over them at that day**; and except they [Gentiles] repent it shall fall upon them, saith the Father, yea, even **upon all the nations of the**

Gentiles [America + the Rest of the 4th Beast 10 Nation Kingdom].
21 And it shall come to pass that **I will <u>establish</u> my people, <u>O house of Israel</u>**.
22 And behold, **this people [children of Lehi] will I establish in this land** [America], unto the fulfilling of the covenant which I made with your father Jacob; and it shall be a **<u>New Jerusalem</u>**. And the **powers of heaven shall be in the midst of this people**; yea, even **I** [Jesus] **will be in the midst of you.**"

Learning Points:

A. Jesus continues his information about the Lost 10 Tribes that the Father hath led away, from yesterday. He now transitions from speaking about the Lost 10 Tribes of Israel yesterday, to speaking mainly of the children of Lehi (Nephites and Lamanites = Native American Indians) today.

B. Today Jesus mentions *The Lion*. That the Children of Israel will go through the un-believing Gentiles like a Lion through sheep.

C. None of the unbelieving Gentiles will be able to stop the Tribes of Israel in their "treading" actions.

D. The remnant of Israel will then be gathered.

E. The people of Israel will have some good technology as "thy horn iron, thy hoofs brass." Their weapons of war will be better than the Gentiles in America have.

F. This phrase of "all the nations of the Gentiles" is an important link to more Gentiles in Europe. And this link will be played out upon the Gentile Beast Kingdom in Europe with the 7 Trumpets and 7 Vials in John's Revelation.

G. The Lord will **establish** his people of the whole House of Israel in their **lands**. The House of Joseph in America and the other tribes eventually in Israel around Jerusalem.

H. (v22) The children of Lehi (Nephites and Lamanites = Native American Indians = Tribe of Manasseh in the House of Joseph) will have America as their covenant land. The New Jerusalem will be built here. The priesthood will be here. And Jesus will visit his Temple when it is built in The New Jerusalem. This is when Jesus will ordain the 144,000 High Priests to go forth and preach and "hunt" the rest of the remnant of Israel for the gathering to Zion.

Author's Analysis:

Almost every book on last-days prophecy, mentions this portion of scripture, "the House of Israel will be like a Lion among the Sheep...and the Gentiles can't stop them." This author has seen at least 4 ways to understand this passage of scripture....as written by other authors.

1) The remnant of Manasseh (Native American Indians) act as the Lion and take down all Gentiles, including members of the Church of God, because everybody has "gone astray." The Church of God needs to be "ordered" by that mighty and strong one.

2) The remnant of Manasseh (Native American Indians) act alone as the Lion and take down the un-believing of the Gentiles.

3) The Lost 10 Tribes come as the Lion and take down the unbelieving Gentiles.

4) The Lost 10 Tribes + the remnant of Manasseh (Native American Indians) act as the Lion and take down the unbelieving Gentiles.

Which one is it?

The way I see it, we should take the "knowns" of the situation and then backtrack to the "unknowns" to fill in the puzzle. We know:
1) That Israel (in some capacity) will be fighting the Gentiles. I understand that these will be the *un-believing* Gentiles.
   a. (Not the believing Gentiles that are of Ephraim that are the ones to hold the Church of God to bring the true Gospel of the Lamb to the rest of the Tribes of Israel.)
2) The unbelieving Gentiles will have formed Daniel's 4th Beast of 10 Nations and America as the conspiring Eagle will be a founding member. Assuming the awesome war-tech that America has at this point and going forward as The Beast of the Gentiles… that war-tech will only get better as it "grinds and crushes" other nations that won't join with it.
3) The "good technology" of Israel (in some capacity) will be better than the un-believing Gentiles… **Think About That For A Second**… How good will this war-tech need to be? Of course, if John the Beloved/Revelator is at their head with the Power of God in his mouth, their "good war tech" won't amount to very much. However… Jesus did say "thy horn iron, thy hoofs brass." So there is some element of really good war-tech that will come into play. (See Appendix 1 on the Lost 10 Tribes)
4) Today, the Tribe of Ephraim as The Church of God has zero war-technology. Today, the Tribe of Manasseh (Native American Indians) has zero war-technologies.

So, odds are, if war-technology is needed and used by the Tribes of Israel against the un-believing super war-tech Gentiles, the only tribes that could have it… are, The Lost 10 Tribes from the North. (More on this subject in Appendix 1)

Jesus continues in 3 Nephi Chapter 20 with some statements from Isaiah again, almost as a clarifying statement to the 1st day's discussion:

(3rd Nephi 20:33-37)
"33 **Then** will the Father **gather them together again**, and give unto them **Jerusalem** for the **land of their inheritance**. [It's about the LAND]
34 **Then** shall they break forth into joy—Sing together, **ye waste places** of Jerusalem; for the Father hath comforted his people, he hath redeemed Jerusalem.
35 **The Father hath made bare his holy arm in the eyes of all the nations; and all the ends of the earth shall see the salvation of the Father**; and the Father and I are one.
36 And **then** shall be brought to pass that which is written: Awake, awake again, and put on thy strength, **O Zion**; put on thy beautiful garments, **O Jerusalem**, the holy city, for henceforth there shall no more come into thee the uncircumcised and the unclean.
37 **Shake thyself from the dust**; arise, sit down, O Jerusalem; loose thyself from the **bands of thy neck, O captive daughter of Zion**."

Learning Points:

A. (v35) There is something **big** to this part about Israel taking down the unbelieving Gentiles in America (and beyond). The statement of the Father making bare his holy arm in the eyes of all the nation. Jesus is *repeating this* from the 1st day's lesson on how **all** the Tribes of Israel will get their land back.

B. And Jesus continues with Isaiah's language that speaks of the **new** Zion Nation and the Jerusalem in Israel in the same verse.

C. The land of Jerusalem and the area round about is for the Lost 10 Tribes of Israel to eventually inhabit...after they make their stop in the Everlasting Hills and help build the New Jerusalem in America.. The land around Jerusalem in Israel is currently inhabited by Muslims. So something will have to take place there, eventually.

D. (v37) This last part of "loose thyself from **the bands of thy neck, O captive daughter of Zion.**" Makes sense that when Israel kicks out the unbelieving Gentiles, they will be the ones to **free** "the captive daughter of Zion." Which from previous passages, we know to be the Church of God being oppressed by the Beast Kingdom ridden by the Whore Church –Babylon the Great – (she is The Tares).

The really big description of these events of the closing of the 6th Seal of John... is in **3 Nephi 21; the *whole* chapter.** I do not want to reprint the whole chapter... however... break it open right now and read it... as if you were reading this book. It's the culmination of the Savior's teaching on this subject... **in even *more* plain terms.**

Summary:

1. Jesus gives "a sign" of the time when the Covenants to Israel (about the **land** + more) will come to pass. It is when Manasseh (Native American Indians) reads these words of the Savior in the Book of Mormon... which comes from the Ephraim Gentiles of the Church of God.

2. When **the day comes**... that the covenant to the House of Israel is to be fulfilled (The **land** +more), then kings shall shut their mouths; they will **see** things they didn't know; and things they haven't heard shall they consider.

3. The "man" that shall declare the great and marvelous work of God unto the Gentiles, seems to be the same man that is leading Israel at that time. This "man" is called by Jesus "my servant." This man will bring forth the Word of God unto the Gentiles and if they don't believe, they will be **cut off** from the people of **Israel** (all tribes – including the Lost 10).

4. The **Lion** that Jesus mentions in this chapter is "a remnant of Jacob" or all the House of Israel (including Lost 10 Tribes). The wording doesn't seem to apply just to Manasseh. Even it says (v13) "their hand." Meaning some other Tribes besides the one that Jesus is speaking to right now which is Manasseh. If this isn't the Jews, or the Ephraimites, or Manasseh...then this can only be speaking of The Lost 10 Tribes (which Jesus confirms at the end of the chapter verse).

5. The unbelieving Gentiles that war against the House of Israel will have their horses, chariots, cities, and strongholds taken down. As well as other wickedness taken down.

6. The New Jerusalem will be built **after** the destruction of the unbelieving Gentiles in the Land of the House of Joseph (America).

7. The preaching to and the gathering of the rest of the scattered House of Israel happens during the construction period of the New Jerusalem.
8. The call goes out to all nations to bring the honest in heart to the New Jerusalem.

Author's Analysis:

Yes, those kings of the earth will see a **great miracle**. They will see the return of the Lost 10 Tribes coming on the new Miracle Ice Bridge/Highway with great Power. (See Appendix 1) And the translated being John the Beloved/Revelator at their head leading them to the Everlasting Hills to Free the Church of God and to take down the Gentile Beast Kingdom in America and beyond. I see this **big** event also as the "strange act" that will divide the people of the earth. Will the people seeing this "strange act" side with the 4th Beast Kingdom with the Whore Church riding it *Or* will they side with the translated being John who wrote the Book of Revelation? That would bring some real division to the Christian world.

John is on a mission to set the Church of God in good order. During this time….*This* could be the Divisive Act that is universally divisive to all people.

- They will see that a *large* miracle was done by God in casting up a highway in the oceans of the North for the Lost 10 Tribes to travel on. That will be a **very big** deal.
- They will see that when the Lost 10 Tribes first come out of their hiding place they will come to the state of Utah in the Everlasting Hills.
- They will all hear John's voice when he speaks to the "Eagle" nation and rebukes it. (Most likely he will introduce himself as a translated being sent by God.)
  - Remember the Christians **know** that John the Revelator wrote Revelations – and they will want to be on **his** side, as most Christians know generally what "tough plagues" happen in that vision.
- They will all see the Translated John the Beloved/Revelator and the Lost 10 Tribes put down The Beast and kick it out of America.
- They will soon see, that the Lost 10 Tribes have scriptures of their own; that will be joined to ours.
- They will soon see America rising again under its Constitution, in the near future.
- AND last of all, they will soon see that the call goes out to the World that America now desires the "pure in heart" to come to the new country of Zion….

When one puts all that together, that may be just the *divisive* Act that God will need to push many current Christians and people of many faiths into the Church of Jesus Christ of Latter-Day Saints, because the miracles will be self evident. His mighty arm will truly have been "revealed".

The special prophecy by Joseph Smith about the American Civil **wars** (plural) shows the same vexation of "the remnant". As do the BIG Plague… and the other last-day signs from the Trumpets and Vials of the Revelation of John.

(D&C 87:5-6)

"5 And it shall come to pass also that **the remnants** who are left of the land will marshal themselves, and shall become exceedingly angry, and **shall vex the Gentiles with a sore vexation**.

6 And thus, with the **sword** and by bloodshed the inhabitants of the earth shall mourn; and with **famine**, and **plague**, and **earthquake**, and the **thunder of heaven**, and the **fierce and vivid lightning** also, shall the inhabitants of the earth be made to feel the wrath, and indignation, and chastening hand of an Almighty God, until **the consumption decreed** hath made a full end of all nations;"

Learning Points:

A. "The remnants" in this section of the D&C, I have always thought was the "the remnants of slaves" as the subject of the previous verse was "slaves." But, *this* verse 5, could be the separation point between the United States Civil War with the North and South… and the next civil war in America.

B. It says that "the remnant" who are left in the land shall marshal **themselves**. This also implies that this scripture is not talking about the Lost 10 Tribes of Israel,… but more speaking of the children of Lehi (Native American Indians). However… given the rest of the scriptures that feel more to be speaking of the "the remnant' as the Lost 10 Tribes returning… this one is a toss-up. If you, as the reader, have more evidence either way, please contact me at the website www.LastDaysTimeline.com.

Mormon had also read the 3ʳᵈ Nephi account when the Savior shared that the Lion shall go-through the Gentiles, if they would not repent. In Mormon 5:

(Mormon 5: 22-24)

"22 And then, **O ye Gentiles**, how can ye stand before the power of God, except ye shall **repent** and turn from your evil ways?

23 Know ye not that ye are in the hands of God? Know ye not that he hath all power, and at his great command the earth shall be rolled together as a scroll?

24 Therefore, **repent ye, and humble yourselves** before him, lest he shall come out in justice against you—**lest a remnant of the seed of Jacob shall go forth among you as a lion, and tear you in pieces, and there is none to deliver**."

Learning Points:

A. Mormon had read the 3ʳᵈ Nephi account of what the Savior said about the wicked Gentiles.

B. Mormon and the Savior were inviting the unbelieving Gentiles to **repent** and come unto Christ and his Church to learn the true points of His doctrine.

C. If the Gentiles didn't repent, "a remnant of the seed of Jacob/Israel" will go through as a lion and none can deliver. This phrase in Mormon also does *not* give us a clue as to *which* part of the Tribes of Israel it will be?

To Summarize What Jesus Told the Children of Lehi (Nephites and Lamanites) About the Lion

A. The Child of Israel will be as a Lion among the Gentiles... if they don't repent and turn unto the true points of Christ's Gospel.
B. This figurative Lion will take down the Gentiles in America and clear the **land** for the host of all Israel.
C. There were many mentions, within the same chapters, about the true Gospel of Christ being among the believing of the Gentiles, and that all Israel will get the Gospel through them.
D. There was talk of a "man" that is the servant of God that will be in the Lord's hands. And that if the unbelieving Gentiles don't listen to that servant, they shall be cut off and destroyed out of the **land**.
E. That when this event happens that the Lion goes through among the unbelieving Gentiles, that *that* is the fulfilling of the covenants the Lord made with Israel about the Land being given to the House of Joseph (Ephraim and Manasseh).
F. That this Lion of the House of Israel, when it goes through and destroys the Gentiles in the land of Manasseh (America), that it will also go among the other lands of the Gentiles (Europe). (Keep this in mind for later, when we speak of The 7 Trumpets and 7 Vials of John's Revelation)

As these points line up very nicely, **we can conclude that the Lion of Ezra's Eagle and the Lion imagery of Jesus in 3rd Nephi are indeed describing the same event.**

The anointed House of Israel led by a "Man" that is sent by God to take down the unbelieving Gentiles out of America.

That is the point that both stories are showing.

It appears that **_after_** the 2nd American Civil War and BIG Plague, the "Remnant of Jacob" (Lost 10 Tribes, or Native American Indians, or **both**) tread down the unbelieving Gentiles still living and fighting in their 4th Beast Kingdom in America.

So, the Lost 10 Tribes returning from the **North** is up next, because they come back **_before_** the New Jerusalem is built-up so they can be sealed. 144,000 High Priests of all 12 Tribes of Israel are to be sealed in their forehead to preach and gather more of the "honest in heart" from the nations and build up the Nation of Zion=Kingdom of God.

13: *The Return of the Lost 10 Tribes of Israel from the land of the North*

The event that will take place to show the world that the Lost 10 Tribes of Israel are alive & well will be the start of something that will end with the destruction of the Anti-Christ/Stout Horn and his 4th Beast Kingdom of the Gentiles at Armageddon. For now, let's simply focus in on their return in one body as a people, from the North countries.

Keeping to the concise nature of this work, I know of many LDS Church resource books and materials that say The Lost 10 Tribes of Israel are being "fished" from among the nations of the earth. Generally that is true, but there are places that the regular missionaries of the church cannot go. They cannot go to where the *bulk* of the Lost 10 Tribes are living. The reason is that they are hidden from the world, on purpose by God the Father, for he has led them away. *Those* are the people that will come to rescue the Church of God from the Gentile 4th Beast Kingdom being ridden by the Whore – Babylon the Great.

How Did They Get Lost?

They were conquered and taken away by Assyria (734BC) before Lehi left Jerusalem in 600BC. That's a long time ago. The record is in the Old Testament of the Bible. See it there.

How Did They Get Free of Assyria?

In the very next chapter of 2nd Esdras, 7 days after receiving Ezra's Eagle; Ezra has another dream from God. (2nd Esdras Chapter 13)

The synopsis of this other vision of Ezra will be included in another edition of this work. (Read Chapter 13 here. http://www.kingjamesbibleonline.org/2-Esdras-Chapter-13/   Side Note: If you read 2nd Esdras 11-16, you will see the whole last-days saga just like John the Revelator saw. This section of the Apocrypha is called "The Apocalypse of Ezra".)

The Lord shows Ezra this piece from the interpretation of the dream:

> (2nd Esdras 13:40-46)
> "40 Those are **the ten tribes**, which were carried away prisoners out of their own land in the time of Osea the king, whom Salmanasar the **king of Assyria** led away captive, and he carried them over the waters, and so came they into another land.
> 41 But they took this **counsel among themselves**, that they would <u>leave the multitude of the heathen, and go forth into a further country, where never mankind dwelt</u>,
> 42 That they might there **keep their statutes**, which they never kept in their own land.
> 43 And they entered into **Euphrates by the narrow places of the river**.

44 For **the most High then shewed signs for them**, and held **still the flood**, till they were passed over.
45 For through that country there was a great way to go, namely, of **a year and a half**: and the same region is called **Arsareth**.
46 Then dwelt they there **until the latter time**; and now when they shall begin to come,"

Learning Points:
A.   The Lost 10 Tribes of Israel escaped from the King of Assyria by a miracle that the Lord held back the waters of a great river Euphrates and allows them to walk up the river a long way out of the land, thus hiding their footprints and making them un-traceable.
B.   Once free, they took counsel and decided *where* they wanted to go. They wanted to leave the heathen nations behind and go even further *north* to a place where no man has dwelt. That is a curious phrase, as there has been mankind all over the planet and even into the very far north in Europe, Asia, and North America. But, the place where they went, in a body, was even further north.
C.   The Most High God showed signs for them and most likely led them directly to the **place** that God wanted them to be planted in his vineyard (Sounds much like Jacob 5 the Allegory of the Olive Tree).
D.   The place is 1.5 years worth of traveling to the north past where they left the Heathen Nations behind.
E.   The region is called Arsareth. This is the location of where the Lost 10 Tribes live until the latter-days, when they will return from that land.

Are They in ONE Body?

Yes, the great bulk of the Lost 10 Tribes of Israel from the North countries are in **one** body. Elder Bruce R. McConkie had this to say:

> (The Millennial Messiah page 319 by Bruce R. McConkie)
> "This inspired language leaves the clear impression that **the gathering** of Israel is one thing and **the restoration** of the Ten Tribes is another.
>
> Why this distinction? Are not the Ten Tribes a part of Israel?
>
> There is a distinction between Israel **as a whole** and the **Ten Tribes** who are **the dominant portion of Jacob's seed**. All scripture comes by the power of the Holy Ghost and is verily true. When special and unusual language is used, there is a reason. Holy writ is not idle chatter; it is the mind and will of the Lord; it says what he wants said."

Learning Points:
A.   The Lost 10 Tribes are in one body and will be restored, not gathered.
B.   These Lost 10 Tribes are the **bulk** of the seed of Jacob/Israel on the Earth.

And here with President Joseph Fielding Smith:

> (Way to Perfection p130 by Smith)

"The Ten Tribes were taken by force out of the land the Lord gave them. **Many of them mixed with the peoples among whom they were scattered.** A **large portion**, however, **departed in one body into the north** and disappeared from the rest of the world."

Learning Points:

A. There was a mixing of the seed, as their multi year journey traveling northward. It appears that some stayed behind and didn't go *all the way north*. It appears they stayed in Northern Europe and mixed.
B. However, the greater majority continued to follow God's prophet and went **all the way north**.

There are lots of questions about where this land of Arsareth actually is. There have been several books written on that subject. I have read them, studied them, and digested them. The basic materials for that discussion are in Appendix 1.

Now that we know that the Lord led them to their location of Arsareth. Let us see <u>how a huge miracle takes place</u> as they come back from the land of the North called Arsareth.

(D&C 133:26-34)

"26 And they **who are in the north countries** shall **come in remembrance** [the covenants of Israel, including the **land**] before the Lord; and **their prophets** shall hear his voice, and shall **no longer stay themselves; and they shall smite the rocks**, and the **ice** shall flow down at their presence.
27 And **an highway shall be cast up in the midst of the great deep.**
28 **Their enemies shall become a prey unto them.**
29 And in the **barren deserts** there shall come forth **pools of living water;** and **the parched ground shall no longer be a thirsty land.**
30 And they shall bring forth **their rich treasures unto the children of Ephraim**, my servants.
31 And the boundaries of the **everlasting hills** shall tremble at their presence,
32 And there shall they **fall down and be crowned with glory**, even **in Zion,** by the hands of the servants of the Lord, even the children of **Ephraim.**
33 And they shall be filled with songs of everlasting joy.
34 Behold, **this is the blessing** of the everlasting God upon **the tribes of Israel, and the richer blessing upon the head of Ephraim** and his fellows."

Learning Points:

A. This is the main scripture that points out directly from the Lord himself in the Doctrine and Covenants how the Lost 10 Tribes will return from the north countries of Arsareth.
B. The Lord will remember his covenant with Israel – including the **land.**
C. The prophets/leaders of the Lost 10 Tribes will hear the Lord's voice and they shall no longer "hide" themselves from the rest of the world. They are doing this on purpose. The bulk of them are in one big body of people. This group is not to

be *gathered* to their lands by missionaries. They are to be *led* to their lands by their prophets.

D. The *large* miracle that God makes bare His Holy Arm in the sight of all the nations has arrived. Apparently, the Lost 10 Tribes will smite rocks and the **ice** of the north will flow down and make a highway for them to cross over the north oceans to land. How far **north** *is* this region of Arsareth? (ice bridge over ocean!)

E. They have enemies. When they come to the Everlasting Hills, they have enemies. That sounds exactly like what the Lion in Ezra's Eagle will have when "the anointed" will save the Saints of God.

F. These enemies will not win at all. These enemies will be like "sport hunting" when they return. In other words, their war-technology will be way more advanced than America under the 4th Beast Kingdom of the Gentiles.

G. They will bring water making technology, *or* the miracles of God to make the desert on the way to the Everlasting Hills (Rocky Mountains) bring forth water; and lots of it.

H. They will bring "treasures" with them and give them to the children of Ephraim/Church of God/Church of Jesus Christ of Latter-Day Saints in Utah (Everlasting Hills). These treasures may be riches…but more than likely, the "treasures" mean they will bring their scriptures… And the Church of God will love to receive those as valued higher than the riches of the earth, by far. I would love to have them.

I. The Lost 10 Tribes will come to the everlasting hills. This part about "trembling at their presence" may mean that there are so many of them, they make the ground rumble. Or it may mean something else. I won't take a direct stance on this.

J. (v32) Is generally understood to mean that Ephraim will give the Priesthood of Melchizedek to them when they arrive. The location where this happens says "Zion." Whether that means the new Nation of Zion with the New Jerusalem *or* whether that means the place of Zion with the Saints of God, this Author doesn't know. *However*, we do know they are coming to the Everlasting Hills, which means Utah, not Missouri. So, that is a clue.

K. The Lost 10 Tribes like to sing.

L. Ephraim has the higher blessing. Many other prophecy writers have said this means the Melchizedek Priesthood is the higher blessing of Ephraim. I do not know.

The Grand Miracle to Reveal God's Arm to All the Nations AND to Divide Them So That They Will Choose

This **grand miracle** of the Ice Highway being cast up and the whole of Lost 10 Tribes being very numerous will get the attention of the entire planet…including the 4th Beast Kingdom of the Gentiles with The Whore Church-Babylon the Great riding it.

> (Isaiah 11:16)
> "16 And there shall be **an highway** for the **remnant of his people**, which shall be left, **from Assyria; like as it was to Israel in the day that he came up out of the land of Egypt**."

(Isaiah 35:3-10)

"3 ¶Strengthen ye the weak hands, and confirm the feeble knees.

4 Say to them **that are** of a fearful heart, Be strong, fear not: behold, your God will come **with** vengeance, even God with a recompence; he will come and save you.

5 Then the eyes of the blind shall be opened, and the ears of the deaf shall be unstopped.

6 Then shall the lame man leap as an hart, and the tongue of the dumb sing: for **in the wilderness shall waters break out**, and **streams in the desert**.

7 And **the parched ground shall become a pool, and the thirsty land springs of water**: in the habitation of dragons, where each lay, shall be **grass with reeds and rushes**.

8 And an **highway shall be there**, and a way, and it shall be called The way of holiness; the **unclean shall not pass over it**; but it shall be **for those**: the wayfaring men, though fools, shall not err therein.

9 **No lion shall be there, nor any ravenous beast shall go up thereon, it shall not be found there; but the redeemed shall walk there**:

10 And **the ransomed of the Lord shall return**, and **come to Zion with songs** and everlasting joy upon their heads: they shall obtain joy and gladness, and sorrow and sighing shall flee away."

Learning Points:

A. During the time in our timeline that the Saints of God think that God has forsaken them because of the oppression of the Gentile Beast Kingdom... we can "Be strong, fear not: behold, your God will come with vengeance... and a "repayment" for you. And "He will save you."

B. The water will break forth in the desert places of Utah and the American West.

C. The Great Highway for the Redeemed of Israel will be cast up in the ice to the North and traveled by the Lost 10 Tribes on their way to the Everlasting Hills. The name of this highway shall be called "The Way of Holiness". And any other "unclean person" that wants to go the other way to where the Lost 10 Tribes came from, in Arsareth will not make it. This is a special ice road for "the anointed" only.

D. No lion or other carnivore animal (like polar bears) shall be on the highway.

E. When the Lost 10 Tribes come over the highway, they love to sing; and they will be happy.

(Jeremiah 16:14-15)

"14 ¶Therefore, behold, the days come, saith the Lord, that **it shall no more be said**, The Lord liveth, that brought up the children of Israel **out of the land of Egypt**;

15 But, The Lord liveth, that brought up the children of Israel **from the land of the north**, and from all the lands whither he had driven them: and I will bring them again into their land that I gave unto their fathers."

Learning Points:

A. This **grand** miracle that is seen by all the nations will be so big that people will *forget* about the parting of the red sea. They will focus on the huge ice highway that came out of the north land of Arsareth to the North American continent on their way to the children of Ephraim in the Everlasting Hills. WOW!

This is a HUGE miracle. It's *bigger* than the parting of the Red Sea when the Lord led the Israelites out of Egypt to the Mountain of God. (See Ron Wyatt's work on the Parting of the Red Sea and the location of Mount Sinai. Appendix 1)

Author's Analysis:
This is **big**. Real BIG. My opinion is that the revealing of the Lost 10 Tribes in their might, with their miracles of technology, and miracles of their prophet leaders will be the *very large* "strange act" that Nephi says will divide the people of the world to choose the Church of God on one hand or the Church of the Devil on the other.

Who Are the Lost 10 Tribe's Prophet Leaders?

(D&C 77:14)
"14 Q. What are we to understand by **the little book** which was **eaten by John**, as mentioned in the 10th chapter of Revelation?
A. We are to understand that **it was a mission**, and **an ordinance**, for **him to gather the tribes of Israel**; behold, **this is Elias**, who, as it is written, **must come and restore all things**."

Learning Points:
A. This "little book" was a mission that John was to eat up. This little book came from the Last of the 7 Angels with the 7 Trumpets that said "there shall be time no longer." He gave John a little book and said to eat it up and it should be sweet to thy mouth but shall make thy belly bitter. In other words, this "mission" to be a translated being till the end of the world and help **gather the Lost 10 Tribes of Israel and RESTORE ALL THINGS** will be sweet *now*, but when he has to prophesy to the nations again and rebuke them…it will feel bitter to John.

More from D&C 77, this time an earlier verse.

(D&C 77:9)
"9 Q. What are we to understand by **the angel ascending from the east,** Revelation 7th chapter and 2nd verse?

A. We are to understand that **the angel** ascending from the east is **he to whom is given the seal of the living God over the twelve tribes of Israel**; wherefore, he crieth unto the four angels having the everlasting gospel, saying: Hurt not the earth, neither the sea, nor the trees, **till we have sealed the servants of our God in their foreheads [the 144,000]. And, if you will receive it, this is Elias which was to come to gather together the tribes of Israel and restore all things.**"

Learning Points:
A. The Lord through the Prophet Joseph Smith just told the Church in the Doctrine and Covenants that John the Beloved/Revelator is the exact person who has the

keys and authority to gather the Lost Tribes of Israel (including the Lost 10), and *restore* all things.

B. And that this Angel rising from the East ***comes before*** the sealing of the 144,000 High Priests which are ordained and sent forth to preach by the Savior himself at the Temple in the New Jerusalem. Thus, that Temple has not been built yet, when John *comes*. Putting him directly in the timeline at the exact point that the Lost 10 Tribes return from the North countries of Arsareth to rescue the Saints of God from the 4th Beast.

(And more… D&C 27:6)

"6 And also with **Elias**, to whom I have **committed the keys** of bringing to pass **the restoration of all things** spoken by the mouth of all the holy prophets since the world began, **concerning the last days**;"

And the next clue is in the calling of the mission itself… in the Book of Revelations Chapter 10. John is speaking to the 7th Angel of the 7th Trumpet who said, "There should be time no longer."

(Rev 10:8)

"8 And the voice which I heard from heaven spake unto me again, and said, Go and take the little book which is open in the hand of the angel which standeth upon the sea and upon the earth.

9 And I went unto the angel, and said unto him, Give me **the little book**. And he said unto me, Take it, and **eat it up**; and **it shall make thy belly bitter, but it shall be in thy mouth sweet as honey.**

10 And I took the little book out of the angel's hand, and ate it up; and it was in my mouth sweet as honey: and as soon as I had eaten it, my belly was bitter.

11 And he said unto me, Thou must prophesy again before many peoples, and nations, and tongues, and kings."

RECAP: John's latter-day mission is to prophesy again before the nations and kings of the earth and call them to repentance… And to do it, from the *lead* of the mighty Lost 10 Tribes of Israel as they return from the North from a massive Ice Highway miracle to save the Church of God from being destroyed by the 4th Beast Kingdom of the Gentiles being ridden by the Whore Church – Babylon the Great.

The Lost 10 Tribes have now returned and have met the Church of God in the Everlasting Hills. They have provided the great Waters in the Desert miracle that the Church of God will desperately need to feed the hungry Gentile masses that walked to the west. They will take down their enemies and finally decimate the last toe-hold of the Beast Kingdom in America. Those bondage shackles are now *cut*. The Saints of God are now *free*.

Onward ye Saints of God to Adam-ondi-Ahman and the New Jerusalem…

14: The Meeting at Adam-ondi-Ahman

This portion in the timeline of the meeting counsel at Adam-ondi-Ahman may come *after* the beginning of construction on the capital city – The New Jerusalem. I have not found specific evidence to put it before or after the building of the New Jerusalem. Some prophecy writers have put it *before*; others have put it *after*.

I feel that it should be tentatively put *before* the New Jerusalem, but not much before. As time passes and more evidence becomes available, this chapter may be moved in the timeline. If you, the reader, have more evidence about the time placement of the Grand Counsel at Adam-ondi-Ahman, please alert me at the website www.LastDaysTimeline.com.

The Grand Counsel of Adam and his children will take place at Adam-ondi-Ahman. This is where all the priesthood holders that have held keys shall return them back to Father Adam and back to the Savior Himself.

If Adam is indeed the Ancient of Days mentioned in Daniel 7, then *this* is the point when the kingdoms of the earth become the kingdoms of our God and his Christ. And that mighty 4th Beast Kingdom of the Gentiles continues to fall from this very moment.

President John Taylor taught:

> (Taylor, The Gospel Kingdom, p. 217)
> "All who have held **the keys** of priesthood will then have to give an account to those from whom they received them.

> …The elders give an account to [stake] presidents of conferences; and presidents of conferences to presidents of [seventy]. Those presidents and the seventies give an account to the twelve apostles; the twelve to the First Presidency; and they to Joseph, from whom they, and the twelve, received their priesthood…. Joseph delivers his authority to Peter, who held the keys before him, and delivered them to him; and Peter to Moses and Elias, who endowed him with this authority on the Mount; and they to those from whom they received them [back to Adam].

> And thus the world's affairs will be regulated and put right, the **restitution of all things be accomplished**, and **the kingdom of God** be ushered in."

Learning Points:
A. It appears that the Kingdom of God = the *new* Nation of Zion will need to have this counsel take place *before* the new nation can come into being….with its capital city at The New Jerusalem in Independence Missouri.
B. The members of the priesthood who have held keys will turn them back to the person who gave them…all the way to Father Adam. And in Daniel Chapter 7, The Savior then comes to collect the Keys from Father Adam. This will represent the Savior's 1st appearance of the 2nd Coming. Meaning, he hasn't come to the

general population of the Church of God at the New Jerusalem Temple to ordain the 144,000 High Priests yet.

The valley today is a big field. It is located in Daviess County Missouri.

Best webpage to see it directly.
https://www.lds.org/scriptures/history-photos/photo-10?lang=eng

The Lost 10 Tribes have returned. The Grand Counsel of Adam-ondi-Ahman is to happen approximately around this time.

It's now time for the Saints of God and their new friends to rebuild America into the new Nation of Zion and the Kingdom of God. The next step is the building of the capital city, the New Jerusalem and its special 24 Temples on 45 acres at the heart of the city.

SECTION 5: The Building of the New Jerusalem Temple and the NEW Zion Nation

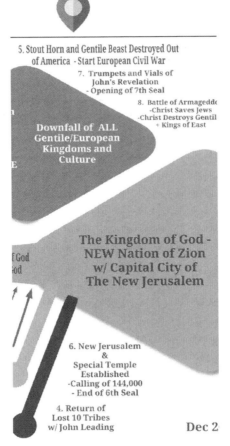

YOU ARE
HERE

5. Stout Horn and Gentile Beast Destroyed Out
of America - Start European Civil War

7. **Trumpets and Vials of
John's Revelation
- Opening of 7th Seal**

8. **Battle of Armageddo
-Christ Saves Jews
-Christ Destroys Gentil
+ Kings of East**

**Downfall of ALL
Gentile/European
Kingdoms and
Culture**

f God
od

**The Kingdom of God -
NEW Nation of Zion
w/ Capital City of
The New Jerusalem**

6. **New Jerusalem
&
Special Temple
Established**
-Calling of 144,000
- End of 6th Seal

4. **Return of
Lost 10 Tribes
w/ John Leading**

Dec 2

15: _The Restoration of the United States Constitution in its Original Form_

When the Saints of God have a "wall/curtain/barrier/gulf" between them and the United States that will be destroying itself, there will need to be some sort of political government. And the clear choice for the principals that match the beliefs of the Saints of God will be to restore the Constitution of the United States to its original form.

Ezra's Eagle Vision says it:

(2nd Esdras 12:18)
"18 That **after the time** of that kingdom there **shall arise great strivings,** and **it shall stand in peril of failing**: nevertheless **it shall not then fall, but shall be restored again to his beginning.**"

Since the last national government had joined the Beast Kingdom of the Gentiles by using treaties, they had permanently shredded the Constitution that protects the equal rights of minority groups. They were engaged in actually _attacking_ their own citizens. Those protected God-given rights will need to be re-enshrined. The people of the Church of God _plus_ the purer Gentiles that walked west to avoid the 2nd American Civil War and BIG Plague will be just the people to re-enshrine it.

The ultimate Government of Zion will be a Theocratic Government, by Jesus as the Law Giver and King of Kings. However, there will be a transition period when the Constitutional Principals will be re-enshrined and lived in a much better way by the people and their federal government. Brigham Young said this:

(Discourses of Brigham Young 6:346-347)
"Theocratic Government -- I believe in **a true republican theocracy, and also in a true democratic theocracy**, as the term democratic is now used; for they are to me, in their present use, convertible terms. 6:346.
What do I understand by a theocratic government? One in which **all laws** are enacted and executed in righteousness, and whose **officers** possess that power which proceedeth from the Almighty. That is the kind of government I allude to when I speak of a theocratic government, or the **Kingdom of God upon the earth**. It is, in short, the eternal powers of the Gods."

(Journal of Discourses 7:13)
"The General Constitution of our country is **good**, and **a wholesome government could be framed upon it**, for it was dictated by the invisible operations of the Almighty; he moved upon Columbus to launch forth upon the trackless deep to discover the American Continent; he moved upon the signers of the Declaration of Independence; and he moved upon Washington to fight and conquer, in the same way as he moved upon ancient and modern Prophets, each being inspired to accomplish the particular work he was called to perform in the times, seasons, and dispensations of the Almighty. **God's purpose,** in raising up these men and inspiring them with daring

sufficient to surmount every opposing power, **was to prepare the way for the formation of a true Republican government**. They laid its foundation; but when others came to build upon it, they reared a superstructure far short of their privileges, if they had walked uprightly as they should have done."

Learning Points:

A. Brigham Young loved the U.S. Constitution as it is stated by Jesus in the Doctrine and Covenants that the framers were raised up for that very purpose.

B. Brigham Young sees the day when a *true republican theocratic* government can be built upon the U.S. Constitution, when the evil men are out of the way.

C. When the laws are passed in righteousness *and* the officers have power (priesthood authorization) from the Almighty God; this will be a Theocracy.

Eventually, Jesus himself will be the Executive (Law Executioner), Legislative (Law Giver) and the Judicial branches (Judge). However, most likely, as he called common judges in Israel as the Bishops of his Church; and he approved of how Moses organized Israel as Jethro taught by breaking up the duties of Government into smaller segments of society; more officers of government will be called forth to govern affairs more locally to the people.

The very best sources for more on this topic of Righteous Government are:

1. The Cleansing of America - by W. Cleon Skousen
2. The Making of America - by W. Cleon Skousen
3. The 5000 Year Leap - by W. Cleon Skousen

These are available at: www.LastDaysTimeline.com/cleon-skousen

The *new* Nation of Zion is the political Kingdom of God. The national government of America *and* the Beast Kingdom's superseding government is also gone. The "wall/band/gulf" has been up around the Saints of God for a while. It's time to start the trek to Jackson County... to begin the rebuilding process.

16: *The Miracle Trek to Arrive in Jackson County*

The trek to Jackson County will be one of miracles. Just as the Children of Israel were led out of Egypt, with the cloud by day and the fire by night, so will this trek be. Elder Orson Pratt had this to say about how we will return to Jackson County:

> (Journal of Discourses, 15:364)
> "We shall go back to Jackson County. Not that all this people will leave these mountains, or all be gathered together in a camp, but when we go back **there will be a very large organization** consisting of thousands, and **tens of thousands**, and they will march forward, the glory of God overshadowing their camp by day in the form of a **cloud**, and a pillar of flaming **fire by night**, the **Lord's voice** being uttered forth before his army. Such a period will come in the history of this people. ..., And his people will go forth and build up Zion according to celestial law.

> Will not this **produce terror upon all the nations of the earth**? Will not armies of this description, though they may not be as numerous as the armies of the world, **cause a terror to fall upon the nations**? The Lord says the **banners of Zion shall be terrible**. ... When the Lord's presence is there, when his voice is heard, and his angels go before the camp, it will be **telegraphed to the uttermost parts of the earth and fear will seize upon all people**, especially the wicked, and the knees of the ungodly will tremble in that day, and the high ones that are on high, and the great men of the earth."

Learning Points:
A. When the Saints of God trek to take back the land in Jackson County that was stolen from them, after purchasing it with monies, it will be tens of thousands that make the trek. Not the millions that inhabit all of the Intermountain West.
B. The camp will go forth with a cloud by day and pillar of fire by night. And the Lord's voice shall be heard.
C. The evil designs of the Stout Horn that had his armies just kicked out of America, will see the report of this. He will see that the God of Israel is with His people. He will feel fear. Remember, this happens during the 6th Seal of John, because the New Jerusalem Temple hasn't been built yet, nor the sealing and mission of the 144,000 High Priests. So the Stout Horn/False Prophet/False Messiah is still strongly ruling the 4th Beast Kingdom of the Gentiles from Europe.

At this time, when the Church of God is to return to Jackson County Missouri to build the New Jerusalem, the Law of Consecration will be re-started and members of the church will be invited to join. (See Appendix 1: Law of Consecration)

> (Brigham Young, Teachings of Brigham Young, Chapter 22)
> "The Lord has declared it to be his will that his people enter into covenant, even as Enoch and his people did, which of necessity must be **before** we shall have the privilege of **building the Center Stake of Zion**, for the power and glory of God will be there, and **none but the pure in heart will be able to live and enjoy it**."

Approximately during this time, when the New Jerusalem hasn't been built yet, but the Saints are in progress moving toward building it, the Lord says that the wicked won't be able to cross the seas to attack. They will be stuck in their own lands; especially the Stout Horn leader of the 4th Beast.

(D&C 61:14-19)
"14 Behold, I, the Lord, in the beginning blessed the waters; but **in the last days, by the mouth of my servant <u>John</u>, I cursed the waters.**
15 Wherefore, the days will come that **no flesh shall be safe upon the waters.**
16 And it shall be said in days to come that **none is able to go up to the land of Zion** upon the waters, but **he that is upright in heart.**
17 And, as I, the Lord, in the beginning cursed the land, even so in **the last days have I blessed it**, in its time, **for the use of my saints**, that they may partake **the fatness** thereof.
18 And now I give unto you a commandment that what I say unto one I say unto all, that **you shall forewarn your brethren concerning these waters**, that **they come not in journeying** upon them, lest their faith fail and they are caught in snares;
19 I, the Lord, have decreed, and the **destroyer rideth upon the face thereof**, and I revoke not the decree."

Learning Points:
A. Note that **John** the Beloved/Revelator is the one who has cursed or will curse the oceans. So, we see John in the last days again doing a labor. John has a big part in the last-days action to bring about Zion.
B. Nobody is going to be safe on the oceans. This could also mean large rivers and lakes as well.
C. The "land of Zion" is the Americas. Eventually all of North and South America. Only those with good upright hearts can come here during this period of time of the roaring waters.
D. The land is blessed by the Lord that the Saints of God may have the fatness of the products of the land. I am grateful for that blessing.
E. There is a destroying angel (The Destroyer) that rides or *will ride* upon the oceans to take down ships that attempt to cross the oceans and large navigable waters.
    a. (**Author's Analysis**): This curse upon the waters that make them *roaring*, may be the large near earth objects mentioned in the first 4 Trumpets in John's Revelation. *However*, the timing of those 4 Trumpets is *after* the 7th Seal. And we are only in the end of the 6th Seal in the timeline right now. So, the timing just doesn't seem right for those to be the reason for the dangerous waters problem.

The Trek has been made. The next thing to do on the Timeline is to start building the special Temple with 24 buildings on 45 acres.

17: The Special Temple Being Erected at the New Jerusalem – The Foundation of Zion

After the area of Jackson County Missouri is cleared out by the 2nd American Civil War, the BIG Plague, the Lost 10 Tribes returning and kicking out the 4th Beast Kingdom from America; the conspiratorial Ezra's Eagle/America has been burned…it's now time to rebuild America and make her desolate places and cities habitable once again. The Church of God with its new helpers will start with the special New Jerusalem Temple and the *new* Nation of Zion – The Kingdom of God.

Clarification Note: the Sept 23, 2017 date is for the Revelation 12 Sign in the stars that is the birth of the political Kingdom of God. It does not mature until after the 4th Beast Kingdom of the Gentiles is kicked out of America.

A Coinciding Event of Civil War

At the same time, with the civil war that started in America's neighborhoods and cities and states; this same spirit of civil war will break forth over in Europe on the home of the 10 Nation Beast Kingdom of the Gentiles and upon the Whore Church. It appears from John's writings that the 4th Beast Kingdom doesn't like the Whore Church riding it and thus destroys the Whore Church by fire. That would seem to be the *end* of the civil war in Europe….just in time for the Battle of Armageddon. (More on this topic coming soon.)

Let us focus on America's re-birth….into the political Kingdom of God with the new Nation of Zion with its capital city "The New Jerusalem" in the heartland of America at Independence, Jackson County, Missouri.

At the center of this new political capital city shall be the biggest and most special Temple of God that has ever been erected by man to his Creator.

This special Temple is best shown in some of the extra-curricular visions of President John Taylor, Joseph Smith Jr. and others. (see Appendix 4 for details)

Elder Orson Pratt saw the plans for this big Temple. This is what he said:

> (Journal of Discourses, 24:24)
> "There will be **24 different compartments** in the Temple that will be built in Jackson County. The names of these compartments were given to us some 45 or 46 years ago; the names we still have, and when we build these 24 rooms, **in a circular form and arched over the center**, we shall give the names to all these different compartments just as the Lord specified through Joseph Smith."

He also said:

> (Journal of Discourses, 24:27-33)

"Perhaps you may ask for what purpose these **24 compartments** are to be built. ...these buildings will be built with a special view to the different orders, or in other words **the different quorums or councils of the two Priesthoods** that God has ordained on the earth. That is the object of having 24 rooms so that each of these different quorums, whether they be High Priests or Seventies, or Elders, or Bishops, or lesser Priesthood, or Teachers, or Deacons, or Patriarchs, or Apostles, or High Councils, or whatever may be the duties that are assigned to them, they will have rooms in the Temple of the Most High God....

But will there be any other buildings excepting those 24 rooms that are all joined together in a circular form and arched over the center—are there any other rooms that will be built—**detached from the Temple? Yes.** There will be tabernacles, there will be meeting houses for the assembling of the people on the Sabbath day. There will be various places of meeting so that the people may gather together."

Learning Points:
A. There will be 24 "compartments" shaped in a circle and arched. I have not seen the exact plans for the 45 acre temple square, but we do know it's circular in shape.
B. There will be compartments or rooms for the different offices of the priesthood.
C. There will be other buildings on the temple square that will be used for meetings and tabernacles.

Once this magnificent Temple is built, the Lord's **glory** and cloud shall rest on it.

(D&C 84:4-5)
"4 Verily this is the word of the Lord, that **the city New Jerusalem** shall be built by the **gathering of the saints**, beginning at this place, even the place of the temple, which temple shall be reared in this generation.
5 For verily this generation shall not all pass away until an house shall be built unto the Lord, and **a cloud shall rest upon it, which cloud shall be even the glory of the Lord, which shall fill the house.**"

Learning Points:
A. The cloud and glory of the Lord will rest upon it in the eyes of all the people.
B. The city of the New Jerusalem shall be built by many Saints of God that are gathered.
C. Twice the Lord says this special Temple will be built "in this generation." I will not attempt to reason on that portion of scripture. I have read many Prophecy books that try to twist that scripture into place. However it happens, I will simply be grateful we have a Temple in the New Jerusalem.

WHO Will Build the New Jerusalem Temple and City?

This question perplexed me for a while when trying to understand this topic. However, if the timeline is correct that the Lost 10 Tribes have returned and have gone to the Saints of God in the Everlasting Hills to give *the miracle of the water in the desert and* to save the Saints of God from the 4th Beast Kingdom of the Gentiles, then they are *with* the believing Gentile Church of God *before* we go to Jackson County.

There are 3 groups that build this Temple:
1. The Gentile/Tribe of Ephraim Church of God: The Church of Jesus Christ of Latter-Day Saints.
2. The Lamanite/Nephite/Judah/Native American/Indian people of the Tribe of Manasseh. These will join with the Saints in protection of the Western United States *and* in the "building party" migration to Jackson County Missouri.
3. The Lost 10 Tribes from the land of the North. These must be present too, as the 144,000 will be called from among their ranks as well.

Remember, that we will need 12,000 of EACH TRIBE to ordain the 144,000 young High Priests to go forth and preach and hunt the rest of Israel from the nations of the earth. This includes 12,000 of Judah.

The special Temple is now being built. The City itself is under construction. But, we are going to have millions of free men living on this continent. It's time to **spread Zion** as mentioned in Isaiah and as the Savior repeated in 3rd Nephi.

18: _Zion Cities are Rebuilt from Vacant Gentile American Cities. The Spread of the Nation of Zion over North and South America_

The _new_ nation of Zion will need places and cities to house the millions of families of the Saints of God. The cities are now vacant and in need of a good cleaning and some good people to inhabit them. It's time for Zion to spread her chords and enlarge her tent.

Joseph Smith Jr says it this way…as already quoted above:

> "…pestilence, hail, famine, and earthquake will sweep the wicked of this generation from off the face of the land, **to open and prepare the way for the return of the lost tribes of Israel from the north country**."

And he continues:

> (Teachings of Joseph Smith, page 362)
> "There has been great discussion in relation to Zion— **where** it is…but I will make a proclamation that will cover a broader ground. **The whole of America is Zion itself from north to south**."

Learning Points:
A. The much needed space for the Lost 10 Tribes returning after 2,600 years from Arsareth in the north has just opened up.
B. The whole of North and South America will eventually be invited to join the _new_ Nation of Zion – the Kingdom of God. And they mostly will accept the invitation as the Kingdom of God becomes a mountain and fills the whole earth.

Isaiah saw the _new_ Nation of Zion expanding. He recorded it this way in Chapter 54:

> (Isaiah 54:1-3)
> "1 Sing, O barren, thou that didst not bear; break forth into singing, and cry aloud, thou that didst not travail with child: **for more are the children of the desolate than the children of the married wife**, saith the Lord.
> 2 **Enlarge the place of thy tent**, and let them **stretch forth the curtains of thine habitations**: spare not, **lengthen thy cords**, and strengthen thy stakes;
> 3 For thou shalt **break forth on the right hand and on the left; and thy seed shall inherit the Gentiles,** and make the desolate cities to be inhabited."

Learning Points:
A. There are many people coming to Zion, and there are _much fewer men_ among them.
B. Zion is to enlarge the tent and stretch out and expand.

C. The seed of the children of Zion shall inherit the unbelieving Gentile cities that are *empty*, because of the Civil War, BIG Plague, and The Lost 10 Tribes returning and taking down Daniel's 4th Beast out of America.

D. The cities of the Gentiles are to be inhabited by the children of Zion… The Saints of God.

The Lifestyle of the People in The New Nation of Zion – The Kingdom of God

This *new* nation of Zion – The Kingdom of God will be built upon the principles of righteousness. And the law that the early Saints of God did not live, will be the law that the latter Saints of God *will live*: The Law of Consecration. (See Appendix 1 for more information on this law)

There will be *new* scriptures among the Saints of God in this new Nation of Zion – The Kingdom of God. Here is a quick list of some of the possible scriptures to be revealed:

- The Lost 10 Tribes will have more scriptures.
- The sealed portion of the Book of Mormon recording of the Brother of Jared with the revelation that must be sealed up, because it gives perfect knowledge.
- The other records kept on plates by the Nephites.
- The writings of John the Baptist.
- The several missing prophets, including Zenos and Zenock.
- The writings of Enoch. Or a complete translation of the current Book of Enoch.
- The complete writings of Abraham.
- The writings of Joseph who was sold into Egypt.
- And many more.

The extra-curricular vision of Patriarch Charles D. Evans shows the future day of the *new* nation of Zion and the type of learning and lifestyle the Saints of God have there. (See Appendix 4)

The Nation of Zion is spreading abroad when more and more people start the gathering process out of the other nations of the world. The call will go out for the pure in heart to gather to Zion to avoid the civil wars happening at this time in the 4th Beast Kingdom of the Gentiles in Europe and other places in the world. Now it's time for Christ to come to his Special New Jerusalem Temple and ordain the 144,000 High Priests to preach and hunt Israel from the nations. This will be the END of the 6th Seal.

19: *Jesus Christ Comes to His Temple - The 144,000 Young High Priests are Ordained and Sent Forth to Preach - Finalizing the 6th Seal*

The *new* nation of Zion is being stretched out to the old Gentile cities. Zion is expanding outward. The *new* special Temple with 24 compartments on 45 acres in the center of the city of the New Jerusalem is now complete. It's time to dedicate the Temple and prepare it to receive the Master of the House.

The scriptures are silent as to **when** the Savior will come to His new Temple. Is it at the Dedication Ceremony? Or is it later? The answer remains to be seen.

John saw the Savior standing at the *new* Temple in Zion and recorded this:

> (Rev 14:1-5)
> "1 And I looked, and, lo, a **Lamb stood on the mount Sion**, and with him an **hundred forty and four thousand**, having his Father's name written in their foreheads.
> 2 And I heard a voice from heaven, as the voice of many waters, and as the voice of a great thunder: and I heard the voice of harpers harping with their harps:
> 3 And **they sung** as it were **a new song** before the throne, and before the four beasts, and the elders: and **no man could learn that song but the hundred and forty and four thousand**, which **were redeemed from the earth**.
> 4 These are they which were not defiled with women; for they are **virgins**. These are they which **follow the Lamb** whithersoever he goeth. **These were redeemed** from among men, being the **firstfruits unto God** and to the Lamb.
> 5 And in their mouth was **found no guile**: for **they are without fault** before the throne of God."

Learning Points:
A. This scripture links Jesus with the 144,000 directly. They follow him. He has redeemed them and made their Calling and Election Made Sure (See Appendix 1: Church of the Firstborn). They are in the Church of the Firstborn… and their mission will be to bring more people to the Church of the Firstborn. So, there will be **lots** of people who have their "calling and election made sure" in the *new* nation of Zion.
B. The 144,000 learn a new song that only they can sing.
C. The 144,000 are young men, because they are virgins and have not yet been married. These are young High Priests. They are also without guile and without fault.
D. Jesus apparently is living in Zion at this time, because these 144,000 follow him everywhere he goes. This scripture could also mean other places, besides Zion.

Joseph Smith said that John the Beloved/Revelator is the **angel** that will hold the 4 other angels of God from delivering their plagues *until* the 144,000 are sealed in their foreheads.

(D&C 77:9)
"9 Q. What are we to understand by the **angel ascending from the east**, Revelation 7th chapter and 2nd verse?

A. We are to understand that the angel ascending from the east is **he to whom is given the seal of the living God over the twelve tribes of Israel**; wherefore, he crieth unto the four angels having the everlasting gospel, saying: Hurt not the **earth**, neither the **sea**, nor the **trees**, till we have **sealed the servants of our God in their foreheads**. And, if you will receive it, **this is Elias which was to come to gather together the tribes of Israel and restore all things**."

And this one later in the same chapter D&C 77:

(D&C 77:14)
"14 Q. What are we to understand by **the little book** which was **eaten by John**, as mentioned in the 10th chapter of Revelation?

A. We are to understand that **it was a mission**, and an ordinance, **for him to gather the tribes of Israel; behold, this is Elias, who, as it is written, must come and restore all things**."

(Below) is the recording of John's Revelation that was mentioned (above)....This scripture immediately precedes the opening of the 7th Seal AND The 7 Trumpets and Vials to be poured out upon the 4th Beast Kingdom of the Gentiles. So, this is very important.

(Rev 7:1-4)
"1 And after these things I saw **four angels** standing on the four corners of the earth, holding the four winds of the earth, that the wind should not blow on the **earth**, nor on the **sea**, nor on any **tree**.
2 And I saw another **angel ascending from the east**, having **the seal of the living God**: and he cried with a loud voice to the four angels, to whom **it was given to hurt the earth and the sea**,
3 Saying, Hurt not the **earth**, neither the **sea**, nor the **trees**, **till** we have **sealed the servants of our God in their foreheads**.
4 And I heard the number of them which were sealed: and there were sealed an **hundred and forty and four thousand of all the tribes of the children of Israel**."

[Then 12,000 of each Tribe of Israel is mentioned by name to be sealed in the 144,000 (Dan is not mentioned)]

Learning Points:

A. Since John is the Angel arising from the East... may very well mean that *John instead of Jesus* is the one to Seal the 144,000 at the Temple in the New Jerusalem. I do not know specifically which one will do the sealing, yet it doesn't matter to our timeline, as we know the sealing happens.
B. John is holding back the first 4 Angels of the first 4 Trumpets against the Gentile Beast Kingdom. This is important, as we will soon see that these first 4 Trumpets/Vials come all at once in a flurry. And the Sea, Land, and Trees are all affected.

The Mission of the 144,000 Young High Priests

Joseph Smith elaborated on the mission of the 144,000 High Priest in the Doctrine and Covenants Section 77.

> (D&C 77:11)
> "11 Q. What are we to understand by sealing the **one hundred and forty-four thousand**, out of all the tribes of Israel—twelve thousand out of every tribe?
>
> A. We are to understand that those who are sealed are **high priests**, ordained unto the holy order of God, to **administer the everlasting gospel**; for they are they who are ordained out of every nation, kindred, tongue, and people, **by the angels** to whom is given power over the nations of the earth, to bring as many as will come to the **church of the Firstborn**."

Learning Points:
A. Here is evidence #2 that John, acting as an Angel, will be the one to ordain the 144,000 and send them out to preach the gospel.
B. Their mission is to preach the gospel and bring as many as will come to the Church of the Firstborn. Again, to *gather* righteous people to Zion out from the rest of the world.
C. The 144,000 will be High Priests sent out to preach.

The *Church of the Firstborn* is an interesting phrase. This is indeed more than regular membership in the Church of God. However, it isn't as elusive as some protagonists of the Church of God have claimed. It is readily described in the Doctrine and Covenants. (See Appendix 1 for details)

The 144,000 young High Priests will have their "calling and election made sure." Joseph Smith had this to say:

> (Teachings of the Prophet Joseph Smith, page 321)
> "Four destroying angels holding power over the four quarters of the earth until the servants of God are sealed in their foreheads, which signifies sealing the blessing upon their heads, meaning the everlasting covenant, thereby **making their calling and election made sure**."

These young High Priests will have the desolation of the nations to deal with during their missions. The 7th Seal is about to open and the Trumpets and Vials of John's

Revelation are to be poured out. These 144,000 will have no normal mission. They will labor in the world during this extremely hard time period.

The 144,000 High Priest's bodies will be changed and elevated to a Translated Being. The plagues and damage to be caused upon the 4th Beast Kingdom of the Gentiles during the beginning of the 7th Seal cannot hurt them. Orson Pratt had this to say about the change in their bodies:

> (Journal of Discourses 15:365-366)
> "The Lord will **purify their bodies until they shall be quickened**, and renewed and strengthened, and they will be **partially changed, not to immortality**, but changed in part that they can be filled with the power of God, and **they can stand in the presence of Jesus, and behold his face in the midst of the Temple**.
>
> This will prepare them for further ministration among the nations of the earth. It prepares them to go forth in **the days of tribulation and vengeance** upon the nations of the wicked when God will [punish] them with **pestilence, plague, and earthquake**, such as former generations never knew."

Learning Points:
A. Elder Pratt says The Lord is the one who changes their bodies into Translated Beings; not a total change to resurrected immortality.
B. The *purpose* of the translated body is so the 144,000 young High Priests can go forth during the Trumpets and Vials to be delivered upon the wicked.

It would appear that our timeline is now going to overlap a bit. The purpose of the Translated body was to protect them against the Trumps and Vials of the 7th Seal of John's Revelation. Thus, when they go out to preach, the 7th Seal is opened. *That* is the mark in the timeline that we were looking for.

The end of the 6th Seal of John's Revelation and the opening of the 7th Seal is when these young High Priests that are Translated go out to preach to the world to call as many as will come to the Church of the Firstborn.

Opening the 7th Seal, After the 144,000 Young High Priests are Translated and Sent Forth to Preach

Let us open the 7th Seal right here in this chapter in our timeline. **What do we see?**

There is a great warning to the wicked people living under the 4th Beast Empire of the Gentiles in Europe.

> (Rev 14:6-12)
> "6 And I saw **another angel [#1]** fly in the midst of heaven, having **the everlasting gospel to preach** unto them that dwell on the earth, and to every nation, and kindred, and tongue, and people,
> 7 Saying with a loud voice, Fear God, and give glory to him; for the **hour of**

his judgment is come: and **worship him** that made heaven, and earth, and the sea, and the fountains of waters.

8 And there followed **another angel [#2]**, saying, **Babylon is fallen**, is fallen, that great city, because she made all nations drink of the wine of the wrath of her fornication.

9 And the **third angel [#3]** followed them, saying with a loud voice, If any man **worship the beast and his image, and receive his mark** in his forehead, or in his hand,

10 The same shall **drink of the wine of the wrath of God**, which is poured out without mixture into the cup of his indignation; and he shall be tormented with **fire and brimstone** in the presence of the holy angels, and in the presence of the Lamb:

11 And the smoke of their torment ascendeth up for ever and ever: and they have no rest day nor night, who worship the beast and his image, and whosoever receiveth the mark of his name.

12 Here is **the patience of the saints**: here are they that keep the commandments of God, and the faith of Jesus."

Learning Points:
A. Angel #1 is sent to preach the Gospel **just** like the 144,000 young High Priests who are translated are sent to do. Also, a command to the 4th Beast Kingdom's people to worship God the Creator, **not the beast.**
B. Angel #2 carries a declaration that Babylon – The Great – Whore of all the Earth, Mother of Harlots – The Great and Abominable Church of the Devil (as taught by Nephi) has fallen and been destroyed by the Beast Kingdom of the Gentiles that she was riding. The exact *time* of this event is very much in debate, as we shall see. But, we do know *how* it happens and approximately *when* it happens, and that gives us some clues.
   a. This scripture, puts the fall of the Whore Church *before* the opening of the 7th Seal, just a bit.
      i. **Author's Analysis**: I do not think the Whore Church Babylon goes down before the Trumps and Vials of the 7th Seal. This Angel #2 is most likely a warning angel telling us that Babylon **will be going down** in the near future. (There is much more on this topic coming up)
C. Angel #3 carries a declaration warning the people of the 4th Beast Kingdom of the Gentiles in Europe that if they worship the Beast, image, or take the mark, instead of God the Creator, they will be the ones targeted by the Trumpets and Vials at the opening of the 7th Seal, which happens *next.*

A Great Missionary Effort to Harvest the Earth is Going On At The Same Time

(Rev 14:14-15)
"14 And I looked, and behold a white cloud, and upon the cloud one sat **like unto the Son of man**, having on his head a **golden crown**, and in his hand **a sharp sickle.**

15 And **another angel [#4]** came out of the temple, crying with a loud voice to him that sat on the cloud, Thrust in thy sickle, and reap: **for the time is come for thee to reap; for the harvest of the earth is ripe.**"

Learning Points:

A. This man on the cloud "like unto the Son of man" is *not* Jesus. Although he has a golden crown and a sharp sickle.

B. Angel #4 commands *the man* on the cloud to **reap** and harvest the souls from the Earth. This is a giant missionary effort led by this man on the cloud. This may be John the Revelator. It still could be Jesus. Or it could be still another person. But, we won't know for sure until we get there and see the 144,000 gathering the wheat into the garners of Zion, in preparation for the field to be burned with the tares of the Whore Church – Babylon the Great. (She is the tares.)

The Much Conjectured ½ Hour of Silence in Heaven – At the Opening of the 7th Seal

At this point, the 6th Seal is now closed. The 7th Seal is now open... and we encounter... about ½ hr silence in Heaven. This is the first thing that we see in the 7th Seal.

> (Rev 8:1)
> "1 And when he had **opened the seventh seal,** there was **silence in heaven about the space of half an hour."**

There has been much said by prophecy writers about this ½ hr of silence in heaven. Many theories have gone forth out of their mouths. However, let's make it very clear first.....

- The ½ hr of silence in Heaven, is *about* a ½ hr. So, it's not exactly precise.
- The ½ hr comes *after* the New Jerusalem has been built and the *new* nation of Zion-The Kingdom of God has been thoroughly established.
- The ½ hr comes *after* Jesus has visited the New Jerusalem.
- The ½ hr comes *after* the ordaining and sealing of the 144,000 young High Priests to preach during the upcoming days of great tribulation.
- The ½ hr comes *after* the closing of the 6th Seal and the opening of the 7th Seal....at just the moment before the pouring out of the Trumpets and Vials in John's Revelation.

Therefore the multitude of theories about what the "½ hr of silence in heaven" *means* are mostly **irrelevant**... because those prophecy writers are assuming that the ½ hr of silence comes at a time *other* than the closing of the 6th Seal and opening of the 7th *after* the New Jerusalem has been built.

There are only 2 theories that make any sense as to the purpose of the ½ hour of silence in heaven.
1. John saw about an actual ½ hr in earth time, which is not much.
2. John saw about a ½ hr in God's Time = about 21 earth years, which is much greater.

If the ½ hr of silence in heaven is in God's time (21 Earth Years) then… that is the time that the 144,000 become members of the Church of the First Born and are making a big call to the world to come to Zion and join the Church of God.

If the ½ hr of silence in heaven is in Earth time, (1/2 hrs on Earth) then… the 144,000 start their preaching directly into the Trumpets and Vials of John's Revelation.

I have no information about either of these scenarios being correct. If you, as the reader, have specific information on this topic, please contact me at the website www.LastDaysTimeline.com.

The Call Will Go Forth To "Gather To Zion"

The "Call" will go forth from these 144,000 young High Priests to **come** unto Zion. This is the time for massive growth in Zion. The Lord will soon use "the carrot" and "the stick" to get the people of Earth to **repent**. The carrot is the message of "come to Zion and be free." The stick is the message that will soon be given in the massive onslaught of the Trumpets and Vials of John's Revelation upon the Earth.

> (D&C45:66-71)
> "66 And it shall be called **the New Jerusalem**, a **land of peace**, a city of **refuge**, a place of **safety** for the saints of the Most High God;
> 67 And the **glory** of the Lord shall be there, and the **terror of the Lord** also shall be there, insomuch that **the wicked will not come unto it**, and it shall be called **Zion**.
> 68 And it shall come to pass among the wicked, that **every man that will not take his sword against his neighbor must needs flee unto Zion** for **safety**.
> 69 And there shall be gathered unto it out of **every nation under heaven**; and it shall be the **only people that shall not be at war one with another**.
> 70 And it shall be said among the wicked: Let us **not go up to battle against Zion**, for the inhabitants of Zion are terrible; wherefore we cannot stand.
> 71 And it shall come to pass that **the righteous shall be gathered out from among all nations**, and shall come to Zion, singing with songs of everlasting joy."

Learning Points:
A. It appears that, as the New Jerusalem city is called these peaceful names: land of peace, city of refuge, place of safety… that the rest of the world will now be in a giant civil war at this time. *And* that does match the timeline nicely. Eventually there will be a civil war in the Gentile Nations of the 4th Beast Kingdom. It has been prophesied.
   a. **Author's Analysis**: The civil war in the 4th Beast Kingdom of Europe will *most likely* be based upon Religion. The Stout Horn leader of the Beast is a man who makes "miracles" in the sight of the people. He is directly led and talks with Satan by evil revelation. And on the other side of the fight is The **state** church – The Whore Church – Babylon the Great who is riding the Beast. However, the Beast, doesn't like to be "ridden", (nor does its leader) and will eventually destroy the **state**

Whore Church in a civil war and by **fire**. The wicked destroy the wicked.

B.   The glory of God will be upon the city. It will **glow**.

C.   The wicked people in North and South America will not come there. Also the main wicked 4th Beast Kingdom will have its hands full in a civil war, so they won't come there either.

D.   The civil war among the world in this scripture appears to be *general*. It is apparent that all people have lost the light of Christ (their conscience). However, we will see in later scriptures in John, that the civil war and the Trumps and Vials are mainly targeting the 4th Beast Kingdom of the Gentiles in Europe. But, it does appear that the civil war is even more wide reaching than their own kingdom.

E.   The righteous are gathered to Zion by the 144,000 young High Priests.

The 144,000 young High Priests have been commissioned and sent forth to gather the pure-in-heart that won't take up the sword against their neighbor in the civil wars of the Gentile nations of Europe's 4th Beast Empire. They are to hunt the Tribes of Israel from among the remaining souls on Earth. However, as I understand it, they are **not** sent to the Gentile Kingdoms of Europe. The Times of the Gentiles have already been fulfilled long ago, when they attacked the Church of God and heavily oppressed it.

There have been a few prophecy book writers that say many of the events surrounding Zion and the New Jerusalem are Millennial events. That those events take place in the Savior's 1000 years of peace. That may very well be so…because once the 6th Seal is closed and the 7th Seal is opened, the Earth is inside the Millennium. The start of the Millennium is the start of the 7th Seal. Thus, **most people on the planet will not know that the Millennium has started.**

Before the unbelieving Gentiles are put out of their evil misery with the 7 Trumpets and Vials of John the Revelator; *first* the Jewish Temple in Jerusalem must be built up… concurrently with the New Jerusalem Temple in Jackson County, Missouri. They happen at **approximately** the same time; which is quite fitting.

20: _The 4th Jerusalem Temple to Be Built By The Jews, BEFORE the Battle of Armageddon_

This is the long awaited moment that the Jews right now (in 2017) have been waiting for. They are able to build their long awaited 4th Temple; where they will finally have a place to offer blood sacrifices to God, once again.

YouTube.com is abuzz about their excitement to be able to build their new Temple. The only problem is they don't know the _location_ of where to build it precisely.

Many of the Jewish religion claim that the current Temple Mount where the Muslim Dome of the Rock is located is the precise location of Solomon's and Herod's Temple. There are other alternatives for the site that make Biblical sense. (See Appendix 1)

Aside from _where_ it should be built, we do know _who_ will build it. It will be built under a Latter-Day Jewish Leader named "David." Joseph Smith spoke of this man:

> (Teachings of Joseph Smith page 339)
> "Although David was a king, he never did obtain the spirit and power of Elijah and the fullness of the priesthood; and the priesthood that he received, and the throne and kingdom of David is to be taken from him and **given to another by the name of David in the last days, raised up out of his lineage."**

And in Zechariah Chapter 6, we see that _this_ David has been spoken of in scripture for a long time.

> (Zechariah 6:12-13)
> "12 And speak unto him, saying, Thus speaketh the Lord of hosts, saying, Behold **the man whose name is <u>The Branch</u>**; and he shall grow up out of his place, and **he shall build the temple of the Lord**:
> 13 Even **he shall build the temple of the Lord**; and he shall bear the glory, and shall sit and rule upon **his throne**; and **he shall be a priest** upon his throne: and the counsel of peace shall be between them both."

Learning Points:
A. This last-days "David" is to be raised up unto the Jews, as a leader. Under his stewardship and in his _future day_, the Jewish Temple will be built.
B. David should be priest (High Priest) and have a throne in Jerusalem.
C. The last-days "David" shall come from the progeny of the old David.

The identity of the latter-day "David" ruler in Jerusalem that is a Priest and shall build the Temple is unknown today. It may be any number of people, and it also may be Christ himself. I have read the books from the prophecy writers and most never mention this person. And the ones that do mention the latter-day "David" are split between Christ himself, or a real man named "David." (See Appendix 1: The Branch)

The physical description of this latter-day Jewish Temple is held in Ezekiel Chapters 40-47. Please see the description there.

The *timing* of the start of construction is of importance to our timeline. Working backwards... we know:

- That when Christ comes on the Mount of Olives to rescue the Jews from Gog's Army (Stout Horn/False Messiah), that the Jews take him and usher him through the East Gate of the city of Jerusalem and into the Temple. So, the temple is completed *before* Christ comes at the end of the Battle of Armageddon.
- That water issues forth from under the Temple from a large earthquake, probably when Christ's feet touch the Mount of Olives to split it. The water flows down to heal the Dead Sea. So, again the temple must be there *before* Christ comes at the end of Battle of Armageddon (Ezek 47:8-9).
- That Gog goes into the Temple during the 3.5 Days that the 2 Witnesses are dead. He commits desecration of the Temple. So, the Temple is there before the 3.5 Days the 2 Witnesses are killed.
- That animal offerings were being made inside the temple, *before* the Battle of Armageddon gets underway and the Gentiles stop the sacrifices in the Temple (See Appendix 1: 4th Jewish Temple).

> (Daniel 9:26)
> "26 And after threescore and two weeks shall Messiah be cut off, but not for himself: and the **people of the prince** that shall come **shall destroy the city and the sanctuary**; and the end thereof shall be **with a flood**, and unto the end of the war desolations are determined.
> 27 And **he shall confirm the covenant with many for one week**: and in the **midst of the week** he **shall cause the sacrifice and the oblation to cease**, and for the overspreading of abominations **he shall make it desolate**, even until the consummation, and that determined shall be poured upon the desolate."

Learning Points:
A. This is the famous scripture that many Christians point to and say that Gog will make a covenant/agreement with the Jews for 7 *years* (maybe a land for peace deal, they say). Then Gog breaks the agreement in 3.5 years; then attacks the Jews after that point... for the remainder of 3.5 years. This very well seems to be the case.
B. 3.5 years into the 7 year commitment, Gog will cause the agreement to be nullified and shall have the Jews *cease* the sacrifices in the Temple. This is how the traditional way of interpreting this scripture goes.
    a. But, if this is true, then the Jews have their Temple and are making animal sacrifices before even this agreement takes place, 3.5 years *before* the Battle of Armageddon.

And again in Daniel Chapter 8, a very similar thing is mentioned. The Stout Horn will **stop** the Sacrifices in the Jerusalem Temple for 3.5 years.

> (Daniel 8:10-14)
> "10 And **it [The Stout Horn] waxed great**, even to the host of heaven; and

it cast down some of the host and of the stars to the ground, and stamped upon them.

11 Yea, **he magnified himself** even to the prince of the host, and **by him the daily sacrifice was taken away, and the place of his sanctuary was cast down.**

12 And an host was given him **against the daily sacrifice** by reason of transgression, and **it cast down the truth to the ground; and it practised, and prospered.**

13 Then I heard one saint speaking, and another saint said unto that certain saint which spake, **How long shall be the vision concerning the daily sacrifice,** and the **transgression** of desolation, to give both **the sanctuary** and **the host** to be trodden under foot?

14 And he said unto me, Unto **two thousand and three hundred days; then shall the sanctuary be cleansed."**

Learning Points:
A. 2300 Days is 6.3 years that the outer court of the Temple will be occupied by the Gentiles of the Stout Horn's Beast Kingdom Armies.
B. The Stout Horn will take away the daily sacrifice of the Temple. Also he shall make a ruckus in the Temple. Remember, it can't be completely destroyed by the Stout Horn or else Jesus would have no place to be taken by the Jews through the East Gate of Jerusalem from the Mount of Olives, when he arrives.

The Jerusalem Temple has been built at approximately the same time as the New Jerusalem Temple was built in America. The 144,000 young High Priests have been sent forth to preach and gather all the pure in heart to Zion. *Now* is the time of the end of the Gentiles. The 7 Trumpets and Vials are about to be poured out by the angels upon the 4th Beast Kingdom of the Gentiles and then they will gather for **their** ultimate destruction at the Battle of Armageddon.

SECTION 6: The Fall of the Gentile Beast Kingdom in Europe by Civil War, John`s Seals, Trumpets, and Vials, While the Nation of Zion/The Kingdom of God is Rising At-Same-Time

YOU ARE
HERE

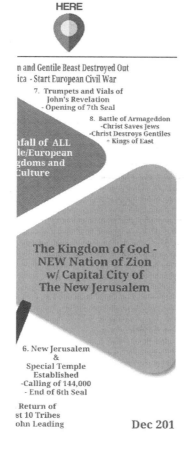

n and Gentile Beast Destroyed Out
ica - Start European Civil War

7. **Trumpets and Vials of
John's Revelation
- Opening of 7th Seal**

8. **Battle of Armageddon
-Christ Saves Jews
-Christ Destroys Gentiles
+ Kings of East**

fall of ALL
le/European
gdoms and
ulture

The Kingdom of God -
NEW Nation of Zion
w/ Capital City of
The New Jerusalem

6. New Jerusalem
&
Special Temple
Established
-Calling of 144,000
- End of 6th Seal

Return of
st 10 Tribes
ohn Leading

Dec 201

21: *The Civil War – The False Prophet`s 4th Beast Kingdom of the Gentiles /VS/ the STATE Church of the Beast Kingdom – Babylon The Great – The Mother of Harlots – The Great and Abominable Church*

To begin the final scene of the wipeout of the 4th Beast Kingdom of the Gentiles, we should start where they are… in the middle of a civil war in their lands. This civil war *may or may not have been* started by the 2nd American Civil War which happened because the **state** religion Whore Church of the Beast attacked the Saints of God. But, no matter *when* this Gentile civil war started, it has spread and has become a large problem for those in Europe and further, at the time before John's Trumpets and Vials are poured out.

Let us connect some dots in the timeline: (assuming the applied scriptures are accurate)

- Step 1: Remember the 144,000 young High Priests who were translated? They were sent out to gather the pure in heart to Zion and were translated to protect them bodily against the 7 Trumpets and Vials of the beginning of the 7th Seal.

- Step 2: All those that would not take up arms against their neighbor would have to flee to Zion because of the fighting in the European Civil War, and beyond.

- Step 3: The Civil War is happening at the same time the 144,000 are going out to gather the pure in heart, which is also right at the beginning of the 7th Seal.

- Step 4: Except for the ½ hr silence in heaven, the 144,000 are going out into the time of the 7 Trumpets and Vials of John.

CONCLUSION: Which means, … The civil war in Gentile Europe is happening at the same time as the beginning of the 7 Vials and Trumps are to be poured out.

If this logic holds true, it is an additional clue as to *who* is fighting in the European Civil war, and beyond.

> Which nations are involved in this European Civil War?
> What is their basis for fighting each other?
> Who are the leaders on each side?

These are important questions for any student of history to understand. However, we are looking into a future that has already happened for the Great Creator. He sees events in history without the limitation of time; as he is All-Knowing. So, let's see what He has to say about these issues.

NOTE: The naming of these entities gets very complicated as many prophets have seen these entities and have called them by different names. We have already drawn links to each of these names throughout this work. Let us define them right here **again**, so you, the reader, can follow along more closely.

- **The Beast Kingdom's final evil leader** that communes with Lucifer directly and takes marching orders from him. The bad guy that rises to power and takes out 3 other kings with his rise. He is a "miracle worker" in the Dark Arts of Satan's miracles. This Man's names are: Gog (Ezekiel) / the False Prophet (John) / the False Messiah (Nephi) / the Stout Horn (Daniel) / the Assyrian (Isaiah). (See also Appendix 1)

- **The 4th Beast Kingdom** itself is the final kingdom on the earth of the Gentiles. It is a confederation of 10 nations that have a **state** Church. This 4th Beast rises as the 3rd Beast (the Leopard Empire) goes down. The people worship The Beast Kingdom and its ideologies, receive the Mark of the Beast and also worship the Beast's Image. Eventually the people worship the Stout Horn himself. This Kingdom has many names: The 4th Beast (Daniel 7) / The Toes with Iron and Clay (Daniel 2) / The Eagle under the 3 Eagle Heads (Ezra-2nd Esdras 11) / Egypt (Isaiah – not defined in this work, yet) / The Scarlet Beast with 7 Heads and 10 Horns (John) / Magog led by Gog (Ezekiel).

- **The Whore Church** is the **state** religion of the 4th Beast Kingdom of the Gentiles. As a **state** religion, it has the power of death upon the Beast Kingdom's citizens. It is an amalgamated religion of many religions on the Earth today (See Appendix 1). This Whore Church has many names: Babylon the Great – Mother of Harlots and Abominations (John) / The Whore of All The Earth (John and Nephi) / The Great and Abominable Church of the Devil (Nephi)

These characters, along with the Jews, are the principal characters in the timeline.

Author's Important Interjection:

If I have identified these characters, through their symbolism correctly, the scriptures will unfold themselves to our open view. ***This is why* identification of the symbols is so important when we read prophecy.**

Many prophecy writers won't directly identify the symbols for fear of *getting it wrong.*

However, if the readers in the Church of God don't properly identify the symbols, the conclusions drawn will be invalid. And this very thing has happened for 100s of years with all prophecy expounders, **including ME.**

If hundreds of people over hundreds/thousands of years have studied their scriptures, asked God for inspiration and have all come out with **different** views of the symbols and **different** identifications; logic tells us…they are all wrong - **including this author.** Remember the archery target in the Introduction of this work?

There are only 2 things I have that are semi-unique:
1. I am living/writing at a **later** time than all the prophecy writers before me.

Thus, the symbols become clearer, because of passing history.

2. I am committed to updating this work for the rest of my life for my children. As new information unfolds, it will be added to this work. This is a lifetime endeavor for me to get the timeline correct; the baton will be passed at the end of my mortal life.

When speaking of the Revelation of John and the destructions that come upon the 4th Beast Kingdom of the Gentiles and the world, we must understand that these figurative things that John saw were real. There was symbolism of beasts, whores, harlots, 2nd beasts, images, and the rest. However, there were also very real things that are to take place: earthquakes, tidal waves, fiery hail, famine, war, and the rest.

So, what John is looking at are the very things that other prophets have been shown by the angels, but he is seeing how **symbolic figures** move through **a timeline filled with real events**.

Some prophecy writers have supposed that all the items are symbolic. And other prophecy writers have supposed that all the items are literal. The mystery of John's Revelation is solved when we differentiate the **symbolic** from the **literal**. And then we properly **identify the symbolic** figures.

And we have just one more problem to deal with… Nephi says it this way:

(1st Nephi 14:23)
"23 Wherefore, the things which he [John the Beloved/Revelator] shall write are just and true; and behold they are written in **the book [the Bible]** which thou beheld proceeding out of the mouth of the Jew; and **at the time** they proceeded out of the mouth of the Jew, or, **at the time** the book proceeded out of the mouth of the Jew, **the things which were written were plain and pure**, and most precious and **easy to the understanding** of all men."

We have already gone over this scripture. The problem is… The Whore Church in the meridian of time, has **altered** much of John's Revelation. *This* is the reason it has been difficult for the prophecy writers to identify the Seals, Trumpets and Vials as it relates to the timeline. With all the symbolic figures tossed into the mix people just get plain lost trying to understand it. So, blame the Whore Church for this complex book of scripture becoming garbled… as the Angel of God teaching Nephi said it was so.

Revelations 14 speaks of Jesus standing upon Mount Zion with the 144,000. This is where our timeline picks up.

We know that America will be restored as at the first, under the Constitution. *And* that the anointed Lion that was hidden (lost 10 Tribes from land of the North) rescues the Saints of God from mass oppression from The 7 crowned Headed 10 Horned Scarlet Beast. Next is when the New Jerusalem Temple is built and Jesus comes to ordain 144,000 high priests from 12,000 of each of the 12 tribes of Israel.

For our timeline purposes, know that the events surrounding the New Jerusalem and Mount Zion happen at the *end* of the 6th Seal. The 12 Tribes are assembled and build the New Jerusalem. And its extra-special Temple in the heart of the city, goes up at the same time.

We will skip this chapter 14 in Revelations, because it doesn't specifically apply to a timeline, other than it happens in America which has now been freed. There is more timeline oriented material in the extra-curricular visions in Appendix 4 that tackle this event in great detail.

Author's Analysis:

This Continuing Civil War in Europe Seems to Be a Religious Civil War.

The Beast's leader the False Prophet/Stout Horn didn't like losing the civil war in America against the new foes, the Lost 10 Tribes of Israel. *Nor* that the territory was lost because of **religious persecution** by the **state** Whore Church upon a group of people…the Saints of God.

Also, the Stout Horn doesn't like the **state** Whore Church – Babylon the Great riding him and his Beast Kingdom. Remember, he has "Dark Arts Power" from Satan to create miracles in the sight of the people. So he is already "sharing" the people's religious attention with this **state** Religion the Whore Church as an organization. Remember, the Stout Horn is *late* to the party of this 4th Beast Kingdom.

Satan is in communication with the Stout Horn Leader, and (remember), Satan is super jealous of The Son of God. Satan doesn't even like his name. So, it makes sense that **when** the time is right, with this maniacal Stout Horn Anti-Christ character *in place* that Satan would want to do away with the **state** Whore Church altogether. And have the people finally worship Lucifer as the supreme god.

The 10 Nations that belong to this 4th Beast Kingdom are in a Civil War. The nations loyal to The **state** Whore Church *vs.* some of the Beast Nations that are loyal to the Stout Horn/False Prophet. This civil war is not limited to *just* Europe. But it certainly is centered there, as Europe contains the principals of the leadership on both sides.

Here are 2 clues to think about:

1. The name of the "Battle of Armageddon" – is a **battle**, not the **war** of Armageddon. **Assumingly**, if 200M men were to come up to a huge battle, there would be a war connected to it. Not just one battle. So it seems that this final **battle** of Gog/Stout Horn against Jerusalem will be part of something much larger. And this civil war in all of Europe would be that **something**.

2. Remember the 4th Beast Kingdom with 7 crowned Heads and 10 Horns **hates** the Whore – Babylon the Great. The Beast Kingdom will make her desolate, eat her flesh, and burn her with fire (more on this scripture to come). This is the final demise of the **state** Whore Church - Babylon the Great. This would also be the end of the civil war. And the very next thing we see… is the Stout Horn/False Prophet, using 3 frog "dark art" ambassadors to gather the

Kings of the East to the battle of Armageddon. Thus, the Whore Church is destroyed before the Battle of Armageddon and the huge army of Gog/Stout Horn/False Prophet is put to a new task.

Given the clues, the duration of this Civil War among the Beast Nations of the Gentiles takes many years. And finally ends with the destruction of the State Whore Church – Babylon the Great. The people in Europe now have a new **state church** – The Church of Lucifer; to worship Lucifer openly; **just like he wanted all along,** along with a semi-global world Government of the Gentiles with Lucifer's Stout Horn/False Prophet/False Messiah in control. *But,* it doesn't last long.

Now that we are settled in… let us take at the Revelation of John and the opening of the 7th Seal in our last-days timeline.

The Civil War in the European 4th Beast Kingdom of the Gentiles is ongoing for a good while. Let us see the judgments of God upon the Beast of Europe.

22: The 7 Trumpets and 7 Vials to be poured out upon the 4th Beast Kingdom of the Gentiles

We have arrived at the 7 Trumpets and 7 Vials to be poured out upon the Beast Kingdom of Europe. These vials represent the **full wrath** of God upon his wicked children. These judgments are **as big as it gets**.

A Word About the Seals, Trumpets, and Vials

As Joseph Smith recorded, concerning the seals in the Revelation of John, in the Doctrine and Covenants Section 77:

> (D&C 77:6-7)
> "6 Q. What are we to understand by the book which John saw, which was sealed on the back with **seven seals**?
> A. We are to understand that it contains the **revealed will, mysteries, and the works of God**; the hidden things of his economy concerning this earth during **the seven thousand years** of its continuance, or its temporal existence.
> 7 Q. What are we to understand by **the seven seals** with which it was sealed?
> A. We are to understand that the **first seal contains the things of the first thousand years, and the second also of the second thousand years, and so on until the seventh**."

Learning Points:
A. The book with 7 Seals contains the things of God done in *each* of the 1000 year periods of the Earth, including the Millennium.
B. Each Seal represents 1000 years. This is very important to know in the timeline when we close the 6th Seal and open the 7th Seal. This will help us "correct" some bad information in the near future.

If these Seals represent 1000 year periods of the Earth, we should be able to look back at the earth's history and see each of the events in the seals. This is the information we are told by Jesus through the prophet Joseph Smith Jr.

A Problem with the Recording of the 6th Seal

Before we get to the Trumpets and Vials of the 7th Seal, we have to close-out the 6th Seal in our timeline. Let us look at it.

(FREE DOWNLOAD of the Excel Spreadsheet of the Seals, Trumpets, and Vials of John's Revelation + the Trumpets of Doctrine and Covenants + D&C 45 timeline of events... **all lined up**... from the www.LastDaysTimeline.com/seals-trumpets-vials)

We will forego the Seals 1-4 as they are in the ancient past, even before the Great Flood. We will concentrate on Seals 5, 6, and 7 (our recent past, and the future).

Seal #5 – Revelation Chapter 6

(Rev 6:9)
"9 And when he had opened the **fifth seal**, I saw under the altar the souls of them that were **slain for the word of God**, and for **the testimony which they held**:
10 And they cried with a loud voice, saying, How long, O Lord, holy and true, dost thou not judge and avenge our blood on them that dwell on the earth?
11 And white robes were given unto every one of them; and it was said unto them, that they **should rest yet for a little season, <u>until their fellowservants also and their brethren, that should be killed as they were, should be fulfilled</u>.**"

Learning Points:
A. The 5<u>th Seal is the meridian of time.</u> It was filled with the early Christian Martyrs that died for their faith at the hands of the Jewish prosecutors (Paul the Apostle used to be one of those prosecutors). Also, it included the major prosecutors from the Roman Empire, until approximately 300 A.D.
    a. The best audio books on this subject are downloadable for FREE on the website www.LastDaysTimeline.com.
        i. The Great Apostasy –by James Talmage
        ii. Foxes Book of the Martyrs – by John Fox
        iii. History of the Early Christian Church – by Cheetham
B. These spirits of the Saints of God who were killed in the 5th Seal were told that they should rest a season, until their fellow servants of God should be killed in the FUTURE. We have already spoken of the oppression of the Saints of God toward the end of the 6th Seal. So, it's only 1 Seal away from these original Christian martyrs in the meridian of time.
    a. If Christ comes at the beginning of the 5th Seal, those Christian martyrs are soon after. Also, the oppression of the Saints of God in the last-days happen at the end of the 6th Seal. That would put about 2000 years between them. That is right on schedule in the timeline "a little season."

And to the **Opening** of the 6<u>th Seal</u>

(Rev 6:12-17)
"12 And I beheld when he had **<u>opened</u> the sixth seal**, and, lo, there was **a great earthquake**; and the **sun became black** as sackcloth of hair, and the **moon became as blood**;
13 And the **stars of heaven fell** unto the earth, even as a fig tree casteth her untimely figs, when she is shaken of a mighty wind.
14 And the **<u>heaven departed as a scroll when it is rolled together</u>**; and **every mountain and island were moved** out of their places.
15 And the kings of the earth, and the great men, and the rich men, and the chief captains, and the mighty men, and every bondman, and every free man, **hid themselves in the dens and in the rocks of the mountains**;
16 And said to the mountains and rocks, **Fall on us**, and hide us from **<u>the face of him that sitteth on the throne, and from the wrath of the Lamb</u>**:
17 For **<u>the great day of his wrath is come</u>**; and who shall be able to stand?"

This scripture is at the **END** of the 6th Seal from Revelation Chapter 7….(paraphrased since we have already gone over this scripture)

Remember the END of the 6th Seal is where we are right now 2017. At the very end of the 6th Seal is when:

- John is the Angel of the East who holds back the 4 angels to **not** hurt the earth, sea, or trees until they have sealed the servants of GOD in their foreheads. (the 144,000)
- The 144,000 young High Priests are ordained and sent forth to preach and to gather the righteous to the *new* Nation of Zion and the New Jerusalem.

Author's Analysis and Learning Points:

Learning Points:

    A. **Wait A Minute**. We have a major problem here. There is *no way* that the 2nd Coming of the Lord to reveal his face and melt the mountains and the islands should come *before* the ordaining of the 144,000 young High Priests in the New Jerusalem.

    B. This scripture… in the Holy Bible… says that *at the beginning* (or opening) of the 6th Seal, approximately 1000 A.D. in our earth's history, shows that all the mountains of our planet flowed down, and all the islands in the ocean fled *and* that the heaven (sky) "departed as a scroll" and rolled up.

    C. Further, that all the important men of the earth hid themselves in caves trying to escape "the great day of the wrath of Jesus."

I don't remember a time in my history books, just after the life of Charlamane 1000 years ago, that the mountains flowed down, the islands fled, and the 2nd Coming of Christ happened.

As a plain reader of the scriptures, I can say that **this scripture is misplaced**. **"Bold" as it may seem**; we know that Nephi told us that the Great and Abominable Church (Babylon the Great) has altered and changed the Word of the Lord in the Book of John's Revelation. *This* is one of the changes.

This scripture is describing the "2nd Coming of the Lord" to a tee. It should be placed at the *end* of the 7 Trumpets/7 Vials, after the Battle of Armageddon, and even a little further in the timeline.

The only things that would be contained in the 6th Seal are: the oppression of the Saints of God; the building of the New Jerusalem; the sealing of the 144,000 young High Priests and their call to preach. That is all that would be logically listed in the 6th Seal.

Who Will Send Forth These 7 Trumpets and 7 Vials upon the 4th Beast Kingdom of the Gentiles?

This is a very good question. When I read the Book of John's Revelation it was assumed that God sent the Angels to deliver the 7 Trumpets and 7 Vials upon the wicked of the world. End of story.

However, after writing this work and paying close attention to detail of the timeline and the Characters involved in the future plot, there may be an alternative that makes sense.

Author Analysis:
I have placed my comments on this part in this "analysis section" to separate my opinion from the main core facts of the work.

Let us consider a scripture about the 2 Witnesses in Jerusalem that hold off the Beast Kingdom's armies for 3.5 years. Revelation 11:

(Rev 11:5-6)
"5 And if any man will hurt them, **fire proceedeth out of their mouth**, and devoureth their enemies: and if any man will hurt them, he must in this manner be killed.
6 These have **power to shut heaven**, that **it rain not in the days of their prophecy**: and have **power over waters** to turn them **to blood**, and to <u>smite the earth with all plagues</u>, as often as they will."

Learning Points:
A. These <u>2 prophets of God, raised up to the Jewish people, have massive power over the elements of the Earth.</u>
B. Fire shoots out of their mouth, power to turn off the clouds and cause a drought for 3.5 years, power over the **water** to turn it to blood to afflict their enemies. To smite the **whole earth** with all sorts of plagues. And to do it as often as they desire to afflict their enemies.

<u>Who are these 2 prophets</u>' enemies? The main enemy of these 2 prophets is none other than the evil leader Stout Horn/Gog/The False Messiah of the 4th Beast Kingdom of the Gentiles (Plus, the armies of the Kings of the East).

How long will these 2 prophets hold the armies of the Beast back from totally decimating Jerusalem?
For 3.5 years they will hold them back. That is a **really long time** to hold back anything, or anyone, or any army. Can the reader think of any feat in the history of modern warfare that a large army of men couldn't accomplish in less than 3.5 years? I cannot. Most total wars are over in less time than that. These 2 prophets have **all the powers necessary** from God to afflict the Beast Kingdom of the Gentiles with the main 7 Trumpets and 7 Vials recorded in John's Revelation.

- <u>The length of time of 3.5 years looks to be about right for the delivery of the 7 Trumpets and 7 Vials upon the Beast's Kingdom of Europe.</u>
- <u>The vials, as we shall see, are interwoven with the trumpets. They are the same.</u>
Note: <u>The vials are directed upon the 4th Beast Kingdom of the Gentiles in Europe. Thus, so are the Trumpets.</u>

- This is not the first time that heavenly angels have been called upon to deliver plagues that a Prophet of God has asked to be delivered. The plagues of God sent upon Egypt were started **by the Prophet Moses** doing an **act**, and then the plague comes upon Egypt. Since we know that the plagues of Egypt are the virtual same as the plagues sent upon this 4th Beast Kingdom, they too may be started *by* the 2 Prophets themselves.

I have *the opinion* (which may change based upon more evidence) that these 2 witnesses/prophets in Jerusalem are the very ones that afflict the Gentiles in their homeland of Europe with the 7 Trumpets and 7 Vials of John's Revelation.

The Opening of the 7th Seal = 7 Plagues (Trumpets and Vials)

The 4th Beast of Europe is engaged in a big civil war *during* the outpouring of these 7 Plagues upon them. *That* is how wicked these people are. None of these judgments get these people to repent. The Light of Christ was gone from their minds long ago. They are controlled by Lucifer now.

As the wicked were swept off the land of the Americas in preparation for the Kingdom of God to grow and expand, so also the wicked are swept off the land of Europe and other places for the Kingdom of God to grow and expand, into the Millennium. Wilford Woodruff had this to say:

> (Wilford Woodruff, Journal of Discourses 2:201)
> "It is the decree of the Almighty God, that the kingdom of heaven shall be established, and shall never again be overthrown, that **judgments shall lay waste the nations, enough at least to give that kingdom room to grow**, and spread, and prosper."

Revelation Chapter 15 is where we will pick-up the timeline. (You should really download a copy of the excel sheet that matches-up the Seals, Trumpets, and Vials from www.LastDaysTimeline.com/seals-trumpets-vials – examine it while you read this section.)

The 7 Trumps match-up to the 7 Vials fairly well. I did not "force" them to fit. If a vial didn't match to a Trump, I have listed it separately. As we review this timeline for the Trumps and Vials of Seal #7, I will put the scriptures that match-up nicely together so you, the reader, can see *if* they match-up for yourself. Remember, this work is a collaborative effort over a lifetime. So, I welcome your input. (Ask questions and post comments on the Discussion Boards on the Website www.LastDaysTimeline.com)

The 7 Trumpets and 7 Vials are going out (Chapter 15). It's time for the honest in heart to *physically* gather to Zion and rebuild her old cities. It is also time to come out of *Babylon the Great*.

> (Rev 8: 1)
> "1 And when he had opened the seventh seal, there was silence in heaven about the space of half an hour."

The first thing that happens after the 7ᵗʰ Seal is opened is the silence in heaven for about ½ hr. Whether this is an earth ½ hr or a ½ hr to God (21 earth years) is spoken of in another chapter of this work. Next the Trumps/Vials are to be delivered upon the 4ᵗʰ Beast Kingdom of the Gentiles in Europe.

(Rev 15:1)
"1 And I saw **another sign in heaven**, great and marvellous, **seven angels having the seven last plagues**; for in them is filled up the wrath of God.";

(Rev 8:2)
"2 And I saw **the seven angels** which stood before God; and to them were given **seven trumpets**."

Learning Points:
A. John was shown by the angel what appears to be another heavenly constellation pattern.
B. It shows 7 angels with the 7 plagues that contain the full measure of the wrath of God.

The angel instructing John takes a detour for a few verses (Rev 15: 2-3) to show the latter-day **modern** Saints of God who were dead in the Celestial Kingdom that had been killed by the Beast Kingdom of the Gentiles. These Saints had gained the victory over the Beast, over his image, over the Mark of the Beast, over the number of the Beast. They sing the song of Moses and the Lamb.

Verses 3 and 4 are the new song. Verse 5 starts with the 7 Angels with 7 Vials of Plagues. Remember the Beast has already gone down in America. These 7 Plagues come upon the rest of the world where the remainder of the Beast's kingdom is still growing, latter-day Gentile Europe.

(Rev 15:5-8)
"5 And **after** that I looked, and, behold, **the temple of the tabernacle of the testimony in heaven** was opened:
6 And the **seven angels came out of the temple, having the seven plagues**, clothed in pure and white linen, and having their breasts girded with **golden girdles**.
7 And **one of the four beasts** gave unto **the seven angels seven golden vials** full of the **wrath of God**, who liveth for ever and ever.
8 And the temple was filled with smoke from the glory of God, and from his power; and **no man was able to enter** into the temple, **till the seven plagues of the seven angels were fulfilled**."

(Rev 8:3-5)
"3 And another angel came and stood at the altar, having **a golden censer**; and there was given unto him **much incense**, that he should **offer it** with the prayers of all saints upon the golden altar which was before the throne.
4 And **the smoke of the incense**, which came with the prayers of the saints,

ascended up before God out of the angel's hand.

5 And the angel took **the censer**, and **filled it with fire** of the altar, and <u>**cast it into the earth**</u>: and there were voices, and thunderings, and lightnings, and an earthquake."

Learning Points:

A. *After* this "new song" part of the vision, the 7 angels collect the plagues from one of the 4 beasts that surround the throne of God.

B. These angels are dressed in white and wearing "golden" inner wrappings, so that John could see into their robes a bit, probably toward the top.

C. Off these 7 angels go to do their business. And none of Father in Heaven's children could enter into his Temple in Heaven until the deeds of these 7 plagues were delivered.

D. It appears that God in his heavenly Temple is not happy about doing this to his children, even as wicked as they are in that 4th Beast Kingdom. God does not want to see **anyone** during this time of the Trumps and Vials.

E. The angel with the golden censer burning incense **throws it** at the earth...And everything begins.

So now in the timeline is when the 7 Trumpets and 7 Vials that we have heard so much about go out from the Temple of Heaven to the earth.

What Do These Destructive Vials Do... AND What Part of the Earth Do They Affect?

<u>Chapter 16 abo</u>ut the **vials** <u>gives us the answers</u>....Because the 7 Vials are related to the 7 Trumpets....So as these few chapters are intermingled, pay close attention as to <u>what location on earth the 7 Vials are hitting...and *who* is their tar</u>get.

(Rev 16:1)
"1 And I heard a <u>**great voice** out of **the temple** saying to the seven angels,</u> <u>**Go your ways**, and pour out the vials of the wrath of God upon the earth.</u>"

Learning Points:

A. The "great voice" can only be God the Father Himself or Jesus Christ, because no other spirit is allowed in the Temple until *after* these 7 angels deliver the 7 vials. It begins.

We can read these Trumps and Vials in interchangeable order. *However*, since not all Vials match perfectly to all Trumpets, interjections will be made. We do know something for sure in this sequence of 7. The first 4 Trumps come all-at-once from *the heavens* or space and fall upon the earth. Remember that the golden censer was filled with **fire** and thrown at the earth...That is exactly what these first 4 plagues look like. They start the process. So, we will match our Vials to the Trumps during these first 4 plagues.

Trumpet #1

(Rev 8:7)

"7 The **first angel** sounded, and there followed **hail and fire** mingled with blood, and they were **cast upon the earth**: and the **third part** of **trees was burnt** up, and **all green grass was burnt** up."

Learning Points:
A. This 1st angel blowing the 1st Trumpet does *not* have a counterpart of an exact match in the Vials. It has a partial match, but not perfect, so I will not force it.
B. This 1st plague is hail that is on fire. Where else have we heard of that before? This is the same as the Fiery Hail that rained down on Sodom and Gomorrah to burn them up. (See Appendix 1) The location of Sodom and Gomorrah today are known. And the type of hail that was on fire is also known today. In fact, I own a piece of the fiery hail that came down upon Sodom and Gomorrah. It did *not* come from Earth. It came down as small asteroids with pure sulfur on fire. Thus, this scene will look like a repeat of Sodom and Gomorrah.
C. The classic question of 'where is the third part' of the Earth that will be affected by these 7 plagues? The answer is....they are directed to fall upon the 4th Beast Kingdom of the Gentiles in Europe. *That* is the 1/3 part of the Earth that gets these plagues of the Trumps and Vials.
   a. Another theory put forth by prophecy writers is that the 1/3 means only 1/3 of the trees in all the world got burned up. I do not subscribe to this notion, because the plagues are directed at the wicked Gentile Beast Kingdom residing in Europe.
D. Notice that this fiery hail from the heavens burns 1/3 of the trees and all grasses. This would cause a great problem with the supply chain in the Beast Kingdom to refuel and feed the huge civil war army of soldiers the Beast Kingdom is maintaining. The supply chain of meat raised on grasses just got cut.

Again, these 7 plagues are to get men to repent. And this common tale of fiery hail coming down to burn up the cities of the Beast Kingdom will feel all too familiar to those that have a heart and have read the scriptures, even a little bit.

A **note** on the Trumpets: Each and every one of these 7 Trumpets that are blown and cast a plague upon the wicked *also* come with an additional blessing upon the Saints of God. Each trumpet 1-7 will reveal the secret acts of men and the history of the earth during the first 1000 years and the second 1000 years and so forth. So, while the wicked are mourning with these Angels blowing their 7 Trumpets, a dual purpose is included to enliven the Saints of God with knowledge that was hidden from the world. This is recorded in D&C88:108. This is also found on the excel sheet that lists the Seals, Trumpets, and Vials in order along with these D&C88 Trumpets and D&C45 last days timeline. Download it from the website www.LastDaysTimeline.com.

Vial #1 – Does Not PERFECTLY Match Trumpet #1

Next up is the 1st Vial. This vial is placed here in the timeline, *only* because it doesn't have a perfectly corresponding Trumpet. *And* John's Revelation says this is #1. So, it is placed at the front of the series. If you, the reader, have more information about the placement of this Vial in the timeline, please contact me at the Website www.LastDaysTimeline.com.

(Rev 16:2)
"2 And the **first** went, and poured out **his vial** upon **the earth**; and there fell
a noisome and grievous sore upon the men **which had the mark of the
beast**, and upon **them which worshipped his image**."

Learning Points of 1st Vial:

A. The 1st angel delivers his Vial upon land and it contains a "noisome and grievous
sore" that *only* comes upon men that are still holding the Mark of the Beast *and*
worshipped the **image** of the Beast.

    a. (important distinction) The sore comes upon those that *both* have
the mark *and* worshipped the Beast's Image. It appears from John's
Revelation that whenever a "bad thing" happens to a person
involving the Mark of the Beast, that the phrase is *always* present
"and worshipped his image." It may be possible to receive the
Mark of the Beast yet not worship the Beast's Image.

    b. NOTE: America is not the place where the Beast rules any longer.
The 144,000 are already ordained at the New Jerusalem Temple
(which is already built) and sent forth among the nations to gather
the elect to the nation of Zion. *This* plague of the "sore" comes only
to the parts of the world which have people under the Beast's
remaining **financial** control. The Mark of the Beast is financial in
nature. So, this sore is going to hit the Gentile nations of **Europe**
that remain with the Beast's Kingdom.

B. Some prophecy writers have claimed this "sore" upon only those that had the
Mark of the Beast is a burning of the mark itself. They claim that if the Mark of
the Beast is an implantable "chip" under the skin that it would burn up or
explode. I have no verification of evidence on this matter, but it seems to make
sense.

Trumpet #2 & Vial #2 – They MATCH - a Quick Continuation of the Items Being Thrown at The Earth

(Rev 8:8-9)
"8 And the **second angel sounded**, and as it were **a great mountain
burning with fire** was cast into the **sea**: and the **third part** of the sea
became **blood**;
9 And the **third part of the creatures** which were in the sea, and had life,
died; and the **third part** of the ships were destroyed."

(Rev 16:3)
"3 And the **second angel** poured out his vial upon the **sea**; and **it became as
the blood** of a dead man: and **every living soul died in the sea**."

Learning Points of 2nd Trumpet and Vial – These 2 match-up nicely.

A. The 2nd angel delivers his Trump and Vial upon the sea or ocean. The ocean turns
red like blood. The scriptures seem to not tell us *which* ocean.

B. And this burning mountain that hits the sea kills every living thing in the ocean.
Since men don't live *in* the ocean, *I assume* this means the souls of animals in the

ocean (fish, whales, ocean birds, etc). This would cause a great stink and degradation. Also, the industry of the Beast Kingdom of the Gentiles would be greatly affected. Besides agriculture and mining, the oceans provide great blessings of God to man to be able to sustain ourselves on the Earth.

    a.   This would also greatly affect the supply chain of the armies fighting in the Civil War in Europe.

C. The 1/3 part of the world again comes up. The 1/3 part is around Europe.

    a.   1/3 of all the ships in the ocean are destroyed around the Beast Kingdom. Presumably, these would be the Beast Kingdom's ocean ships for <u>shipping</u> supplies to the armies and to their nation. Now, the Beast Kingdom doesn't have any way to get mass trade from far away lands of Asia and Africa. This would also stop all the oil shipments. This would affect their vehicles and their military machines.

D. This burning mountain hitting the ocean, seems to be a large asteroid event. However, this asteroid isn't large enough to be that catastrophic to the whole globe, but just to inflict damage upon the Gentile 4th Beast Kingdom of Europe.

Trumpet #3 & Vial #3 – They MATCH – More Continuation of Items Being Hurled at The Earth

The 3rd Trumpet and Vial appear at the same time from *the heavens* or space. Something bigger is coming this time; this is the **big** one.

    (Rev 8:10-11)
"10 And the **third angel sounded**, and there **fell a great star from heaven, burning** as it were a lamp, and **it fell** upon the **third part** of the rivers, and upon the **fountains of waters**;
11 And the name of the star is called **Wormwood**: and the **third part** of the **waters became wormwood**; and many **men died** of the waters, because they were made **bitter**."

    (Rev 16:4-7)
"4 And the **third angel** poured out his vial upon **the rivers** and **fountains of waters**; and they became **blood.**
5 And I heard the angel of the waters say, Thou art righteous, O Lord, which art, and wast, and shalt be, because thou hast judged thus.
6 **For they have shed the blood of saints and prophets**, and thou hast given them **blood to drink**; for they are worthy.
7 And I heard another out of the altar say, Even so, Lord God Almighty, true and righteous are thy judgments."

Learning Points of 3rd Trumpet and Vial:

A. The 3rd angel delivers his Trump and Vial upon the rivers and ground water springs. The water turns to blood. Somehow, a burning star either touches the earth or it comes close to the earth and affects the rivers and springs of water to cause them to be poisoned.

    a.   This "burning star" could just be a *bigger* asteroid that is burning in the atmosphere. It appears to be *bigger* than the one before it that was like a mountain. This asteroid could do some real damage. And it hit on **land**. Again, most likely right in the Beast Kingdom of Europe. These plagues are to get them to repent.

      i. (**Author's Analysis**): And if the 2 prophets in Jerusalem are sending these plagues upon the Beast, it is to get them to leave Jerusalem alone, by killing their supply chains.

    b. After the oceans turned red like blood, the last sources of water to drink were the rivers and springs. These are going to turn to blood too in the Beast's Kingdom of Europe.

    c. The food of the land is already burned up and grasses gone. There are no more beef cattle. The fish are dead. The shipping availability is destroyed. And now, no more water in the homeland of the Beast Kingdom. No wonder Gog/The Stout Horn eventually comes up to the Battle of Armageddon in Jerusalem. His base homeland is destroyed.

      i. (**Author's Analysis**): This homeland destruction may be why Gog/The Stout Horn's army has been built so large that it attacks Jerusalem. If evil people have nothing in their homeland, they may be feeling revengeful against the 2 Prophets that caused all this damage. And they have **nothing to lose**. Everything is gone. They can't even drink the water. No wonder the wicked of the Beast Kingdom "give gifts" to each other when the 2 Prophets of God are killed in Jerusalem.

B. The angel that delivered the vial says that the **people who live in the place**, where the vial is delivered have **murdered the Saints of God and Prophets of God**. Again this seems to suggest the angels are going after **The Beast Kingdom**, not the Saints of God dwelling in the Nation of God in the Americas. So, this is another confirmation to say that these plagues are going to hit Gentile Europe where the Beast resides.

C. The 1/3 part again shows up. The place is Gentile Europe.

D. The wormwood poison is in the rivers and springs of water. Men will die if they drink that water.

Remember this study is focused on the timeline, *place* and *what*. (What is to happen *when* and *where*.)

Trumpet #4 – Dust and Smoke From the Impact

The 4th Angel Trumpet has no corresponding Vial. It's the darkness of the land after the meteors strike the Beast Kingdom of Europe and the raging uncontrolled fires from the fiery hail/asteroids.

    (Rev 8:12-13)

"12 And the **fourth angel sounded**, and the **third part** of the **sun was smitten, and the third part** of the **moon**, and the **third part** of the **stars**; so as the third part of them **was darkened**, and **the day shone not** for a third part of it, and **the night likewise**.

13 And I beheld, and heard an angel flying through the midst of heaven,

saying with a loud voice, **Woe, woe, woe**, to the inhabiters of the earth by reason of **the other voices of the trumpet of the three angels, which are yet to sound!"**

Learning Points of 4th Trump and 5th Vial:
A. After getting hit with presumably 2 asteroids and lots of fire from the fiery asteroid hail, the Beast Kingdom of the Gentiles would be very smoky, dusty and dirty. There would be huge forest fires left to burn with lots of ash in the air. Plus the dust kicked up by the large burning star asteroid object that hit land affected the waters. Plus, the coast-line along the ocean areas is destroyed. There is a lot of darkness.

And this little add-on from the Angel

(Rev 8:13)
"13 And I beheld, and heard an angel flying through the midst of heaven, saying with a loud voice, **Woe, woe, woe**, to the inhabiters of the earth **by reason of the other voices of the trumpet of the three angels, which are yet to sound!"**

This little "tack on" scripture at the end of the 4th Trumpet, gives us a clue... that these first 4 Trumpets all happened at the same time and from the same extra-terrestrial source. The fire from the censer of God's altar had been hurled to the earth. These Trumps (1st – 4th) were part of the same exhibit.

Vial #4 – An Outlier Event – The Sun Scorches Men

This is the end of the super-easy match-ups of the Trumps and the Vials. It gets more complicated from here. This *next* Vial #4 is an **outlier** with no firm concrete match-ups with a Trumpet. It is placed here in the timeline only because it comes before Vial #5. If you, the reader have more data about the firm placement of this #4 Vial, please contact me through the website www.LastDaysTimeline.com.

(Rev 16:8)
"8 And the **fourth angel** poured out his vial upon **the sun**; and power was given unto him to **scorch men with fire**.
9 And **men were scorched with great heat**, and **blasphemed** the name of God, which **hath power over these plagues**: and **they repented not** to give him glory."

Learning Points of 4th Vial:
A. The 4th angel delivers his Vial upon the sun. The sun turns up the heat. This is *real Global Warming.*
B. Men are scorched with fire and great heat from the sun.
C. Yet, these men don't repent and turn to God. They curse God.
D. Again, this vial is directed upon those that are *not* the Saints of God, but are currently serving the Beast Kingdom. They are living in the part of the world

where the remaining Beast is actively ruling over its Gentile people with wickedness, Europe.

Author's Analysis:
With my current understanding of how the sun works in relationship to the earth, it appears that the earth is going to get a large solar flare directed right at it. This would also come with a large Electro-Magnetic Pulse (EMP). An EMP of this magnitude would take down all communications, transportation, and computers. Everything electronic would be fried, **on that side of the world** that gets it.

Again, it appears that these vials of plague are directed right at the remaining 4th Beast of Gentile Europe, not America and the Nation of Zion –The Kingdom of God.

Trumpet #5 & Vial #5 – They MATCH – An Attack Using Stun Weapons on the 4th Beast Kingdom of the Gentiles

Trumpet #5 has corresponding Vial #5. This Trump #5 is an important event. It is a commonly misconstrued scripture. I know this, because every prophecy writer that tries to explain this scripture comes to a different opinion. Thus, it is hard to understand. Let us see if we can get to the bottom this Trump #5.

(Rev 9:1-11)
"1 And the **fifth angel sounded**, and I saw **a star fall** from heaven unto the earth: and to (**JST- the angel**) was given **the key** of the bottomless pit [*Greek*- pit of the abyss].
2 And **he [the angel]** opened the bottomless pit [*Greek*- pit of the abyss]; and there arose **a smoke** out of the pit, as the **smoke of a great furnace**; and the sun and the **air were darkened by reason of the smoke** of the pit.
3 And there came out of the smoke **locusts** upon the earth: and unto them was **given power, as the scorpions** of the earth have power.
4 And it was **commanded them** that they should **not hurt the grass** of the earth, neither any **green thing**, neither any **tree**; but **only those men which have not the seal of God** in their foreheads.
5 And to them it was given that **they should not kill them**, but that they should be tormented **five months**: and their **torment was as the torment of a scorpion**, when he striketh a man.
6 And in those days **shall men seek death**, and shall not find it; and shall **desire to die**, and death shall flee from them.
7 And the **shapes of the locusts** were like unto **horses prepared unto battle**; and on their **heads** were as it were **crowns like gold**, and **their faces were as the faces of men**.
8 And they had **hair as the hair of women**, and their **teeth were as the teeth of lions**.
9 And they had breastplates, as it were **breastplates of iron**; and the **sound of their wings was as the sound of chariots** of many horses running to battle.
10 And they had **tails like unto scorpions**, and there were **stings in their tails**: and their power was **to hurt men five months**.
11 And they had **a king over them**, which is the **angel** of the bottomless pit

[GREEK- pit of the abyss], whose name in the Hebrew tongue is **Abaddon**, but in the Greek tongue hath his name **Apollyon**."

(Rev 16:10)
"10 And the **fifth angel** poured out his vial upon **the seat of the beast**; and **his kingdom was full of darkness**; and they gnawed their tongues for pain,
11 And blasphemed the God of heaven because of **their pains and their sores**, and **repented not** of their deeds."

Learning Points from the 5th Trump and 5th Vial

A. NOTE: this Vial #5 could also be explained as connected to Trump #4. Both have darkness. But, Trump #5 has darkness *and* stinger pain.
B. There is a lot to cover here. (v1) The star that fell appears to be the Angel that holds the key to the pit of the abyss… that holds all these locust men.
   a. Most prophecy writers assume that the "bottomless pit" is analogous to "hell" holding Satan's minions. However, this simply is *not true*. These locust/people/machines that come out of the pit of the abyss do damage to the Beast Kingdom, upon its own capital city. They are the good guys.
C. (v2) The smoke in the pit of the abyss that darkens the earth over the 4th Beast Kingdom could come from many sources. The source may be a natural cause, such as large volcanoes near the opening of the pit of the abyss. The darkness is caused by something. It could also mean that there are so many of the "locust men" that they are like clouds of smoke that darken the sky.
D. (v3) The locusts come out of the pit of the abyss. However, these are *not* locusts. They are men in machines. John had a hard time describing them. Let us continue to look at some of the features of these machines.
   a. The common reason John called these men looking machines locusts, was because there were **lots of them**. And they **flew**. (v9) These were flying machines that had wings that sounded like chariots.
   b. These men inside machines were *commanded* by their leader Abaddon to *not* hurt the trees or grass, because the fires in the Beast Kingdom have already wiped 1/3 of them out. They need to grow back and establish the eco-system in that area. *But*, their leader Abaddon commanded these men in the flying machines to **sting** men for 5 months. And the attack was to be upon the Capital City/Nation of the Beast Kingdom itself.
E. These locust men have faces, breastplates, crowns like gold upon their heads and long hair.
F. The "teeth as lions" may actually mean these men had sharp teeth. Or it may mean something else.
   a. There is another reference to **lions** that destroy wicked Gentiles.
G. Apparently, it's the flying machine's tails that do the ***stinging***. In modern weaponry the shooting mechanisms are usually faced forward. These **stingers** could be faced forward, or backward, however one wants to interpret this scripture. A case could be made for both.
H. The 5th angel delivers his Vial upon **the capital city** of the Beast Kingdom of the Gentiles itself. This "seat of the beast" is certainly directed **at the beast**. This

"seat" could be a capital city *or* a primary country that rules the Beast Kingdom. **This is the *biggest* clue that these Trumpets and Vials are focused on the Beast Kingdom itself, and not willy-nilly to the whole world.**

I. The pain that causes them to gnaw their tongues for pain. This Vial #5 is the **sting** from these *Locust Men in flying machines*. The pain from the stings is very real. It is so intense that men want to die and they chew their tongues for pain.

J. These locust men in flying machines had a **king** named Abbadon/Appolyon. Abbadon is translated as *The Destroyer*. Note, this Leader of the Locust Men **is the angel** that had the key to open the pit of the abyss.

    a. (**Author's Analysis**): Abbadon is a Destroying Angel. Just like the destroying angel in the plagues against the Pharaoh in Egypt. Except here, he leads a large fighting force of men in flying machines.

K. The men of this capital city/country of the Beast don't repent, but curse God.

This scripture from Joel Chapter 2, seems very similar in describing this army... and here the Lord says this is His army.

(Joel 2:2-5 and 10-11)

"2 A day of **darkness and of gloominess**, a day of clouds and of **thick darkness**, as the morning spread upon the mountains: **a great people and a strong**; there hath **not been ever the like**, neither shall be any more after it, even to the years of many generations.

3 A **fire devoureth before them**; and behind them a flame burneth: the land is as the garden of Eden before them, and **behind them a desolate wilderness**; yea, and **nothing shall escape** them.

4 The appearance of them is as the **appearance of horses; and as horsemen, so shall they run.**

5 Like the <u>noise of chariots on the tops of mountains shall they leap</u>, like the **noise of a flame of fire** that devoureth the stubble, as **a strong people** set in battle array."

(skipping a few verses for brevity)

"10 The **earth shall quake before them**; the **heavens shall tremble**: the **sun and the moon shall be dark**, and the stars shall withdraw their shining: 11 And <u>the Lord shall utter his voice before his army</u>: for <u>his camp is very great</u>: for he is strong that executeth his word: for the day of the Lord is great and very terrible; and who can abide it?"

Learning Points:

A. This army comes very thick, like heavy dark clouds, that spread as the morning spreads **over** the mountains.

B. This army of the Lord is such that there has never been an army like this one. His camp is huge.

C. This army burns up the land when it *flies* on the tops of the mountains.

D. The machines of this army sound like roaring fire.

E. The machines of this army are like horses and chariots with drivers (horsemen)

F. Nothing shall escape the power of this army. They always win.

G. This is *not a perfect match* to John's Trumpet #5, because there is fire left *after* this army flies over the area, instead of not hurting the green things. *However*, this may be a better match for Trumpet #6 where 1/3 of the Beast Kingdom is wiped out. Remember, this is the Lord's army that is this size and doing these things upon the wicked.

This huge army is **not Gog's army** attacking Israel as is supposed by many prophecy writers. This army is the Lord's army doing His work against the Stout Horn's 4th Beast Kingdom of the Gentiles. This idea is non-traditional in Christianity.

Author's Analysis:
Without getting too technical, this army is a good army with advanced flying machines that **sting** wicked people living in the vicinity of the Beast Kingdom's capital in Europe. This force is massively successful at their job because they came right into the location where the Stout Horn *should have* air superiority, over his own capital city or nation.

There is a mention of lions with teeth that destroy wicked Gentiles. This is feeling quite familiar. Also, these men don't do permanent harm to these wicked Gentiles, yet. Abadon's flying forces sting the 4th Beast Gentiles or paralyze their military efforts against Jerusalem for 5 months.

I believe that we are looking at the same strong military technology that just brought down the Beast Kingdom in the Americas and chased them out of there. But here, they are called and summoned to war as the 5th Plague to help take down the Beast Kingdom of the Gentiles. Thus, these people in these flying machines, led by an Angel of God are most highly likely, the Lost 10 Tribes of Israel that came out of the north.

Thus the 'pit of the Abyss' is another clue as to *where* the Lost 10 Tribes are currently residing in the north countries.

(Pure speculation): The reader may be thinking, "Didn't the Lost 10 Tribes already return to America?" Yes they did. However, as the people of the Church of God will not all go to the New Jerusalem right away, the Lost 10 Tribes coming from the north land of Arsareth may also not all come at the same time. Thus, they may have more re-enforcements to their military that will come at this later date to help in the fight against Gog/The Stout Horn.

This may also mean that the "destroying angel" who is a King and leader over these men in flying machines as dense as locusts, would be John the Beloved/Revelator - Just like John did when he led the Lost 10 Tribes to kick out the strong forces of the Stout Horn from the Americas.

Trumpet #6 – From Stun to Kill

The *next* Trump #6 does *not* match-up with Vial #6 in the timeline. Seemingly the words "River Euphrates" line up. However, Joseph Smith corrected this. And by doing so, shows that Trump #6 was about the Army of God doing some more work upon the Beast Nation of the Gentiles.

While Vial #6 is about an actual river drying up, so that the Kings of the East could march their armies across it to get to Jerusalem to add re-enforcements to the attack.

In Trump #6, the army of God shall commence after the 5 months of stinging. God uses his invading flying army upon the capital city/nation of the Beast Kingdom of the Gentiles. After the **stinging** doesn't work...this is the next step for this flying army of God, led by a destroying angel...

> (Revelation 9:13-21)
> "13 And the **sixth angel sounded**, and I heard a voice from the four horns of the golden altar which is before God,
> 14 Saying to the sixth angel which had the trumpet, Loose **the four angels which are bound in [JST- the bottomless pit]**.
> 15 And the **four angels were loosed**, which **were prepared** for an hour, and a day, and a month, and a year, for **to slay the third part of men.**
> 16 And the **number of the army of the horsemen were two hundred thousand thousand**: and I heard the number of them.
> 17 And thus **I saw the horses** in the vision, and **them that sat on them**, having **breastplates of fire**, and of **jacinth**, and **brimstone**: and the **heads of the horses were as the heads of lions**; and out of **their mouths issued fire** and **smoke** and **brimstone**.
> 18 By **these three** was the **third part of men killed**, by the **fire**, and by the **smoke**, and by the **brimstone**, which issued **out of their mouths**.
> 19 For their **power is in their mouth**, and **in their tails**: for **their tails were like unto serpents, and had heads**, and with them **they do hurt**.
> 20 And the rest of the men which were not killed by these plagues yet **repented not** of the works of their hands, that they should not worship devils, and idols of gold, and silver, and brass, and stone, and of wood: which neither can see, nor hear, nor walk:
> 21 Neither repented they of their murders, nor of their sorceries, nor of their fornication, nor of their thefts."

Learning Points of 6th Vial:
A. The Army of God is still using the flying machines with men inside to do more damage. After the 5 months is over and the men in the Beast Kingdom of Gentile Europe are still not repenting, neither is Gog/The Stout Horn....it's time to take it up a notch and go from "stun to kill"
B. The 4 Angels in the "bottomless pit" or "pit of the abyss" were preparing for this day in the fight. They knew that they would have to do additional damage to the Beast Kingdom's armies. They slay 1/3 of them. 2/3 is still left living. And they don't repent.
C. This "an hour, a day, a month, and year" has for **many** prophecy writers been assumed that this means this attack will last about 13 months. It could mean that, but it could mean that this army of God was simply prepared for this moment to do this job. I take no stance on either meaning.

D. These war machines with drivers seem to do much greater harm than the previous machines with "stings in their tails." These *new* war machines don't seem to fly. *But* they probably still do. Because there is a link: Their mouths have power to do the killing and their **tails** have the power of stinging or maybe worse. Again modern war machines don't have tails. But, these war machines have tails like snakes that "hurt" or sting. The fact that the flying war machines in Trumpet #5 had **tails**, and the flying war machines in Trumpet #6 have **tails** that hurt, is the link that *probably* they are the same army doing the same deeds to the wicked Gentiles of the 4th Beast. They have simply have gone from "stun to kill".

E. Out of these *new* war machines, their front 'mouth' had the weapons to kill... Fire, Smoke, and Brimstone.

F. The 200,000,000 army. It has always been *assumed* by the prophecy writers, that Gog has raised the 200,000,000 army to attack Israel from *this scripture*. Since this 200,000,000 strong fighting force of God's Army upon the wicked 4th Beast Kingdom of the Gentiles, **couldn't** be Gog's/Stout Horn's army. This army is raised against Gog/Stout Horn as a plague…to slay 1/3 of his men or army.

G. And again, we see the Heads of Lions.

Author's Analysis:

Again, the links are *many* that Trumpet 5 and Trumpet 6 are the same Army of God led by the destroying angel John with the 10 Tribes of Israel. They have some super war technology that takes down 1/3 of the 4th Beast Kingdom's army.

That 200,000,000 army is *not Gog's army*. It's the Lord's army. This fact will be somewhat hard to breach into the culture of the Christians of America, since every time someone speaks of Gog's big army against Jerusalem, they quote it as 200,000,000. This is the scripture where they get that idea.

The scripture says "**two hundred thousand thousand**" but this number may not be reliable because of the Great and Abominable Church – The Whore Church – Babylon the Great has changed this book of scripture. Let us just say, it will be a *huge force* sent by God upon the Stout Horn, that the world has never seen or will ever see again, until the battle at the end of the Millennium.

What do you, the reader, think about this section of scripture? It is one of the hardest nuts to crack in all of scripture. Contact me on the website www.LastDaysTimeline.com.

Vial #6 – Drying Up The River and Preparing The Kings of the East to JOIN with the 4th Beast Kingdom of the Gentiles in the Battle of Armageddon

The 6th Vial is coming up; the gathering for the Battle of Armageddon. The Gentile lands of Gog/Stout Horn are so decimated; he needs extra help from allies to assist him in taking down the 2 prophets in Jerusalem after 3.5 years of fighting them. So, he calls upon his three trusted and self taught "dark arts" ambassadors to gather more men to add to his armies.

(Rev 16:12-16)

"12 And the **sixth** angel poured out his vial upon **the great river Euphrates**; and the water thereof was **dried up**, that **the way** of the **kings of the east** might be prepared.

13 And I saw **three unclean spirits** like frogs come out of the **mouth of the dragon**, and out of the **mouth of the beast**, and out of the **mouth of the false prophet**.

14 For they are **the spirits of devils, working miracles**, which go forth **unto the kings** of the earth and of the whole world, **to gather them to the battle** of that great day of God Almighty.

15 Behold, **I come as a thief**. Blessed is he that watcheth, and keepeth his garments, lest he walk naked, and they see his shame.

16 And **he gathered them** together into a place called in the Hebrew tongue **Armageddon**."

Learning Points of 6th Vial:

A. The 6th angel delivers his Vial upon the river Euphrates. This may be the Euphrates River in Egypt itself or another big river to the East of Jerusalem.

B. The reason for this vial was to clear this big river so the kings of the East could send their armies to the battle of Armageddon.

C. The three bad spirits "like frogs" have as their main purpose to gather nations to the big battle against Jerusalem (Armageddon). They work miracles before the Kings of the East to get them to **sign-on** their troops to this battle between The Remaining Beast VS Israel.

  a. These 3 frog/evil spirits could be men, like ambassadors that work "dark art" miracles. *Or* they could be real spirits that do approximately the same thing.

D. This little statement by Jesus "I come as a thief" is an interesting interjection right here between v14 and v16. This little piece doesn't add to the story plot line at all. *Yet*, it is to show the Saints of God who have been watching the signs of the times that "this is it" "the end is near" "Jesus is coming back".

Author's Analysis:

There are multiple ideas from prophecy writers around these *kings of the East.*

1. These kings may be "the East" as in **all the way** east like China. We know the Battle of Armageddon force that shows up on the battlefield for 3.5 years will be large and grow larger. The remaining man power for that army has been estimated by the prophecy writers to come from China (Again, thinking that the force needs to be 200,000,000).

2. These kings may be a much closer *East*. Directly east of Israel lays the lands of the Middle East and millions of Muslims. (Syria, Jordan, Iraq, Iran, Afghanistan, Pakistan, Saudi Arabia(S.East)) So, it is highly likely to be the Muslims that come to battle Israel.

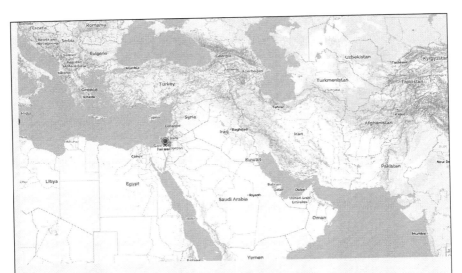

We know that this battle of Armageddon is instigated by the remainder of The Beast Kingdom in Gentile Europe. But, it appears the Stout Horn/Gog needs more man power, so he enlists some "dark art miracle workers" (3 frogs) to go and enlist these other nations to join the battle.

I take no position on "which" nations will show up specifically.

We have seen the first 6 Trumpets and 6 Vials poured out. This next and *last* Trumpet and Vial needs a Chapter of its own. As it stretches many, many days, and has the final Battle of Armageddon *inside* of it.

23: The Many Days of the 7th Trumpet and 7th Vial – The Battle of Armageddon

The 7th Trumpet and 7th Vial do match up very well. However, they are complicated, when compared to the other Trumpets and Vials. Plus, there are some other scriptures in the Doctrine and Covenants Section 29 and 88 which add some clarity to the picture.

I feel that this Trump #7 and Vial #7 is a wild show spanning many days. These last Trumpets and Vials encompass quite a bit of time leading right up to the ushering-in of the 1000 Millennium Years as a Terrestrial Earth.

NOTE: This 7th Trumpet and 7th Vial are fairly complicated. It would be very easy for this Author to miss something. So, if you the reader have information about the fitting of the pieces, then contact me at the website www.LastDaysTimeline.com.

Let us Go Through This Sequence STEP-BY-STEP

The 3 evil Frog Men have gathered the armies of the Kings of the East to combine them with the forces of Gog/The Stout Horn leader of the 4th Beast Kingdom of the Gentiles at the gathering place outside of Jerusalem for the final showdown at the Battle of Armageddon. Let us start off with Vial #7, it is fairly straight forward and allows us to set the stage.

> (Rev 16:17-21)
> "17 And the **seventh** angel poured out his vial into **the air**; and there came **a great voice** out of the **temple of heaven**, from the throne, saying, **It is done.**
> 18 And there were **voices**, and **thunders**, and **lightnings**; and there was **a great earthquake**, such as was not since men were upon the earth, so mighty an earthquake, and so great.
> 19 And the **great city was divided into three parts**, and the **cities of the nations fell**: and **great Babylon came in remembrance before God**, to **give unto her the cup of the wine of the fierceness of his wrath.**
> 20 And **every island fled away**, and the **mountains were not found.**
> 21 And there fell upon men a **great hail out of heaven**, every stone about **the weight of a talent**: and men **blasphemed God** because of the plague of the hail; for **the plague thereof was exceeding great.**"

Learning Points of 7th Vial (LAST VIAL):
A. The 7th angel delivers his Vial upon the *air*, into the atmosphere of Earth.
B. The voice of God the Father or Jesus Christ says "all the vials have been delivered – **It Is Done.**"
C. Then the Earth experiences a huge earthquake and large natural upheavals that move mountains and makes *every* island sink.
D. Plus a very large hailstorm from the heavens with large sized hail. 1 Talent = 58.9 Kg = 130 Lbs. That would destroy about every structure that man has made. (See weight of a talent   https://en.wikipedia.org/wiki/Talent_(measurement))

a. This is interesting hail. It comes from "out of heaven." These may not be common cloud hail at all, but a meteor shower that does this decimation. The huge size *and* the wording of the scripture make a meteor shower more plausible than standard cloud hail.
b. Or, it just may be 130 Lbs regular hail chunks.

E. The men of Gentile Europe's Beast still don't repent.

F. This Vial #7 / Trumpet #7 is the last of the 7 plagues. This is also the first time when we see the phrase "the plague thereof was exceeding great."

G. Babylon – The Great, will be covered in the next section in *detail*. But notice, that *after* the Earthquake and Hailstorm is released, that God now starts to focus on Babylon –The Great to take it down. This is the **timeline** element of *when* Babylon goes down = **After** the 7th Vial earthquake and hailstorm/meteor shower.

    a. (**Author's Analysis**): However, we do know that The Beast Kingdom itself is the one that destroys the Whore Church's capital city with fire. And the smoke goes up forever. So, Gog can't be killed in the Battle of Armageddon quite yet. The Whore Church must be destroyed by Gog **before** the Battle of Armageddon.

When one thinks about the Last Trumpet including the "mountains flowing down" and the "islands fleeing" as the Earth becomes a terrestrial sphere, plus the other items mentioned; this Vial could cover quite a great many days or months. There is more evidence of this in the next set of scriptures. The 7th Trump.

The whole 7th Trump is contained over 2 full chapters (Rev 10-11). This is the reason this section has confused so many people. There is a **beginning** to this Trump, and an **end** to this Trump. Thus, it encompasses a great deal of time…And there are lots of things that happen **inside of it,** including the final Battle of Armageddon. Let us begin.

    Paraphrasing to save time (Rev 10:1) Read the scripture directly here: https://www.lds.org/scriptures/nt/rev/10?lang=eng
- (v1) A large angel comes in a **cloud** with a **rainbow over his head,** with glory, and flaming legs/feet.
- (v2) The large angel had **a little book,** and placed his feet upon the sea and earth.

(Rev 10:3-4)
"3 And cried with a loud voice, as when a **lion roareth**: and when he had cried, **seven thunders uttered their voices.**
4 And when the **seven thunders had uttered their voices,** I was about to write: and I heard a voice from heaven saying unto me, Seal up those things which the seven thunders uttered, and write them not."

    (v5) The angel lifted up his hands

(Rev 10:6-7)
"6 And sware by him that liveth for ever and ever, who created heaven, and the things that therein are, and the earth, and the things that therein are, and

the sea, and the things which are therein, that **there should be time no longer:**

7 But in the **days of the voice of the seventh angel,** when **he shall begin to sound,** the **mystery of God should be finished,** as he hath declared to his servants the prophets."

(v8-11) John takes the little book and eats it. It is sweet to the mouth but bitter to the belly.

(Rev 10:11)
"11 And he said unto me, **Thou must prophesy again before many peoples, and nations, and tongues, and kings."**

Learning Points:

A. This is the 7th Angel with the 7th Trump. He speaks as a lion roars. Again we see the Lion mentioned. There is something about the Lion and John the Beloved/Revelator with the Lost 10 Tribes of Israel. The symbolism of the Lion was the tribe of Judah's standard. There may also be other symbolism connected as well.

B. This angel proclaims "There shall be time no longer." So, this angel puts the Earth on a different time, or no time at all. Remember *time* is calculated by rotations of the Earth, and the Earth circling the Sun. Thus, for Time to be *ended*, the earth must leave its orbit around the sun. And many Church leaders have said such would occur. (see below)

C. This angel's 7th Trump has **days** that it shall sound. This is the big clue, that this 7th Trump takes a good period of time. There is a "beginning" and an "end" to this Trump.

D. There will be 7 Thunders that have voices during the days of this Trump. This is the **linking evidence** to the 7th Vial above.

E. The little book that was eaten is John's latter day mission to prophecy *again* before the nations. As we have already covered in this work. (D&C 77:14)

F. In the *days* of the 7th Trumpet and 7th Vial the **mystery** of God should be finished. This scripture may be alluding to the fact that each of these angels, as they blow their trumpet also gives an account of the history of the earth for a specific 1000 year period to the Saints of God. Thus the mysteries and true history of those years may be known (see Doctrine and Covenants 88:108).

It appears that the Earth will be moved into a new orbit as we move into the Millennium. Many early brethren have preached this doctrine from the pulpit. Daniel H. Ludlow said this:

(A Companion to Your Study of the Doctrine and Covenants, Ludlow, Appendix A, page 278)
"One of the predicted events associated with the second coming of Jesus Christ is that "the stars shall fall from heaven.".... As the earth moves through the stars of its present heaven to its new position, these stars will appear to be falling in relationship to the movement of the earth."

Learning Points:

A. Ludlow says the scene of the **stars falling from heaven**, is actually the Earth moving through the stars. This is an interesting concept.

John is to Measure the Jerusalem Temple at the Time of The Battle of Armageddon

Now let us continue with the 2nd part of Trumpet #7. The ending is the whole of the next Chapter #11. These verses *are* important so we will talk about each of them. This is the Battle of Armageddon *inside* the 7th Trump. This is a **very important fact**; the Battle of Armageddon happens *__within the days__* of the 7th Trump...as we shall soon see.

(Rev 11:1-2)
"1 And there was given me a reed like unto a rod: and the angel stood, saying, Rise, and **measure the temple of God**, and the altar, and them that worship therein.
2 But **the court which is without the temple <u>leave out</u>**, and measure it not; for **it is given unto the Gentiles**: and the holy city shall they **tread under foot forty and two months**."

Learning Points:
A. The large 7th Angel, from the last chapter, tells John to measure the Jerusalem Temple that was recently rebuilt by King David of Jerusalem.
B. However, John was instructed *not* to measure the outer court, as it is "given unto the Gentiles." Prophecy writers have guessed forever that the outer court was to be left off the Jerusalem Temple, because the Muslim Dome of the Rock is sitting upon the place of the Temple. There are 2 things wrong with this. 1. The Muslims are not Gentiles in the scriptures (See Appendix 1: Gentiles). The Europeans are. 2. If the Dome of the Rock is sitting upon the Holy of Holies of Solomon's Temple, then *of course*, the Temple would need to be built on it, not just beside it.
   a. **(Author's Analysis)** I do not believe the Jerusalem Temple will need to be built on the Dome of the Rock. However, I have very little evidence at hand to support this opinion.
C. The city of Jerusalem shall be under siege of the Gentile armies of the Stout Horn/Gog/False Prophet for 3.5 years.

The 2 Special Witnesses/Prophets in Jerusalem to Hold Back the Armies of the 4th Beast Kingdom of the Gentiles + Kings of the East

(Rev 11:3-6)
"3 And I will give **power unto my two witnesses**, and they shall prophesy a **thousand two hundred and threescore days**, clothed in sackcloth.
4 These are the two olive trees, and the two candlesticks standing before the God of the earth.
5 And if any man will hurt them, **fire** proceedeth out of their mouth, and **devoureth their enemies**: and if any man will hurt them, he must in this manner be killed.
6 These have **power to shut heaven**, that it **rain not** in the days of their

prophecy: and have **power over waters to turn them to blood**, and to **smite the earth with all plagues, as often as they will."**

Learning Points:
A. We have covered this section of scripture before.
B. The 2 witnesses in Jerusalem are 2 prophets raised up unto the Jewish Nation in their time of need.
C. They shall prophesy 3.5 years.
D. They have the power of God over the elements. This scripture is evidence that these 2 Prophets are the ones calling the plagues contained in the 7 Trumpets and 7 Vials.

(Rev 11:7-12)
"7 And when they shall have **finished their testimony**, the **beast** that ascendeth out of the bottomless pit shall make war against them, and shall overcome them, and **kill them**.
8 And their **dead bodies shall lie in the street** of the great city, which spiritually is called Sodom and Egypt, where also our Lord was crucified.
9 And they of the people and kindreds and tongues and nations shall see their dead bodies three days and an half, and shall **not suffer their dead bodies to be put in graves**.
10 And **they** that dwell upon the earth shall **rejoice** over them, and **make merry, and shall send gifts** one to another; because these two prophets **tormented them that dwelt on the earth**.
11 And after three days and an half the **Spirit of life from God entered into them, and they stood** upon their feet; and **great fear** fell upon them which saw them.
12 And they heard **a great voice from heaven** saying unto them, **Come up hither**. And they **ascended up to heaven in a cloud**; and their enemies beheld them."

Learning Points:
A. At the end of the 3.5 years, these 2 prophets are murdered by the armies the Stout Horn/Gog plus Kings of the East. They are not buried. Their bodies remain in the streets of Jerusalem. The armies and people in the 4th Beast Kingdom of Europe give gifts to each other and have a merry celebration that these 2 men of God have been killed.
B. The rejoicing and gift sending is because these 2 prophets tormented them that dwelt on the earth. *Not* just in the immediate vicinity of the Battle of Armageddon around Jerusalem. This is clue #2 that these 2 Prophets have been the ones **calling for** the plagues of the 7 Trumpets and 7 Vials upon the 4th Beast Kingdom of the Gentiles plus their companions in arms.
C. After 3.5 days of laying in a mangled heap on the street in Jerusalem, they are suddenly resurrected. And the armies of the Stout Horn/Gog immediately had great fear. For now they know, that God truly is on the Jew's side. (As if the miracles alone weren't enough to convince them. This is how hard-hearted the armies and people of this 4th Beast Kingdom have become. They are desensitized to miracles.)

D. And as these 2 prophets of God are rising up in the cloud… Jesus is descending to greet the Jews… in the very same hour.

Jesus Returns to the Mount of Olives and It is Split in ½ and the Jews Meet Their Messiah…(sort of)

(Rev 11:13)
"13 And the **same hour** was **there a great earthquake**, and the **tenth part of the city fell**, and in the earthquake were slain of men seven thousand: and the remnant were affrighted, **and gave glory to the God** of heaven."

Learning Points:
A. This IS IT. This is the scripture, right here, of when Jesus visits the Jews on the top of the Mount of Olives. However, in this 2nd part of the Book of Revelation series of events, it does not mention it. (This is recorded in Ezekiel and in the Doctrine and Covenants)
B. As the 2 prophets are rising in the cloud, Jesus is descending. When his foot touches the Mount of Olives, there is a huge earthquake and the mountain splits in half. This is probably the same earthquake that causes water to flow out from under the Jerusalem Temple and that runs down to heal the Dead Sea. All of this in just a few sentences.
C. 1/10th of Jerusalem crumbles, 7000 men are slain (presumably of the Stout Horn's Army).
D. The remainder of the army has continuing great fear, *but* some of them **repent**. Finally. The miracles have broken through to some of them. They give glory to the God of Heaven.

NOTE: The Battle of Armageddon, between the hosts of the Stout Horn/Gog leader of the 4th Beast Kingdom of the Gentiles *and* the 2 Prophet/Witnesses in Jerusalem is one of the most discussed topics in all of scripture. This large battle scene is discussed in several books of scripture. To save time, most of the discussion about this battle will be in Appendix 1. Remember, we are focused on a timeline of the last-days events. (What happened, when and where.) Please see Appendix 1 for all the details on the Battle of Armageddon.

The most important thing to our timeline about the Battle of Armageddon, is *not* that Jesus comes to the Jews. *It is* that the Battle of Armageddon happens *inside* the *days* of the 7th Trumpet and 7th Vial. This is one long Trumpet blast with several events that take place *inside* it.

(Rev 11:14-19)
"14 The **second woe** is past; and, behold, the **third woe** cometh quickly.
15 And the **seventh angel sounded**; and there were **great voices in heaven**, saying, The kingdoms of this world are become the kingdoms of our Lord, and of his Christ; and he shall reign for ever and ever.
16 And the four and twenty elders, which sat before God on their seats, fell upon their faces, and worshipped God,
17 Saying, We give thee thanks, O Lord God Almighty, which art, and wast, and art to come; because **thou hast taken to thee thy great power, and hast**

reigned.

18 And the nations were angry, and thy wrath is come, and **the time of the dead**, that they **should be judged**, and that thou shouldest give **reward unto thy servants the prophets, and to the saints**, and them that fear thy name, small and great; and shouldest **destroy them which destroy the earth.**
19 And the **temple of God was opened in heaven**, and there was seen in his temple the ark of his testament: and there were **lightnings, and voices, and thunderings, and an earthquake, and great hail**."

Learning Points:

A. There are "woes" within this 7th Trumpet. If the 1st woe is the 2 prophets and their plagues cast upon the 4th Beast Kingdom, then the 2nd woe is the Battle of Armageddon that wipes out the Stout Horn/Gog and 5/6th of his armies. The 3rd woe in this sequence is the great earthquake, thunders with voices, lightning, and the great hail that weighs 130lbs per stone. I see that there could definitely be several other definitions for these 3 woes.

B. Finally, the 7th Angel has fully blown the 7th Trumpet. Notice it happened *after* the Battle of Armageddon.

C. We see the same **linking events** link the 7th Trumpet to the 7th Vial: loud voices in heaven, thunders with voices, lightning, and a **big** earthquake, plus huge hail.

D. Focusing on the events around the throne of God, the 24 Elders around the throne fell down worshipfully and stated that Jesus has finally taken His great power and reigned as King of Kings and Lord of Lords on the Earth. So, at this point, he has conquered the evil men, and has claimed this World for himself as a political ruler in righteousness.

    a. Theses 24 Elders further state: that this is the time that the *dead* prophets and saints of God are to be judged and awarded for their works. So, the 1st Resurrection and Judgment happens *within* **the 7th Trumpet and 7th Vial**, as we move toward the Millennium. This is a key fact. What else happens in this 7th Trumpet?

    b. "Destroy them which destroy the earth." This seems a lot like the Lord's actual 2nd coming in the clouds. He melts the earth with fervent heat and prepare it for the Millennium. Yes, this happens *within* the 7the Trumpet and 7th Vial as well.

    c. NOTE: The Temple of God in Heaven is **re-opened**. Remember, it was closed that no man may enter during the discharge of the 7 angels with their 7 Vials? Now, the Temple in Heaven is re-opened. "It is done."

Author's Analysis:

This 7th Trumpet and 7th Vial has a *lot* of events to put into one trumpet. This trumpet has many "**days**", which could mean months. I do not think this 7th Trump takes years. Even with the final Battle of Armageddon *inside* it.

If the 2 prophets in Jerusalem are sending these 7 Trumpet and 7 Vial plagues upon the 4th Beast Kingdom *while* that kingdom is building a force larger and larger at their gate for 3.5 years, then the *days* of this 7th Trumpet would really only describe the **final** battle of the build-up of military forces around Jerusalem.

The main points to remember are:

1. The 7 Vials and the 7 Trumpets overlap almost perfectly with each other. There are only 2 outliers that don't perfectly match up. The other 5 perfectly match up. (See the Downloadable Excel Sheet on the Website www.LastDaysTimeline.com/seals-trumpets-vials)
2. The 2 prophets in Jerusalem have the same powers needed to produce the 7 Trumpets and 7 Vials upon their enemy, the 4th Beast Kingdom of the Gentiles
3. The enemy of the 2 prophets is the same entity that the 7 Vials are targeting; the 4th Beast Kingdom of Gentile Europe. Led by Gog/The False Prophet/The Stout Horn/The False Messiah.
4. The whole **final portion** of the final Battle of Armageddon takes place *inside* the 7th Trumpet and 7th Vial. Jesus comes to the Jews on top of the Mount of Olives inside the *days* of the 7th Trumpet.

Remember, the Book of John's Revelation is divided into 3 main parts:
1) The 7 churches.
2) The events of the last days through the eyes of the Saints of God/or Jews.
3) The events of the last days through the eyes of the rest of the world.

This is the end of the Battle of Armageddon account with the 2 prophets as recorded in the 2nd part. There is no mention of the Whore Church – Babylon the Great. There is no mention of Jesus coming to the Jews on top of the Mount of Olives. There is no mention of the after-math of the Battle of Armageddon and the Supper of the Lord. All of these items are found in Ezekiel, Isaiah, and Doctrine and Covenants. See Appendix 1 for the details.

However, this is not the end of the 7th Trumpet and 7th Vial. This is the *middle*. The Christ must reveal his face and melt the mountains and have the islands flee, first. And He must move the Earth from its present orbit. We are only getting warmed up in this sequence.

However, there is one more **big** part of the Book of John's Revelation. A part… that an Angel of God specifically pulled John aside to show him; a part that makes everything surrounding the 4th Beast Kingdom of the Gentiles become crystal clear. The Whore Church – Babylon the Great. What it is; and how it goes down.

24: *The Whore Church – Babylon The Great – The Great and Abominable Church of the Devil is Destroyed by the 4th Beast Kingdom. End of the Civil War*

Now, only in Revelation Chapter 17, toward the end of the book, do we fully understand the real motivations behind The Beast. It is a false **state** religion that is taken-down during the 7th Trumpet/7th Vial. The same **state** religion that was heavily oppressive to the Saints of God and to other Christian faiths around the world. Let us see what it is, and come full circle.

We are going to stick to our timeline and cover the "What happens When and Where." The majority of the identification of the Whore Church will be in Appendix 1. It is very in-depth. As you, the reader, are using this work to see the clues and evidence for the last-days timeline, make sure to read the section on the Whore Church – Babylon the Great in Appendix 1. It was of vital importance to John that the Angel called him aside specifically to show him the meaning of **this Symbol of the Whore** that is riding the 4th Beast Kingdom of the Gentiles.

According to our timeline, we are after the Battle of Armageddon but before the 2nd Coming of Christ in the Clouds to burn the earth and cleanse it by fire.

Both last-days sections of the Book of John's Revelation show that the Whore Church gets destroyed by fire **after** the Battle of Armageddon.

However….keep this little scripture in mind:

> (Rev 17:16-17)
> "16 And **the ten horns** which thou sawest upon the **beast, these** shall **hate the whore**, and shall **make her desolate and naked**, and shall **eat her flesh**, and **burn her with fire**.
> 17 For God hath put in **their hearts** to fulfil his will, and to agree, and give their kingdom unto the beast, until the words of God shall be fulfilled."

Remember, it's the 10 Kings of the 4th Beast Kingdom of the Gentiles that take down the Whore Church. These evil men are fulfilling God's Will in doing it.

Continuing the timeline is the destruction of the Whore Church by Fire. This apparently takes place **after** the Battle of Armageddon. John's Revelation Chapter 18…

> (Rev 18:4-20)
> "4 And I heard another **voice from heaven**, saying, **Come out of her, my people**, that ye be not partakers of her sins, and that ye **receive not of her plagues**.
> 5 For **her sins** have reached unto heaven, and God hath remembered her iniquities.
> 6 **Reward her even as she rewarded you**, and **double unto her double**

according to her works: in the cup which she hath filled **fill to her double**.
7 How much she hath **glorified herself**, and lived **deliciously**, so **much torment and sorrow give her**: for <u>she saith in her heart, I sit a queen, and am no widow</u>, and shall see no sorrow.
8 Therefore shall **her plagues come in one day**, death, and mourning, and famine; and she shall be **utterly burned with fire**: for strong is the Lord God who judgeth her.
9 And **the kings of the earth, who have committed fornication** and lived deliciously with her, shall bewail her, and **lament for her**, when they shall see **the smoke of her burning**,
10 <u>Standing afar off for the fear of her torment</u>, saying, Alas, alas, **that great city Babylon, that mighty city! for in one hour is thy judgment come.**
11 And **the merchants** of the earth **shall weep and mourn over her**; for no man buyeth their merchandise any more:
12 The merchandise of gold, and silver, and precious stones, and of pearls, and fine linen, and purple, and silk, and scarlet, and all thyine wood, and all manner vessels of ivory, and all manner vessels of most precious wood, and of brass, and iron, and marble,
13 And cinnamon, and odours, and ointments, and frankincense, and wine, and oil, and fine flour, and wheat, and beasts, and sheep, and horses, and chariots, **and slaves, and souls of men**.
14 And the fruits that thy soul lusted after are departed from thee, and all things which were dainty and goodly are departed from thee, and thou shalt find them no more at all.
15 The **merchants** of these things, which **were made rich by her**, shall **stand afar off** for the **fear of her torment**, weeping and wailing,
16 And saying, Alas, alas, that great city, that was clothed in fine linen, and **purple**, and **scarlet**, and **decked with gold, and precious stones, and pearls!**
17 For **in one hour** so great riches is come to nought. And every **shipmaster**, and all the company in ships, and sailors, and as many as trade by sea, **stood afar off**,
18 And cried when they saw **the smoke of her burning**, saying, <u>**What city is like unto this great city!**</u>
19 And they cast dust on their heads, and cried, weeping and wailing, saying, Alas, alas, that great city, wherein **were made rich all that had ships in the sea by reason of her costliness!** for in **one hour is she made desolate**.
20 <u>Rejoice</u> over her, thou heaven, and ye holy apostles and prophets; **for God hath avenged you on her**."

Learning Points:
A. This whole section describes the destruction to come upon the church named "Babylon-The Great" that is in the city with 7 Mountains. It is a message <u>**from**</u> God <u>**to**</u> "my people" or the Saints of God.
B. God issues a warning call to have all of "my people" who are in the area of the city on the coast leave and exit, *before* the destruction happens.
C. Babylon-The Great will receive *double* what she dished out to the Saints of God. The destruction and oppression that she oppressed the Saints of God with under

the 10 nation Red Beast in America… that same massive destruction *times two* will be coming upon her. This is instructive of the type of "oppression" that she gave the Saints of God.

    a. (**Author's Analysis**) I read one theory that was pretty good on this "fill to her double" subject. If the manner that she lived deliciously with the merchants of the earth was that she put up **gold** for the backing of the paper money of the original Beast Kingdom. Then she ran the printing presses to print more paper notes than there were gold in the vaults (classic fractional reserve banking), then this "fill to her double" may mean that the currency hyper-inflates, before the actual physical destructions happen upon her. (Just a theory-nothing more.)

D. This church Babylon-The Mother of Harlots says "to herself" that she is a *married* Queen, and not a lone widow. This is instructive of the type of doctrine being preached inside the church itself. Remember, the true Church of God is the Bride to her Bridegroom Christ. Since Christ is the King of Kings, then the true Church is his **Queen**. However, this church is a **whore**. She has prostituted herself out to the Kings of the Earth and has fornicated with them. This Whore is left desolate and alone from Jesus the Bridegroom.

E. Listen to the clues about her destruction. Her destruction will be in only one hour. It's fast. The city will burn and leave a large smoke cloud that can be seen by the ships in the ocean, nearby. The shipmasters and merchants are going to stand "afar off" for fear of the type of torment this city church is going through. After the destruction, there will be no more people doing any business at all in the city. Which means nobody is going to live there. Remember, this is a man-made destruction by the other 7+1 Kings of the Red 4th Beast that hate the whore and burn her up. The wicked destroy the wicked. What <u>type of destructive force</u> does that sound like to you?

    a. (**Author's Analysis**) This sounds like a nuclear bomb to me. This is the only place in scripture that actually directly sounds like a nuclear bomb (See Appendix 1 for information on World War 3).

    b. This scripture above says that "the kings of the earth will lament for her" and feel bad that she is utterly destroyed. That seems opposite to what we read in Rev 17:16 that the 10 horned Red Beast will hate the whore and make her desolate and naked, and shall eat her flesh and burn her with fire. Likely, we are talking about different kings who will bewail her compared with the 10 nation Beast that will actually do the destruction upon her. Some nations will lament, and other nations will rejoice over her destruction.

F. The church and city Babylon-The Great is a port city at this time. Or is very near to the ocean. There are many shipmasters, sailors, and companies of ships. There is a lot of commerce and delivery of goods.

G. **Key point for the timeline**: The church and city "Babylon - The Great" is *the* richest (or close to it) city on the planet. There are no other cities like this city for its sale of goods and services. It's awesome, which means, whatever city this is, it will be the best in the world.

H. The merchants of the earth were the great men of the earth. The biggest corporations and name brand businesses of the future will be actively trading with this city on 7 mountains. They trade in all manner of goods and services.

They are made super rich by selling their goods and delivering them through shipping into this area of the world.

        a.   Note: This scripture says these merchants are dealing with all manner of goods including **slaves** and the souls of men. It appears that slavery is active, once again, in the lands of Gentile Europe.

I.   God commands that the Saints of God rejoice over her destruction.

Author's Analysis:

I raise a question: If the Miracle-Man Stout Horn/Gog/Anti Christ/False Prophet/False Messiah is dead at the end of the Battle of Armageddon, why does the Beast destroy the Whore by fire?

Possible answers:
1. The remaining 7 Kings of the 4th Beast Kingdom destroy the Whore Church *after* the Stout Horn leader is already dead.
2. The order of the destruction of this Whore Church may be **misplaced** in the Scriptures. Maybe it comes *before* the Battle of Armageddon. (Unlikely, given that we have 2-3 points of evidence that points to *this time* in the timeline. But, there is evidence that points the Whore Church's capital city being destroyed *before* the final Battle of Armageddon. So, we can't rule it out.)
3. Maybe the Stout Horn/Gog does destroy the Whore Church's capital city right before he dies in Jerusalem, thus making it concurrent with the coming of Jesus to the Jews.

I would personally like the Whore Church's capital city get bombed *before* the Battle of Armageddon. It makes more sense in the timeline. However, I do not know the mind of God in all things; therefore the timeline of scripture is what I will stick with. Remember, we are commanded by God to *rejoice* over this event.

I do not have the definite answers to this question. If you, the reader, have further evidence as to *when* the Whore Church capital city is burned, contact me at the website www.LastDaysTimeline.com.

Jesus Comes on the White Horse

Onto Chapter 19 of John's Revelation.

The first several verses deal with the hosts of heaven praising God for destroying The Whore - Babylon The Great – The Great and Abominable Church of the Devil; *and* that the Church of God has finally made herself ready for the Bridegroom Jesus.

Also, that Jesus comes on a white horse with the armies of heaven and is proclaimed King of Kings and Lord of Lords. This happens at the Battle of Armageddon in Jerusalem in the timeline.

This is one of the points of evidence to show that the destruction of the Whore Church –Babylon the Great, actually takes place *before* the final Battle of Armageddon. So, it is possible for this Whore Church to be destroyed *before* the Battle of Armageddon. So, make a note - this scripture evidence exists.

Jesus Comes to the Jews to Rescue Them From the Gentile and Heathen Armies

The Book of Revelation of St. John is lacking in detail concerning the coming of Christ to the Jews to rescue them. This prophecy is taught in clear detail in the Doctrine and Covenants.

(D&C 45:47-53)
"47 Then shall the arm of the Lord fall upon the nations.

48 And then shall the Lord **set his foot upon this mount**, and it shall **cleave in twain**, and the **earth shall tremble**, and reel to and fro, and the heavens also shall shake.

49 And the Lord shall utter his voice, and all the ends of the earth shall hear it; and the nations of the earth shall mourn, and they that have laughed shall see their folly.

50 And calamity shall cover the mocker, and the scorner shall be consumed; and they that have watched for iniquity shall be hewn down and cast into the fire.

51 And then shall the **Jews look upon me and say: What are these wounds in thine hands and in thy feet?**

52 **Then** shall they **know that I am the Lord**; for I will say unto them: These wounds are the wounds with which I was wounded in the house of my friends. I am he who was lifted up. **I am Jesus that was crucified. I am the Son of God.**

53 And then shall they weep because of their iniquities; then shall **they lament because they persecuted their king.**"

Learning Points:
A. When Jesus sets his foot upon the mount the earth will have a great earthquake in the Jerusalem area.
B. The attacking nations of the Gentiles and Heathen will know their folly. They will be burned. Gog/Stout Horn/False Prophet will fall on the hills of Israel with the rest of his army.
C. The Jews finally meet their God. It was Jesus of Nazareth all along. The Son of the Father. Their mass conversion to Christianity happens at once. They mourn because the Jews of the past had persecuted their God, yet they recover and take him into the Temple.

This grand prophecy is also detailed in Zechariah chapter 14.

The Supper of the Great God

On our Timeline, we are still in the 7th Trumpet and 7th Vial. After the Battle of Armageddon is the Supper of the Great God.

The Supper of the Great God is the birds eating the flesh of the Gentile Beast armies and the kings of the East (See Appendix 1: Heathen) after they are decimated on the Battlefield by Jesus. It takes 7 months to mass bury the dead.

Let us jump in toward the end of the chapter in Verse 20

> (Rev 19:20-21)
> "20 And **the beast** was taken, and with him **the false prophet** that **wrought miracles** before him, with which **he deceived them that had received the mark of the beast**, and them that worshipped his image. These **both** were cast alive into a lake of fire burning with brimstone.
> 21 And **the remnant were slain** with the sword of him that sat upon the horse, which sword proceeded **out of his mouth**: and all **the fowls were filled with their flesh**."

Learning Points:
A. The False Prophet – Many prophecy writers have tried to make a distinction as to "who" the False Prophet is. However, it appears from the False Prophet's description that he is the same person as "The Anti-Christ/the Stout Horn/Gog" that rules over the 10 nation Red Beast conglomerate kingdom of the Gentiles. The False Prophet is The Anti-Christ. They are the same.
    a. Remember, the Whore-Babylon the Great-The Great and Abominable Church of the Devil is *possibly* already destroyed by the time the battle of Armageddon takes place. So, it appears that the False Prophet cannot be a major religious figure at the front of the Whore Church. Having the Whore Church destroyed first, would free-up man power from the civil war to attack Jerusalem. This *logically* makes sense to me; however there is evidence on both sides of that question. So, we cannot rule out either side, yet.
B. At the Battle of Armageddon is also when The Anti-Christ/Stout Horn is killed. He is personally at the battle at the head of this super army of the Red Beast and the Kings of the East.
C. The Red Beast of 10 Gentile Nations and the Stout Horn are finally put down and decimated by Jesus Christ himself at the Battle of Armageddon. This is when humanity is freed from the Red Beast.
D. The Supper of the Great God with the birds eating the dead armies' flesh commences.

The Christ has came to the Jews in Jerusalem. The capital city of the Whore Church – Babylon the Great is now destroyed by fire. The enemies are defeated. Now it's time to tie up the loose ends.

There is a period between the Battle of Armageddon when Jesus is now on the ground with the Jews in the Temple of Jerusalem and when the *full* 2nd coming of Christ happens.

25: _The 2nd Coming of Christ to Burn the Earth - Melt the Mountains and Restore this World to a Terrestrial Sphere, and Move this Planet in Space_

There is no timeline for these next events. They all happen _after_ the Battle of Armageddon, and before the terrestrial world of the millennium. I will put them in a _seemingly_ correct order. However, these events could definitely come in a different order in real life, as we arrive there through time. As more verified material comes into view, this work will be updated accordingly. Let us dig in.

7 Months to Bury the Dead – After Armageddon

After the Battle of Armageddon, the dead will be buried by the Jews for 7 months… and their machines of war will supply the Jews with fuel for 7 years.

> (Ezekiel 39: 9-15)
> "9 And they that dwell in the cities of Israel shall go forth, and shall set on fire and **burn the weapons**, both the shields and the bucklers, the bows and the arrows, and the handstaves, and the spears, and they shall **burn them with fire seven years**:
> 10 So that they shall **take no wood out of the field**, neither cut down any out of the forests; for they **shall burn the weapons with fire**: and they shall **spoil those that spoiled them**, and rob those that robbed them, saith the Lord God.
> 11 And it shall come to pass in that day, that I will give unto Gog **a place there of graves in Israel**, the valley of the passengers on the east of the sea: and it shall **stop the noses** of the passengers: and <u>**there shall they bury Gog and all his multitude**</u>: and they shall call it The valley of Hamon-gog.
> 12 And <u>**seven months**</u> shall the house of Israel be burying of them, that they may cleanse the land.
> 13 Yea, all the people of the land shall bury them; and it shall be to them a renown the day that I shall be glorified, saith the Lord God.
> 14 And they shall sever out men of continual employment, passing through the land to bury with the passengers those that remain upon the face of the earth, to cleanse it: after the **end of seven months** shall they search.
> 15 And the passengers that pass through the land, when any seeth a man's bone, then shall he set up a sign by it, till the buriers have buried it in the valley of Hamon-gog."

Learning Points:
A. Weapons of war and machines of war to be used as fuel for 7 years.
   a.   *********Does this mean there will be 7 years minimum, until Christ comes again and appears in the clouds of heaven?** It definitely may. The only other explanation would be that the Jews are burning weapons of war for fuel during the Millennium. Mark this scripture down as the timeline possibility of at least 7 years after the Battle of Armageddon until Christ returns.

B. The Jews will be burying the dead for 7 months. They will even have teams of men in full time employment digging ditches and putting the bodies in. The valley to the East of the sea coast is the spot that will be designated. It's going to stink for a while.

C. Gog/The Stout Horn, the mighty "dark miracle working" evil leader of the 4th Beast Kingdom of Gentile Europe will be killed in Israel during the final Battle of Armageddon. His grave site will be in Israel, along with all his armies.

A New Missionary Call to the Heathen Nations

After The Christ rescues the Jews from the Heathen Nations and Gentile Nations attacking Jerusalem, a new missionary call will go forth to claim back the Heathen Nations. Remember, the Times of the Gentiles is well past.

> (D&C 45:52-54)
> "52 Then shall they know that I am the Lord; for I will say unto them: These wounds are the wounds with which I was wounded in the house of my friends. I am he who was lifted up. I am Jesus that was crucified. I am the Son of God.
> 53 And then shall they weep because of their iniquities; then shall they lament because they persecuted their king.
> 54 **And then** shall **the heathen nations be redeemed**, and they that knew no law shall have part in the first resurrection; and it shall be tolerable for them."

The Heathen will want the missionaries, after Jesus returns to the Jews.

> (Zechariah 8:23)
> " 20 Thus saith the Lord of hosts; **It shall yet come to pass**, that there shall come people, and **the inhabitants of many cities**:
> 21 And the inhabitants of one city shall go to another, saying, Let us go speedily to pray before the Lord, and to seek the Lord of hosts: I will go also.
> 22 Yea, many people and strong nations **shall come to seek the Lord of hosts in Jerusalem**, and to pray before the Lord.
> 23 Thus saith the Lord of hosts; **In those days** it shall come to pass, **that ten men** shall take hold out of all languages of the nations, even **shall take hold of the skirt of him that is a Jew, saying, We will go with you: for we have heard that God is with you.**"

The Offering in Righteousness by the Future Levites

The Jews in Jerusalem will have built their new 4th Temple to offer blood sacrifices. They will be offering up animals *before* the Battle of Armageddon, as already shown. But now, Gog is dead and the 4th Beast Kingdom of Europe is destroyed, they will want to offer them again to their *new* Messiah and Savior, Jesus the Christ. And they will, for a short time, offer animal sacrifices as part of the "restitution of all things."

> (Teachings of the Prophet Joseph Smith p172)

"Sacrifice to Be Part of Restoration - It will be necessary here to make a few observations on the doctrine set forth in the above quotation, and **it is generally supposed** that sacrifice was entirely done away when the Great Sacrifice [i.e.,] the sacrifice of the Lord Jesus was offered up, and that there will be no necessity for the ordinance of sacrifice in future; but those who assert this are certainly not acquainted with the duties, privileges and authority of the Priesthood, or with the Prophets.

The offering of sacrifice has ever been connected and forms a part of the duties of the Priesthood. It began with the Priesthood, and will be continued **until after** the coming of Christ, **from generation to generation**. We frequently have mention made of the offering of sacrifice by the servants of the Most High in ancient days, prior to the law of Moses; which ordinances will be continued when the Priesthood is restored with all its authority, power and blessings."

(D&C 13:1)
"1 Upon you my fellow servants, in the name of Messiah I confer the Priesthood of Aaron, which holds the keys of the ministering of angels, and of the gospel of repentance, and of baptism by immersion for the remission of sins; and this shall never be taken again from the earth, until **the sons of Levi do offer again an offering unto the Lord in righteousness.**"

Learning Points:
A. As I read this, there will be animal sacrifices long into the Millennium, from "generation to generation," not just a one-time sacrifice and done. It will be an ongoing effort.
B. The Aaronic Priesthood is to be taken from the Earth *after* the sons of Levi do offer *again* an offering in righteousness to the Lord. This **act** would conclude the need for the Aaronic Priesthood, as a preparatory priesthood for the Melchizedek Priesthood.

NO RAIN for 1 Year Before Christ Comes – Drought?

The year that the Lord comes again in the clouds as the final 2nd Coming of Christ, there shall be no rainbows; which probably means no **rain**. Joseph Smith said this:

(Teachings of the Prophet Joseph Smith p340)
"I have asked of the Lord concerning His coming; and while asking the Lord, He gave a sign and said, "In the days of Noah I set a bow in the heavens as a sign and token that in any year that the bow should be seen the Lord would not come; but there should be **seed time and harvest during that year**: but whenever you see **the bow withdrawn**, it shall be a token that there shall be **famine, pestilence, and great distress among the nations**, and that the coming of the Messiah is not far distant. But I will take the responsibility upon myself to prophecy in the name of the Lord, that Christ will not come this year, as Father Miller has prophesied, for we have seen the bow."

Learning Points:
A. The rainbow is the signal. When there is no rainbow for a **year**, then the Lord can come in that year. What makes a rainbow? The sunlight passing through rain droplets as they are falling from the clouds. If there is no rainbow anywhere on earth… that must mean there are no clouds or rain on earth. That surely would be a shocking event unto itself.
   a. Note: This could be interpreted as part of the plagues that the 2 prophets in Jerusalem put upon their attacking enemies. That they "shut up heaven" and therefore there would be no rain. We won't know, until we get to this point in the timeline.
B. Also, specifically the Lord mentioned the rainbows as the signal for seed time and harvest time. Thus, meaning a drought and a famine during this year with no rainbow.

Let The Mountains Melt and The Islands Flee – The Wicked Shall Be As Stubble – The GLORIOUS 2nd Coming of Christ

It's the *end of the world*, as it is said. Jesus is now to approach the Earth in full glory. The elements melt with fervent heat. All people shall see Him together. The Saints of God in Zion are caught up to meet him amongst the clouds, only to return to the earth as a terrestrial sphere for the Millennium.

The **sign** of the Coming of the Lord will be seen in the sky. And then the veil lifts and the Lord's face is revealed. This would be the spot in the timeline for the **melting of** the Mountains that they flow down. The islands flee away, The land masses re-assemble as the days before Peleg. This means, that this portion of the Lord's 2nd Coming is still within the 7th Trumpet and 7th Vial. Amazing.

> (D&C 88:95-98)
> "95 And there shall be **silence in heaven for the space of half an hour**; and immediately after shall the **curtain of heaven be unfolded**, as a scroll is unfolded after it is rolled up, and **the face of the Lord shall be unveiled**;
> 96 And the **saints** that are upon the earth, who are alive, shall be quickened and be **caught up** to meet him.
> 97 And they who have **slept in their graves** shall come forth, for their **graves shall be opened**; and they **also shall be caught up** to meet him in the midst of **the pillar of heaven**—
> 98 They are Christ's, the **first fruits**, they who shall descend with him first, and they who are on the earth and in their graves, who are first caught up to meet him; and all this by the voice of the sounding of the trump of the angel of God."

Learning Points:
A. There is another period of ½ hr of silence in heaven. This again could mean 21 earth years before Christ comes… *after* the Whore Church – Babylon the Great is destroyed by Fire. (See vs 94). Or again, it may mean just ½ hr of earth time.
B. The Saints of God living at that time, or in their graves, shall be caught up to meet Jesus in the pillar of heaven… while Jesus is descending.

C. The graves will be opened. Obviously spirits don't need their graves opened to be with Jesus in the pillar; *only* if they are to receive their resurrected bodies at this time. This is the Morning of the 1st Resurrection.

And what a bright morning on the Earth it shall be. The sun will hide its face in shame at the glorious brightness of Jesus.

> (D&C 133:46-49)
> "46 And it shall be said: Who is this that cometh down from God in heaven with **dyed garments**; yea, from the regions which are not known, clothed in his glorious apparel, traveling in the greatness of his strength?
> 47 And he shall say: I am he who spake in righteousness, mighty to save.
> 48 And the Lord shall be **red in his apparel**, and his garments like him that treadeth in the wine-vat.
> 49 And so great shall be the glory of his presence that **the sun shall hide his face in shame**, and the moon shall withhold its light, and **the stars shall be hurled from their places**."

Learning Points:
A. When Jesus comes in his **glory**, he will have red apparel. This is not for his other appearances on the Earth. Just for this special 2nd coming in Glory.
B. Jesus will be so bright, that the sun and moon won't even show their light. They will be overcome with the light and glory and **fire** emanating from Jesus' immediate person. *This* is the Glory that will burn the earth and melt the elements with fervent heat and rejoin the continents. It makes the mountains to flow down and the islands to flee. The wicked men which are left on the earth, which are not caught-up to Jesus as his Saints of God, will simply be left on the earth to burn with the rest of the elements. Nothing more, nothing less.
C. And finally, the stars hurled from their normal places. To upgrade the Telestial Earth to a Terrestrial Earth like the Garden of Eden, the Earth will be **moved** before the start of the Millennium to a place that is Terrestrial. (The same thing happens again at the end of the Millennium, and the Earth moves to a place that is Celestial.)

The mountains flowing down; the islands fleeing; the stars hurled from their places... This is the ending of the 7th Trumpet and 7th Vial in John's Revelation. The final end.

Now, it's wide open... for a **new** beginning... for YOU.

SECTION 7: The Millennium and Beyond

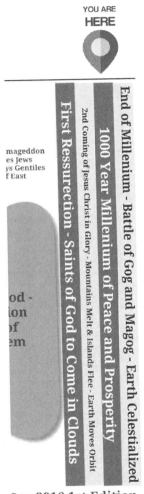

YOU ARE **HERE**

mageddon
es Jews
ys Gentiles
f East

End of Millenium - Battle of Gog and Magog - Earth Celestialized

2nd Coming of Jesus Christ in Glory - Mountains Melt & Islands Flee - Earth Moves Orbit

1000 Year Millenium of Peace and Prosperity

First Ressurection - Saints of God to Come in Clouds

od -
ion
of
em

Dec 2016 1st Edition

26: Satan is Bound – The 1000 Year Millennium of Peace and Prosperity and The Battle of Gog and Magog – The Celestialized Earth

The remainder of John's Revelation Chapters 20-22 will be summarized for brevity. Read the record itself for further clarification. I have defined this work to be about the prophecy timeline of future events to the millennium. This section will be short.

Chapter 20 of John's Revelation: (Remember Satan is bound *inside* the 7th Trumpet and 7th Vial. This is one *long* sequence of events inside one Trumpet.)

1. Satan is bound by an angel and thrown into the "Bottomless Pit." This same pit is where the Lost 10 Tribes of the north came out of to rescue the saints of God in America near the Everlasting Hills.
2. Satan will be loosed for a short time at the end of the Millennium to test the souls of men born during the Millennium at the battle of Gog and Magog. There will be **one** holdout left for good. The evil armies will surround it and then fire will come down out of the sky to burn them up and save the righteous.
3. Judgment is delegated to the leadership of the 12 Tribes of Israel.
4. Many men are resurrected that were beheaded in the **last days**, because of their testimony of Jesus which they wouldn't give up for the Beast or the mark of the Beast, nor his image. The *first* resurrection is started.
5. After the Battle of Gog and Magog, **at the end of the Millennium**, the Earth dies and is resurrected in Celestial glory.
6. Next, is the Final Judgment of all men, and the only judgment for the men remaining in Hell suffering for their own sins. They too are judged and resurrected at this time, at the end of the Millennium.

Chapter 21 of John's Revelation:

1. This *new* heaven and a new earth is a Celestialized earth. This new Celestial Earth will get a new Holy City, and only 1 this time. This new city is also as a bride for Jesus.
2. Now, that this earth is a celestial sphere of fire and glass appearance, God the Father himself will come and abide with the Celestialized children of Him that made their spirits. God the Father lives on all the Celestialized Spheres he wishes, including this one.
   a. SIDE NOTE: Notice the earth went through the same mortal progression that Man must go through? Birth at the creation; and wickedness before the flood. Baptism by the flood. Reception of the Holy Ghost by burning at Christ's coming. The Millennium of Peace and a boost to the terrestrial sphere. Death at the end of the Millennium. Resurrection into Celestial glory of a new heaven and new earth. And finally, a Celestialized sphere with fire and the appearance of glass, enjoying the presence of The Father.
3. The new Holy Jerusalem is the celestial city that descends upon the new Celestial earth. It has 12 gates with the 12 names of the Tribes of Israel on them. The city has 12 foundations with the 12 original Apostles of Jesus written on them. The length, width, **and height** are all 12,000 furlongs. This is a **cube** shaped city.

4. There is no Temple or need of light in this city as God the Father is with the Celestialized people written in the Lamb's Book of Life.

Chapter 22 of John/s Revelation:
1. There is a **real** river with the water of life flowing out from the throne of God *and* the Lamb. The **real** Tree of Life is in this area of the river. The Tree of Life has 12 fruits that are rotated by month. The leaves of the tree are used for healing of the nations.
2. Christ identifies himself as the *Root of David*, not to be confused with the *Root of Jessie*. Christ wraps-up the vision to John the Revelator.

SECTION 8: Take-Aways and Conclusion of The Timeline

27: What Should You Do With This Information?

Congratulations! You, the reader, now know more about the exact events to take place from December 2016 through the last-days and the 2nd Coming of Jesus Christ. The timeline has been presented in a concise format.

I would like to take a moment to share the best **physical** preparedness resources and **spiritual** preparedness resources with you, the reader. Let us start off with physical preparedness. I believe that if a man cannot eat, then it is harder to listen to the Word of the Lord.

The BEST Physical Preparedness Resources:

- Every book title by Joel Skousen – get them all. This man has spent his whole life preparing for these storms. He is an expert in that field. Joel has multi-pack lists of different family needs like: food storage, communications, bartering items, weapons. Listen to him. (See www.LastDaysTimeline.com/joel-skousen)

- Crafts and Skills Preparation – To prepare for yourselves and others: food, clothing, shoes, heating fuel, shelter, water gathering. These types of skills will be absolutely needed among your neighborhood. The best general resources for these types of skills are YouTube.com and How-to books. They are the cheapest. The books will serve you well during the crisis itself, as print-books will still be available to you in your library.

- Disinfection and Disease Control – Jim Phillips has the very best resources in this area. (See www.LastDaysTimeline.com/jim-phillips)

- For inexpensive sources of food heating, light, and other disaster needs read *The Nuclear War Survival Guide* by Cresson Kearny. There is a lot more in the book than just nuclear war survival tactics. (Download this great work for FREE at www.LastDaysTimeline.com/nuclear-war-survival-skills)

- A giant updated list of tried and tested food storage companies, gardening techniques, water filtration, sanitation supplies, cooking supplies, alternative fuels, and general preparedness items will be maintained on the website www.LastDaysTimeline.com.

These supplies will be needed when the problems in America begin when Ezra's 3 Eagle Heads start to take control. This is when the 3rd Beast of Daniel goes down and the 4th Beast rises. You will need enough supplies to manage that storm.

The BEST Spiritual Preparedness Resources:

- If you are not yet a member of the Church of Jesus Christ of Latter-Day Saints, go to www.mormon.org and Chat **live** with a missionary. They will give you a **free** copy of the Book of Mormon. A great many scriptures in this work, came from this wonderful Book. I am sure glad I "listened" when they knocked on my door many years ago. Have them over to your home for **free** and listen to their message. You'll be shocked and surprised at what they share with you.

- If you are already a Member of the LDS Church, your Gift has already been given to you. Use the Gift of the Holy Ghost to ask your Father in Heaven **more questions**. Ask Him for information. Ask Him. He will cause pure information of truth to pour into your mind. He did that for me. The promise is the same for you.

The truths of God are held within the Church of Jesus Christ of Latter-Day Saints. There are no other religious teachings on Earth as deep as what are to be found in the restored church of Jesus Christ.

I am also a student of religions and of history. I can tell you that Satan has put up a gauntlet of churches and religions on this earth. He will even have one enthroned as a **state** religion in the 4th Beast Kingdom. The way through that gauntlet is for you, the reader, to focus on TRUTH. It is the only thing that matters.

The Book of Mormon is **truth**. In fact, God said in the last days, He would cause **truth** to spring forth out of the Earth. And He always keeps His promises.

The Church of Jesus Christ of Latter-Day Saints is the "Church of God" that is in the Everlasting Hills that the future Lost 10 Tribes of Israel will come to. The Melchizedek Priesthood of God is held within the Church. John the Beloved/Revelator will lead them to this people… for John himself gave the Melchizedek Priesthood to this people. A prophet of God, holding the keys of the kingdom, stands at the lead of this Church. The prophet directs us toward the Savior. And the Savior directs us toward the Father.

All members of the Church, and some non-members, would agree that Joseph Smith Jr. was a prophet of God and that the Lord called upon him to restore the ancient Church of Jesus Christ; and Joseph did so.

In the future, the Lost 10 Tribes will return from the land of Arsareth in the North led by John the Beloved/Revelator. Together with the other Tribes of Israel, we will build the new Nation of Zion. We will live the law of consecration. We will see the Savior come to his New Jerusalem Temple. He will be among us then.

If the Church was restored in the past and is true in the future...for the Savior will mark it with his own presence. Then the church is **true today**, in the middle.

Always align yourself with the **truth**.

Build your house of testimony upon the rock of the Savior Jesus Christ. Have faith in his power to **save**. Use Faith as a Verb and show your faith by your actions day to day. Repent and Come unto Him.

THE END...is only your beginning.   www.LastDaysTimeline.com

APPENDIX 1 - Who is Who & What is What... With the Evidence Data to Support the Conclusion

4th Jewish Temple to Be Built in Jerusalem

The last Jewish Temple to be built upon the earth will be built during the last days. The Latter-Day King David "The Branch" (see Appendix 1) shall have the honor of completing the 4th Jewish Temple.

The modern Jewish nation of Israel established in 1949, has been collecting and assembling the needed components to the temple for decades. They only lack the knowledge of the exact location of where to place it. And since they admit that there is no prophet of God with authority among them, they are seeking to place it on the old spot. They just don't know where that spot is. This controversy is all abuzz on www.YouTube.com

Of several possible spots:
1. It is commonly thought that the current Muslim Dome of the Rock is the site of the old Jewish Temple. That poses a problem, as it's a holy site to the Muslims. For the Jewish rabbis that believe this is the spot, they are waiting on God to clear the area before they will build.
2. The spot that the Jews call the Wailing Wall, is thought to be the old wall of the Temple of Herod. However, this is a problem, as there were not one brick left of the old Temple left standing after the sac of Jerusalem in 70AD by the Romans. So, as the theory goes, this wall called The Wailing Wall is actually the wall of the Roman Fort Antonia which overlooked the old Temple of Herod. The Jewish rabbis that like this spot claim that the 4th Jewish Temple could be built along side the Muslim Dome of the Rock...leaving off the outer courtyard area.
3. There is a spot of ground that is currently BARE to the South of the current "Temple Mount", on a hill. This may have been the actual site of the Temple of Herod, that was overlooked by the Roman Fort Antonia. Very few Jewish people consider this spot a legitimate spot for the Temple of Herod.
4. There may be a 4th legitimate spot that the Jews haven't thought of, yet.

5.   There are some LDS prophecy book authors that say the Jews won't build their 4th Temple to God until after Christ comes to them. It would be an LDS temple. Thus, the Dome of the Rock problem is eliminated entirely.

   a.   I do not subscribe to this view, because the sacrifices must be stopped by the Stout Horn during the lead-up to the final Battle of Armageddon.

Regardless of placement, the latter-day King David of Jerusalem will be the builder of it. It shall be built BEFORE the final Battle of Armageddon. The Jews would have already offered animal sacrifices in it, BEFORE Gog/Stout Horn would have stopped the sacrifices. (See the main portion of The "Last Days" Timeline Book)

The Church of the Firstborn

In the privately authored books of members of the church today, there are plenty of nuances surrounding the Church of the Firstborn.

1. I have read some that equate the Church of the Firstborn to the Church of Jesus Christ of Latter-Day Saints itself. Applying the Parable of the 10 Virgins to The Church provides that about 50% of the membership would be faithful and receive that station of The Church of the Firstborn. In the sense of a <u>long TIMELINE</u> going thru the Temple at Jackson County Missouri with Christ visiting his Saints AND extending through the 1000 year Millennium…that statement makes sense.

2. Then other books written by members of the church; the complete opposite view is taken. That it's an elite club that only the special leaders of the church are partaking of, plus a few others. In the current <u>short TIMELINE</u>, this statement makes sense.

I wanted to know which version was correct.

The Church of the Firstborn are those members of The Church of Jesus Christ of Latter-Day Saints that will receive all that the Father hath including the Celestial Kingdom.

> (D&C 88:3-5)
> "3 Wherefore, I now send upon you **another Comforter**, even upon you my friends, that it may abide in your hearts, even the Holy Spirit of promise; which **other Comforter** is the same that I promised unto my disciples, as is recorded in the **testimony of John**.
> 4 **This Comforter is the promise** which I give unto you of eternal life, even **the glory** of the celestial kingdom;
> 5 Which glory is that of **the church of the Firstborn**, even of God, the holiest of all, through Jesus Christ his Son—"

Learning Points:

A. The promise that is recorded in the testimony of John was seen in fulfillment on the Day of Pentecost in the book of the Acts of the Apostles.
B. The Holy Spirit of Promise is what does the sealing and glorifying.
C. The Holy Spirit is received and then glory starts to appear. This is the same glory as the Celestial Kingdom. AND the glory of the Celestial Kingdom is the glory of the Church of the Firstborn. These phrases are all intertwined.

> (D&C 93:20-22)
> 20 For if you keep my commandments you shall receive of **his fulness**, and be **glorified** in me as I am in the Father; therefore, I say unto you, you shall **receive grace for grace**.
> 21 And now, verily I say unto you, I was in the beginning with the Father, and **am the Firstborn**;
> 22 And all **those who are begotten through me** are partakers of the **glory** of the same, and are **the church of the Firstborn**.

Learning Points:
A. We see those that keep Jesus' commandments receive of Jesus' fullness and glory.
B. Those that are "begotten" through Jesus are partakers of the glory through Jesus and are the Church of the Firstborn. Again, this has to do with following the commandments.

> (D&C 78:20-21)
> "20 Wherefore, do the things which I have **commanded you**, saith your Redeemer, even **the Son Ahman**, who prepareth all things before he taketh you;
> 21 For **ye are the church of the Firstborn**, and **he will take you up in a cloud**, and appoint every man his portion."

Learning Points:
A. Again we see "follow the commandments" as being a prerequisite to becoming part of the Church of the Firstborn.
B. The name of God the Father is "Ahman". Many Latter-Day Saints believe that the name of God is "Elohim", however that is His title. It means "Chief of the Gods". But our Father in Heaven's name is Ahman. (See "Mormon Doctrine" by Bruce R. McConkie. Also See LDS Hymn "The Time is Far Spent" by Eliza R. Snow)
C. The Church of the Firstborn will be called up to the cloud when Jesus comes to melt the elements of the earth with the heat of His glory.

There have been many Saints who have had their Calling and Election Made Sure, as they were SEALED up unto eternal life and made members of the Church of the Firstborn.

> (https://www.lds.org/ensign/1976/07/accepted-of-the-lord-the-doctrine-of-making-your-calling-and-election-sure?lang=eng)
> "The promise of becoming **a member of the church of the Firstborn** is also made to Latter-day Saints. (See D&C 76:50–60.) In our dispensation

many Saints have made their calling and election sure. (See, e.g., D&C 124:19.) Noteworthy among these was William Clayton, to whom the Prophet said:

"Your life is hid with Christ in God, and so are **many others.** Nothing but the unpardonable sin can prevent you from **inheriting eternal life** for you are **sealed up** by the power of the Priesthood unto eternal life, having taken the step necessary for that purpose." (History of the Church, 5:391.)"

There is a need to SEAL UP the 144,000 young High Priest servants of God in their forehead before they go out to preach during the time of the 7 Trumpets and 7 Vials of John's Revelation are being poured out upon The 4th Beast Kingdom of the Gentiles in Europe. This takes place after the special Temple in the New Jerusalem in Jackson County Missouri is built. Joseph Smith said:

(Smith, Teachings of the Prophet Smith, p. 366)
"There will be **144,000 saviors on Mount Zion**, and with them an **innumerable host** that no man can number. Oh! I beseech you to go forward, go forward and make **your calling and your election sure.**"

Learning Points:
A. The 144,000 young High Priests will have their calling and election made sure. They will be members of the Church of the Firstborn.
B. There will be an innumerable host that will also receive these blessings. Not to be called on missions, but to receive membership in the Church of the Firstborn and have their Calling and Election made Sure.

The main point….is that a member of the Church of the Firstborn has had their Calling and Election Made Sure. What does that mean?

There is an ordinance that is performed in many of the larger Temples of the Church of Jesus Christ of Latter-Day Saints. It is the ordinance of having your Calling and Election Made Sure. This ordinance is performed in the Holy of Holies. This special room is not in all temples of the Church, just some of the larger temples.

I will not say more concerning this ordinance, however there is only one picture that has ever been taken of the Holy of Holies. It is printed in the book "House of the Lord" by James E. Talmage 1921 reprinted edition.

However, the image of the Holy of Holies also appears on Wikipedia.org
https://en.wikipedia.org/wiki/Holy_of_Holies_(LDS_Church)

Given that this image is in the public domain, I have reprinted it here in the highest resolution possible.

This is the PLACE of the ordinance of having ones Calling and Election Made Sure.

Notice the room is round. It has a vaulted ceiling. This image comes from the Salt lake Temple in 1921.

Also, the stained glass window in the center of the image is the depiction of the Prophet Joseph Smith being visited by God the Father and Jesus Christ in person.

Very fitting depiction for this room, as this is where that very deed happens.

When the ordinance of having ones Calling and Election Made Sure is performed and SEALED by the Holy Spirit of Promise, that person is now a member of the Church of the Firstborn.

If this ordinance hasn't happened for you yet, wait for the New Jerusalem period when Jesus will visit personally. For it will happen for an innumerable host of the Church of God. Look forward to it.

(published in the US before 1923 and public domain in the US.)

The Dedication of the Land of Israel by Orson Hyde

Orson dedicated the land of Israel for the return of the Jews from on top of the Mount of Olives just outside of Jerusalem. In 1841, Jerusalem was controlled by the Ottoman Turks, which recently retook the city in 1840. (See https://en.wikipedia.org/wiki/Timeline_of_Jerusalem)

Just OUTSIDE the city wall, was the Mount of Olives. This is the site where Orson Hyde dedicated the whole land of Israel for the return of the Tribe of Judah.

Today, in modern times, the Church of Jesus Christ of Latter-Day Saints owns a 5 acre plot toward the PEAK of the Mount of Olives. The Orson Hyde Memorial Garden sits over the area where The Lord Jesus Christ will place his feet when he comes to rescue the Jews from the attacking Gentile 4th Beast Kingdom lead by The Stout Horn/Gog.

| Orson Hyde Memorial Garden on 5 acres toward the Top of the Mount of Olives | Orson Hyde Memorial Garden Plaque That Contains Elder Hyde's Original Dedicatory Prayer |

The 4 Beasts of Daniel Chapter 7 are Last-Days Kingdoms

There has been much speculation over the millennia as to which kingdoms represent these 4 Beast Kingdoms in Daniel Chapter 7. In fact many different Bible translations and concordances place these 4 Beasts of Daniel into the Timeline of Nebuchadnezzar's Dream of the Statue of the Man that is broken by the stone cut without hands (Daniel chapter 2 - See Appendix 1). They try to label these 4 Beasts as kingdoms of the ancient past.

Something like this:
The Flying Lion = Nebuchadnezzar's Babylon
The Rib Eating Bear = Media and Persia
The Leopard = Greece
The 4th = Rome

However, these spurious interpretations cannot be. Period!

The **whole revelatory vision** must be taken into account, not just segmenting out any 4 large ancient kingdoms.

The items below are listed in the Daniel Chapter 7 vision. Did these things come to pass yet?
- In the 4th Kingdom, were there 10 rulers colluding together in the big kingdom?
- Was there a "little stout horn" ruler that came up at the end of the kingdom which took down 3 other rulers?
- Did this Stout Horn ruler attack the Saints of God?
- Did the Stout Horn ruler have his throne cast down by the Ancient of Days? The traditional Latter-Day Saint definition of the Ancient of Days is Adam/Michael?
- Did the Ancient of Days come?
- Was the Ancient of Days dressed in bright white and have hair that was light? Was his throne like a fiery flame?
- Did a thousand thousands minister unto him? Were the books opened and judgment set?

- Did the Stout Horn Leader speak great blasphemy against God?
- Was the 4th Beast Kingdom being led by the Stout Horn ruler cast down and burned?
- Did the Beast Kingdoms 1-3 continue in their kingdoms AFTER the 4th Beast Kingdom was burned?
- Did the Beast Kingdoms 1-3 have their dominion taking away by the Son of man that came in the clouds of heaven?
- Did the one like the Son of Man visit the Ancient of Days?
- Did the one like the Son of Man's kingdom grow forever and became an everlasting dominion?

Obviously, the 2nd Coming of Jesus Christ and his everlasting political kingdom that is to be setup in The New Jerusalem has not happened yet. Thus, when the entire revelatory vision of Daniel Chapter 7 is taken into account, **and** the other information contained in Ezra's Eagle; **Daniel Chapter 7's four beasts are last-days kingdoms.**

The 4 Important Latter-Day Leaders: The Stem, The Rod, The Branch, and The Root – All of Jesse

There are 4 great leaders of the last days.
1. The Stem
2. The Rod
3. The Branch
4. The Root

The question as to who these latter-day important leaders are has been the side-focus of many prophecy writers. I would rather make it short and very sweet for you the reader.

The main scripture that mentions them all together, showing that they don't overlap each other and are in fact separate people is shown in both the Book of Mormon as Jacob quotes Isaiah 11 :

> (2nd Nephi 21:1)
> "1 And there shall come forth a **rod** out of the **stem** of Jesse, and a **branch** shall grow out of his **roots**."

> (Isaiah 11:1 perfect match)
> "1 And there shall come forth a **rod** out of the **stem** of Jesse, and a **Branch** shall grow out of his **roots**:"

Who is The Stem?

This question was cleared up quickly for the Saints of God by Joseph Smith Jr. in the Doctrine and Covenants

(D&C 113:1-2)

"1 Who is **the Stem** of Jesse spoken of in the 1st, 2d, 3d, 4th, and 5th verses of the 11th chapter of Isaiah?

2 Verily thus saith the Lord: **It is Christ.**"

So, we have identified The Stem as the Lord Jesus Christ himself. Consider this portion of the small parable of "The Vine" in John.

(John 15: 4-6)

"4 Abide in me, and I in you. As **the branch** cannot bear fruit of itself, except **it abide in the vine**; no more can ye, except ye abide in me.

5 **I am the vine, ye are the branches**: He that abideth in me, and I in him, the same bringeth forth much fruit: for without me ye can do nothing.

6 If a man abide not in me, he is cast forth as a branch, and is withered; and men gather them, and cast them into the fire, and they are burned."

Jesus Christ is the true vine (or STEM). Easy....lets go to the next one.

Who is The Rod?

This definition was partially cleared up by the prophet Joseph Smith in the Doctrine and Covenants. Although a perfect definition is not had from the prophet.

(D&C 113:3-4)

"3 What is **the rod** spoken of in the first verse of the 11th chapter of Isaiah, that should come of the Stem of Jesse?

4 Behold, thus saith the Lord: It is **a servant in the hands of Christ**, who is partly a descendant of **Jesse** as well as of **Ephraim**, or of the **house of Joseph**, on whom there is **laid much power**."

Learning Points:

A. The man whose name is "The Rod" is not fully identified well. However, we do know some characteristics about him.

B. The Rod is a servant of Christ. By definition, a prophet of God.

C. He is a human that was born into the earth, because he is a descendant of Jesse and Ephraim.

  a. Ephraim is usually associated with the white Gentile Europeans. Jesse was the Father of King David. King David is associated with the Jews....Thus, the man named "The Rod" will be part white European Gentile and part Jew....by family tree.

D. This man will have much power given to him in the last-days.

There are more scriptures about "The Rod". Most of the evidence doesn't point to a specific living man today. There has been speculation that "The Rod" was Joseph Smith. However, this is not true because of this statement by Brigham Young

(Journal of Discourses 2:268–69.)

"It is the house of Israel we are after, and we care not whether they come from the east, the west, the north, or the south; from China, Russia, England,

California, North or South America, or some other locality. ... The Book of Mormon came to Ephraim, **for Joseph Smith was a pure Ephraimite**, and the Book of Mormon was revealed to him."

Obviously the Prophet Joseph was not partly of Jewish descent. Thus, he was not "The Rod". So, the man called "The Rod" will continue to be a mystery. More evidence relating to this important last-days prophet will continue to be compiled for a future edition of this work. Contact me at www.LastDaysTimeline.com if you, the reader, have more definitive information.

Who is The Branch?

There is a special last days servant named King David that will be raised up to the Jews. The 4th Jewish Temple will be built under his administration. Here is the evidence:

> (Zechariah 6:12-13)
> "12 And speak unto him, saying, Thus speaketh the Lord of hosts, saying, Behold **the man** whose **name is The Branch**; and he shall grow up out of his place, and **he shall build the temple** of the Lord:
> 13 Even **he shall build the temple** of the Lord; and he shall bear the glory, and shall **sit and rule upon his throne**; and **he shall be a priest** upon his throne: and the counsel of peace shall be between them both."

Learning Points:
A. The man whose name is "The Branch" shall build the temple. So, who is the man named "The Branch"?
B. This man shall grow up out of his place.
C. This man shall have a throne in Israel and rule from upon it.
D. This man shall be a priest.

Consider what the Prophet Joseph Smith said about the man called The Latter Day King David.

> (History of the Church, vol 6, page 253)
> "Although David was a king, he never did obtain the spirit and power of Elijah and the fullness of the Priesthood; and the Priesthood that he received, and the throne and kingdom of David is to be taken from him and **given to another by the name of David in the last days, raised up out of his lineage."**

Learning Points:
A. There will be a king of Israel named "David" in the last days. This latter-day king will come from the posterity of the old King David.

And Orson Hyde knew of what the Prophet Joseph said on this subject, because Elder Hyde dedicated the land of Israel for the return of the Jews in 1841 using this language:

(http://emp.byui.edu/satterfieldb/rel341/Orson%20Hyde%20Prayer.htm)
"Thou, O Lord, did once move upon the heart of Cyrus to show favor unto Jerusalem and her children. Do Thou now also be pleased to inspire the hearts of kings and the powers of the earth to look with a friendly eye towards this place, and with a desire to see Thy righteous purposes executed in relation thereto. Let them know that it is Thy good pleasure **to restore the kingdom unto Israel**--raise up **Jerusalem as its capital**, and constitute her people a distinct nation and government, **with David Thy servant, even a descendant from the loins of ancient David to be their king."**

The Branch is identified as the latter-day King David of Jerusalem.

Who is The Root?

Joseph Smith did clear up this definition very well in 2 separate sections of the Doctrine and Covenants.

(D&C 113:5-6)
"5 What is the **root** of Jesse spoken of in the 10th verse of the 11th chapter? 6 Behold, thus saith the Lord, it is a **descendant of Jesse**, as well as of **Joseph**, unto whom **rightly belongs the priesthood**, and **the keys** of the kingdom, for **an ensign**, and **for the gathering of my people in the last days.**"

Learning Points:
A. The man whose name is "The Root" is also a man that was born onto the earth.
B. He has a similar family tree as "The Rod". "The Root" comes thru Jesse, father of King David of the Jews. "The Root" is partly of Jewish ancestry AND Joseph. Which could be either Ephraim (white European Gentiles) or Manasseh (Native American Indians).
C. The man called "The Root" has a native right to the Priesthood. Also to the Keys of Kingdom of God that handle the Gathering of Israel in the last days.

Consider these next scriptures from Isaiah 11 concerning WHO has the task and mission to gather Israel in the last days, including the Lost 10 Tribes of the North.

(Isaiah 11:10-13)
"10 And in that day there shall be a **root of Jesse**, which shall stand for **an ensign** of the people; to it shall **the Gentiles seek**: and his rest shall be glorious.
11 And it shall come to pass in that day, that the Lord shall set his hand **again the second time to recover the remnant of his people**, which shall be left, **from Assyria**, and from Egypt, and from Pathros, and from Cush, and from Elam, and from Shinar, and from Hamath, and from the **islands of the sea.**
12 And he shall set up **an ensign** for the nations, and shall assemble **the outcasts of Israel**, and gather together the **dispersed of Judah** from the **four corners** of the earth.

13 The envy also of Ephraim shall depart, and the adversaries of Judah shall be cut off: Ephraim shall not envy Judah, and Judah shall not vex Ephraim."

Learning Points:
A. Again the man called The Root shall raise the Ensign. And one more clue is given....The Gentiles shall seek to it. This certainly sounds like the Ensign that Joseph Smith raised up to the Gentiles. BUT, remember, in the last days John the Beloved/Revelator will raise the Ensign to the Gentile Nations by kicking out the 4th Beast Organization from America. Making America a land of safe haven from the Gentile Beast's exploits.
B. (v11) In The Root's day, the 2nd great gathering shall commence.
    a. Notice the reference to Assyria. This is the nation that the Lost 10 Tribes escaped from, before they went North. This appears to be a reference to the Lost 10 Tribes.
    b. There are a lot of nations listed here. Some make symbolic sense. Egypt may be America. Islands of the Sea is sometimes referenced again as America. There is probably more here to research.
C. (v12) The Root shall assemble the outcasts of Israel. This has direct reference to the Lost 10 Tribes. They weren't scattered as much as they were "outcasted". With another reference from "The four corners of the earth." And this man "The Root" shall also assemble Judah to Jerusalem.

The main thrust of The Root is shown here.

> (D&C 77:14)
> "9 Q. What are we to understand by the **angel ascending from the east,** Revelation 7th chapter and 2nd verse?
> A. We are to understand that the angel ascending from the east is **he to whom is given the seal of the living God over the twelve tribes of Israel**; wherefore, he crieth unto the four angels having the everlasting gospel, saying: Hurt not the earth, neither the sea, nor the trees, **till we have sealed the servants of our God in their foreheads**. And, if you will receive it, **this is Elias** which was to come **to gather together the tribes of Israel** and **restore all things**."

> Later in the same chapter, John the Beloved Revelator is declared to be the Elias.

> (D&C 77:14)
> "14 Q. What are we to understand by the little book which was eaten by **John**, as mentioned in the 10th chapter of Revelation?
> A. We are to understand that **it was a mission**, and an ordinance, for **him** to **gather the tribes of Israel**; behold, **this is Elias**, who, as it is written, must come and **restore all things**."

Learning Points:
A. John the Beloved/Revelator is to be the Elias that is to COME in the last days to gather the tribes of Israel, including the Lost 10 Tribes and restore all things. That sounds important.

As shown, the man called "The Root" has the same last days mission as the Elias to prepare the way before the Lord Jesus Christ, to restore all things, and to gather all Israel, including the Lost 10 Tribes.

"The Root" is John the Beloved/Revelator.

The Final Breakdown
The Stem = Jesus Christ
The Rod = ?
The Branch = latter day King David of Jerusalem
The Root = John the Beloved/Revelator

The Special Plague Disease of Flies and Maggots

This is a special plague. What is it? The answer is revealed in Doctrine and Covenants.

> (D&C 29:17-20)
> "17 And it shall come to pass, because of the wickedness of the world, that I will take vengeance upon the wicked, for they will not repent; for **the cup of mine indignation is full**; for behold, **my blood shall not cleanse them** if they hear me not.
> 18 Wherefore, I the Lord God will **send forth flies** upon the face of the earth, which shall take hold of the inhabitants thereof, and **shall eat their flesh, and shall cause maggots to come in upon them;**
> 19 And **their tongues shall be stayed that they shall not utter against me;** and their **flesh shall fall from off their bones, and their eyes from their sockets;**
> 20 And it shall come to pass that the beasts of the forest and the fowls of the air shall devour them up."

The murderers of the Prophet Joseph Smith at Carthage Jail swore that Brigham Young had cursed them. They called this disease that afflicted them "The Curse of Brigham Young". This from the book "The Fate of the Persecutors of the Prophet Joseph Smith" by N. B. Lundwall:

> (See "Fate of the Persecutors of Joseph Smith" by N.B. Lundwall. "Also Autobiography of Parley P. Pratt, pp.474-77)
> "A colonel of the Missouri mob, who helped to drive, plunder and murder the Mormons, **died in the hospital** at Sacramento, 1849. Beckwith had the care of him; he was **eaten with worms-a large black-headed kind of maggot-which passed through him by myriads, seemingly a half pint at a time**! Before he died these maggots were crawling out of his mouth and nose! He literally rotted alive! Even the flesh on his legs burst open and fell from the bones! They gathered up the rotten mass in a blanket and buried

him, without awaiting a coffin!

A Mr._____, one of the Missouri mob, **died in the same hospital** about the
same time, and under the care of Mr. Beckwith. His **face and jaw on one
side literally rotted**, and half of his face actually fell off! **One eye rotted
out, and half his nose, mouth and jaw fell from the bones!** The doctor
scraped the bones, and unlocked and took out his jaw from the joint round to
the center of the chin. The rot and maggots continued to eat till they ate
through the large jugular vein of his neck, and he bled to death! He, as well
as Townsend, stank so previous to their death, that they had to be placed in
rooms by themselves, and was almost impossible to endure their presence,
and **the flies** could not be kept from blowing them while alive!"

Again, this special plague of flies and maggots is reserved only for the most wicked
of God's children.

The Abomination of Desolation & The Desolation of Abomination

There are two definitions for The Abomination of Desolation. Lets discuss both of
them:

1. That Jerusalem will be under siege and the Temple will be desecrated. The Bible
    Dictionary tells us of both definitions as well:

    > (Bible Dictionary-Abomination of Desolation)
    > "Conditions of desolation, born of abomination and wickedness, were to
    > occur *twice* in fulfillment of Daniel's words. The first was to be when the
    > Roman legions under Titus, in A.D. 70, laid siege to Jerusalem (Matt. 24:15;
    > JS—M 1:12).
    >
    > Speaking of the last days, of the days following the Restoration of the gospel
    > and its declaration "for a witness unto all nations," our Lord said: "And
    > again shall the abomination of desolation, spoken of by Daniel the prophet,
    > be fulfilled" (JS—M 1:31–32). That is, Jerusalem again will be under siege."

    Here is the same interesting approach by Professor Stephen E. Robinson of BYU
    Farms. He shares with us that the Abomination of Desolation has to do with the
    Temple of God, and God's holy presence within it.

    > (http://publications.mi.byu.edu/fullscreen/?pub=1397&index=6)
    > "The term abominable is used in the Old Testament to describe what
    > God hates, what cannot fail to arouse his wrath. In Daniel, the
    > abomination of desolation is that thing so hateful to God that its
    > **presence in the temple causes the divine presence to depart**, leaving
    > the sanctuary desolate. In the Old Testament, the terms translated into

English as abominable or abomination (Hebrew roots shiqqutz, tarab, piggul; Greek Septuagint and New Testament bdelugma) are usually associated with **idolatrous worship or gross sexual immorality**."

2. The 2nd definition comes from the Bible Dictionary as well. The Abomination of Desolation is simply the judgments poured out upon the wicked in the last days. Presumably when the Times of the Gentiles are finished, that the wipeout of America and Europe by the BIG Plague AND with the 7 Trumpets Vials of John the Beloved/Revelator.

> (Bible Dictionary-Abomination of Desolation)
> "In a general sense, abomination of desolation also describes the latter-day judgments to be poured out upon the wicked wherever they may be. And so that the honest in heart may escape these things, the Lord sends His servants forth to raise the warning voice, to declare the glad tidings of the Restoration, lest "desolation and utter abolishment" come upon them. The elders are commanded to reprove "the world in righteousness of all their unrighteous and ungodly deeds, setting forth clearly and understandingly the desolation of abomination in the last days" (D&C 84:114, 117; 88:84–85)."

I have concluded that the scriptures say it both ways. So, we as the reader must KNOW which way The Lord intended the meaning to be. As both meanings are correct and true.

The Everlasting Hills Are The Rocky Mountains

Most Latter-Day Saints have heard that the Rocky Mountain range is the Everlasting Hills mentioned in the scriptures, but they don't know specifically why.

The "shadow of the Everlasting Hills" is mentioned in each of the Sunday broadcasts of The Music and the Spoken Word presentations by the Mormon Tabernacle Choir.

This information was learned through a 1980s presentation called *The Conversion of a Jew*. It shares the fireside conversion story of a Jewish man that converted to the LDS Church.

In this fireside talk, the Jew that converted to the LDS Faith mentioned that the Everlasting Hills are called this in Hebrew because the mountain chain we call the Rocky Mountains, is the same as the Andes Mountain chain in South America. In fact this long mountain chain stretches under the ocean from the North Pole to the South Pole. (See https://en.wikipedia.org/wiki/Pacific_Coast_Ranges)

These ranges continue under the ocean from Alaska down thru Chile and Argentina. From the tip of North America down to the Southern tip of Chile and Argentina.

Everlasting Hills (North)

Everlasting Hills (South)

Gentiles, Heathen, and the Tribes of Israel

When speaking of the Gentiles, the Heathen, or the Tribes of Israel, the definitions get pretty muddy. The terms are used by various prophets in our cannon differently. Let us tackle The Tribes of Israel first. The LDS Guide to the Scriptures tells us:

> (The Guide to the Scriptures, Israel)
> "Abraham's grandson Jacob, whose name was changed to Israel, had twelve sons. Their descendants have become known as the twelve tribes of Israel or the children of Israel. These are the twelve tribes: Reuben, Simeon, Levi, Judah, Issachar, and Zebulun (the sons of Jacob and Leah); Dan and Naphtali (the sons of Jacob and Bilhah); Gad and Asher (the sons of Jacob and Zilpah); Joseph and Benjamin (the sons of Jacob and Rachel) (Gen. 29:32–30:24; 35:16–18)."

Learning Points:

A. The 12 Tribes of Israel are the descendants of the 12 sons of Jacob. Easy.

The 12 sons of Jacob inherited Gods promises to Abraham through the Abrahamic Covenant. The covenant that flowed through Abraham, Isaac, and Jacob (Israel) is the source of God's promises to man.

The strict Israelite Nations would include the nations of the Lost 10 Tribes in Arsareth (See Appendix 1: Lost 10 Tribes) and the current 2017 Jewish Nation of Israel in the Middle East. However, Israel's bloodlines are spread far and wide to many nations today.

The Heathen – Who Are They?

> Note: I am an author looking to find the definitions that the Lord has stated to make sense of the scriptures. The term "Heathen" can have some negative connotations among some people. I do not mean any harm by using the term. Thank you

The Heathens are idol worshipers, engaged in idolatry generally. The idols represent their multiple gods. The idols have taken on different forms. Usually made of silver, gold, or wood, but also the worship in special groves of trees.

> (Psalms 135:15-18)
> "15 The **idols of the heathen are silver and gold**, the **work of men's hands**.
> 16 They have mouths, but they speak not; eyes have they, but they see not;
> 17 They have ears, but they hear not; neither is there any breath in their mouths.

18 They that make them are like unto them: so is every one that <u>trusteth</u> in them."

The Heathen nations that have the majority of their citizens worshiping idols has changed over the years. Many nations that were idol worshipers are now Christians. So, today the Heathen nations would be the nations that hold the great number of people that are current idol worshippers.

(JST, Luke 3:5-6)
"5 For behold, and lo, he shall come, as it is written in the book of the prophets, to take away the sins of the world, and to bring salvation unto the **heathen nations**, to gather together those who are lost, who are of the **sheepfold of Israel;**
6 Yea, even the dispersed and afflicted; and also to prepare the way, and make possible the preaching of the gospel **unto the Gentiles;**"

The Lord's use of the word "heathen" in modern times to Joseph Smith means that there are plenty of heathens on the Earth in modern times. This use of the word, seems to mean people who have never heard of the Gospel of Jesus Christ before, and they will be judged less hard than a house that rejected the Gospel outrightly.

(D&C 75:21-22)
"21 And you shall be filled with joy and gladness; and know this, that in the day of judgment you shall be judges of that house, and condemn them;
22 And it shall be more tolerable **for the heathen** in the day of judgment, than for that house; therefore, gird up your loins and be faithful, and ye shall overcome all things, and be lifted up at the last day. Even so. Amen."

There will be a missionary outreach to Heathen Nations after Christ comes to the Jews on the Mount of Olives at the end of the Battle of Armageddon. Again we see the Lord in modern times using the word "heathen" as synonymous with not knowing the Gospel of Christ.

(D&C 45:53-54)
"53 And then shall they weep because of their iniquities; then shall they lament because they persecuted their king.
54 **And then** shall **the heathen nations be redeemed, and they that knew no law** shall have part in the first resurrection; and it shall be tolerable for them."

This next scripture from the Old Testament seems to be talking about the people living around the Nation of Israel just before the Battle of Armageddon. Which at the moment 2017, would be the Muslim Nations or Islamic Nations that want to attack Israel.

(Joel 3:11-12)
"11 Assemble yourselves, and **come, all ye heathen**, and gather yourselves together round about: thither cause thy mighty ones to come down, O Lord.

12 Let the **heathen** be wakened, and come up to the valley of Jehoshaphat: for there will I sit to judge all the heathen round about."

So, if this scripture comes into play, it seems the Heathen are not only Idol Worshipers, as the Muslims are not. They are anti-idol worship. However, the Lord uses "Heathen" to describe these people around the Nation of Israel as well. So, under this broader definition the Islamic Nations would be considered Heathen by the Lord. Here is another scripture from the Old Testament describing the "Supper of the Lord" which takes place after the Lord comes on the Mount of Olives to rescue the Jews.

(Ezekiel 39:21)
"20 Thus ye shall be filled at my table with horses and chariots, with mighty men, and with all men of war, saith the Lord God.
21 And I will set **my glory among the heathen**, and **all the heathen shall see my judgment that I have executed**, and my hand that I have laid upon **them**.
22 So the house of Israel shall know that I am the Lord their God from that day and forward."

The Heathen will be at the Battle of Armageddon as the attackers of the Nation of Israel. Thus, the Heathen would include the Muslims by the Lord's definition. The Heathen Nations are then defined including the Middle Eastern countries of the Muslims, plus more.

The Gentiles – Who Are They?

We are getting to the point now. As the Israelite Nations are the Lost 10 Tribes Land of Arsareth and the Nation of Israel for the Jews. The Heathen Nations being the Middle East and the idol worshipers even further to the East and South. The Gentile Nations are to be located. Lets hunt for them. This will be an easy hunt.

The Gentiles are usually associated with Japheth, the elder son of Noah.

(Bible Dictionary: Gentile)
"The word *Gentiles* means "the nations" and eventually came to be used to mean all those not of the house of Israel. It is first used in Genesis with reference to the **descendants of Japheth** (Gen. 10:2–5)."

(Bible Dictionary: Japheth)
"Eldest son of Noah (Moses 8:12; see also Gen. 5:32; 6:10; 7:13; 9:18, 23); his blessing (Gen. 9:27). His descendants were dispersed over the **European coasts of the Mediterranean and the districts adjoining the Black and Caspian seas**."

Japheth went North after the Great Flood from the resting place of the Ark in Turkey (See Appendix 1: Ron Wyatt).

Paul was the "Apostle of the Gentiles". Paul was a Roman citizen and traveled the empire freely. The Romans of Europe were Gentiles.

(Romans 11:13)
"11 I say then, Have they stumbled that they should fall? God forbid:
but rather through their fall **salvation is come unto the Gentiles**, for to
provoke them to jealousy.
12 Now if the fall of them be the riches of the world, and the diminishing of
them the riches of the Gentiles; how much more their fulness?
13 For **I speak to you Gentiles**, inasmuch as **I am the apostle of the
Gentiles, I magnify mine office:**"

The big controversy in the early Church of Christ led by Peter, was rather Gentiles
who were uncircumcised should be allowed into the Church of Christ. Peter received
the vision of the sheet falling from heaven with "unclean" animals as food. God
commanded Peter in Acts chapter 10 to send the Gospel to the Gentiles.

(Acts 10:1-2)
"1 There was a certain **man in Cæsarea called Cornelius, a centurion of
the band called the Italian band,**
2 A devout man, and one that feared God with all his house, which gave
much alms to the people, and prayed to God alway."

Cornelius, the Roman solider had a vision to send for Peter.

(Acts 10:44-47)
"44 While Peter yet spake these words, the Holy Ghost fell on **all them**
[included the Gentiles] which heard the word.
45 And they of the circumcision which believed were astonished, as many as
came with Peter, because that on **the Gentiles also was poured out
the gift of the Holy Ghost.**
46 For they heard them speak with tongues, and magnify God. Then
answered Peter,
47 Can any man forbid water, that these should not be baptized, which have
received the Holy Ghost as well as we?"

The Romans in Europe are the Gentiles. There are *lots* more scriptures that point to
the Europeans being the Gentiles. Thus, the Christian Nations of Europe, **and the
nations they colonized** are the Gentile Nations.

Author's Analysis:
My take on all of these definitions are that The Israelite Nations are easy to define
as the Nation of Israel in the Middle East and the Land of Arsareth where the Lost
10 Tribes are dwelling. In addition, there are populations of Israelites all over the
world.

The Gentile Nations are the so-called western nations or Christian Nations.
Including: Europe, North America, South America, Australia, New Zealand, and
South Africa. There may be more areas.

The Heathen Nations are the rest of the world. Including: the Middle East, Africa,

---

and Asia generally. There may be more areas.

These are big sweeping generalizations. There are populations of different groups of people in many countries of the world, away from their homelands. So, these are not strict country or continent groupings at all.

I am attempting to make sense of the scriptures as the Lord has stated them. If you have more insight to get better definitions than what I have stated, please contact me at the website www.LastDaysTimeline.com

The Great Whore of All the Earth – Babylon the Great that Rides the Scarlet Beast, The Mother of Harlots, The Great and Abominable Church, The Tares

DISCLAIMER: This author makes it known to all the world that he does NOT formally or informally associate any Church with the Great and Abominable Church of the Devil or the Whore of All the Earth named "Babylon the Great" nor her Harlots.

Most people don't know that these names all represent the same entity. We will explore the identity of this entity below.

Nephi son of Lehi, as recorded in The Book of Mormon, shows an angel of the Lord giving a communication of the beginning of a Great and Abominable Church in Europe by the Gentiles. This is important to yet future prophetic events.

(1ˢᵗ Nephi 13:1-3)
"1 And it came to pass that the angel spake unto me, saying: Look! And I looked and **beheld many nations and kingdoms**.
2 And the angel said unto me: What beholdest thou? And I said: I behold many nations and kingdoms.
3 And he said unto me: These are **the nations and kingdoms of the Gentiles**."

Learning Points:
A. The Gentiles live in an area of the world with lots of nations. They are plentiful.
B. This part of the Angel's vision to Nephi was not part of the last Chapter 12 vision. This is something (or somewhere new).

(1ˢᵗ Nephi 13:4-5)
"4 And it came to pass that I saw **among the nations of the Gentiles** the formation of **a great church**.

5 And the angel said unto me: Behold the formation of a church which is **most abominable** above all other churches, which **slayeth the saints of God**, yea, and tortureth them and bindeth them down, and yoketh them with a **yoke of iron**, and **bringeth them down into captivity**."

Learning Points:
A. it is among the Gentile nations that this great church forms.
B. it is a "great church" or say large church. The angel of the Lord said this was a "church", not a secret combination organization, not a synagogue, not a general group of wickedness. We must admit that the word "church" was used. Lets not overlay our own Frame of Reference on top of this. Remember, this is the angel's language in heaven, not even Nephi's language.
C. THIS church is most abominable above all other churches
D. It has the power to kill people, and has done it. Also to tortureth them and bind them down in captivity or a form of slavery. This is no ordinary church of today. What church could get away with that in today's modern world? ANSWER: there isn't any. The governments of most Gentile nations have Freedom of Religion. We are looking at a **time period** that pre-dates the modern world. Back in a time when THE CHURCH was A STATE RELIGION. And the STATE had those powers over death of it's people. So, the real question is "WHEN and WHERE?".....and we are about to receive our answer.

(1st Nephi 13:6-10)
"6 And it came to pass that I beheld this great and abominable church; and I saw the devil that he was the founder of it.
7 And I also saw gold, and silver, and silks, and **scarlets**, and fine-twined linen, and all manner of **precious clothing**; and I saw many harlots.
8 And the angel spake unto me, saying: Behold the gold, and the silver, and the silks, and the scarlets, and the fine-twined linen, and the precious clothing, and the harlots, are the desires of this great and abominable church.
9 And also for the praise of the world do **they destroy the saints** of God, and bring them down into captivity.
10 And it came to pass that I looked and beheld **many waters**; and they divided the Gentiles from the seed of my brethren."

Learning Points:
A. The devil had personal business in founding this Great and Abominable Church.
B. The church leaders went after precious metals (money of the day), nice scarlet red clothing, and whores.
C. (v9) This church is separate than the lovers of Jesus Christ as the Saints of God. This wicked church actually binds them in a form of captivity. There are many forms of captivity: outright physical slavery, financial slavery with debt, state religion. I believe that the State Religion and persecutions of the Saints of God is on the right track....at this early time period we are viewing.
D. (v9 – "WHEN") Also the implication from "they destroy the saints of God", is that there must be Saints of God for this evil church to destroy. So, the logic flows that this is a TIME PERIOD when the Christian gospel was on the Earth. I believe that **the time** of the formation of the Great and Abominable Church of

the Devil was during the late persecutions of the Saints of God by the Roman Empire and the founding of the State Church of Rome by Constantine the Great.

E. (v10 – "WHERE") Lots of ocean water was between the nations of the Gentiles and the Americas, where the Lamanite seed was dwindling in unbelief. So, NOW we have fairly reasonable **location data** of this Great and Abominable Church of the Devil. I believe we are talking about Europe.

Author's Analysis:

Based upon the above evidence, I am led to the opinion that the Great and Abominable Church that the angel is showing to Nephi was created by the Gentiles in Europe at about 300-350 AD. It was a State Religion with power over death for those that believed differently than the State Religion.

At this same time and same place, we have a large State Religion being formed in the empire of Rome by Emperor Constantine the Great as the state religion of Rome and her lands; using the Edict of Milan in 313AD and the First Counsel of Nicaea in 325AD. Emperor Theodosius I made this new form of Christianity, the state religion of the Roman Empire in 380AD. Not general wickedness of the world. Not a secret combination. Yet a real church.

See:
1. https://en.wikipedia.org/wiki/Constantine_the_Great
2. https://en.wikipedia.org/wiki/Edict_of_Milan
3. https://en.wikipedia.org/wiki/First_Council_of_Nicaea

Once the First Counsel of Nicaea in 325AD is completed and the new Nicene Creed is established, the new **reformed Christian Church** is no longer persecuted as a whole. However, only the new state religion is condoned. The other believers of Christianity all over the Roman Empire that don't "kiss the ring" of the new religion's leader (Constantine), that is not baptized into the church until his death, are heavily persecuted and still killed. Much of northern Africa were Christians at this time and didn't like the new Roman brand of Christianity. Many were killed and tortured to repent. This torture and death was carried by the Roman Inquisition into the countries it controlled with religion.

In fact, after the Roman Empire fell, the nations that remained were part of the "Holy Roman Empire".

The Great Apostasy happened where true Christianity morphed into a false form of **state** mandated Christianity.

Visit the website www.LastDaysTimeline.com to get FREE audiobook copies of these resources to show what happened in this time period of European history:
1. *The Great Apostasy* – by James E Talmage
2. *Foxes Book of Martyrs* – by John Fox
3. *History of the Christian Church* – by Cheetham

Continuing with Nephi's account...

Summary: In 1ˢᵗ Nephi 13 verses 11 thru 19, The angel instructs Nephi that there will be a scourging of the Lamanites by those Gentiles from Europe. In the timeline, we see that one man comes first and then many multitudes of Gentiles come from Europe to the Americas. They were white. The Gentiles went forth out of captivity of the same State Religion that had them captive. The mother Gentiles had a war with the Gentiles in America. Miraculously, the weaker Gentiles in America won the war by the power of God. They were free from all nations.

The events that correspond to the timeline of events is the 1492 first sailing of Columbus. Then many more Europeans come as Pilgrims and Puritans. And the Revolutionary War with Great Britain against the 13 Colonies. We are now in 1776-1785ish in Nephi's Timeline. And the official United States of America is born as 13 Colonies and then we see more of what these Gentiles do and **why** they came.

(1ˢᵗ Nephi 13:20-23)
"20 And it came to pass that I, Nephi, beheld that **they did prosper** in the land; and I beheld a **book**, and it was carried forth among them.
21 And the angel said unto me: Knowest thou the meaning of the book?
22 And I said unto him: I know not.
23 And he said: Behold it **proceedeth out of the mouth of a Jew**. And I, Nephi, beheld it; and he said unto me: The book that thou beholdest **is a record of the Jews**, which contains the **covenants** of the Lord, which he hath made unto the house of Israel; and it also containeth many of the **prophecies** of the holy prophets; and it is **a record like unto the engravings which are upon the plates of brass**, save **there are not so many**; nevertheless, they contain the covenants of the Lord, which he hath made unto the house of Israel; wherefore, they are of great worth unto the Gentiles."

Learning Points:
A. The source of the Gentile humility before God and their knowledge of God came from this Book that proceeded out of the mouth of a Jew. The record of the Jews that contain the covenants of God and Israel and many future looking prophecies. This book is **the Bible** in no uncertain terms. Nephi even mentioned the word "BIBLE" in several prophecies in 2ⁿᵈ Nephi.
   a. Also the Old Testament is specifically mentioned because the plates of brass that Nephi went back to Jerusalem to get had much of the Old Testament. However, the angel tells Nephi that the plates of brass have more of the Old Testament than we have now.

Soon we will see what happened to the Bible by that Great and Abominable Church.

(1ˢᵗ Nephi 13:24-29)
"24 And the angel of the Lord said unto me: Thou hast beheld that the book proceeded forth from the mouth of a Jew; and **when** it proceeded forth from the mouth of a Jew it contained the **fulness of the gospel** of the Lord, of whom the twelve apostles bear record; and they bear record according to the truth which is in the Lamb of God
25 Wherefore, these things **go forth from the Jews in purity unto the**

Gentiles, according to the truth which is in God.

26 And **after** they go forth by the hand of the twelve apostles of the Lamb, **from the Jews unto the Gentiles**, thou seest the **formation of that great and abominable church**, which is most abominable above all other churches; for behold, **they have taken away from the gospel of the Lamb many parts which are plain and most precious; and also many covenants of the Lord have they taken away.**

27 And all this have they done that they might pervert the right ways of the Lord, that they might blind the eyes and harden the hearts of the children of men.

28 Wherefore, thou seest that **after** the book hath gone forth **through the hands of the great and abominable church, that there are many plain and precious things taken away from the book**, which is the book of the Lamb of God.

29 And **after** these plain and **precious things were taken away it goeth forth unto all the nations of the Gentiles**; and after it goeth forth unto all the nations of the Gentiles, yea, even across the **many waters** which thou hast seen with the Gentiles which have gone forth out of captivity, thou seest—**because of the many plain and precious things which have been taken out** of the book, which were plain unto the understanding of the children of men, according to the plainness which is in the Lamb of God— because of these things which are taken away out of the gospel of the Lamb, an **exceedingly great many do stumble**, yea, insomuch that Satan hath great power over them."

Learning Points:

A. The section was added to bolster the proof of the Great Apostasy. And to show WHO and WHAT the Great and Abominable Church is. This is the key scripture to DEFINE what entity is the Great and Abominable Church AND to state what they have done.

    a. The Great and Abominable Church of the Devil is NOT "general wickedness" as some LDS writers have stated.

    b. The Great and Abominable Church is a Gentile organization in Europe.

    c. The Great and Abominable Church has controlled the Bible and New Testament of the 12 Apostles of the Lamb. Thus, this is a not a Jewish Organization as some writers have stated.

    d. The Great and Abominable Church have changed the ordinances and stripped away parts of the Bible. They must have had control of the Bible in the "early days" to have the authority to strip it. They must have had the ordinances at one time to have the authority to change them.

    e. Remember: The Great and Abominable Church is a State Religion with powers over life and death.

    f. A great many Gentiles do stumble in doctrine and understanding because of what this Great and Abominable Church originally stripped out of the Bible.

    g. The Gentiles carry the Bible from Europe across the waters to the Americas.

Remember, we are focusing on the Who and Why of the Great and Abominable Church.

Note: How can we, the members of the LDS church, discuss the Great Apostasy that was so accurately documented by Apostle James E. Talmage, without discussing the history of the Roman **state** church?

Now, lets look at the links from Nephi's vision shown by an angel of God, to John's vision shown by an angel of God.

> (1 Nephi 13:7-8)
> "7 And I also saw **gold, and silver, and silks, and scarlets**, and fine-twined linen, and all manner of precious clothing; and I saw **many harlots**.
> 8 And the angel spake unto me, saying: Behold the **gold, and the silver, and the silks, and the scarlets**, and the fine-twined linen, and the precious clothing, and **the harlots**, are the desires of this great and abominable church."

>> (1st Nephi 14:10 – skipping around to focus on the language the Angels used to describe to Nephi and John of this Whore Church entity.)

> (1 Nephi 13:10-11)
> "10 And he said unto me: Behold there are save two churches only; the one is the church of the Lamb of God, and the other is the **church of the devil**; wherefore, whoso belongeth not to the church of the Lamb of God belongeth to that great church, which is **the mother of abominations**; and **she is the whore of all the earth**.
> 11 And it came to pass that I looked and beheld **the whore of all the earth**, and she **sat upon many waters**; and she had dominion over all the earth, **among all nations, kindreds, tongues, and people."**

>> (1st Nephi 14:16 – skipping around to focus on the language the Angels used to describe to Nephi and John of this Whore Church entity.)

> (1 Nephi 13:16)
> "16 And as there began to be wars and rumors of wars among all the nations which belonged to **the mother of abominations**, the angel spake unto me, saying: Behold, the wrath of God is upon **the mother of harlots**; and behold, thou seest all these things—"

>> (Comparing Revelations 17:1 skipping a few verses to focus on The Whore Church)

> (Rev 17:1, 4-6, and 15)
> "1 And there came one of the seven angels which had the seven vials, and talked with me, saying unto me, Come hither; I will shew unto thee the judgment of **the great whore that sitteth upon many waters**."

"4 And the woman was arrayed in **purple and scarlet colour**, and decked with **gold and precious stones** and pearls, having a golden cup in her hand full of abominations and filthiness of her fornication:
5 And upon her forehead was a name written, **Mystery, Babylon the Great, the Mother of Harlots and Abominations of the Earth.**
6 And I saw the woman drunken with **the blood of the saints**, and with the blood of the **martyrs** of Jesus: and when I saw her, I wondered with great admiration."

"15 And he saith unto me, The **waters** which thou sawest, where the whore sitteth, are **peoples, and multitudes, and nations, and tongues.**"

Learning Points:
A. The name of the Great and Abominable Church of the Devil is "Babylon the Great".
B. The Great and Abominable Church of the Devil is a Whore Church. As Jesus has his bride, this church is a whore, a false bride.
C. The Great and Abominable Church is the Mother of Harlots, and Mother of Abominations.
D. The Great and Abominable Church cares for gold, silver, precious clothing, and harlots
E. The Great and Abominable Church sits on many waters or people, nations, and tongues and is a worldwide false church of Christ.
F. This Whore Church dresses in purple and red.
G. This Whore Church loves gold, precious stones, and pearls.
H. This whore church has killed plenty of Saints of God in her days. Lots of blood. As we have seen in Nephi's time, the foundation of this church STATE religion of Rome killed many of the Christians that didn't believe the doctrine of this new church. AND as we have seen in our future to 2017, this church riding the Beast will kill many last-day Saints of God who were standing, as seen by John, in a Celestial Sphere and had overcame "The Beast, the mark of the Beast, and the number of his name."
I. The Whore Church = Babylon the Great = The Great and Abominable Church of the Devil. They are all one entity, described by 2 angelic visions to 2 prophets of God: Nephi and John.

Note: there are more references the Whore, Mother of Harlots, etc…in the next few chapters of 1st Nephi. The point has been sufficiently established.

Author's Analysis:
On the topic of The Great Whore – The Great and Abominable Church - Babylon the Great – Mother of Harlots, it would make sense too, that this entity is also a church, just like the Bride of Christ is his Church. Much more detail will come shortly.

Remember back to 1st and 2nd Nephi and his description, also from an angel sent from the presence of God? The angel used the same descriptors: Babylon, Mother of Harlots, Church of the Devil. Indeed this "Great Whore" IS A CHURCH.

The Book of Mormon does indeed add greater light than the Bible alone. I have read many books by church authors and non-church authors on this topic of "The Whore riding the Beast". However, not until the realization came while reading the scriptures from front to back with my own family did it click upon the entity of "The Whore – Babylon the Great".

I have read the theories of the authors of books in our modern age. Here are some:
1. The Whore –Babylon the Great is the secret combination of money powers that rule from behind the curtain of today's political super-structure.
2. The Whore –Babylon the Great is a general band of secret combinations.
3. The Whore – Babylon the Great are the principals of bad government foisted upon the world's citizenry.
4. The Whore – Babylon the Great is Islam
5. The Whore – Babylon the Great is general societal wickedness (ie. Babylon is "the World")

After reading all those theories it makes one's head spin as to the true nature of "The Whore" who is going to mount and control The Scarlet Beast kingdom with 7 crowned heads and 10 horns/The 4th Beast Kingdom of the Gentiles.

The answer is pretty good inside the John's Revelation itself. BUT, the firm concrete answer lays with Nephi. Man has been "speculating" about The Whore for 1000s of years, since this was written by John. But, only in the 1830's could the picture have become very clear; and it was the grand vision of Nephi that gave us the answer by a prophet of God in the Book of Mormon. (read the 1st section of this work again about **the formation by the Gentiles** of The Great and Abominable Church of the Devil)

Nephi's Great and Abominable Church of the Devil – The Mother of Harlots formed by the Gentiles, is the exact same entity as John's "Babylon the Great" – Mother of Harlots who is mounting the 4th Gentile Beast Kingdom.

Nephi stated that the rest of the vision he was viewing was recorded by the Apostle of the Lamb named "John". Linking their visions again.

<u>The entity that will ride the 4th Beast Kingdom is The Whore Church "Babylon the Great". THIS is the amalgamated STATE religion of the 4th Beast Kingdom.</u>

This is the entity that had the 4th Beast Kingdom severely oppress the Saints of God during the Beast's beginnings in America with the 3 Eagle Heads of Ezra's Eagle and early days of the Stout Horn/Anti-Christ, BEFORE the Lost 10 Tribes return to rescue the Saints of God - BEFORE the BIG Plague – BEFORE the 2nd American Civil War.

I do not pull punches; Let the evidence point the way and then draw conclusions based upon the evidence. I expect this of myself. I also feel this is a harsh statement. But, it doesn't matter how this author feels about it. The truth alone matters.

When I first joined the LDS Church many years ago, this statement in Joseph Smith History seemed very harsh as well:

(Pearly of Great Price - Joseph Smith History 1:18)

"18 My object in going to inquire of the Lord was to know **which of all the sects was right**, that I might know which to join. No sooner, therefore, did I get possession of myself, so as to be able to speak, than I asked the Personages who stood above me in the light, which of all the sects was right (for at this time it had never entered into my heart that all were wrong)—and which I should join.

19 I was answered that I must join none of them, for **they were all wrong**; and the Personage who addressed me said that all **their creeds were an abomination** in his sight; that those professors were all corrupt; that: "they draw near to me **with their lips**, but **their hearts** are far from me, they teach for doctrines the commandments of men, having **a form of godliness**, but they deny **the power** thereof."

Aren't most of these people in other Christian denominations good God fearing men or women? Aren't many of them willing to die for the Savior? It's NOT the people. It's the doctrine & leadership. The "creeds" or official doctrine is "an abomination" in Jesus' sight.

Remember, the angel showing John's vision and Nephi's vision used this "Whore – Babylon the Great", as a **symbol** for the Saints of God to recognize her riding the 4th Beast Kingdom of the Gentiles in the last days. If we as the Saints of God do not **correctly** identify this Whore symbol for what it truly is, we are going to miss the big picture. As this symbol of The Whore-Babylon the Great is **central** to the big picture of the 10 nation Beast Kingdom that will deeply oppress the Saints of God and martyr them in the LAST DAYS.

The more I defined the Whore Church of John the Revelator with Nephi's Great and Abominable Church, the scriptures began to open up. See Jesus' meaning of the parable of The Wheat and the Tares. Read the whole chapter, it's short, but focus in on this verse.

(D&C 86:3)

"3 And after they have fallen asleep **the great persecutor of the church**, the **apostate, the whore**, even **Babylon**, that maketh **all nations to drink of her cup**, in whose hearts the enemy, even **Satan**, sitteth to reign—behold **he soweth the tares**; wherefore, the tares choke the wheat and drive the church into the wilderness."

Then 2 sections later…

(D&C 88:94)

"94 And another angel shall sound his trump, saying: That **great church**, the **mother of abominations**, that made **all nations drink of the wine of the wrath of her fornication**, that **persecuteth the saints** of God, that **shed their blood**—she who **sitteth upon many waters**, and upon the islands of the sea—behold, **she is the tares of the earth**; she is bound in bundles; her bands are made strong, no man can loose them; therefore, she is ready to be

burned. And he shall sound his trump both long and loud, and all nations shall hear it."

This Whore Church named "Babylon the Great" **IS the Tares** in the Parable of the Wheat and the Tares. And she will eventually be burned with fire. Just as the parable says would happen to the Tares. This entity that murders the Saints of God in the early days and the last days, will be burned by the 4th Beast Kingdom of the Gentiles that she is riding.

There are lots more examples like this in the Doctrine and Covenants. However, for brevity, we will take up our next topic.

This author not the first person to think about the Whore Church-"Babylon the Great" and the Great and Abominable Church being the Roman **state** church. In fact, most of the early brethren and some of the later brethren knew this doctrine, stated the doctrine in writing to the church, and then were asked by the First Presidency to change their writings to a better tone.

> (Orson Pratt – The Seer 1853)
> "Q. Who founded the **Roman Catholic Church**?
> **A. The Devil,** through the medium of Apostates, who subverted the whole order of God by denying immediate revelation, and substituting in the place thereof, tradition and ancient revelations as a sufficient rule of faith and practice.
>
> Q. But did not the first Protestant Reformers receive their ordination and authority from the Catholics?
> A. Yes: and in this manner they received all the authority that **their mother church** was in possession of; and **the mother having derived her authority from the Devil,** could only impart that which his Satanic majesty was pleased to bestow upon her. . . ."

Orson Pratt was a mathematician and member of the original Quorum of the Twelve Apostles under Joseph Smith. The entire book of Apostle Orson Pratt was disavowed by the First Presidency in 1865 under Brigham Young for having "doctrines we cannot sanction." So, these are Pratt's OPINIONS and were not official church doctrine. However, it shows what was on the mind of one of the greatest scholars of the early LDS Church.

> (Bruce R. McConkie's 1st Edition of Mormon Doctrine)
> "It is also to the Book of Mormon to which we turn for the plainest description of **the Catholic Church as the great and abominable church.**"

The First Presidency pressed him to make changes to this portion of the 2nd edition of "Mormon Doctrine". The 2nd edition instead stated:

> (Bruce R. McConkie's 2nd Edition of Mormon Doctrine)
> "The titles church of the devil and great and abominable church are used to identify all churches or organizations of whatever name or nature—whether

political, philos'ophical, educational, economic social, fraternal, civic, or religious—which are designed to take men on a course that leads away from God and his laws and thus from salvation in the kingdom of God."

Again, these personal opinions of an Apostle in the Quorum of the Twelve Apostles are not doctrine. The ideas are simply a notion of what the brethren have on their mind. The brethren have made it clear there is no official position on the entity that is Nephi's Great and Abominable Church or John's "Babylon the Great" that is burned in the last days.

There are more strict guidelines set by the First Presidency that the Roman Catholic Church is not to be identified with Nephi's Great and Abominable Church of the Devil or the Whore Church "Babylon the Great" nor her Harlots.

> DISCLAIMER: This author makes it known to all the world that he does NOT formally or informally associate any Church with the Great and Abominable Church of the Devil or the Whore of All the Earth named "Babylon the Great" nor her Harlots.

Law of Consecration

The Law of Consecration/United Order is a law of the Celestial Kingdom. If the Saints are to abide there, they must willingly live this law to it's fullest. Brigham Young stated:

> (Journal of Discourses, 13:3)
> "If the people called Latter-day Saints do not become one in temporal things as they are in spiritual things, they will not redeem and build up the Zion of God upon the earth"

Some LDS authors proclaim that Joseph Smith's Law of Consecration was different than Brigham Young's United Order. This may very well be true.

The most researched and easy-to-digest sources on the Law of Consecration are:
1. "Approaching Zion" by Hugh Nibley
2. "The Cleansing of America" by W. Cleon Skousen. This book was published post-humusly by Skousen's family members after the 2008 financial crises.
3. "The Naked Communist" by W. Cleon Skousen. This book shows the wide difference between Communism/Socialism and the Lord's Law of Consecration

From these books is it learned that The Law of Consecration is voluntary. It is established at GOD'S command. Not the command of men.

Socialism and Communism is NOT the same thing as the Law of Consecration.

Communism uses the power of force (at the point of a gun) by the government to **TAKE** property from one and give it to another. Socialism is the exact same. Except Socialism comes to pass by being "voted in" by the people. Communism comes from a violent takeover of the existing government. The Law of Consecration is built upon voluntary action and is based upon charity/love.

The General Authorities of the LDS Church have warned against Communism/Socialism for centuries. (16-17 decades)

The Lost 10 Tribes Location

This topic of the Lost 10 Tribes has been the focus of many books, unto themselves. This small appendix portion, will only be a PRIMER.

What do we KNOW from the scriptures a few things about the Lost 10 Tribes:
1. The Lost 10 Tribes headed out of Assyria, going North for a many years.
2. They were led by prophets when they left, who were following the pillar of smoke. God was leading them; and God could have led them anywhere.
3. They were in a large body when they left, and they will be in a large body when they return.
4. They left and went to the utmost North. When they return they will come from the utmost icy North.
5. God will lead them by prophets again from the North.
6. Their return direction shall be from the icy North, to the North American continent, to the Everlasting Hills. To receive their blessings from the believing Gentile/Ephraimite Church of God.
7. WHEN – They will be returning just after the 2nd American Civil War/BIG Plague and before Jesus comes to the New Jerusalem Temple.
8. They live in a land called Arsareth.
9. John the Beloved/Revelator is with them and preparing them.

The above material points are the "knowns" of the equation. The "unknown" is WHERE are they building up their kingdom of Arsareth in the middle time.

Logic would tell us, that if they went to the NORTH in one body, and are going to return from the NORTH in one body, then they are probably still in THE NORTH in one body.

Some LDS writers have stated that the Lost 10 Tribes are dispersed among the nations and that we are gathering them with missionary work. The Lord had this to say to the Nephites at approximately 34AD. The Lost 10 Tribe's location was known unto the Father and Jesus would visit them as a group.

(3 Nephi 17:4)

"4 But now I go unto the Father, and also to **show myself unto the lost tribes of Israel**, for they are not lost unto the Father, for **he knoweth whither he hath taken them.**"

The Lost 10 Tribes were confirmed to be a distinct people hundreds of years after their escape from Assyria when the Savior visited them around 34 AD. In the book Articles of Faith by James E. Talmage, as included in the Missionary Library, had this to say:

(James E. Talmage, Articles of Faith, Chapter 18, page 340)
"From the scriptural passages already considered, it is plain that, while many of those belonging to the Ten Tribes were diffused among the nations, a sufficient number to justify the retention of the original name were **led away as a body and are now in existence in some place where the Lord has hidden them**. To them the resurrected Christ went to minister after His visit to the Nephites, as before stated."

They are still in one body, together, living their lives in a the cozy spot the Lord has hidden them. President Joseph Fielding Smith, in modern times, gives us even more details.

(Joseph Fielding Smith, The Signs of the Times, pages 185-186)
"First let us say something further about the restoration of the ten 'lost tribes of Israel.' Strange to say, notwithstanding all that has been written, <u>there are many members of the Church who think that these 'lost tribes' were scattered among the nations and are now being gathered out and are found through all the stakes and branches of the Church</u>. They reach this conclusion because the general opinion is that these tribes went into the North, and it is the northern countries from whence most of gathered Israel has been found. . . . Whether these tribes are in the north or not, I am not prepared to say. As I said before, they are 'lost' and until the Lord wishes it, they will not be found. All that I know about it is what the Lord has revealed, and He declares that they will **come from the North**. He has also made it very clear and definite that **these lost people are <u>separate and apart</u> from the scattered Israelites now being gathered out**. If this be not true, then the commission of Moses to the Prophet Joseph Smith is without meaning, wherein we read: 'Moses appeared before us, and committed unto us the keys of the gathering of Israel from the four parts of the earth, **and the leading of the ten tribes from the land of the north.**' The statement that the tribes are to be **led from the north** harmonizes perfectly with the words of Jeremiah (Jer. 16:14-15) and Section 133, verses 26 to 34."

Learning Points:
A. The Lost 10 Tribes are in one body as a distinctly separate and hidden people.
B. They will return in the same direction as they left, North.
C. The members of the church that think the Lost 10 Tribes are scattered and are being gathered by missionary work are not correct.

D. Moses' commission of Priesthood Keys to the Prophet Joseph Smith was to gather the scattered, **and** to lead the Lost Tribes from the North; as 2 different commissions.

E. As Moses appeared before Joseph Smith and Oliver Cowdery in the Kirtland Temple on April 3,1836, the Lost 10 Tribes were still in a distinct body at that point, as Moses singled them out "and the leading of the ten tribes from the land of the north".

The Lost 10 Tribes were in a distinct body:
- When they left Assyria.
- In 34 AD when the Savior visited them.
- In April 3, 1836 when Moses committed the Keys to lead them from the North.
- When they shall return from the North, yet future to 2017.

It is highly likely they are still in a distinct body right now in 2017. Living in a hidden location the Lord is reserving for a time to bring them forth.

There are only a few theories that have been postulated as to the actual location of the Lost 10 Tribes that make sense.
1. They went to a separate planet, somehow.
2. They are living in the North

There have been Joseph Smith "quotes" written in journals of members on BOTH sides of this fence. Literally, the journals are saying that Joseph Smith said both things. How odd!

The "Separate Planet" Argument

This argument was postulated by some of the early brethren surrounding Joseph Smith Jr. But, later amplified by books and materials that are more modern in nature. They claim the Lost 10 Tribes vanished similar to the City of Enoch that was translated. Joseph Smith's words were recorded by Bathsheba Smith:

> (Juvenile Instructor 27 page 344)
> "the ten tribes were **not on this globe**, but a **portion of this earth cleaved off** with them, went **flying into space**, and when the Earth reels to and fro like a drunken man, and the stars from heaven fall, **it would join on again**."

Eliza R. Snow wrote this in poetry:

> (Millennial Star 13:272, September 1852)
> "And when the Lord saw fit to hide
> The "ten lost tribes" away,
> Thou, **earth, wast sever'd** to provide
> **The orb** on which they stay."

W. Cleon Skousen believed this doctrine in the book "The Cleansing of America":

> (The Cleansing of America, Skousen p36)

"What did the Lord mean by the "great deep"? Is He referring to the depths of the ocean or the **depths of outer space**? If the Lord is referring to outer space, then perhaps a number of passages of scripture become more meaningful."

[Then Skousen goes on to reference 3 scriptures to elaborate upon the point of "they are on another planet in outer space"]

The postulates of the Separate Planet Theory have some problems to deal with:
1. Why did the Lord lead the Lost 10 Tribes of Israel for YEARS to the North, if he was to have them just hop to another planet?
2. If there was another "lobe" hooked to the Earth on the North, what happened to the other Southern lobe?
3. Is there any physical evidence at all, relating that the Earth had an extra "lobe" or two hooked to it at the North in the past?
4. Where would such a "lobe" go? How fast would it get there? Was this "lobe" just for the Lost 10 Tribes of Israel to ride to their destination? (how convenient a theory)
5. Why would the "lobe" from the far-away-planet return to the NORTH? Why not drop them off at the Everlasting Hills?

I do not buy this theory of The Lost 10 Tribes of Israel are living on "a Separate Planet". It COULD be this way, however I do not see any evidence at this time to support it.

The "Living in the North" Argument and Evidence

The main quote of Joseph Smith that the supporters of this theory give is by Benjamin Johnson, written in his autobiography:

(My Life's Review, Benjamin Johnson 1818-1905, p. 93)
"Sometimes when at my house I asked him questions relating to the past, present and future; ... one of which I will relate: I asked **where the nine and a half tribes of Israel** were. 'Well,' said he, 'you remember the **old caldron or potash kettle** you used to boil maple sap in for sugar, don't you?' I said yes. 'Well,' said he, '**they are in the north pole in a concave just the shape of that kettle. And John the Revelator is with them, preparing them for their return."**

Learning Points:
A. From the above quote, we see that really there are 9.5 Lost Tribes of Israel, because we know the whereabouts of Judah, Ephraim, and Manasseh. I *assume* this is what the statement is speaking of. It definitely may be something different.
B. The Earth has a concave portion that is shaped like a large caldron/kettle. Thus, it's deep and wide on the inside. Plenty of space for a large group of people to inhabit and grow for 2600 years.

Elder George Reynolds, in his 1895 book "Are We Israel?" had this to say:

(Are We of Israel?, 1895 George Reynolds, page 10)
"The Ten Tribes [are] hidden by Divine Providence **in the far off frozen regions of the north**, and environed by a **belt of snow and ice** so impenetrable that no man in modern days has reached them."

Orson Pratt also knew of this doctrine taught by the Prophet Joseph:

(Journal of Discourses, 18:23-26)
"I do know, from that which is reported by those who have tried to find a passage to the pole, that **there is a warmer country off there**.... There is **a tract of country around the pole, some seven or eight hundred miles in diameter**, that no man among the nations that we are acquainted with, has ever explored. But how much of that land may be fit for habitation I am not prepared to say, for I do not know. I know it would be a very easy matter for the Lord God, by the aid of great mountain ranges encircling them around about, to produce **a band of ice which would prevent other nation and people very easily reaching them**."

W. W. Phelps who wrote the LDS hymn "Praise to the Man" said this:

(a Letter from W.W. Phelps to Oliver Cowdery (October 1835) recorded in "Messenger and Advocate, vol 2, number 1, page 94)
There may be **a continent at the north pole**, of more than **1300 square miles**, containing **thousands of millions** of Israelites"

Brigham Young said this on the subject:

(The Journal of Wilford Woodruff 1867, vol. 6, p. 363)
"The nations will have nothing to do with the preparing of the way for their return. But when the time has come for their return, the Lord will do the work. <u>They are on a portion of earth separated from this globe in the north which cannot be seen from this earth</u>."

Learning Points:
A. The place where the Lost 10 Tribes are hidden has a band of snow and ice around it, that prevents people from getting there easily.
B. Yet, there is a warmer country up there of 700-800 miles diameter (or 1300 square miles)
C. There may be "thousands of millions" of the Lost 10 Tribes living there
D. The portion of the earth, cannot be seen by us, from this vantage point.

This "Living in the North" theory, was the main theory of the brethren of the church in the early days. However, from 1890s to 1940s, when the North polar regions were being well explored by dog sled, ship and airplane; with no findings of extra continents up there; the book writers of the church started to change to the different theory of "a Separate Planet".

But How Did the Lost 10 Tribes Get Into that North Polar Opening?

In the Church's Millennial Star publication on the 30th of March 1867 published from Liverpool England, there was a large article about the Lost 10 Tribes of Israel with much speculation by the Brethren. It was not doctrine but is a good example of what the early brethren were thinking about concerning the method of how the Lost 10 Tribes got into this land of the North called "Arsareth". They originally arrived there by the same means they will be returning from the North countries. The early brethren conjectured this as well.

> (Millennial Star, Vol. 29, No. 13, 30 March **1867**, p. 201
> http://contentdm.lib.byu.edu/cdm/compoundobject/collection/MStar/id/1077 1/rec/29)
> "We are told by Jeremiah and other Jewish Prophets, that they will return from the north. (Jer. 16: 15; also 31: 8.) consequently they must have been led in a northerly direction, and very probably passed between the Black and Caspian Seas, and continued through Russia to the extreme northern shore of Europe, which would bring them about 2500 miles to the north: but this could not be considered "a year and a half's" journey; indeed it would not be an average of 5 miles a day. From many intimations of ancient prophecy, **they evidently had a highway made for them in the midst of the Arctic ocean, and were led to a land in the neighborhood of the North Pole**. This region would be about 4000 miles north of their Assyrian residence; and could be traveled in 18 months time at an average of a little less than 8 miles per day."

(**Side Note**: on Page 202 of that same publication shows the early brethren still had the apocryphal Bible book of Esdras in their King James Version in 1867. They were quoting from 2nd Esdras 13)

This is the text that the early brethren were quoting in the Apocrypha.

> (2nd Esdras 13:40 in the Apocrypha)
> "40 Those are the **ten tribes**, which were carried away prisoners out of their own land in the time of Osea the king, whom Salmanasar the king of **Assyria** led away captive, and he carried them over the waters, and so came they into another land.
> 41 But they took this counsel among themselves, that they **would leave the multitude of the heathen, and go forth into a further country, where never mankind dwelt,**
> 42 That they might there **keep their statutes**, which they never kept in their own land.
> 43 And they entered into Euphrates by the narrow places of the river.
> 44 For **the most High then shewed signs for them**, and held **still the flood**, till they were passed over.
> 45 For through that country there was a great way to go, namely, of **a year and a half**: and the same region is called **Arsareth**.
> 46 Then dwelt they there **until the latter time**; and now when they shall begin to come,"

Learning Points:

A. The Lost 10 Tribes "got lost" because they escaped from the King of Assyria by being led by the Lord directly with signs for them to follow. It was the Lord's will that they escaped.
B. The Lord held back the river, so they could walk in it and not be tracked by the Assyrians
C. The Lost 10 Tribes wanted to repent and keep the Law of Moses.
D. They traveled 1.5 years to the North. That would put them in the WAY North.
E. They live in one big body in a land called Arsareth, where they will dwell until the last days.

This material lines up nicely with the Doctrine and Covenants 133:26-34 account of how they will return from the North in one body.

This is a DEEP rabbit-hole. The more this topic is studied, the deeper it goes. No pun intended. Start with YouTube.com. That may open your eyes. Then go to the books for the rest of the details. And always relate the material back to the scriptures.

The Ram and The He Goat Vision– Daniel 8

This vision of Daniel is a lesser known vision that isn't discussed much. It describes the rise of the Stout Horn/False Prophet/Gog of Magog. It even locates the PLACE of where he will rise from. Let us begin:

> (Daniel 8:1-4)
> "1 In the third year of the reign of king Belshazzar a **vision** appeared unto me, even unto me Daniel, **after that which appeared unto me at the first.**
> 2 And I saw in a vision; and it came to pass, when I saw, that I was at Shushan in the palace, which is in the province of Elam; and I saw in a vision, and I was by **the river of Ulai.**
> 3 Then I lifted up mine eyes, and saw, and, behold, there stood before the river **a ram** which had **two horns**: and the two horns **were high**; but <u>one was higher than the other</u>, and the higher <u>came up last</u>.
> 4 I saw the ram pushing **westward**, and **northward**, and **southward**; so that **no beasts** might stand before him, neither was there any that could deliver out of his hand; but he did according to his will, and **became great.**"

Learning Points:
A. NOTE: this "Ram and He Goat" vision of Daniel will be played out twice. Once early, with Persia, Media, and Greece. Only some of the bullet points came to pass during the first partial fulfillment. The second FULL fulfillment will take place in the Last-Days. So, everything we see here, is applicable directly to our future from 2017.
B. The Ulai River is in Persia, near the city Suhshan. (See http://biblehub.com/topical/u/ulai.htm). The Ulai River is in modern day western **Iran** above the town of Shush.

C. It appears that Iran/Persia will push to the North (Eastern Europe); to the South (Saudi Arabia); to the West (Iraq, Syria, Jordan, and …..**Israel).** But NOT to the East (Afghanistan, Pakistan).

D. Two horns are going to come up in Iran/Persia. Usually HORNS on Beasts, represent Kings in Nations. At least that is the common meaning we have read in many other scriptures. One horn/leader will come up first and it will be HIGH. However, the second horn/leader will be even higher.

E. (v4) no beasts/kingdoms will be able to stand against Iran/Persia as it really starts to exert force upon it's neighboring kingdoms to the North, South, and West.

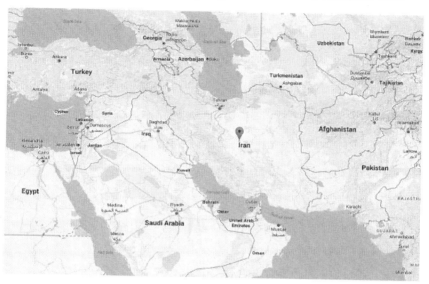

God's Interpretation:
Later in this same vision in Daniel Chapter 8; the angel Gabriel gives the meaning of the symbols:

> (Daniel 8:20)
> "20 The **ram** which thou sawest having **two horns** are the **kings of Media and Persia.**"

Learning Points:
A. The Ram is the nation and the 2 horns are the leaders. Of Media and Persia. Persia is Southern Iran and Media is Northern Iran. So, we are talking about modern day Iran. (See https://en.wikipedia.org/wiki/Persian_Empire)

Iran/Persia has a good run at pushing against it's neighbors as the primary AGGRESSOR. But, it will meet it's match from the big neighbor on it's West.

(Daniel 8:5-7)

"5 And as I was considering, behold, **an he goat came from the west on the face of the whole earth**, and **touched not the ground**: and the goat had **a notable horn** between his eyes.

6 And he came to the ram that had two horns, which I had seen standing before the river, and **ran unto him in the fury of his power**.

7 And I saw him come close unto the ram, and he was moved (Hebrew: enraged) with choler against him, and **smote the ram, and brake his two horns**: and there was **no power in the ram** to stand before **him**, but he cast him down to the ground, and **stamped upon him**: and there was none that could deliver the ram out of his hand"

Learning Points:

A. A He Goat nation comes from the WEST. This retaliation of the He Goat is a counter, from the PUSH that Iran/Persia was initiating first.

B. The He Goat has a BIG HORN. Most of the time, the horns are leaders. So, this is BIG STRONG leader.

C. The He Goat flies and doesn't touch the ground on it's counter attack. Thus, a flying counter attack.

D. The counter attack by the He Goat is a large group. Because the "He Goat" was on the face of the whole earth. That is pretty hard for a single man to do. But, not for a whole nation or group of nations.

E. There is a big battle. Just possibly near the river that is in Western Iran....near where Daniel was standing, north of the town of Shush, Iran.

F. If the Ram is Persia/Iran, then the 2 horns would be leaders of Iran. The He Goat breaks to 2 horns/leaders of the Ram.

G. The He Goat just destroys the Ram. Casting him to the ground, stamping on him, etc. It wasn't much of a fight.

Now.....the Ram nation is gone. What happens to an unstable region when the power dynamics change?

There is a vacuum and it must be filled.

(Daniel 8:8-12)

"8 Therefore the **he goat waxed very great**: and when he was strong, the **great horn was broken**; and for it (Hebrew: Instead of it) came up **four notable ones** toward the four winds of heaven.

9 And **out of one of them** came forth a **little horn**, which **waxed exceeding great**, toward the **south**, and toward the **east**, and toward the **pleasant land**.

10 And **it waxed great**, even to the **host of heaven**; and **it cast down some of the host** and of the **stars to the ground**, and **stamped upon them**.

11 Yea, **he magnified himself** even to the **prince of the host**, and **by him the daily sacrifice was taken away**, and the **place of his sanctuary was cast down**.

12 And an host was given him **against the daily sacrifice** by reason of transgression, and it **cast down the truth** to the ground; and it practised, and prospered."

Learning Points:

A. A He Goat nation (or alliance of nations) waxes great.
B. When this nation is strong, the BIG Horn breaks. So, the BIG leader is gone.
C. When the BIG leader goes down, 4 smaller leaders come up. THEN LATER, **THE STOUT HORN** OF DANIEL chapter 7/Gog of the land Magog/The False Prophet/The False Messiah, rises in one of these 4 kingdoms. The bad leader that is directly led by Lucifer; that eventually takes over the whole Gentile 4th Beast of Europe.
D. This little stout horn leader waxes great to the South and East and "toward the pleasant land". The direction of the pleasant land is unknown me.
E. This evil leader The Stout Horn, even destroys some of the "host of heaven". This could mean angels (not likely). But, it could also be a tie-in to God's Army that will attack the 4th Gentile Beast in the 5th and 6th Trumpet/Vial of John's Revelation.
F. This evil Stout Horn leader magnified himself in the face of the prince of the host....or the leader of the host of heaven.....or the army of God. Who is the leader of the army of God? Wouldn't that be Michael? And isn't the Ancient of Days to come in Daniel chapter 7? But, if we look at who is leading the Lost 10 Tribes of Israel, that would be John the Beloved/Revelator. So, we have a toss-up as to who it will be. I see that both interpretations have their strong points.
G. The evil Stout Horn takes away the Daily Sacrifice in the Temple of the Jews in Jerusalem. This is another reference that says the Temple of the Jews will be completed before the Battle of Armageddon.
H. (v12) There is a host (or army) given to The Stout Horn to attack the Jews in Jerusalem. And eventually after 3.5 years, the Stout Horn's army wins (for only 3.5 days) and casts down the truth IN the Temple....and commits the Abomination of Desolation upon the House of the Lord and his holy presence leaves the Temple. At least that is what this scripture sounds like is happening to me.

God's Interpretation:

More of the Angel Gabriel's interpretation of the elements of the Dream…

(Daniel 8:21-25)

"21 And the **rough goat** is the **king of Grecia**: and **the great horn** that is between his eyes is the **first king**.

22 Now that being broken, whereas **four stood up** for it, **four kingdoms shall stand up out of the nation**, but not in his power.

23 And in the **latter time of their kingdom**, when the **transgressors** are come to the full, **a king of fierce countenance**, and understanding **dark sentences**, shall stand up.

24 And **his power shall be mighty**, but **not by his own power**: and he shall **destroy wonderfully**, and shall prosper, and practise, and **shall destroy the mighty and the holy people**.

25 And through **his policy** also he shall cause **craft to prosper** in his hand; and he shall **magnify himself in his heart**, and **by peace shall destroy many**: he shall also **stand up against the Prince of princes**; but he **shall be**

broken without hand."

Learning Points:

A. The rough He Goat is the area of Grecia. The BIG horn is the main 1st king. The He Goat kingdom splinters into 4 parts. **The Stout Horn Leader comes from Grecia**. Where is Grecia?

B. (v22) it looks like 4 large factions stand up in this nation, after the BIG horn leader is gone.

C. (v23) and in the last times of this kingdom, when the people have been very corrupted, then this dark Stout Horn leader comes to power.

D. (v24) this Stout Horn leader has power from Satan, as the other scriptures surrounding this evil leader point out. Lucifer himself leads this man personally and communicates with him through evil revelation.

E. (v24) The Stout Horn leader will destroy the strong and holy people. Again, this is a reference to an attack on the Church of God in America…as already mentioned in many other scriptures. But, remember, this Stout Horn also attacks the Jews in Jerusalem. Lucifer is trying to wipe out all religions and force all mankind to worship him directly.

F. (v25) The Stout Horn leader will destroy people in "peaceful ways"….or by armed peace-keepers….or by peaceful intents.

G. (v25) The Stout Horn will stand up to the Prince of princes, but the Stout Horn loses. Now, we know that The Stout Horn will die on the battlefield in Israel at the end of the Battle of Armageddon, and be buried in Israel. That would mean that Jesus would be the Prince of princes. But, it could still also mean Michael/Adam. Or yet still John the Beloved/Revelator. The scripture doesn't give us a lot of clues to help us narrow it down.

This last scripture about the Little Stout Horn rising up with such a clear description of the same Stout Horn in Daniel chapter 7,….is how we know this a LAST-DAYS scripture, and NOT speaking specifically about Alexander the Great of the Greek Empire in earlier times. Many online Bible concordances have stated this. However, after Alexander the Great….then what?

- Did the Greek Kingdom break up into 4 parts, specifically? NO
- Did a little horn rise up and oppress the People of God? NO
- Did a little horn rise up and thrust down and trample the Host of Heaven? NO
- Did a little horn contend with the Prince of Princes? NO

Thus, this "Ram and the He Goat Vision" is a LATTER DAY scripture, just as Daniel Chapter 7 is a latter day scripture.

So, the big question is….Where is Grecia in modern days? (because that will tell us where the Stout Horn will come from. Lets look at the map.)

According to Bible.com, the Hebrew doesn't use the term Greece or Grecia, but the term Yawan or Javan. This is the name of one of the sons of Japheth, Noah's son. It is believed that this son Javan did inhabit with his kindred the islands of the Mediterranean Sea. Which would include the old kingdom of Greece. But, this very well could include anyplace around the Eastern Med. From Turkey, to Eastern

Europe, to Russia, anywhere in that area of the world. (See
https://bible.org/seriespage/7-kingdom-greece)

It could just mean another name for the Gentiles of Europe.
At this point, we know a little more, but not definite on the location of the Stout Horn, just yet.

Secret Combinations

This will be a fast primer on Secret Combinations. There are many excellent books and resources on this topic already. I will *not* give a lot of proof of the points in this section. The books and resources will provide ample proof. It is advisable to *all* reading this section to research this topic thoroughly. It is **vitally important** that you know the *truth* of this topic. It might not be pretty or easy to digest, but by learning the truth you will be set free.

List of Quick Facts About Secret Combinations

All Nations, Tongues, and Peoples have Secret Combinations

(Ether 8:20)
"20 And now I, Moroni, do not write the **manner of their oaths** and combinations, for it hath been made known unto me that **they are had among all people**, and they are had among the Lamanites."

They Have Been with Us from The Very Beginning of This World

(Moses 5:51)
"51 For, **from the days of Cain, there was a secret combination**, and their works were in the dark, and they knew every man his brother."

Secret Combinations are Satan's Main "go-to" Method of Corrupting the People by Getting Control of the Leadership of Society.

(2 Nephi 9:9)
"9 And our spirits must have become like unto him, and we become devils, angels to a devil, to be shut out from the presence of our God, and to remain with the father of lies, in misery, like unto himself; yea, to that being who beguiled our first parents, who transformeth himself nigh unto an angel of light, and **stirreth up the children of men unto secret combinations of murder and all manner of secret works of darkness.**"

The term "secret works of darkness" in the scriptures is another name for "secret combination." Also anytime you see the words "secret", "secret acts", "secret works", "works in the dark", "covenant with Satan", they can usually be applied to "secret combination." They are all synonyms.

The *leadership* of the people is what Lucifer is looking to control. If one has influence over the leadership, one has influence over the people. So, the goal of Lucifer is to get control of the leadership levels of society. The rich, the powerful, the government.

Note: The poor street gangs and organized crime syndicates do not have much influence, compared with **large producers** of **goods, services, commodities, media influence, and money**; also **government** officials that regulate the lives of the people.

(3 Nephi 7:6)
"6 And **the regulations of the government were destroyed, because of the secret combination** of the friends and kindreds of those who murdered the prophets."

The Point of a Secret Combination is to Be Able to Commit All Manner of Sin, Without Being Brought to Earthly Justice.

Including murder, sexual sin, theft, robbery, evil control and wielding of power over others, etc. without being punished on the Earth.

This is the main mission, to get gain and power through the use of **organized sin and** to have **no Earthly consequences** for it.

Every One of the Secret Combination Groups Have: Secret Words, Secret Handshakes, Secret Signs, and Secret Oaths Made One to Another.

(Helaman 6:22)
"22 And it came to pass that they did have their signs, yea, their **secret signs,** and their **secret words**; and this **that they might distinguish a brother who had entered into the covenant,** that whatsoever wickedness his brother should do he should not be injured by his brother, nor by those who did belong to his band, who had taken this covenant."

(Ether 8:20)
"20 And now I, Moroni, do not write the **manner of their oaths** and

combinations, for it hath been made known unto me that **they are had among all people**, and they are had among the Lamanites."

Secret Combinations are Parasitical by Nature. This is Their Achilles Heal.

The secret combinations *need* a host to feed from. Without a host to steal from, the combination dies off.

This was shown with the Nephite battles with The Gadianton Robbers secret combination in 3rd Nephi Chapters 3-6. At first, The Robbers were in the mountains and raiding (stealing) food, cattle, and property from the outlying districts of the Nephites. They were hauling this stash back to the mountains to consume. There were wars of protection against The Robbers. However, The Robbers were winning.

Lachoneous, Chief Governor of the Nephites, received an epistle from Giddianhi, leader of the Gadianton Robbers secret combination. In the epistle Giddianhi gave us a deep look into the thought patterns of secret combinations. It is recorded in 3rd Nephi 3:2-10.

(3 Nephi 3:7)
"7 Or in other words, yield yourselves up unto us, and unite with us and become acquainted with our **secret works**, and become our brethren that ye may be like unto us—not our slaves, but our brethren and **partners of all our substance**."

(3 Nephi 3:9)
"9 And behold, I am Giddianhi; and I am the governor of this **the secret society of Gadianton**; which society and the works thereof I know to be **good**; and **they are of _ancient date_ and they have been handed down unto us**."

Instead of succumbing to Giddianhi's demands, Lachoneous bravely plotted a way to beat The Robbers secret combination. Over the next few chapters, Lachoneous decided to "starve them out into the open." So Lachoneous amassed 7 years worth of provisions to the land of Zarahemla, a long way away from the mountains where The Robber's home base was located. With no plundered goods from the Nephites, The Robbers were helpless and weak. They lost and the Nephites won, because there was nothing left to steal. There was no host to feed on.

The Achilles Heal of needing a host, was proven true in recent times when the Communist secret combination was toppled in 1989-1991 in Russia's USSR. America outspent the USSR in the arms race and buckled their economy with a large debt to GDP ratio among other things. (See: https://en.wikipedia.org/wiki/Cold_War_(1985%E2%80%9391))

Secret Combinations are Operated on a Need-To-Know Basis, Only

There are levels within these secret combinations. Thus, the lower levels know very little, but the upper levels know the whole plot, mission, and goals. The lower levels are being duped into cooperation to accomplish the goals of the upper levels. The levels operate on a need-to-know basis to protect the secret overall plans at the top. (See *Strategic Relocation* by Joel Skousen at www.LastDaysTimeline.com/strategic-relocation)

The Evil People at The Very Top Levels Worship Lucifer as God.

The evil people at the very top of the levels – the pinnacle, receive their marching orders from Lucifer himself as he appears before them. They make promises with him and Lucifer makes promises to them for wealth, power, and ability to commit sin with no Earthly justice. Also, the false promise of the ability to commit sin with no Heavenly justice. This is the main oath with Satan that is talked about in the scriptures. The top people practice Luciferianism as their religion….just like Cain did. (See *Hiding in Plain Sight* by Ken Bowers. Also his audio presentations on YouTube.com)

This is the same oath binding process that Cain made with Lucifer to become Master Mahan, or master of the great secret.

> (Moses 5:31)
> "31 And Cain said: Truly I am Mahan, the **master of this great secret, that I may murder and get gain.** Wherefore Cain was called **Master Mahan**, and he gloried in his wickedness."

The Lord Says The Murdering and Sin That Happens Inside a Secret Combination is The Most Wicked Sin

Most of the church has been taught that individual sexual sin is the most grievous sin next to sinning against the Holy Ghost. However, consider how organized sexual sin and organized murder inside a secret combination where there is **no earthly justice** for those exact same acts would calculate. That situation would be worse.

> (Ether 8:20)
> "18 And it came to pass that they formed a secret combination, even as they of old; which **combination is most abominable and wicked above all, in the sight of God;**"

How Lucifer Works in His Earthly Kingdom

As you could imagine by the short fact list above….if Lucifer has people on Earth doing his bidding and worshiping him, they are in the form of a secret combination. This is how Lucifer is able to use the riches of the earth to buy up armies and navies as well as false priests who subject the people. Also kings as tyrants who rule with blood and horror. **THIS** is the method he uses to do it.

A Quick History of Secret Combinations in the World

1. The first secret combination on earth was that of Cain harkening to the leadership of Lucifer. This group was called the Mahanites. Cain was Master Mahan. (See

"The First 2000 Years" by W. Cleon Skousen)

2. This Mahanite secret combination grew huge before the Flood of Noah. This group was the main reason that the people were so wicked and there was much violence. They were wiped out in the Great Flood. (See *The First 2000 Years* by W. Cleon Skousen at www.LastDaysTimeline.com/first-2000-years). Enoch was called to actively preach against this secret combination of the Mahanites, before the Great Flood.

(Moses 6:28-29)
"28 And for these many generations, ever since the day that I created them, have they gone astray, and have denied me, and have sought their **own counsels in the dark**; and in their **own abominations** have they **devised murder**, and have not kept the commandments, which I gave unto their father, Adam.
29 Wherefore, **they have foresworn themselves**, and, **by their oaths**, they have brought upon themselves death; and **a hell I have prepared for them**, if they repent not;"

The Great Flood happened under Noah, Enoch's Great-Grandson, *after* the City of Enoch was gathered and taken up. The only thing left on the Earth was the giant Mahanite secret combination which was very violent. The wicked kill the wicked as they seek for power.

(Moses 8:27-30)
"27 And thus Noah found grace in the eyes of the Lord; for Noah was a just man, and perfect in his generation; and he walked with God, as did also his three sons, Shem, Ham, and Japheth.
28 The **earth was corrupt** before God, and it was **filled with violence**.
29 And God looked upon the earth, and, behold, it was **corrupt**, for all flesh had corrupted its way upon the earth.
30 And God said unto Noah: The end of all flesh is come before me, for the earth is **filled with violence**, and behold I will destroy all flesh from off the earth."

Once the City of Enoch was taken up, and Noah's family had prepared the Ark, **Lucifer had won**. All the righteous people were taken out of the population and now only Lucifer's secret combination oath makers were in charge of society. However, the Earth is God's footstool, so He wiped the Mahanite secret combination off the planet and into Hell. We see that Lucifer does *not* have power to save his evil oath making people from God's eternal judgment.

3. The Jaredites in the Book of Mormon were the next group of people in scripture to embrace Satan's direct leadership through a secret combination. Their whole civilization destroyed itself because of it. (See "The Book of Mormon" by God)

4. The Nephites/Lamanites in the Book of Mormon were also destroyed by Secret Combinations, attested to by Moroni in Ether 8.

5. Moroni gives a direct warning to modern day Gentiles in America (that's us) that we WOULD HAVE Secret Combinations and that we are not to let them get over

us in Government or the whole society would crumble down (See Ether 8:22-24). And as shown in Ezra's Eagle as America since 1929, we have had these evil people in place behind the scenes. **They are already above us**. Long before anyone reading this book was born. (See *The Creature from Jekyll Island* by G. Edward Griffin. See *Awakening to Our Awful Situation* by Jack Monnett)

6. What is the end-game for these secret combinations? Lucifer's end-game is to have massive influence and control over the Earth's people so that he can get them to sin. This is the same planned use-of-force he had from the beginning. However, when he gains that control of the Earth, the logical extension is the eradication of the people of God, so that all the remainder of the people will worship him directly as their god. This is what the 4th Beast Kingdom of the Gentiles with the evil Stout Horn leader who performs miracles by Lucifer's power will attempt to do.

Waking-up and Taking Action

One older church member, remembered Ezra Taft Benson and Spencer W. Kimball speaking against secret combinations; and for good constitutional government. He was annoyed that the Prophets and Apostles of God were speaking about "politics". However, the lumping of secret combinations into the *political grouping* in his mind **is not accurate**. Secret combinations are not about politics, they are using the *normal political system* against the people to maintain their power and expand it, toward global government. The US Constitution with it's God-given rights that are unalienable, is one layer of God's block on these evil people. Yet, they are eroding the God given constitutional protections fast.

> (Ezra Taft Benson, July 1972, Civic Standards for the Faithful Saints) "Now undoubtedly Moroni could have pointed out many factors that led to the destruction of the people, but notice how he singled out the secret combinations, just as the Church today could point out many threats to peace, prosperity, and the spread of God's work, but it has **singled out the greatest threat** as the **godless conspiracy**. **There is no conspiracy theory in the Book of Mormon —it is a conspiracy fact**.

> Then Moroni speaks to us in this day and says, "Wherefore, **the Lord commandeth you**, when ye shall see these things come among you that ye shall **awake to a sense of your awful situation**, because of this **secret combination** which shall be among you" (Ether 8:14.)

> The Book of Mormon further warns that "**whatsoever nation** shall uphold such secret combinations, to get power and gain, **until they shall spread over the nation, behold they shall be destroyed. ...**" (Ether 8:22.)

> This scripture should alert us to what is ahead unless we repent, because there is no question but that as people of the free world, we are increasingly upholding many of the evils of the adversary today. **By court edict godless conspirators can run for government office, teach in our schools, hold office in labor unions, work in our defense plants, serve in our merchant

marines, etc. As a nation, we are helping to underwrite many evil revolutionaries in our country.

> Now we are assured that the Church will remain on the earth until the Lord comes again—but at what price? The Saints in the early days were assured that Zion would be established in Jackson County, but look at what their unfaithfulness cost them in bloodshed and delay.
>
> President Clark warned us that "we stand in danger of losing our liberties, and that **once lost, only blood will bring them back**; and once lost, we of this church will, in order to keep the Church going forward, have more sacrifices to make and **more persecutions to endure than we have yet known**. ..." (CR, April 1944, p. 116.)"

The people of God want nothing to do with secret combinations. If you are in one, exit it now. Prepare for the future by aligning yourself with righteousness.

(Ether 8:19)

"19 For **the Lord worketh not in secret combinations**, neither doth he will that man should shed blood, **but in all things hath forbidden it**, from the **beginning** of man."

Study the modern secret combinations as they move toward the 4th Beast Kingdom of the Gentiles spoken of in the chapters on Ezra's Eagle. Prepare to see the 3 Eagle Heads come to active power in society. They will be moving Gentile society toward a more global government. So, that Lucifer may enact his final-end-game plans, through the evil Stout Horn leader.

Show your family's non-support of secret combinations by studying them and not participating with their **large productions** of **goods, services, commodities, media influence, and money**; also **government** officials that regulate the lives of the people. Prepare early by withdrawing your family from these large institutions of Gentile society, and substituting smaller institutions and wiser life decisions for your family instead. Vote with your wallet, your feet, and your media choices.

Note: I am being enigmatic with you, the reader, on this topic of *modern* secret combinations. Most readers can see these issues in the scriptures of the past. Less readers can see these issues in current *modern* day society right in front of their noses, as they interact with the branches of the *modern* Gadiantons everyday. The Gadiantons of today want it that way. Start reading to learn how deep this issue goes. **If you are to wake-up, this is your path...read the books.** YouTube.com will only help a little. The books on this topic will help a lot. Then you can make wise lifestyle choices for your family. Remember, they need a host to feed on. Deprive them of it for your family. (See book list on secret combinations at www.LastDaysTimeline.com/secret-combinations)

As stated earlier, getting a firm grip on this material of secret combinations is *absolutely vital* to your understanding of God's prophecy of the future, as it involves secret combinations.

The Stout Horn - Who is The Ultimate "Bad Guy" Who Leads the 4th Beast of the Gentiles? And What Are His Names?

The nature of this evil leader becomes the nature of The 4th Beast Kingdom itself. THAT is important.

The leadership at the top of a nation usually controls the direction of policies set by that nation. This is true in America. It is true in Great Britain, and other Gentile Nations at this time, 2017. There are no "direct voting democracies" in the world. Most of the Gentile Nations of Europe have a "Representative" form of voting for policies and governmental bills that will become *the law of the land*. The people elect their Representatives; and the Representatives VOTE. In some of the European Nations at this time, there are **some** appointment of leaders happening, but they are in the minority at this time.

In Germany's European Union in 2017, which is interpreted to be Daniel's 3rd Beast; the Representative Congress of the EU is already setup as the European Parliament. (See https://en.wikipedia.org/wiki/European_Parliament)

This European Parliament WITH IT'S EXECUTIVE (ie. President) which is elected from it's own Members, is already in place. This Parliament, sets some policy within it's member countries that cannot be changed by their LOCAL National Presidents and Congresses because of the TREATIES that they have signed, in the past.

(See https://en.wikipedia.org/wiki/Elections_to_the_European_Parliament)

"The two legislative powers of the Ordinary Legislative Procedure are **directives** and **regulations**."

"A directive **requires the member states** to pass the new law individually, a process called "transposition." The difference in the timing of completing transposition is the "democratic deficit.""

"A regulation **acts on all the member states** at once and is effective immediately."

This is how the EU VAT Tax came into being. (See https://en.wikipedia.org/wiki/Politics_of_the_European_Union)

This European Parliament and the Council of the European Union have finally matured. It took more than 50 years to bring us to this point. They have their own Executive Branch (President), Legislative Branch (European Parliament), Judicial Branch (European Courts of Justice), Central Bank, Legal Code, etc….And all of this was done by TREATY from the individual Member Nations.

These are the "nations of the Gentiles" that Nephi saw.

Author's Analysis:
When the 4th Beast is to be built, after the 3rd Beast goes down, as Daniel Says, it will be a combination of the first 3 Beasts, PLUS the Eagle as stated by Ezra.

The EU was built by the Gentiles from the late 1940s, after World War II, to today 2017. This is the exact same time that the 14 evil feathers/US Presidents have built America under the "behind the scenes" leadership of the secret combination Eagle Heads.

When the time comes for the 3 Eagle Heads of Ezra's Eagle to build the 4th Beast, which is an amalgam of the former 3 Beasts of Daniel chapter 7, with the Eagle of the United States of America, they will use the former institutions and build on top of them….and as always, taking more and more POWER from the people of those member nations.

So, the NEW 10 Nation 4th Beast will most likely have some semblance to the current political systems of the countries before it. However, as time goes on, it appears that more and more power will be vested in ONE MAN. Daniel's Stout Horn.

Remember, "necessity, is the mother of invention". These political opportunists don't want "to waste a crisis". When things are going good, "there is no need for a change". It's only when things are going badly that a "change" is needed.

So,…something MOST LIKELY will need to go very badly for a radical shift of blending the United States of America into the European Union. AND it must happen at the same time. For if America had a big problem, and the EU was going well, there would be no need to blend them. National Sovereignty would not be the issue. Most likely this is a FINANCIAL CRISIS that would need to take place.

The SOLUTION that these 3 conspiring Eagle Heads would "cook up" is the very same plan they have had all along, to merge America's power with the European Union's Treaty System of Government, with many DIRECT unelected leaders at the top, that can make rules for member nations without them having any say over it.

What Are the Names of Daniel's "Stout Horn" Leader?

Daniel Chapter 7 reveals that the "Stout Horn" ruler is LATE to the party. The 3 Eagle Heads of Ezra's Eagle have already built the global government organization of the Gentiles with at least 10 original Member States.

During this **TIME** of the 3 Eagle Heads from Ezra's Eagle, taking an ACTIVE role in creation of this 4th Beast, this is MOST LIKELY the time when the new money system would need to be created. AND the **TIME** that the Whore Church – Babylon the Great would have to "mount" the NEW 4th Beast.

AFTER the formation of the 4th Beast, a more powerful MAN comes to power. And he works "Dark Art Miracles" to mystify the world's populations. He takes down 3 of the former "kings" or leaders of the 10 Nation Beast. He also doesn't like the Whore Church riding HIS Kingdom. Remember, he is a man of "dark miracles of deception" as shown by John the Revelator

This MAN called the Stout horn will only last 3.5 years in the power of his office as "king or leader" of the Beast Kingdom. The mouth….of the Stout Horn….is the Antichrist MAN of John's Revelation Chapter 13.

Although John actually never uses the term "Antichrist", this is the term that the rest of the Christian World uses as a proxy for this MAN'S name. John uses the term "False Prophet" for the name of this MAN who is LEADER of the Beast Kingdom of the Gentiles.

>(Revelation 13:5)
>"5 And there was given unto him [the Beast] **a mouth** speaking great things and blasphemies; and power was given unto him to continue forty and two months [3.5 years]."

>(Revelation 19: 20)
>"20 And the beast was taken, and with him **the false prophet** that **wrought miracles** before him, with which he deceived them that had received the mark of the beast, and them that worshipped his image. These both were cast alive into a lake of fire burning with brimstone."

>(Revelation 16:13)
>"13 And I saw three unclean spirits like frogs come out of the mouth of **the dragon** [Satan], and out of the mouth of **the beast** [the 4th Beast Kingdom], and out of the mouth of **the false prophet** [the leader of the Beast taking orders from Satan]."

This Stout Horn shall not be a good person. He is the culmination of all the political intrigue and state-craft of all the ages, being led by Satan himself. What is his agenda?

Remember, Satan has always had a war with the Saints of God since he was sent down to the earth. His war in heaven is still ongoing. <u>His mission has always been to use the powers of Government against the Church of God.</u> (That would be a book unto itself)

This time is no different. Listen to the mission of this "mouthpiece" of the 4th Beast Kingdom...

<u>(Revelation 13:6)</u>
"6 And he opened **his mouth** in **blasphemy against God**, to blaspheme **his name**, and his **tabernacle**, and **them that dwell in heaven**.
7 And it was given unto him **to make war with the saints**, and **to overcome them**: and power was given him **over** all kindreds, and tongues, and nations.
8 And all that dwell upon the earth **shall worship him [the Beast]**, whose names are not written in the book of life of the Lamb slain from the foundation of the world."

And in Nephi 25:16, this is Nephi speaking of the return of the Lost 10 Tribes of Israel, with a marvelous work and a wonder to DIVIDE the children of men to choose the Church of God held by the Ephraimite Gentiles that DO BELIEVE. Or the STATE Church of Babylon the Great that is riding the 4th Beast Kingdom....AND he speaks of a **FALSE MESSIAH** that should come.

<u>(2nd Nephi 25:17)</u>
"17 And the Lord will set his hand again the second time to restore his people from their lost and fallen state. Wherefore, he will proceed to do a marvelous work and a wonder among the children of men.
18 Wherefore, he shall bring forth his words unto them, which words shall judge them at the last day, for they shall be given them for the purpose of convincing them of **the true Messiah**, who was rejected by them; and unto the convincing of them that they need not look forward any more for a Messiah to come, for there should not any come, **save it should be a false Messiah which should deceive the people**; for there is save one Messiah spoken of by the prophets, and that Messiah is he who should be rejected of the Jews."

<u>This MAN who works Dark Art Miracles by Satan's Power will deceive the people, even the people of Israel.</u>

In Daniel Chapter 8, recorded just 2 years after Daniel Chapter 7 with the 4 Beasts...Daniel receives the Vision of the Ram and the He Goat. This fierce Little Stout Horn King of the Last Days will rise up and...

(Daniel 8:10-12)

"10 And it waxed great, **even to the host of heaven; and it cast down some of the host** and of **the stars to the ground, and stamped upon them.**
11 Yea, he magnified himself **even to the prince** of the host, and by him the daily sacrifice was taken away, and **the place of his sanctuary was cast down.**
12 And an host was given him against the daily sacrifice by reason of transgression, and **it cast down the truth to the ground; and it practised, and prospered."**

In Daniel 8:23-25 – this is God's interpretation of the Dream of the Ram and the He Goat, about that MAN who shall rule the 4th Beast

(Daniel 8:23-25)

"23 And **in the latter time of their kingdom** [last days of the 4th Beast Kingdom], when the **transgressors are come to the full** [end of the Times of the Gentiles], a **king** of **fierce countenance**, and **understanding dark sentences**, shall stand up.
24 And his power shall be **mighty**, but **not by his own power** [it's Satan's power]: and he shall **destroy wonderfully**, and **shall prosper**, and **practise**, and **shall destroy the mighty and the holy people**.
25 And **through his policy** also he shall cause **craft** to prosper in his hand; and he shall magnify himself in his heart, and **by peace shall destroy many**: he shall also stand up **against the Prince of princes**; but **he shall be broken without hand."**

Learning Points:

A. This Stout Horn is one BAD GUY. He comes at the **END** of the 4th Beast Kingdom of the Gentiles. Also, around the time when the Times of the Gentiles are fulfilled....when they SIN against the Gospel....and ACTIVELY ATTACK IT and the Church of God. (just before the Civil war among the Gentile Kingdoms of the 4th Beast)
B. This King has a war-like fierce countenance and he uses Dark Sentences. This has allusion to those Dark Art Miracles that John and Nephi says the False Prophet will employ.
C. This LAST King/Leader of the 4th Beast will have much success in his state-craft.
D. He shall attack the Church of God.
E. It seems that he will "come in peace", then start to destroy.
F. He shall attack the "Prince of princes". This seems like the "Ancient of Days" as spoken 2 years earlier in Daniel Chapter 7. This could be Adam or John the Beloved/Revelator. Only time will tell which one.

Also in Daniel 8: there is a CLUE to the location of the "Stout Horn" Leader of the Beast...I am not looking at the whole vision here, just for clues on WHERE the "Stout Horn" will come from. (See Appendix 1)

(Daniel 8:8-9)

"8 Therefore the **he goat** waxed very great: and when he was strong, the great horn was broken; and for **it came up four notable ones** toward the four winds of heaven.

9 And **out of one of them came forth a little horn**, which waxed exceeding great, toward the south, and toward the east, and toward the pleasant land."

And more…in the interpretation by God of the Vision…

(Daniel 8:19-22)
"19 And he said, Behold, I will make thee know what shall be **in the last end** of the indignation: for at the time appointed the end shall be.
20 The **ram** which thou sawest having two horns are the **kings of Media and Persia**.
21 And the **rough goat** is the **king of Grecia**: and the great horn that is between his eyes is the first king.
22 Now **that [great horn] being broken**, whereas **four stood up for it, four kingdoms shall stand up out of the nation (Grecia)**, but not in his power."

Learning Points:
A. Lets follow this line of thought in the vision…The Ram has 2 horns which are the kings of Media and Persia (Media is northern Iran and Persia is southern Iran = the whole of Iran)
B. The rough He Goat is the king of Grecia (Grecia is the area, to the North West of Turkey. Today, this is Eastern Europe: Greece, Bulgaria, Romania, Serbia, Hungary, and a bit of Russia.) Eastern Europe/Russia takes down Iran.
C. 4 Kingdoms arise out of Eastern Europe/Russia (Grecia)…….
D. And out of 1 of these 4 Grecian new kingdoms rise the STOUT HORN, at the front of one of the dominant kingdoms.
    a. **(Author's Quick Analysis)** It appears from this passage that the Stout Horn rises from a section of Eastern Europe or Russia.)

In Ezekiel chapters 38-40 show the Battle of Armageddon that John saw. And here mentions the leader of the Armies that come up to the Battle of Armageddon as Gog, the leader of the land of Magog.

(Ezekiel 38:2)
"2 Son of man, set thy face against **Gog, the land of Magog**, the **chief prince of Meshech and Tubal**, and prophecy against him,"

Learning Points:
A. This man named GOG is the leader of the armies that come up to Armegeddon. Thus, Ezekiel is saying that the Stout Horn of Daniel 7 and 8 is the same as this evil leader "Gog of Magog". The names are synonymous. Two names for the same evil last-days leader. And there are yet more names for him.
B. This passage in Ezekiel 38 also shows WHERE this evil man will come from. Meshech and Tubal. There are many people, (too many blogs with good and proper map images to mention) that put Meshech and Tubal and even Magog itself… inside modern day **TURKEY**.

Author's Analysis:
When the bullet points are put together with the other scriptures in this series; it is clear that each Prophet of God saw this one evil MAN who leads the Beast Kingdom of the Gentiles thru the ages and called him by different names, including:

- The Stout Horn Ruler of the 4th Beast Kingdom in Daniel's writings
- The Antichrist/False Prophet in John's writings
- The False Messiah in Nephi's writings
- Gog of Magog in Ezekiel's writings
- The Assyrian in Isaiah's writings

He comes at the END of the 4th Beast. Right at the perfect spot on the TIMELINE...when the Gentiles shall "sin against my gospel"....and the Times of the Gentiles be fulfilled. This is the moment. This is the spot in the TIMELINE when the missionaries are called home from the Gentiles...and the attacks start upon the Church of God by the Whore Church – Babylon the Great who is riding the 4th Beast Kingdom.

Wow. And this False Prophet who is the Leader of the Beast Kingdom, is the turning point in the TIMELINE. He turns up the heat on the Saints of God and oppresses them to the max....UNTIL the Civil war starts within the Beast Kingdom itself. This Stout Horn Leader is a "supernatural" character. He makes miracles in the sight of men. He won't like to be ridden by the STATE Church of the Beast Kingdom.

Remember, this False Prophet/Stout Horn evil leader comes at the END of the 4th Beast Kingdom and only rules 3.5 years total. That is not a lot of time to get through the Persecution Phase, have the Trumpets and Vials of Revelation hurled at Europe, and have the final gathering and Battle of Armageddon where he dies on the Israel's mountains next to the battlefield.

Turkey, Russia, or Europe

I have read many prophecy books and opinions, that the Stout Horn/Antichrist ruler of the 4th Beast Kingdom will come from Russia. And it VERY WELL could be that way.

I do not take a stance on the location the last Ruler of the Beast will come from. But, I would like to be thorough in this discussion with the evidence at hand.

Today 2017, Turkey is a Muslim country. This might be related to the beheadings of the Saints of God that were seen by John in the Celestial Kingdom of those who overcame The Beast. This would also make sense that the Muslims would HATE the Jews in Israel and want to push them into the sea, during the Battle of Armageddon. This would also make sense that the Muslims would want to do-away with the presiding STATE Church of the Beast if that church was decidedly Christian in nature, thus a civil war.

He may even be a man that was born in Turkey and grew up in Russia or Eastern Europe. Remember, the scribes of the Jews had a hard time pinpointing where the

Messiah would come from because of the writings of different earlier prophets speaking of different locations. It was confusing to them to properly read prophecy of the future. And so it goes with us.

There is much evidence on both sides of this discussion. I do not think it matters very much about WHERE he comes from. Just that he comes at the right TIME in our TIMELINE...and what he DOES with The Beast Kingdom that is in his control.

Fortunately, We Do Know WHEN, HOW, and WHERE He DIES. It is recorded in Ezekiel 39.

> (Ezekiel 39:2-4)
> "2 And I will turn thee back, and leave but the sixth part of thee, and **will cause thee to come up from the north** parts, and **will bring thee upon the mountains of Israel**:
> 3 And I will smite thy bow out of thy left hand, and will cause thine arrows to fall out of thy right hand.
> 4 **Thou shalt fall upon the mountains of Israel**, thou, and all thy bands, and the people that is with thee: I will give thee unto the ravenous birds of every sort, and to the beasts of the field to be devoured."

And more...

> (Ezekiel 39:11-12)
> "11 And it shall come to pass in that day, that **I will give unto Gog a place there of graves in Israel, the valley** of the passengers on the east of the sea: and it shall stop the noses of the passengers: and **there shall they bury Gog and all his multitude**: and they shall call it The valley of Hamon-gog.
> 12 And seven months shall the house of Israel be burying of them, that they may cleanse the land."

Learning Points:
A. This Stout Horn/Gog from Magog will be brought by the Lord to witness the battle 1st hand. Not in his homeland of the North, but AT the battlefield on the top of mountain overlooking the scene. Just like a General would be doing.
B. The Stout Horn/Gog will be killed at the end of the Battle of Armageddon and will be buried in a valley with all his army....after they are eaten by the birds as the "Supper of the Great God"

Thus, the end of The Stout Horn/Gog...and the very end of the 4th Beast Kingdom of the Gentiles with him.

Nebuchadnezzar`s Dream of the Giant Statue Broken by the Rock Without Hands

This dream of Nebuchadnezzar's that was interpreted by Daniel is somewhat important to our Last Days Timeline. BUT, since it is applicable only at the end of the vision, it was not included in the main timeline of the book. It would have reached too far back in time. We will consider it here in the Appendix 1. Let us begin.

The first section of this scripture in Daniel Chapter 2 tells the readers that Nebuchadnezzar chose to TEST his own staff of magicians, astrologers, and sorcerers to READ HIS MIND. They obviously could not do it, except for Daniel, a slave in Babylon. Daniel praises God for saving their lives by showing him the vision that the King had.

> (Daniel 2:31-33)
> "31 Thou, O king, sawest, and behold a great image. This great image, whose brightness was excellent, stood before thee; and **the form thereof was terrible.**
> 32 This image's **head was of fine gold,** his **breast and his arms of silver,** his **belly and his thighs of brass,**
> 33 His **legs of iron,** his **feet part of iron and part of clay.**"

Learning Points:
A. The giant statue image was that of a man.
   a. Head was gold.
   b. Chest and arms was silver.
   c. Belly and upper legs were brass.
   d. Lower legs (calves) were iron
   e. Feet were iron mixed with clay

> (Daniel 2:34-35)
> "34 Thou sawest till that **a stone** was cut out without hands, which **smote the image upon his feet** that were of iron and clay, and brake them to pieces.
> 35 Then was the iron, the clay, the brass, the silver, and the gold, broken to pieces together, and became like the chaff of the summer threshingfloors; and the wind carried them away, that **no place was found for them:** and **the stone that smote the image became a great mountain,** and filled the whole earth."

Learning Points:
A. The King watched the vision develop until a stone cut without human hands smashed into THE FEET. Then the stone broke up the entire rest of the statue.
B. The winds came and carried away the pieces of the statue entirely with no place for them to be found.
C. The stone itself grew into a great mountain and filled every land of the earth.

Now for God's interpretation of the Dream of King Nebuchadnezzar.

(Daniel 2:36-38)

"36 This is the dream; and we will tell **the interpretation** thereof before the king.

37 Thou, O king, art a king of kings: for the God of heaven hath given thee a kingdom, power, and strength, and glory.

38 And wheresoever the children of men dwell, the beasts of the field and the fowls of the heaven hath he given into thine hand, and hath made thee ruler over them all. **Thou art this head of gold."**

Learning Points:

A. The kingdom of Babylon under King Nebuchadnezzar II in 603BC is the 1st Kingdom Head of Gold.
  a. This is the same King of Babylon that sacked Jerusalem and took the Jews prisoners, destroyed the Temple of Solomon, and constructed the Hanging Gardens of Babylon. The same King of Babylon that Lehi and Ishmael's family escaped by leaving to the Americas. (See https://en.wikipedia.org/wiki/Nebuchadnezzar_II)

The kingdoms will break down and become less powerful over time.

(Daniel 2:39)

"39 And after thee shall arise another [silver] kingdom inferior to thee, and another third kingdom of brass, which shall bear rule over all the earth."

Learning Points:

A. Most prophecy writers consider the Silver 2nd kingdom as the Persian Empire.
B. And the Brass 3rd kingdom as the Greek Empire starting with Alexander the Great conquering Persia around 332BC

NOTE 1: We have 3 kingdoms moving through time. AND that they start and stop almost together. Babylon was taken down by Persia. Persia was taken down by Greece. BUT.....if this 4th kingdom is a LAST DAYS kingdom, there is a BIG JUMP IN TIME.

NOTE 2: This whole statue image has only 4 kingdoms; NOT 5. The iron legs and the iron+clay feet and toes were of the same kingdom, but that it morphed over time.... in the same area of land in the world.

NOTE 3: The 4 kingdoms move through time. The head is earliest, and the feet are latest.

(Daniel 2:40-43)

"40 And the **fourth kingdom** shall be **strong as iron**: forasmuch as iron breaketh in pieces and subdueth all things: and as iron that breaketh all these, **shall it break in pieces and bruise.**

41 And whereas thou sawest the **feet and toes, part of potters' clay, and part of iron**, the **kingdom shall be divided**; but there shall be in it of **the strength of the iron**, forasmuch as thou sawest the iron mixed with miry

clay.
42 And as the **toes of the feet were part of iron, and part of clay,** so the kingdom shall be **partly strong, and partly broken.**
43 And whereas thou sawest **iron mixed with miry clay,** they shall **mingle themselves** with the seed of men: but **they shall not cleave one to another,** even as iron is not mixed with clay."

Learning Points:
A. The Iron 4th Kingdom is very hard. It breaks and bruises other kingdoms. It conquers and subdues other kingdoms. This 4th kingdom is aggressive to it's neighbors. This qualifies for ROME as the 4th kingdom. There may be others identifications. Go to www.LastDaysTimeline.com to contact me.
B. As time goes by, we exit the solid iron part of Rome's legs, and we split into iron mixed with clay feet. This would represent the Byzantine Empire of Europe - time period of 600AD. Partly strong and partly broken.
C. Then to the Iron and MIRY Clay Toes that don't mix together, would be the classical nations of Europe today. Wow, that brings us right to the modern age….**in the last-days.**

> (Daniel 2:44-45)
> "44 And **in the days of these kings** [the toes] shall the **God of heaven set up a kingdom,** which shall never be destroyed: and the kingdom shall not be left to other people, but **it shall break in pieces and consume all these kingdoms,** and it shall stand for ever.
> 45 Forasmuch as thou sawest that the stone was cut out of the mountain without hands, and that it brake in pieces the iron, the brass, the clay, the silver, and the gold; the great God hath made known to the king what shall come to pass hereafter: and the dream is certain, and the interpretation thereof sure."

Learning Points:
A. In the days of these kings of the broken down European Nations….The Kingdom of God is to be created by God Himself.
B. The political Kingdom of God we know as the Nation of Zion, shall eventually consume and absorb all the nations on Earth.

This is it. The simple version of the interpretation of Nebuchadnezzar's Dream. We have seen that in the Timeline portion of this work that Gentile Europe is indeed the problem that will need to be handled by God to usher in Christ's 1000 year millennium.

The Rapture Doctrine and "The Callout"

The doctrine of the "Rapture of the Church" is believed by many non-LDS Christians. Even in the mass of Christianity, this doctrine is controversial. It is included in this work, as a reference point only.

They look to the prophecies in the Book of Revelation and think that they are so bad, that God would not want his righteous Christians living through it, so God would "rapture" them away in the blink of an eye. 2 will be grinding at the wheel and one will be taken. Etc....

https://en.wikipedia.org/wiki/Rapture *

There is no place for the Pre-Tribulation Rapture Doctrine in the LDS talks by the General Authorities of the LDS Church.

In and of itself, the doctrine is quite new. It appears on the Christian scene in the early 1830s.

HOWEVER, there is a variation of the doctrine that is quite legitimate for the LDS faith. Lets look at it.

(JST Luke 17:36-40)
"36 And they answered and said unto him, **Where, Lord, shall they be taken**?
37 And he said unto them, Wheresoever **the body** is gathered; or, in other words, whithersoever **the saints are gathered**, thither will the eagles be gathered together; or, thither will **the remainder be gathered** together.
38 This he spake, signifying the **gathering of his saints**; and of **angels descending and gathering the remainder unto them**; the **one from the bed**, the **other from the grinding**, and the **other from the field**, whithersoever he listeth.
39 For verily there shall be new heavens, and a new earth, wherein dwelleth righteousness.
40 And there shall be no unclean thing; for the earth becoming old, even as a garment, having waxed in corruption, wherefore it vanisheth away, and the footstool remaineth sanctified, cleansed from all sin."

Learning Points:
A. Joseph Smith translated the New Testimate quite differently than the way the King James scholars did.
B. This is a scripture to say that where the majority of the Saints are Gathered (probably to Utah or the New Jerusalem as these locations hold the greatest numbers of members.), the Angels will move people and stuff FROM other parts of the world TO the main gathering places of the Saints of God.
C. Notice the listing of activities of the people when this occurs: while sleeping, while working, while farming. It seems that when this Angelic Gathering takes place, it will be very quick. The Saints of God themselves won't be prepared for it; obviously on one side of the world, they will be **SLEEPING** when it happens.
D. I do not think that there is much to be prepared for here, OTHER than personal righteousness.

E.   The TIMELINE of this event is very uncertain. So, there is no need to place it into the main Timeline unless more evidence comes to light.

The "Callout" and Going "Righteous Camping"

The "callout" idea among Latter-Day Saints is an interesting point. The idea goes like this:
- The bad times are going to happen across the whole earth.
- The Church has places prepared to house the righteous Saints to give God's special protection

There are some problems with these ideas. However, they could come to pass under certain conditions. Here is what I can see at this time:

1. An economic downturn, no matter how harsh would not justify "going camping" in the wilderness of Utah through the winter.
2. A massive persecution by the Government would not be the reason the righteous would get "called out" of the population to go "camping". The Government would most likely find those locations. Unless a pure miracle of God would protect the locations.
3. The 2nd American Civil War would not justify "going camping". As this civil war would be started by God for the pure purpose of keeping the Government busy and not attacking the Saints of God.
4. The BIG Plague – This may justify a "callout to go camping". But usually a quarantine condition of being in separate houses would be better at containing a plague. Not the joint living areas of the wilderness. But, it is still possible under this condition.
5. A giant earthquake in utah – This may justify a "callout to go camping". But, only if it was known by the prophets ahead of time and instructed to the people ahead of time. As, *after* the quake, the services needed (gas and roads) would not be available to move the cargo needed to the camping site.
6. After these events, would be the return to Jackson County to build Zion. Thus not a "Callout camping" condition. The Trumpets and Vials of John's Revelation come **AFTER** the 144,000 young High Priests are sent out to preach from the New Jerusalem Temple in Jackson County.

Remember, most of the "callout" and "going righteous camping" ideas are coming from the modern dreams and visions book authors.

The real "callout" happens when the new Nation of Zion is established and the call goes out to the righteous of the world to come and gather.

The Ron Wyatt Discoveries

Ron Wyatt (1933-1999) was a plain man. However, he loved his scriptures. He read them everyday. And he wanted to see all these things in the Bible for himself. So, he traveled to the Holy Land and the regions round-about for nearly 25 years.

Ron Wyatt was coined as "The Real Indiana Jones". He spent many years searching the Middle East for artifacts as an armature archeologist. He found much. This is very relevant to the Last Days TIMELINE because Ron was told by an angel that his discoveries would be valid and come to much light in the days of the Mark of the Beast....Which comes in the 4th Beast Kingdom of the Gentiles. Since the discoveries are so utterly FANTASTIC and REAL, they are valid source materials to be quoted for this work. Enjoy

Ron Wanted to Find the REAL Noah's Ark

Instead of climbing Mt Ararat in Turkey and looking for it, like everybody else does; he prayed and asked God to locate it. God made the taxi driver's cab break down in just the right 3 spots.

God showed him 3 specific spots that helped with locating the evidence of the REAL Noah's Ark in Turkey.
1. The first time his taxi "broke down" was on the road in a mountain next to Mt. Ararat. It was the location of Noah's Ark
2. The second time the taxi "broke down" was at the location of the Drogue Stones that weighted the ark in the water and kept it from capsizing.
3. The third location the taxi "broke down" was at the remnants of Noah's stone house. And Mrs. Noah was buried in the yard. She was 18 foot tall. Aparently humans grew a lot taller and older before the Great Flood.

The ark site came complete with: metal rivets, petrified timbers, drogue stones, petrified cat hair, petrified dung, and petrified antlers. Just what you would expect at Noah's Ark.

Apparently, the real Noah's Ark was an ancient tourist destination for the early Christians and Jews. It was lost only to modern man. However, the nation of Turkey has now put up a Tourist Center near the Ark to show the discovery to the world. This archeological site is significant for the Christans, Muslims, and Jews.

The video detailing this information is available FREE at www.LastDaysTimeline.com/noahs-ark . Come and see for yourself.

Ron Wyatt Found the REAL Sodom and Gomorrah

They are located along the Western Edge of the Dead Sea. This area now is a great white dusty salt area, where nothing grows. However, the houses and buildings of the people can still be found. Including burned human bones encrusted in limestone, that was caused by burning sulfur that fell from the sky.

I own a piece of pure 99.8% sulfur that fell upon this area and burned the cities of Sodom and Gomorrah. This pure 99.8% sulfur fell as white hot brimstone hail. The sulfur is so pure, that no other natural sulfur deposit on Earth matches it's purity. Thus, this didn't come from Earth. It came from the stars. Just as God's Word has said.

This same sort of occurrence is to happen upon the 4th Beast Kingdom of Gentile Europe during the 7 Trumpets/Vials of John.

The video detailing this discovery is available free on the website www.LastDaysTimeline.com/sodom-and-gomorrah

Ron Wyatt Discovered THE Exact Location the Israelites Crossed the Red Sea

The Israelites were held in Egypt for many years. The exact dates are in question. However, there was a prophecy by Joseph that stated that a man would be raised up named "Moses" to release them from bondage.

In due time, Moses was raised up and did lead them out of the land of Egypt. However, many professional archeologists today claim that the Israelites were never in Egypt and that there was no Moses.

Remember Egypt is a Muslim nation and the Jews in Israel today are not well liked by Egypt. There was even a short war between Egypt and Israel. So, the controversy continues. But, what if there was physical evidence to substantiate the Hebrew scriptures?

Ron Wyatt went to Egypt to look for that evidence. While he was there, he discovered exactly how the Pyramids were made. It wasn't aliens. It was plain "simple machines" like we find in physics class put to good use. See www.LastDaysTimeline.com/red-sea-crossing

The key to finding where the place where the "Red Sea" crossing happened, was to find where the Israelites started from. By using the scriptures, Ron Wyatt found the starting place and the ending place of the "Red Sea" crossing on the Gulf of Aqaba on the East side of the Sinai Peninsula.

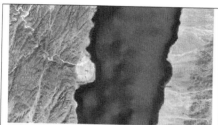

Neweibaa Beach on the Gulf of Aqaba today. The ocean boarder between Egypt and Saudi Arabia

Premier discovery at the site was a gold 4 spoked chariot wheel

The trail of artifacts of broken Egyptian chariots, chariot wheels from the time period, and human bones inside coral, were strewn across the sea floor from one side to the other in a straight path.

From the image above, notice the small wadi, that empties onto the Beach from the Left. That is the place that Pharaoh's armies were hemmed-in and the fire/smoke of God restricted their access to the beach, until the Israelites had cleared the other side, into the Saudi Arabian desert.

There were Israelite Marker Pillars found on both sides of this sea trench to mark the crossing location, just as it said in scripture.

See the whole story here www.LastDaysTimeline.com/red-sea-crossing

If the Red Sea Crossing led to Saudi Arabia, Then Mount Sinai Would Also be in Modern Day Saudi Arabia

Ron Wyatt simply continued to follow the trail of the Israelites into Saudi Arabia. The Saudi Arabian authorities arrested Ron and his 2 sons in the 1980s. He was set free after several months and brought back the pictures of what he had found.

He found that the largest mountain in North West Saudi Arabia currently named by the Saudis to be "Jabal al-Lawz" was indeed Mount Sinai for ancient Israel.
- Where the 10 commandment tablets were carved out by the finger of God.
- Where the golden calf was created.
- Where the laws of animal sacrifice were given.
- Where the Ark of the Covenant was molten of Gold.
- Where the 1st Israelite Temple in the Wilderness was created and carried forth.

Mount Sinai = Jabal Al Lawz in Saudi Arabia

Large cracked rock with water erosion on its base.

Jabal al-Lawz is relatively close to the Neweibaa Beach "Red Sea Crossing" was located. The site contains Hebrew symbols and writing, and a large alter where the golden calf (Egyptian Idol) sat. Also containing bull symbols of the Egyptian god.

Also on the way to the Mountain of God-Mount Sinai, was the Wilderness of Sin where the Manna was first given. The giant rock split in half by Moses' rod with water pouring out onto the desert floor is also present with evidence.

Mount Sinai was also blackened on top where the presence of God put the mountain on fire.

This means that the desert wanderings for 40 years of the Israelites were in the deserts of modern day Saudi Arabia.

Much more evidence than this was found. See the video on the site for the most information. www.LastDaysTimeline.com/mount-sinai

The Greatest Discovery of All by Ron Wyatt

After discovering Noah's Ark, the location of the cities of Sodom and Gomorrah, the Israelite's Red Sea crossing point, and Mount Sinai being in the location the Bible directed it would be in.....Ron spent the next 7 years of his life excavating in one spot in Jerusalem for the Ark of the Covenant.

In the excavation area, named "Jeremiah's Grotto" after several seasons of digging a series of small tight caves were found and excavated out from loose stone that had been poured into them for concealment long ago.

After much work, the caves were excavated and Ron was able to crawl into a further chamber and make the discovery.

The Ark of the Covenant was located inside a large stone box the size of a small car. The rest of the temple elements of tables and candlesticks were present. The stone box had been cracked on the lid. There was an adjacent crack on the top of the cave above the box.

There was dark black liquid residue that had dried on the top of the cave crack, on the crack in the lid of the stone box, and also found on the top of the Ark itself.

The dark black liquid residue had dripped from the ground above, thru the rock crack, thru the crack in the stone box, and finally rested upon the mercy seat of the Ark of the Covenant.

That sounds pretty fantastic. What was the dark black liquid residue?

Ron was commanded by an angel inside the cave to take pictures and document everything. Then take a sample of the liquid residue.

Ron did so and took the sample of the dried liquid residue to an Israeli lab to have it analyzed; and took the images to the Israeli government. They kept the pictures and covered up the excavated cave once more; safe and sound. However, Ron still had the Israeli lab results of the dried liquid residue.

I will leave the lab analysis results for those that watch the video on the website. www.LastDaysTimeline.com/ark-of-the-covenant

This is the part that is significant to our Last Days Timeline. The Angel that had Ron take the pictures of the Ark said that this evidence would come forth during the "Mark of the Beast Period". And that makes sense to me, as that is the period of the 4th Beast of the Gentiles and the building of the 4th Jewish Temple in Jerusalem, before the last Battle of Armageddon. The exact moment that those sacred items will be needed by the Jews, according to the TIMELINE.

Author's Analysis:
I feel there is some evidence lacking on the Ark of the Covenant discovery. Where are the pictures?

However, the lab results show something incredible. I count this as some pretty big evidence of the discovery of the Ark of the Covenant.

Note: if Ron Wyatt would have said he discovered the Ark and this was his first discovery, I would not have been persuaded. HOWEVER, this was Ron Wyatt's 5th big discovery of places in the bible that plenty of people have been searching for, over

100s of years.

With a chain of important Biblical discoveries under his belt, I will take Ron at his word plus a little evidence that the Ark of the Covenant and temple items have been found and are in the hands of the Israeli authorities at this time.

The "United Nations of Churches"

There are some parts of John's Revelation that put the future **state** church that rides the 4th Beast Kingdom in some relation to the Muslims in the future.

(Revelation 20:4)
"4 And I saw thrones, and they sat upon them, and judgment was given unto them: and I saw the souls of them that were **beheaded for the witness of Jesus**, and for the word of God, and which had not worshipped **the beast**, neither his **image**, neither had **received his mark upon their foreheads**, or in their hands; and they lived and reigned with Christ a thousand years."

Author's Analysis:
(pure speculation) This part about **beheading** is very interesting. It's one of those "little clues" that gets different author's thinking. I have read a book that mentioned, from this clue, that it is quite possible that the Roman Catholic Church could roughly-amalgamate with Islam in the future. Not a full "blend" of doctrine but a unification on some fronts.

In the early days of Islam under Muhammad, there were overtures made toward the Roman Catholic Church to COMBINE with Islam and worship Allah together. In that day, the Roman Catholic Church declined. However, in modern times the Catholic Church has made some major outreaches toward Islam and other religions.

(Second Vatican Council, Lumen Gentium 16, November 21, 1964)
"But the plan of salvation also includes those who acknowledge the Creator, in the first place among whom are the Muslims: these profess to hold the faith of Abraham, and together with us they adore the one, merciful God, mankind's judge on the last day."

This page has loads of the Quotes from Roman Catholic Popes and Cardinals "making" nice with Islam:
http://www.usccb.org/beliefs-and-teachings/ecumenical-and-interreligious/interreligious/islam/vatican-council-and-papal-statements-on-islam.cfm

Just this month, November 2016, the current Pope Frances made a large overture to the 5 major world religions of: Roman Catholicism, Protestant Christian, Jewish, Muslim, Jainism. He wants the dialog to start that we may "all agree" on **LOVE** as the common element of religion. And that we may start to come together on the subjects we agree on.

On the surface, that sounds awesome. However, that very well may develop into something much more sinister.

Here is Pope Frances in a Muslim mosque praying toward Mecca during the Call to Prayer. (See www.LastDaysTimeline.com/united-nations-of-churches)

Here is a Fox News story on Islamic Prayers being held at the Vatican (See www.LastDaysTimeline.com/united-nations-of-churches)

Pope John Paul II kissing the Koran of Islam

Something is going on with the "unification" of religions. And the Pope is at the center of it and calling for it.

(Here is the pure speculation part) If Islam does indeed merge in the common beliefs with the Roman Catholic Church, there certainly could be a time where **beheading** is practiced again; because that method of putting a person to death by the Government may be coming from Islam's Sharia Law.

I do *not* think that all religions (Christian, Muslim, Hindu, Jainism, and more) will get together and put all doctrinal differences aside and unite. That seems the most unlikely future scenario.

However, the creation of a "United Nations of Churches" organization seems much more likely. A counsel of that magnitude could become a powerful force for money and organizational financing for the churches. That may be all the "control force" necessary. And over time, the control mechanisms would be set in place for the persecution of all "fundamentalist religions" that don't conform. The removing of the "503C church" non-profit organization label could be removed by Governments. Then the persecution by the Inquisitors. Then the outright attacks by STATE military. (again, pure speculation)

This "United Nations of Churches" concept is the most likely prospect for the Whore Church that rides the 4th Beast Kingdom of the Gentiles. It is not invented yet in the year 2017. However, an organization like this would be able to be "all inclusive" to most mainstream religions of the world, except for the fundamentalist religions.

World War 3 with Russia and China

I have been on the side of World War 3 for more than 8 years. Having read all the material that could be obtained on the subject, including:

- War strategy books
- Best spots for Relocation books
- Preparation items books
- Books on the secret combinations behind the nations that would fight WW3.
- Bunker building books
- Prophecy books including WW3

The Last Days Timeline work that we are engaged in right now, has shown me a few things. When heavy research is done into the Timeline, there are very few events that could be attributed to a nuclear weapon. Off the top of my head, only the fiery destruction of the Great Whore Church's capital city looks like nuclear weapons.

I have found a few things that would make a large difference to this debate as to whether this would happen in our future to 2017....Here are the valid points on WW3 with Russia and China.

1. Since scripture doesn't specifically mention WW1 or WW2, that I am aware of, then there definitely could be WW3, and yet still not be mentioned.
2. Ezra's Eagle didn't mention WW2, although it fell into the post 1929 TIMELINE. However, it also didn't mention The Korean War, Vietnam, Iraq, etc. So, it just means that the scriptures are silent about it.
3. There is an upcoming battle war with Iran, mentioned in The Prophesy of the Ram and He Goat (see Appendix 1). However, this war with Persia/Iran, doesn't look like a nuclear exchange between Russia/China and America.
4. If Russia (The Bear) is to be included in the new global government of the 4th Beast Kingdom between Germany's Europe (Leopard), England (Dancing Lion), and America (Ezra's Eagle), it would be unlikely that there would be a large war with Russia/China that would kill a huge number of Americans and Europeans and then turn right around and offer them a union with joint governmental powers. If anything, Russia would likely join the Union first, the back stab the union later with an attack. That seems like a more likely scenario to me.
5. There is medium level evidence about nuclear weapons NOT WORKING the way the public has been shown in movies. Bruce Cathy from New Zealand has some proven theories about how nuclear bombs work that would preclude them from being used in a real world war setting. They may not be able to be used on the quick-draw as ASSUMED. Bruce has written books and YouTube Videos on the topic. (Note, I have NOT researched deeply into this subject. But, the material is out there to be researched.)

Where Did This Prophecy Theory of WW3 Come From?

In 1962, the highest selling prophecy book was first released called "Prophecy – Key to the Future" by Duane Crowther. This is a highly recommended book. You probably already have a copy on your bookshelf.

In this book, Crowther puts forth that WW3 would take place in "the period of preparatory wars". When I read that information many years ago, it sounded quite credible. HOWEVER, this book was first printed in 1962. I own the 2002 edition. And still over 40 years of publication....there has not been WW3. It didn't happen in 40 years....even though it was predicted as being "right around the corner" 40 years ago.

So, where did Crowther get the idea that WW3 was going to happen and why did he include it in his Timeline?

Crowther got the idea from "Patriarchal Blessings" given from patriarchs that have long passed into the Spirit World by now 2017. There was no other evidence besides these 2-3 Patriarchal Blessings in his book that WW3 was to take place. No scriptures...Nothing.

This book was so widely read among the Latter-Day Saints that the ideas in it, became part of our culture.

NOTE: I am not saying that WW3 can't happen; for it surely can. However, I do not see it in the Timeline. The only reference to Russia and China doing anything is the famed "White Horse Prophecy" by Joseph Smith (See Appendix 4)...which Crowther used as a source document for his book.

If you, the reader, would like to research this topic of WW3, the very best book on the topic is "Strategic Relocation" by Joel Skousen. (available on the site: www.LastDaysTimeline.com/strategic-relocation)

APPENDIX 2 – "Last Days" Topics Not Yet Covered in This Work. However, They are Acknowledged to Exist Surrounding the Topic of "Prophecy"

1. **The 2nd Beast (Rev 13:11)** - This 2nd Beast looks like a goat with 2 horns. It will be covered in a future release of this work.

2. **The Bible Code** – a giant computer based searchable "word find" in the old Testimate (generally). This code is known by the Jews to exist. The magic comes from searching key figures in politics and society and looking around at other words located around the primary search term. Much more legitimate information on this topic will come in a future release of this work.

3. **The Constitution of the United States** – and it's prophetic role in the future. See the book The Making of America by Cleon Skousen as the best book on the subject. The Doctrine and Covenants says that The Constitution is of GOD.

4. **Daniel's Remaining Prophecies**
   a. **Daniel chapter 9's vision** of the Angel Gabriel and the 70 weeks.
   b. **Daniel chapter 10's vision** of the Golden Man and the interpretation by the angel Gabriel. Persia, then Greece, just like in Daniel Chapter 8
   c. **Daniel chapters 11 and 12's vision** of the 3 kings in Persia plus a 4th king which is richer. He is the Stout Horn of Daniel 7. This vision builds upon the Ram and He Goat Vision. The "dark one" is

the Stout Horn that is late to the party. Michael shall deliver the Saints of God from this dark leader. Daniel sees the successive kings and their wars, leagues, and conflicts that lead up to the Second Coming of Christ. Daniel tells of the two resurrections— The wise will know the times and meanings of his visions.

    d. NOTE: all of these will be covered in a future edition of this work.

5. **David Croly** – This gentleman made predictions that actually came true long after his death. The future predictions sound very close to the actual future timeline as told by scripture for the future of America. We will get to the bottom of the predictions in a future release of this work.

6. **Doctrine and Covenants related last-days scriptures**. There is much recorded in the Doctrine and Covenants of the Church pertaining to the future. That material will be fit into the TIMELINE of a future release of this work.

7. **Enoch's Vision in Moses chapter 7**. Enoch saw the future last-days vision as well. His recordings will be inserted into the TIMELINE of a future release of this work.

8. **Ezekiel's Visions**
    a. Chap 28 - Tyre and Sidon are England and thus, they were brought down in the 1st Beast of Daniel, England at the same time Israel got their land back. (Just a guestimate at this point. More research is needed.)
    b. Chap 29, who is Egypt and who is Babylon to Ezekiel? Is America Egypt and Babylon the new Beast?
    c. Chap 32 – Ezekiel laments Egypt's fall.
    d. Chap 33 – the people of Judah are messed up again, because of sin.
    e. Chap 34 – Jesus will gather all of Israel – the lost 10 tribes included.
    f. Chap 35 –Mount Seir (Jordan today) and Idumea is Edom of the Edomites (Jordan today).
    g. Chap 36 – Lost 10 Tribes restored to their own lands in Israel in their traditional covenant lands.
    h. Chap 38 – The battle of Gog and Magog (battle of Armageddon) will usher in the 2nd Coming
    i. Chap 39 – the battle of Gog and Magog (battle of Armageddon) is over and 7 years to destroy the weapons of war and 7 months to bury the dead in mass graves. Supper of the Great God.
    j. The Battle of Armageddon is greatly described in Ezekiel.
    k. Lots of future last-days material in Ezekiel. It will all be covered in a future edition of this work. Stay tuned to the website www.LastDaysTimeline.com for future releases. Make sure you are on the email list for updates.

9. **Ezra's Remaining Prophecies** – *The Apocalypse of Ezra*

a. **Vision of the Man From the Sea (2nd Esdras 13)** the man who burns up the enemies… and calls the Lost 10 Tribes to him. 2nd Esdras 13 shows the man blasting away the army with sparks and tempest out of his mouth. It's either John OR it's Christ at the New Jerusalem. There is a link to the "mountain built without hands" between Ezra's vision and Daniel's vision of King Nebuchadnezzar's dream of the stone "cut without hands" that takes over the rest of the kingdoms.

b. **The comparison of 2nd Nephi 21/Isaiah 11 with 2nd Esdras 13** as John the Beloved/Revelator comes with the Lost 10 Tribes to take down the Beast in America. They are almost identical on how this man breaks down the enemies of the Saints of God.

c. **2nd Esdras 14-16** the same vision as John the Beloved/Revelator's of the Trumpets and Vials. Plus, the destruction of the Whore Church Babylon by the Beast, the Battle of Armageddon, plus the civil wars; which are between Babylon Church and the Beast.

d. NOTE: all of these will be covered in a future edition of this work.

10. **Isaiah's Prophecies** - "The Assyrian", one of the most important characters in Isaiah is the same as the Stout Horn last ruler of the Beast Kingdom. Also, Isaiah saw the whole panoramic vision of the last-days. It will be included and added to the TIMELINE in a future edition of this work.

11. **Jacob's Allegory of the Olive Tree** – In Jacob chapter 5, this allegory gives the future states and locations of the Lost 10 Tribes of Israel, and all the rest of Israel. It will be included in a future edition.

12. **Joel's Prophecies**
    a. **Joel 1: 17-20 burned grass and trees**. Sounds similar to the Trumpets 1-4 of the asteroid or even the later prophecy of John the Revelator of Trumpets 5-6 of the Locust Flying Machine men.
    b. Joel 2:2-3 and lots more of Joel.
    c. These will be covered in a future edition of this work.

13. **JST Matthew 26** – Recorded in the Pearl of Great Price is a translation of Matthew 26 from the Bible. However, the Prophet Joseph Smith JR. made some very important edits and adjustments about the future last-days. It will be included in a future edition of this work.

14. **Luke 21** – The Savior's teachings to his Apostles in Jerusalem concerning the *end of the world*. This is important material to be included in a future edition.

15. **Mark of the Beast in John's Revelation** – The mark of the beast was covered in this work already. However, a more in-depth study of this mark and it's relationship to buying and selling within the 4th Beast Kingdom of the Gentiles will be given in a future release of this work.

16. **Moroni's Prophecies** of the future.

17. **Nostradamous** – A "made for tv" classic prognosticator of old. In a future edition of this work, we will get to the root of his prophecies and bring the whole truth to you the reader. Good and Bad.

18. **The Plagues of John the Revelator match the Plagues of Egypt in Exodus.** This will be discussed in a future edition of this work.

19. **Sir Isaac Newton's** prediction of the Return of Christ based upon the measurement of the Sacred Cubit of the Arm of God and the Great Egyptian Pyramid to come to 2050AD. Also, Newton wrote another work called *Observations upon the Prophecies of Daniel and the Apocalypse of St. John.* This historic book is where the academics get the idea that Rome is the 4th Beast of Daniel. (Download it FREE at www.LastDaysTimeline.com/isaac-newton)

APPENDIX 3 - Quick Book Reviews – The Good and The Bad

To save space in this work, all book reviews will be done on the website www.LastDaysTimeline.com/book-reviews

Go there now, and see the big list of last days prophecy books that have been reviewed, plus others.

APPENDIX 4 – Extra Curricular Prophecies with Reliability Ratings

John Taylor`s Vision

This vision was recorded in the journal of Elder Wilford Woodruff while serving under President John Taylor. Elder Woodruff was a prolific journaler during his lifetime. He recorded each evening, the events of the day and important happenings. President Taylor held the reigns of the church a short time after President Brigham Young. He was the only person around the Quorum of the 12 Apostles to know the French language. Thus, this revelation is ascribed to President John Taylor.

I think that this vision has some merit. It is put on the (medium) scale of reliability. It WAS USED in our TIMELINE to HELP determine the placement of the BIG Plague. The remainder of the descriptions of the BIG Plague were evidenced by **scripture** when the "Times of the Gentiles are come in". Either way, the evidence of scripture shows that this BIG Plague happens before the New Jerusalem period…and yet future to 2017.

As you will see, the mini-timeline that is shown, is very short and limited. All of these events could happen in the space of 1-3 years. It would come AFTER the 2nd American Civil War and shows the BIG Plague directly before the building of the New Jerusalem. **Caution**: It is graphic.

(Wilford Woodruff's Journal, 6/15/ 1878, "A Vision, Salt Lake City, Night of Dec 16, 1877")
"I went to bed as usual at about 7:30PM. I had been reading a revelation in the French language. My mind was calm, more so than usual if possible, so I composed myself for sleep, but could not. I felt a strange feeling come over me and apparently became partially unconscious. Still I was not asleep, nor exactly awake, with dreary feeling. The first thing that I recognized was that I was in the tabernacle of Ogden, Utah. I was sitting in the back part of the building for fear they would call on me to preach, which however they did, for after singing the second time they called me to the stand.

I arose to speak and said that I didn't know that I had anything especially to say, except to bear my testimony of the Latter-day work, when all at once it seemed as if I was lifted out of myself and I said, "Yes, I have something to say and that is this: Some of my brethren have been asking, "What is becoming of us? What is the wind blowing?" I will answer you right here what is coming **very shortly.**"

I was then **in a dream**, immediately in the city of Salt Lake, and wandering around in the streets and in all parts of the city, and **on the doors of the houses I found badges of mourning** and I could not find a house but was in mourning. I passed my own house and found the same sign there, and I asked the question, "Is that me that is dead?" Someone gave me the answer, "No, you will get through it all."

It seemed strange to me that I **saw no person in the streets** in all my wandering around the country. I seemed to be in their houses with **the sick**, but saw no funeral procession, nor anything of the kind, but the city looking still and as though **the people were praying**. And it seemed that **they had controlled the disease**, but what the disease was I did not learn; it was not made known to me. I then looked over **the country, north, east, south, and west**, and the same mourning was in every land and in every place.

The next thing I knew I was just **this side of Omaha**. It seemed though I was above the earth, and looking down upon it. As I passed along upon my way east I saw **the road** full of people, **mostly women**, with just what they could **carry in bundles on their backs**, traveling **to the mountains** on foot. I wondered how they would get through with such a small pack on their backs. It was remarkable to us[?] that there were **so few men among them**. It didn't seem to me as though **the cars** were running, the **rails looked rusty** and the roads abandoned; and I have no conception of how I traveled as I looked down upon the people.

I continued **east** by the way of Omaha and Council Bluffs, which were **full of disease**. There were **women everywhere**. The state of <u>**Illinois and Missouri were in a tumult, men killing one another, women joining the fighting, family against family**</u> in the most horrid manner.

I imagined next that I was in **Washington** and I found desolation there. The **White House was empty** and the Halls of Congress the same, and everything **in ruins**. The people seemed to have left the city and left it to take care of itself.

I was in **Baltimore**. In the square where the Monument of 1812 stands in front of the Charles Hotel. I saw **dead piled up so as to fill the street square**. I saw mothers cutting the throats of their own children for their blood. I saw them suck it from their throats to quench their own thirst and then lie down and die. The **water of Chesapeake Bay was stagnant**, and the stench arising from it on account of their **throwing their bodies into it** so terrible, that the very smell carried death with it. I saw **<u>no man</u>** except they were dead or dying in the streets and very few women. Those I saw were crazy and in an ugly condition. Everywhere I went I beheld the same sights all over the city; it was terrible beyond description to look upon.

I thought this must be the end; but no, I was seemingly in an instant in the city of **Philadelphia**. There everything was still. No living soul was there to greet me. It seemed the **whole city was without any inhabitants**. In the south of Chestnut Street and in fact everywhere I went, the putrefaction of the dead caused such a stench that it was impossible for any living thing to breathe, nor did I see any living thing in the city.

Next I found myself in **Broadway, in the city of New York**, and there it seemed the people had done the best they could to **overcome the disease**, but in wandering down Broadway I saw the bodies of beautiful women lying, some dead and others in a dying condition, on the sidewalks. I saw men come out of cellars and ravish the persons of some that were yet alive and then kill them and rob their bodies of all the valuables they had upon them. Then before they could get back to the cellar they would **roll over a time or two and die** in agony. In some of the back streets I saw them kill some of their own offspring and eat their raw flesh, and in a **few minutes** die themselves. Everywhere I went I saw the same scene of horror and destruction and death and rapine.

No carriages, buggies, or cars were running; but death and destruction were everywhere. Then I saw **fire start** and just at that moment a mighty East wind sprang up and **carried the flames over the city** and **it burned** until there was not a single building left standing there, even **down to the waters edge**. Wharves and shipping all seemed to burn and follow in common destruction where the "great city" was a short time ago. The **stench** from the bodies that were burning was so great that it was carried a long distance cross the Hudson Bay and **carried death and destruction wherever it penetrated**. I cannot paint in words the horror that seemed to compass me about; it was beyond description of man.

I supposed this was the end; but it was not. I was given to understand the same horror was being enacted all over **the country, east, west, north, and south**. Few were left alive, still there were some.

Immediately after I seemed to be standing on the **left bank of the Missouri River**, opposite the **City of Independence**, but there **was no city**. I saw the **whole state of Missouri and Illinois and all of Iowa, a complete desert with no living being there**. A short distance from the river however, I saw twelve men dressed in **temple robes**, standing in a square or nearly so (and I understood it represented the Twelve Gates of the New Jerusalem.) Their **hands were uplifted** in consecration of the ground and laying the corner stone of **the temple**. I saw myraids of angels hovering over them, and saw also **an immense pillar of clouds** over them and heard the angels singing the most heavenly music. The words were "**Now** is established the Kingdom of God and his Christ, which shall never more be thrown down."

I saw **people coming from the river** and from the desert places a **long way off** to **help build the temple** and it seemed that hosts of angels all helped to get material to build with and I saw some of them who wore temple clothes come and **build the temple and the city**, and all the time I saw the **great pillar of clouds hovering** over the place.

Instantly, however, I found myself again in the tabernacle at Ogden. And yet, I could still see the building go on and I got quite animated in calling on the people in the tabernacle to listen to the beautiful music, for the angels were singing the same music I had heard before. "Now is established the Kingdom of God and his Christ, which shall never more be thrown down."

At this I seemed to stagger back from the pulpit and Brother Francis D. Richards and some others caught my arm and prevented me from falling. Then I finished so abruptly. Still even then I had not fainted, but was simply exhausted.

Then I rolled over in bed and **awoke** just as the city clock was striking twelve."

Learning Points:
A. There is a lot to cover here. Let us get to it. President Taylor was DREAMING this vision while asleep in 1877. This vision confines itself to the land of America.
   a. President Taylor was flying right down Highway 80. See the lineup: 1. Salt Lake City, 2. Omaha Nebraska, 3. slight detour south to the corner of Missouri and Illinois, 4. Using Hwy 70, jumping straight East to Washington DC, 5. and Baltimore (only 20mins apart up Hwy 95), 6. continuing Hwy 95 to Philadelphia, 7. continuing Hwy 95 to New York City. 8. Huge leap back to the City of Independence Missouri to start the New Jerusalem.
B. President Taylor started in Salt Lake City. It was the opening scene of the BIG Plague.
C. There were badges on the doors of the houses; and almost all houses had the badges. This seems to say that almost all houses are affected by the BIG Plague. However, we can ASSUME that many people are alive. They were praying. The rest of the country of America did NOT fare that well.
D. Overall description factors of the BIG Plague: It was overcome fairly well in Salt Lake City. New York City also had some who overcame it. It seems to spread by the stench, or by the wind itself. It appears to be airborne. There are no flies or maggots seen.
   a. It kills pretty quickly; apparently not in weeks or days, but in hours and minutes. As beautiful women were laying in the streets of new york, not even able to get home to nurse themselves, but simply wallowing in the streets and dying quickly. Also, men who were perfectly able to move themselves were coming in contact with the disease and then "rolling over a time or two and dying". Nothing on earth currently in 2017 would represent this level and speed of death. Not the special Flies and

Maggots disease. Not the bubonic plague which takes days and weeks. Not Ebola of Africa which takes days and weeks. Not nuclear radiation poisoning from nuclear fallout dust which takes several days to bleed to death internally. (See "Nuclear War Survival Skills" by Cresson Kerny – available with review at www.LastDaysTimeline.com) This disease will cause the bodies to be piled high without anyone to bury them. THAT is fast.

E. A large number of women, alone (no men)– are traveling on the highways from East to the Western Rocky Mountains. They are walking as no cars or trains are working, for some time.

    b. Notice President Taylor didn't see any huge earthquake rift in the center of the country, preventing these Gentile women from crossing it and getting to the West.

F. Nothing takes men alone out of the population as well as WAR. President Taylor saw the end of the 2nd American Civil War...overlapping the BIG Plague. Apparently the BIG Plague won't even stop the fighting. The last scene of the civil war takes place in Illinois and Missouri. As the war had been stopped everywhere else, as was seen. So, the 2nd American Civil War comes BEFORE the BIG Plague, as shown in this vision of President Taylor.

G. The giant pillar of cloud hovering over the place of the New Jerusalem Temple shows that the Lord did lead the men there to dedicate the new Temple.

H. There were "other helpers" of unknown distant origin helping to build the city and temple. They came UP the Missouri River itself. They brought building materials with them. The Saints of God would be coming from the West to East. So, this is another group of people. As we KNOW that only the Tribes of Israel are to build the New Jerusalem, it's probably not more of Ephraim. It's most probably not the Jews from Jerusalem. It's probably NOT the Lost 10 Tribes of Israel from the NORTH. So, the only tribe left would be Manasseh (the Native American Indians of this western hemisphere).

    a. NOTICE: that President Taylor didn't mention ANY huge miracle of the Lost 10 Tribes returning yet. This would be the time, that they would come from the North. After the 2nd American Civil War and the BIG Plague. Right around the time to start building the New Jerusalem and fend off aggression of the 4th Beast Kingdom. However, it doesn't appear in this vision to see any aggression from any outside source. However, this vision is pretty short in time span. We do know the Lost 10 Tribes will be at the New Jerusalem by the time the Temple is dedicated or soon after....because the 144,000 young High Priests will be from every tribe of Israel, including the Lost 10 Tribes from the North lands of Arsareth.

"The White Horse Prophecy" by Joseph Smith

The famous White Horse Prophecy by Joseph Smith. This is the most explored extra-curricular prophecy of them all.

A Word on Joseph Smith's White Horse Prophecy

Note: I have found out why over the years, so many prophecy book writers keep coming back to the Joseph Smith White Horse Prophecy... it's because it has the most length and detailed description.

The classic LDS Prophecy book "Prophecy-Key to the Future" written in 1962 by Duane Crowther is the best selling Prophecy book of all time. You, the reader, have probably read it or have it on your shelf. In that book, Crowther did a masterful job of pulling together all the quotes from early prophets and apostles that spoke about the exact topics and points that were written in the original White Horse Prophecy by Joseph Smith.

This prophecy has been read by nearly all the LDS Church Leaders from the beginning. We know this, because the **early church authorities** believed it and preached it over the pulpit; and made additional declarations concerning the teachings within it.

I have read it and digested it, but have chosen to *not* use it as a primary source for this work. However, many of the early brethren did.

The **latter church authorities** have preached against it and outrightly denounced it specifically, several times, over many decades.

The original source of the prophecy was recorded by Edwin Rushton and Mosiah Hancock. It even has it's own Wikipedia page.
https://en.wikipedia.org/wiki/White_Horse_Prophecy

With all the controversy around this prophecy, there is some research needed to verify if any of the early church authorities had ever believed the elements taught within it. Duane Crowther has done just that research.

In Crowther's book "Prophesy Key to the Future" he masterfully details almost 90% of the prophecy's elements as being believed by the early church authorities such as Brigham Young, Heber C. Kimball and others. This author highly recommends that you buy a copy, if you don't already own one. (the book is available at www.LastDaysTimeline.com/prophecy-key-to-the-future)

As it stands, the prophecy is at a "medium/low" rating. It is hard to prove or disprove. It does have several elements that have already come to pass after the original recording by Rushton and Hancock. And that is a KEY to any prophecy being reliable.

This prophecy was NOT used as a source in the TIMELINE of this work, unless specifically stated.

On or about the sixth day of May. 1843, a grand review of the Nauvoo Legion was held in Nauvoo. (Illinois) The Prophet Joseph complimented them for their good discipline and evolutions performed. The weather being hot, he called for a glass of water. With the glass of water in his hand he said, "I drink to you a toast to the overthrow of the mobocrats."

The next morning a man who had heard the Prophet give the toast returned to visit the Mansion of the Prophet. And so abused him with bad language. That the man was ordered out by the Prophet. It was while the two were out that my attention was attracted to them and hearing the man speaking in a loud tone of voice. I went toward them; the man finally leaving. There were present the Prophet Joseph Smith. Theodore Turley and myself. The Prophet began talking to us of the mobbings and drivings and persecutions we as a people have endured. But, said he, "We will have worse things to see; our persecutors will have all the mobbings they want. Don't wish them any harm. For when you see their sufferings you will shed bitter tears for them."

While this conversation was going on we stood by his south wicket gate in a triangle. Turning to me he said: "I want to tell you something. I will **speak a parable like unto John the Revelator. You will go to the Rocky Mountains.** And you will be a **great and mighty people, established there,** which I will call the White Horse of Peace and Safety. When the Prophet said you will see it, I asked him, "Where will you be at that time?" He said, "I shall never go there. Your enemies will continue to follow you with persecutions and will make **obnoxious laws against you in Congress to destroy the White Horse,** but you will have a friend or two to defend you to throw out the worst part of the laws, so they will not hurt much. You must continue to petition Congress all the time, they will treat you like strangers and aliens, and they will not give you your rights but will govern you with strangers and commissioners; you will **see the Constitution of the United States almost destroyed**; it will <u>hang by a thread, as it were</u>, as fine as the finest silk fiber."

At this point the Prophet's countenance became sad; he said, "I love the constitution. It was made by the inspiration of God. And **it will be preserved and saved by the efforts of the <u>White Horse</u> and the <u>Red Horse</u>. Who will combine in its defense.** The White Horse will raise an ensign on the tops of the mountains of peace and safety. The White Horse will find the **mountains full of minerals** and they will become very rich. You will see **silver** piled up in the streets. You will see **gold** shoveled up like sand.

Gold will be of little value even in a mercantile capacity, for the people of the world will have something else to do in seeking for salvation "The time will come when the banks in every nation will fail and **only two places will be safe where people can deposit their gold and treasures.** These places will be the **White Horse** and **England's vaults."**

"A terrible **revolution will take place in the land of America,** such as has never been seen before; for <u>the land will be literally left **without a supreme government.** And every species of wickedness will run rampant. Father will</u>

be against son, and son against father, mother against daughter, and daughter against mother. The most terrible scenes of murder and bloodshed and rapine that have ever been looked upon will take place.

"Peace will be taken from the earth and there will be **no peace only in the Rocky Mountains. T**his will cause **many hundreds and thousands of the honest in heart to gather there**; not because they would be saints but for safety and **because they would not take up the sword against their neighbor.**

"You will be so numerous that you will be in **danger of famine**, but not for the want of seed time and harvest, but because of **so many to be fed**. Many will come **with bundles under their arms** to escape the calamities, and there will be no escape except by fleeing to Zion.

"Those that come to you will try to keep the laws and be one with you, for they will see your unity and the greatness of your organization. The **Turkish Empire or the Crescent will be one of the first powers that will be disrupted**, for freedom must be given for the gospel to be preached in the Holy Land.

"The Lord took of the best blood of the nations and planted them on the small islands now called **England and Great Britain**, and gave them great power in the nations for a thousand years and their power will continue with them, that they may **keep the balance of power and keep Russia from usurping her power over all the world. England and France are now (1843) bitter enemies, but they will be allied together and be united to keep Russia from conquering the world.**

"The **two Popes, Greek and Catholic**, will come together and be united. The Protestant religions do not know how much they are indebted to Henry the VIII for throwing off the Pope and establishing the Protestant faith. He was the only monarch who could do so at the time, and he did it because this nation, England, was at his back to sustain him. One of the peculiar features in England is the established red coat, a uniform making so remarkable a mark to shoot at, and yet they have conquered wherever they have gone. The reason for this will be known by them some day. The Lion and the Unicorn of Israel is their ensign, the wisdom and statesmanship of England comes from having **so much of the blood of Israel in the nation.**

"While the terrible revolution of which I have spoken has been going on, **England will be neutral** until it becomes so inhuman that **she will interfere to stop the shedding of blood**. England and France will unite together to make peace, not to subdue the nations; they will find the nations so broken up and so many claiming government, till there will be no responsible government. **Then it will appear to the other nations or powers as though England had taken possession of the country.** The **Black Horse** will flee to the invaders and will join with them, for they will have **fear of becoming** slaves **again**. Knowing England did not believe in slavery, fleeing to them they believe would make them safe. Armed with British bayonets, **the doings of the "Black" Horse will be terrible.**"

Here the Prophet said he could not bear to look longer upon the scene as shown him in vision and asked the Lord to close the scene.

Continuing, he said. "During this time the great White Horse will have gathered strength sending out Elders to gather the honest in heart **among the Pale Horse, or people of the United States**, to stand by the Constitution of the United States, as it was given by inspiration of God.

"In these days **God will set up a kingdom never to he thrown down**, for other kingdoms to come unto. And these kingdoms that will not let the Gospel be preached will be humbled until they will.

"**England, Germany, Norway, Denmark, Sweden, Switzerland, Holland, and Belgium**, have a considerable amount of the blood of Israel among their people WHICH must be gathered.

Then nations will submit to the Kingdom of God. **England will be the last** of these kingdoms to surrender, but when she does, she will do it as a whole in comparison as she threw off the Catholic power. The **nobility know that the gospel is true** but it has not enough pomp and grandeur and influence for them to embrace it. They are proud and will not acknowledge the Kingdom of God, or come unto it, until **they see the power which it will have**. Peace and safety in the Rocky Mountains will be protected by **a cordon band of the White Horse and the Red Horse**.

"The coming of the Messiah among this people will be so natural, that "only" those who see Him will know that He has come, but He will come and give His laws unto Zion, and minister unto His people. This will not be His coming in the clouds of heaven to take vengeance on the wicked of the world.

"The **Temple in Jackson County will be built in this generation**. The saints will think there will not be time to build it. but with all the help you will receive you can put up a great temple quickly. They will have **all the gold, silver, and precious stones; for these things only will be used for the beautifying of the temple;** all the skilled mechanics you want, and **the Ten Tribes of Israel** will help you build it. When you see **this land bound with iron you may look toward Jackson County.**"

At this point he made a pause, and looking up as though the vision was still in view, he said." There is a land **beyond the Rocky Mountains that will be invaded by the heathen Chinese** unless great care and protection are given." Speaking of the heathen nations he said, "Where there is no law there is no condemnation, and this will apply to them.

Power will be given the White Horse to rebuke nations afar off, and they will be one with the White Horse, but when the law goes forth they will obey; for the law will go forth from Zion. **The last great struggle Zion will have to contend with will be when the whole of the Americas will be made the Zion of our God. Those opposing will be called Gog and Magog, some of the nations of the world led by the Russian czar** and their power will be great, but all opposition will be overcome and then this land will be the Zion of our God."

The 1st Prophecy of Patriarch Charles D. Evans

This 1st of 2 prophecies by Springville Utah Patriarch Charles D. Evans was recorded by him during an evening in the 1890s.

There is much said in this account about "labor" and "capital". So, obviously he was living in an early time when Unions were beginning to fight the business owners. However, the big fights didn't happen until the 1910s and 1920s.

It is rated "medium/low" simply because it is hard to disprove. A reputable Patriarch in the church had a vision. Who is to say he didn't have it?

> (*Contributor*, Vol. 15, 1893; *TRUTH* 1:12, pp. 161-163; see also *Visions of the Latter Days*, p. 55)
> "While I lay pondering in deep solitude on the events of the present, my mind was drawn into a reverie such as I had never felt before,--a strong solicitude for my imperiled country utterly excluded every other thought, and raised my feelings to a point of intensity which I did not think it possible to endure.
>
> While in this solemn, profound, and painful reverie of mind, to my infinite surprise, a light appeared in my room, which seemed to be soft and silvery as that diffused from a northern star. At the moment of its appearance, the acute feeling I had experienced instantly yielded to one of calm tranquility.
>
> Although it may have been at the hour of midnight, and the side of the globe whereon I was situated, was excluded from the sunlight, yet all was light and bright and warm as an Italian landscape at noon, but the heat was softer or more subdued.
>
> As I gazed upward, I saw descending through my bedroom roof, with a gently gliding movement, a personage clothed in white apparel, whose countenance was smoothly serene, his features regular, and the flashes of his eye seemed to shoot forth scintillations, to use an earthly comparison,

strongly resembling those reflected from a diamond under an intensely illumined electric light, which dazzled but did not bewilder.

Those large, deep, inscrutable eyes were presently fixed upon mine, when instantly placing his hands up on my forehead his touch produced an indescribable serenity and calmness, a calmness not born of earth, but at once peaceful, delightful and heavenly. My whole being was imbued with a joy unspeakable. All feelings of sorrow instantly vanished. Those lines and shadows which care and sorrow impress upon us were dispelled as a deep fog before a blazing sun.

In the eyes of my heavenly visitor, for such he appeared to me, there was a sort of lofty pity and tenderness, infinitely stronger than any such feeling I ever saw manifested in ordinary mortals. His very calm appeared like a vast ocean stillness, at once overpowering to every agitated emotion.

By some intuition, or instinct, I felt he had something to communicate to sooth my sorrows and allay my apprehensions. Thereupon addressing me, he said:

"Son, I perceive thou hast grave anxieties over the perilous state of thy country, that thy soul has felt deep sorrow for its future. I have therefore come to thy relief and to tell thee of the causes that have led to this peril. Hear me attentively.

"Seventy-one years ago [1823], after an awful apostasy of centuries, in which all nations were enshrouded in spiritual darkness, when the angels had withdrawn themselves, the voice of prophets hushed, and the light of Urim and Thummim shown not, and the vision of the seers closed, while heaven itself shed not a ray of gladness to lighten a dark world, when Babel ruled and Satan laughed, and Church and Priesthood had taken their upward flight, and the voice of nations, possessing the books of the Jewish prophets, had ruled against vision and against Urim, against the further visits of angels, and against the doctrine of a church of apostles and prophets, thou knowest that then appeared a mighty angel with the solemn announcement of the hour of judgment, the burden of whose instructions pointed to dire calamities upon the present generation. This, therefore, is the cause of what thou seest and the end of the wicked hasteneth."

My vision now became extended in a marvelous manner, and the import of the past labors of the Elders was made plain to me. I saw multitudes fleeing to the place of safety in our mountain heights. The church was established in the wilderness. Simultaneously the nation had reached an unparalleled prosperity, wealth abounded, new territory was acquired, commerce extended, finance strengthened, confidence was maintained, and peoples abroad pointed to her as the model nation--the ideal of the past realized and perfected--the embodiment of the liberty sung by poets and sought for by sages.

"But," continued the Messenger, "thou beholdest a change. Confidence is lost, wealth is arrayed against labor, labor against wealth, yet the land abounds with plenty of food and raiment, and silver and gold are in abundance. Thou seest also the letters written by a Jew have wrought great confusion in the finances of the nation which, together with the policy of many wealthy ones, has produced distress and do produce further sorrow."

Factions now sprang up as if by magic; capital had entrenched itself against labor throughout the land; labor was organized against capital. The voice of the wise sought to tranquilize these two powerful factors in vain. Excited multitudes ran wildly about; strikes increased; lawlessness sought the place of regular government.

At this juncture I saw a banner floating in air whereupon was written the words, **"BANKRUPTCY, FAMINE, FLOODS, FIRE, CYCLONES, BLOOD, PLAGUE."** Mad with rage, men and women rushed upon each other. Blood flowed down the streets of cities like water. The demon of bloody hate had enthroned itself on the citadel of reason; the thirst for blood was more intense than that of the parched tongue for water. Thousands of bodies lay untombed in the streets. Men and women fell dead from the terror inspired by fear. Rest was but the precursor of the bloody work of the morrow. All around lay the mournfulness of a past in ruins. Monuments erected to perpetuate the names of the noble and brave were ruthlessly destroyed by combustibles.

A voice now sounded aloud these words, "Yet once again I shake not the earth only, but also heaven. And this word yet once again signifies the removing of things that are shaken, as of things that are made; that those things that cannot be shaken may remain."

Earthquakes rent the earth in vast chasms, which engulfed multitudes; terrible groanings and wailings filled the air; the shrieks of the suffering were indescribably awful. Water wildly rushed in from the tumultuous ocean, whose very roaring under the mad rage of the fierce cyclone, was unendurable to the ear. Cities were swept away in an instant, missiles were hurled through the atmosphere at a terrible velocity, and people were carried upward only to descend an unrecognizable mass. Islands appeared where ocean waves once tossed the gigantic steamer. In other parts, voluminous flames emanating from vast fires, rolled with fearful velocity, destroying life and property in their destructive course.

The seal of the dread menace of despair was stamped on every human visage; men fell exhausted, appalled and trembling. Every element of agitated nature seemed a demon of wrathful fury. Dense clouds, blacker than midnight darkness, whose thunders reverberated with intonations which shook the earth, obscured the sunlight. Darkness reigned unrivaled and supreme.

Again the light shone, revealing an atmosphere tinged with a leaden hue, which was the precursor of an unparalleled plague, whose first symptoms were recognized by a purple spot which appeared on the cheek or on the back of the hand, and which, invariably, enlarged until it spread over the entire surface of the body, producing certain death. Mothers, on sight of it, cast away their children as if they were poisonous reptiles. This plague, in grown persons, rotted the eyes in their sockets and consumed the tongue as would a powerful acid or an intense heat. Wicked men, suffering under its writhing agonies, cursed God and died, as they stood on their feet, and the birds of prey feasted on their carcasses.

I saw in my dream the Messenger again appear with a vial in his right hand, who addressing me, said: "Thou knowest somewhat of the chemistry taught in the schools of human learning, behold now a chemical sufficiently powerful to change the waters of the sea."

He then poured out his vial upon the sea and it became putrid as the blood of a dead man, and every living soul therein died. Other plagues followed which I forbear to record.

A foreign power had inroaded the nation, which, from every human indication, it appeared would seize the government and supplant it with monarchy. I stood trembling at the aspect, when, lo, a power arose in the west which declared itself in favor of the Constitution in its original form; to this suddenly rising power, every lover of constitutional rights and liberties throughout the nation gave hearty support. The struggle was fiercely contested, but the Stars and Stripes floated in the breeze, and bidding defiance to all opposition, waved proudly over the land.

Among the many banners I saw, was one inscribed thus: "The government based on the Constitution, now and forever"; on another, "Liberty of Conscience, Social, Religious, and Political."

The light of the Gospel which had but dimly shone because of abomination, now burst forth with a luster that filled the earth. Cities appeared in every direction, one of which, in the center of the continent, was an embodiment of architectural science after the pattern of eternal perfections, whose towers glittered with a radiance emanating from the sparkling of emeralds, rubies, diamonds, and other precious stones set in a canopy of gold, and so elaborately and skillfully arranged as to shed forth a brilliancy which dazzled and enchanted the eye, excited admiration and developed a taste for the beautiful, beyond anything man had ever conceived.

Fountains of crystal water shot upwards their transparent jets, which, in the brilliant sunshine, formed ten thousand rainbow tints at once delightful to the eye. Gardens, the perfection of whose arrangement confound all our present attempts at genius, were bedecked with flowers of varied hue to develop and refine the taste and strengthen a love for these nature's chastest adornments.

Schools and universities were erected, to which all had access; in the latter, Urims were placed for the study of the past, present, and future, and for obtaining a knowledge of the heavenly bodies, and of the construction of worlds and universes. The inherent properties of matter, its arrangements, laws, and mutual relations were revealed and taught and made plain as the primer lesson of a child. The conflicting theories of geologists regarding the foundation and age of the earth were settled forever. All learning was based on eternal certainty. Angels brought forth the treasures of knowledge which had laid hid in the womb of the dumb and distant past.

The appliances for making learning easy surpass all conjecture. Chemistry was rendered extremely simple, by the power which the Urims conferred on man of looking into and through the very elements of every kind; a stone furnished no more obstruction to human vision than the air itself. Not only were the elements and all their changes and transformations plainly understood, but the construction, operations and laws of mind were thus rendered equally plain as those which governed the coarser elements.

While looking through the Urim and Thummim, I was amazed at a transformation, which even now is to me marvelous beyond description, clearly showing the manner in which particles composing the inorganic kingdom of nature are conducted upward to become a part of organic forms; another astounding revelation was a view clearly shown me of the entire circulation of the blood, both in man and animals.

After seeing these things and gazing once more upon the beautiful city, the following passage of scripture sounded in my ears: "OUT OF ZION, THE PERFECTION OF BEAUTY, GOD SHINETH."

On this I awoke to find all a dream. I have written the foregoing, which is founded on true principle, under the caption of a dream, partly to instruct and partly to check the folly of reading silly novels now so prevalent.

CHARLES D. EVANS
Springville, Utah"

The 2nd Prophecy of Patriarch Charles D. Evans

This 2nd prophecy of Charles D. Evans happened in 1882 while he was a Bishop. This shows that a brother in the Church was having visions right along his life. Most LDS members are not familiar with this 2nd vision.

As this was recorded in 1882, this was before Ezra's Eagle in 1929.

Rating: a good brother in the church had a vision and it was recorded early. It is hard to prove or dis-prove. It is rated low-medium.

"While I continued to stare and marvel at the wondrous work before me, all of a sudden the scene vanished, and a new era, resultant, however, from the forces of the religious agencies before mentioned, burst upon my view. The history of American Independence, with the actors therein, passed before me. The Constitution of the United States was emblazoned upon an immense distance. **Civil and religious toleration was general throughout the land**. Man rejoiced in the privilege of worshipping God according to the dictates of conscience. Prosperity reigned. Angels smiles. Heaven approved. The fetters of political and religious intolerance, forged by the monarchs of the eastern world, were sundered, shall it be said forever? Such was my thought. I was full of joy at the sight; big tears of joy rolled down my cheeks, when all of a sudden, my attention was directed to a personage standing by my bedside, and who was attired in a white and flowing robe. Addressing me, he said, 'Son of Mortality, look.'"

"I looked and beheld a scene most revolting to my senses, from the fact that it was the reverse of the prosperity and religious freedom I had before witnessed. I saw the **representatives of one branch of the Republic holding in their hands fetters they themselves had forged.**

"The personage, again addressing me, said, "'Knowest thou the meaning of these?'

"I answered, 'No.'

"He replied, 'These are **the chains with which certain sons of the Republic, who have tasted the fruit of the tree of liberty, desire to bind their fellows. These are they who seek to subvert the cause of human freedom.** These seek to **enslave one portion of the children of freedom who differ from them in religious belief and practice.** Know thou, my son, that their object is **filthy lucre**. They **plot** to take away human rights, and to destroy the freedom of the soul, to possess the homes of the industrious without fee or reward. Their souls shall be in derision, and the heavens shall laugh at their folly. Their calamity slumbereth not. But cast thine eyes **eastward** and look.'

"I looked and beheld that the bands that held society together during the reign of the republic, were snapped asunder. Society had broken loose from all restraints of principle and good conscience. Brotherhood had dissolved. Respect for common rights and even the rights of life and property had fled from the land. I saw **faction after faction** arise and contend with each other. **Political strife** was everywhere. Father and son alike contended in these awful feuds. The spirit of deadly hate... passed through the Republic. Blood was written every banner. The spirit of bloodshed appeared to possess every heart.

"Turning to the person in white I exclaimed, 'Surely this means the total destruction of our nation.'"

"Touching my eyes with his finger, he replied: 'Look again.'

"I looked and beheld that many who were angry with the rulers of the Republic, for the **subversion of the Constitutional law**, and their wholesale **plunder of the public moneys**, arose and proclaimed themselves the **friends of the Constitution in its original form**. These looked around for some others to sustain the country's flag inviolate, pledging themselves and their fortunes and sacred honours to that end.

"A voice was suddenly heard declaring these words: 'In the distant mountain tops are to be found the true lovers of freedom and equal rights, a people who have never made war upon each other. Go there, for only there can your lives and property be secure from the spoiler. There alone can the flag you love wave proudly for the protection of all people, irrespective of creed and color.'

"While thus engaged I cast my eyes to the far west, when suddenly appeared **on Ensign Peak**, near Salt Lake City, a beautiful flag whereon was written these words: 'Friends of Human Liberty throughout the world, all hail! We greet you under the flag of freedom, our country's flag.' One shout of 'Welcome' from the Mountain Sons of Freedom rent the air. I beheld that the multitude wept with joy. **The laws were again administered in purity**. The people prospered. Tyrants were hurled down. All religious bodies were equally protected before the law. No North, no South, no East, no West, but one unbroken nation whose banner waved for all the world. On this I awoke in tears of joy."

"The Independent American Party Prophecy" by Joseph Smith

This is a quick little prophecy recorded by Mosiah Lyman Hancock in 1844. It speaks of existing things. However, it is hard to verify true or false. It is what it is.

If the recording date of this prophecy is accurate, some of these predictions have already come true. That would qualify it for medium-high reliability status.

(Autobiography of Mosiah Hancock 1844)
"There will be **two great political parties** in this country. One will be called the **Republican**, and the other the **Democrat** party. These **two parties will go to war** and out of these two parties will spring another party which will be the **Independent American Party**.

The **United States will spend her strength and means warring in foreign lands** until other nations will say, 'Let us divide up the lands of the United States'; then the people of the US will unite and swear by the blood of their forefathers, that the land shall not be divided. Then the country will go to war, and they will fight until **one half of the US Army will give up**, and the rest will continue to struggle. They will keep on until they are very ragged and discouraged, and almost ready to give up --- when **the boys from the mountains** rush forth in time to save the American Army from defeat and ruin. And they will say, 'Brethren, we are glad you have come; give us men, henceforth, who can talk with God'. Then you will have friends, but you will save the country **when its liberty hangs by a hair, as it were.**"

"The Cardston Temple Prophecy" by Sols Caurdisto

The following is a letter that was written by a non-LDS woman named "Sols Caurdisto" that went through the Cardston Canada Temple in 1933 in a regular Temple Open House, before the Temple was dedicated.

This vision received by Sols Caurdisto has been the basis for many of the "dreams and visions" prophecy books that have been written by Latter-Day Saints. This vision is somewhat important to the reader of this work, to be aware that it exists. But, it is of "low-grade" source material.

Proving it false is most hard to do; yet so is proving it true. This could be a real vision given to a member of the Quaker faith in 1933. However, it also may be a complete hoax. There is no way to know, until the events in this vision start to come to pass in the exact order that the vision says.

The account was not included in any of the workable TIMELINE for this book.

Cardston, Alberta Canada

December 14, 1933

Robert W. Smith, Esq. Salt Lake City, Utah

Dear Brother Smith:

I am pleased to answer your letter of December 1st-first as to the letter of a non-member who wrote of "impressions" received while going through the Temple before it was dedicated, the truth of which letter you ask me to verify and which I am pleased to do.

It was a Quaker lady who was a magazine writer from eastern Canada. She has some relatives in Lethbridge, about 60 miles from Cardston; and being so deeply impressed on her first visit, she had them bring her a second time - this time I was acting as guide. She would sit in each room and never said a word to any in the company, but seemed to be in deep meditation all the time.

When she reached her own home several weeks after, she wrote this letter which has caused so much comment all over the Church. We have never been able to understand how she seemed to know so much about our faith and our belief in our future life and works after death. I never learned her real name. She visited us along in 1921. I have never heard from her since that time, but the letter is genuine, and of her own "impressions!" received while in the Temple while on the two visits she mentions.

Sincerely your Brother,

0/S Elder J. Wood, Pres. Alberta Stake

This is her actual letter of her visions:

We have been to the Temple erected by your church wherein are to be performed the sacred rites in accordance with your faith. The first time I was strongly impelled to describe to you my impressions. I did so but before the completion of the letter, I received some news that so affected me that acting upon the spur of the moment, I destroyed the document in its entirety.

The continued feeling within me of dissatisfaction as to something left undone, coupled with the desire upon the part of the members of my household who had not visited the temple, led to our second visit to Cardston, in which you so kindly consented to accompany us, notwithstanding the inclement weather and personal inconvenience to yourself which the journey entailed.

It was because of this and many other evidences of your friendship that has given me the privilege to presume to bother you with what after all may be foolish fantacies of a too impressionable mentality. To me it does seem so, for never before in my life have such powerful impressions been infringed upon my inner consciousness as during my visit thru the Temple. Especially was this true at our second visit. The impressions of our first visit were repeated with such overwhelming intensity and variety of detail that I must positively inform you of my experience.

It seems to me it were a sacred duty upon my part to do this, and knowing as I do that your friends will lightly ridicule what to me is a personal matter, I am going to give you in detail my experience in the hope, that if it is well, maybe it is something more than imagination, that you and others of your faith may wisely analyze and correctly use whatever may be gleaned from this letter.

A fortress in time of storm, was the first thought that shaped itself in my mind with my first view of this ancient, yet modern temple; mellowed with the spiritual usage of ancient civilization and customs, yet alert, virile, and watchful.

A grand, solemn, strong, beautiful, useful house of spiritual progression which seemed to be the embodiment of architectural expression of ancient civilization and glories suddenly re-incarnated and for a future and higher civilization than our own. Strength and beauty exaggerated the more flimsy houses and buildings of the town and gave a painfully obvious example of how the soul within is expressed thru the material body, either in the individual or nation, or a race, either in the man or his architecture. Try how I would I could not get away from the feeling that the town itself was inferior to the latest building, so new and yet so old. Even the electric lights failed to change this thought, that the Temple and the town represented two different epochs of humanity? spiritual development expressed in architecture. The town embodied the present epoch, science, art, invention harnessed purely for trade or commerce, irrespective of past or future development. The Temple embodies the accumulated knowledge of the ancient world combined with the modern inventions of science and inspiration as the road to a higher future development so near at hand. Let me put it down even another way.

There is a place called Cardston. A Temple linking the past with the present has been built at Cardston and the town has become a collection of flimsy huts nestling at the foot of the Temple which will continue to function for the spiritual purposes for which it is raised.

Just as the exterior impressions compared with the present and future epochs so did the interior also reflect comparison. Of the beautiful and artistic effects I need not dwell; abler pens can describe the interior from this viewpoint. Sufficient for me to say that the shape of the Temple is a cross, that each apartment is symbolical in artistic and structural effects of some stage of humanity's progress thru the ages. In fact, everything physical is a stepping stone to spiritual progress as such is typified in these ceremonies.

All this was kindly and intelligently explained to us by Mr. Duce on one occasion and by Mr. Wood on the second visit; but I am afraid I was very indifferent and inattentive upon both occasions, for which I tender them my sincere apologies. I had no intentions of being rude or discourteous, but from the moment of entering the Temple until leaving, I was placed in the position of having, as it were, to listen to and grasp a dual narrative all the time, with the result that so engrossed was I at times that I am afraid I was so absent-minded as to appear inattentive if not positively stupid.

I have stated that my impression of the exterior of the building was that of a place of waiting for a higher civilization than our present one. This would suggest a condition of emptiness, but that is not what I mean. An ordinary newly erected building has no atmosphere at all until it has been inhabited some time; after which, it has, as it were, a living atmosphere. What kind of an atmosphere this is, is largely determined by the spiritual development and thought of the persons using and inhabiting the building. This applies especially to places of worship or consecration, and is very noticeable to a sensitive person. Sometimes such an atmosphere is agreeable, exalting, etc.; sometimes very much the reverse, depending upon the spiritual harmony or otherwise of the persons under this atmospheric rule; but was not so as far as it was concerned while outside the Temple.

I could not understand the overwhelming scene of ancient atmosphere which the building actually possessed in its very granite blocks in spite of the fact that I know a few months previous these stones had been laid, yet the feeling of age predominated. I dismissed the feeling as well as I could by thinking that the place of the structure was responsible for the suggestion of age, but when I entered the Temple, how quickly I found there was nothing to suggest to me that present atmosphere of which I have spoken, but was it empty? Emphatically no! Time and again as I listened to the speaker explaining some phase of the building or its meaning, I would be seeing beyond him some illustration of kaleidoscopic nature, depicting what he was describing, only more completely and vividly. The characters were so plain to me that I required all my self control to keep silent from room to room. This continued and only ceased when we were out in the frost and snow once more.

There was no set plan for presenting these pictures to me. It seemed as if when I thought something mental, a picture instantly presented itself in explanation of some word of the conductor, which would have the same effect. I was not afraid, only awed by the wonder of it all and the fearful impressive feeling that I received which seemed to imbed every little detailed scene into my brain, from which it will ever remember and record; and vivid as all of it was, these incidents herein related are the ones upon which I received instructions.

The scenes which I observed of an historical character seemed chiefly to verify and amplify the speaker's outline of past history, and so I do not feel impressed to record such, except to state that the same patriarchal characters whom I observed directing and influencing the early movements of the Church, were the same down through every age and epoch, and as the scenes advanced to more modern times, I saw among these spiritual characters and counselors, persons whose features I had previously observed as being in the material body on other historical occasions.

It seemed as though the temple was filled with the actual spiritual bodies of these previous leaders of your church, each seeming to have the work that person was engaged in whilst in the flesh. In that temple I saw persons who were leaders of your church, during its march across the American desert now engaged in helping these higher patriarchs under whose orders they seemed to be working. It was these latter spiritual leaders, if I may use that term, who seemed to be instructed to show me the scenes here recorded.

I can give no time as to the happening, except that the impressions I received were of actual present or immediate future.

I saw first a brief but comprehensive sketch of the present state of the world, or as you would term it, the Gentile Kingdoms. Each country in turn was shown, its anarchy, hunger, ambitions, distrusts and warlike activities, etc., and in my mind was formed from some source the words, "As it is today with the Gentiles."

I saw international war again break out with its center upon the Pacific Ocean, but sweeping and encircling the whole globe.

I saw that the opposing forces were roughly divided by so-called Christianity on the one side, and by the so-called followers of Mohammed and Buddha on the other. I saw that the great driving power within these so-called Christian nations, was the Great Apostasy of Rome, in all its political, social and religious aspects. I saw the worldwide dislocation and devastation of production and slaughter of people occur more swiftly and upon a larger scale than ever before. I saw an antagonism begin to express itself from those so-called Christian nations against your people. I saw those with a similar faith to yours in the far east begin to look toward Palestine for safety.

I saw the international world war automatically break down, and national revolution occur in every country, and complete the work of chaos and desolation. I saw geological disturbances occur, which helped in this work as if it were intended to do so. I saw the Cardston Temple preserved from all of this geological upheaval. I saw the international boundary line disappear as these two governments broke up and dissolved into chaos. I saw race rioting upon the American continent on a vast scale.

I saw hunger and starvation in this world; I saw disease produced by hunger, strife and chaos complete the end of this present order or epoch. How long these events were in reaching this consummation I do not know, but my impression was from the outbreak of the international war these things developed into a continuous procession, and almost ran concurrently, as it is with a sickness, the various symptoms are all in evidence at one and the same time, but in different stages of development.

My intensified thought was "What of the Church," if such is to become of the Kingdoms of the earth? Was immediately answered by a subconscious statement. "As it is in the church today," and I saw these higher spiritual beings throughout the length and breadth of the air, marshalling their spiritual forces, and concentrating them upon the high officials of your church upon earth.

I saw the spiritual forces working upon those officers, impressing and moving them, influencing and warning them. I saw the spiritual forces begin to unfold these things into the minds of your elders and other high officials, especially during their spiritual devotions and official duties, and those activities which exalt the mind of the individual or groups. I saw the impressions take hold and inspire the more receptive and spiritual men, until it was all clearly revealed to them in the way the spiritual patriarch desired.

Again I seemed to hear the words, "As it will be." I saw the high officials in council, and under inspired guidance issue instructions to your people to re-consecrate their lives and energies to their faith, to voluntarily discipline themselves, by abstaining from all those forms of indulgence which weaken the body, sap the mentality and deaden the spirit, or waste the income.

I saw further on, instructions given whereby places of refuge were prepared quietly but efficiently by inspired elders. I saw Cardston and the surrounding foothills, especially north and west, for miles, being prepared as a refuge for your people quietly but quickly.

I saw elders still under divine guidance, counseling and encouraging the planting of every available acre of soil in this district, so that large supplies would be near the refuge. I saw the church property under cultivation of an intensified character, not for sale or profit, but for the use of the people. I saw artesian wells and other wells dug all over that territory so that when the open waters were polluted and poisoned that the people of the church and their cattle should be provided for.

I saw the fuel resources of the district develop in many places and vast piles of coal and timber stored for future use and building. I saw the territory carefully surveyed and mapped out, for the camping of a great body of the people of the church. I saw provision also made for a big influx of people who will not at first belong to the church, but who will gather in their tribulation.

I saw vast quantities of surgical appliances, medicines, disinfectants, etc., stored in the temple basement. I saw inspiration given the elders whereby the quantity, quality and kind of things to be stored were judged, which might not be attainable in this territory in time of chaos. I saw defensive preparations working out the organizations of the camps on maps.

I saw the mining corridors used as places of storage underground; I saw the hills surveyed and corrals built in sequestered places for cattle, sheep, etc., quietly and quickly. I saw the plans for the organization of the single men and their duties, the scouts, the guards, the nurses, the cooks, the messengers, the children, the herders, the temple guards, etc.. I saw these things going on practically unknown to the Gentile world, except the Great Apostasy, whose knowledge and hatred is far reaching, in this day of its temporary power. This was going on piece by piece as the Elders were instructed so to do.

I saw the other officials obeying the inspired instructions, carrying their message and exhorting the people to carry out, from time to time the revelation given them, whilst all around throughout the Gentile world the chaos developed in its varying stages, faction against faction, nation against nation, but all in open or secret hostility to your people and their faith. I saw your people draw closer and closer together, as this became more tense and as the spiritual forces warned them through the mouth of your elders and your other officers. I saw the spiritual forces influencing those members who had drifted away, to re-enter the fold. I saw a greater tithing than ever before. I saw vast quantities of necessaries supplied by members whose spiritual eyes had been opened. I saw a liquidation of properties and effects disposed of quietly but quickly by members of the church, as the spiritual influences directed them.

I saw the inspired call sent forth to all the church, to gather to the refuges of Zion. I saw the stream of your people quietly moving in the direction of their refuge. I saw your people moving more quickly and in larger numbers until all the stragglers were housed. I saw the wireless message flashed from Zion's refuge to Zion's refuge in their several places that all was well with them, and then the darkness of chaos closed around the boundaries of your people, and the last days of tribulation had begun.

Sols Caurdisto

"The President of Greek Extraction Prophecy" by George Albert Smith

The account is by George Albert Smith recorded by David Hughes Horne, P.E.

This one was recorded in late 1988 or early 1989. The dating was unclear. David Horne was a neighbor to President George Albert Smith in 1946.

However, noting the date of recording is so far beyond when President George Albert Smith lived (April 4, 1870 to Apr 4, 1951), that there surely could be some big problems with the validity of this prophecy.

Nov 8, 1988 was a Presidential election. It is noted here that in 1988 there were lots of "election year" issues as Republican George H.W. Bush was running against Democrat Michael Dukakis who was "non-white". Thus, the reference about a Greek President. And Michael Dukakis was leading in the polls going into the election. George Bush ultimately won.

Also in 1988, The Strategic Defense Initiative by Ronald Regan was in full swing and would not eliminate nuclear weapons, but actually increased them.

So, it appears at first glance that this prophecy was talking about the issues of the day in the election year of 1988 when David Horne came forth and provided the prophecy.

However, not everything in this Prophecy can be ruled out, either. This account has a "low rating".

> "Then President Smith said, "I have had a troublesome vision of another great and terrible war that made the war just ended look like a training exercise, and people died like flies. It began at a time when the Soviet Union's military might dwarfed that of the United States, and we, that is the United States, would have missiles that carried an atomic bomb in Europe. I saw the United States withdraw its missiles to appease the Soviet Union, and then the war began." He also said that we would have big missiles in deep holes he described like grain silos which the Soviets would try to destroy by their own missiles. They would hit military installations and some cities also. He said that the president at that time would be of Greek extraction.

> *Until then all the presidents would be of British or Northern European ancestry.* He continued that the U.S. would be bound by numerous entangling alliances and would take away weapons owned by the people. He talked some about the initial attack and the ground warfare, but I can't remember enough to document all their tactics and in which countries various things occurred. One tactic, especially in Europe, was to transport tanks in thousands of big trucks like semi trailers on the super highways to have them located where they wanted them when the war was to begin. During that explanation I asked, "What about the Atomic Cannon?" to which he answered, "I didn't see anything like that." Then he said, "The aftermath was dreadful. Think of the worst, most difficult times of the depression." He turned to us children and said, "You won't remember the depression," which was true. I didn't know there was a depression as I was growing up; the sun came up every morning, flowers bloomed, we went to school, and there was church every Sunday. But he repeated to our parents, "Think of the worst condition of the depression. Can you think of something?" to which our father answered, "Oh yes!" Then President Smith continued, "You know how Sunday School picnics are complete with salad, chicken, root beer, and dessert, and everyone has a wonderful time. That worst time of the depression will seem like a Sunday School picnic when compared with how conditions will be after that great war." When he finished speaking, he turned around and went to the front door. As I left I thought to myself, "What he said is really important. I've got to remember it!" "

"Salt Lake City Classed With the Wicked Cities of the World Prophecy" by Heber C. Kimball

This prophecy was stated by Heber C. Kimball in 1931. It was published in the Church Newspaper the Deseret News. This prophecy has a "medium/high rating".

(Heber C. Kimball - Deseret News, May 23, 1931)
"An army of Elders will be sent to the four quarters of the earth to search out the righteous and warn the wicked of what is coming. **All kinds of religions will be started** and **miracles performed** that will deceive the very elect it that were possible. Our sons and daughters must live pure lives so as to be prepared for what is coming.

After a while **the gentiles will gather by the thousands to this place, and Salt Lake City will be classed among the wicked cities of the world.** A spirit of **speculation and extravagance** will take possession of the Saints, and the results will be **financial bondage. Persecution comes next** and all true Latter-day Saints will be **tested to the limit.**

Many will apostatize and others will be still not knowing what to do. Darkness will cover the earth and gross darkness the minds of the people. The **judgments of God will be poured out on the wicked** to the extent that our **Elders from far and near will be called home**, or in other words the gospel will be taken from the Gentiles and later on carried to the Jews.

The western boundary of the **State of Missouri will be swept so clean** of its inhabitants that as President Young tells us, when you return to that place, there will not be left so much as **a yellow dog to wag his tail**. Before that day comes, however, **the Saints will be put to tests** that will try the integrity of the best of them. The **pressure will become so great** that the more righteous among them will cry unto the Lord day and night until deliverance comes.

Then **the prophet and others will make their appearance** and those who have remained faithful will be selected to return to Jackson County, Missouri, and take part in the upbuilding of that beautiful city, **the New Jerusalem.**"

Learning Points:
A. This whole statement by Elder Kimball seems to be exactly in-line with the TIMELINE concerning the persecution upon the Saints by the Whore Church that Nephi saw in vision. However, Elder Kimball gave us more TIMELINE clues.
B. First, comes many religions that perform seemingly real miracles. Good ones that deceive people. So, these are either "real miracles", or they are miracles like the magicians perform now in 2017, but are held to a more religious standard.

C. Second, comes large numbers of Gentile Americans to Salt Lake City. In 2017, this has already taken place to a large extent. Salt Lake City is about 50% non-LDS at this point.

D. Third, comes a BOOM TIME with that will result in much speculation and extravagance among the people of Utah. With much DEBT as a result.

E. Fourth, comes The Great Persecution of the Saints of God that Nephi saw in vision.

F. Fifth, the judgments are poured out…that clean out the area of Jackson County Missouri. According to our TIMELINE, these judgments would be The 2nd American Civil War and the BIG Plague. Which are exactly the same judgments used to clear out the East Coast of the USA and the central region of our country for the Lost 10 Tribes to return.

G. Sixth, it is time to Build Jackson County Missouri into the New Jerusalem with the special Temple and the Nation of Zion.

WOW, I did not read this prophecy of Elder Kimball until AFTER the main section of the Last Days Timeline Book was written. It is amazing what the Prophets of the Lord can see. This is why we sustain them as Prophets, Seers, and Revelators.

From the added 1st portions of this quick timeline by Elder Kimball, we see that there will be a BOOM time, BEFORE the persecution. This makes complete sense as this would be the "good times" needed to make the capital city of the Whore Church on 7 Hills very rich…..so that in mounting and riding the 4th Beast Kingdom of the Gentiles, the Whore Church would gain in power and riches. Then that power and riches of the STATE Religion would be used against the Saints of God in The Great Persecution, that Nephi saw.

This also means that the BOOM TIME, that this prophecy by Elder Kimball is speaking of, is AFTER the 4th Beast of the Gentiles is formed.

"New York City, Boston, and Albany Prophecy" by Wilford Woodruff

Elder Wilford Woodruff of the 12 Apostles serving under Brigham Young in 1863 speaking to the youth at a conference in Logan Utah, had this to say about New York City, Boston, and Albany New York: (medium/high rating)

(In Lundwall, *Temples of the Most High.* pp. 97–98.)
"Now, my young friends, I wish you to remember these scenes you are witnessing during the visit of President Young and his brethren. Yea, my young friends, treasure up the teachings and sayings of these prophets and apostles as precious treasure while they are living men, and do not wait until they are dead. A few days and President Young and his brethren, the prophets and apostles and Brothers Benson and Maughan, will be in the spirit world. You should never forget this visitation. You are to become men

and women, fathers and mothers: yea, the day will come, after your fathers, and these prophets and apostles are dead, you will have the privilege of going into the towers of a glorious Temple built unto the name of the Most High (pointing in the direction of the bench), east of us upon the Logan bench; and while you stand in the towers of the Temple and your eyes survey this glorious valley filled with cities and villages, occupied by tens of thousands of Latter-day Saints, you will then call to mind this visitation of President Young and his company. You will say: That was in the days when Presidents Benson and Maughan presided over us; that was **before New York was destroyed by an earthquake**; it was **before Boston was swept into the sea**, by the sea heaving itself beyond its bounds; it was **before Albany was destroyed by fire**; yea, at that time you will remember the scenes of this day. Treasure them up and forget them not.' **President Young followed and said**: 'What Brother Woodruff has said is revelation and will be fulfilled.'"

If you live in one of these 3 cities, be prepared to leave, or leave early. President Young said this would happen. You know *when* this would happen based upon the Timeline.

"Revelation in Wilderness of San Francisco Mountain in Arizona Prophecy" by Wilford Woodruff

This revelation was given to Elder Woodruff while an Apostle in the Quorum of the Twelve. It was received on Jan 26, 1880. It is believed by me to be authentic.

However, the problem arises that this revelation about the future was received by an Apostle, not the President of the Church. So, this revelation may have been for Elder Woodruff alone; not intended for general circulation. In this revelation is appears that Elder Woodruff is actually giving a prophetic "Thus saith the Lord" unto John Taylor, Orson Pratt, and all the rest of the Quorum of the Twelve. This doesn't seem to sit right with the counsel that the Prophet receives revelation for the whole church. And Elder Woodruff was NOT yet the President of the Twelve, which came a few months later in 1880.

True or not, it at least was recorded by Elder Wilford Woodruff and gives us insight as to the thoughts of some of the early brethren at the time. Read it and judge it for yourself. This revelation holds a "low/medium rating".

> (Wilford Woodruff's Journal: 1833-1898 Vol. 7, p.61 (entry after December 31, 1880))
> "Thus saith the Lord unto my servant Wilford Woodruff
>
> I have heard thy prayers, and will answer thy petitions. I will make known unto thee my will concerning the **nation who encumber the land of promise**. And also concerning Zion and her inhabitants. I have already

revealed my will concerning the nation through the mouth of my servant Joseph, who sealed his testimony with his own blood, which testimony has been in force upon all the world from the hour of his death.

What I the Lord have revealed in that testament and decreed upon this nation, and all the nations of the Earth shall be fulfilled, saith the Lord of Hosts. I the Lord have spoken and will be obeyed. My purposes shall be fulfilled upon this nation, and no power shall stay my hand. The hour is at the door when my wrath and indignation shall be poured out upon the wicked of this nation. Their murders, blasphemies, lyings, whoredoms and abominations have come up before my face and before the heavens and the wrath of mine indignation is full.

I have **decreed Plagues to go forth** and lay waste mine enemies and not many years hence they shall not be left to pollute mine heritage. The Devil is ruling over his kingdom and my spirit has no place in the hearts of the rulers of this nation, and the Devil stirs them up to defy my power, and to make war upon my saints. Therefore let mine apostles and mine elders who are faithful obey my commandments which are already written for your profit and guidance.

Thus saith the Lord unto my servant John Taylor and my servant Wilford Woodruff and my servant Orson Pratt and to all the residue of mine Apostles. Have you not gone forth in my name without Purse or scrip and declared the gospel of life and salvation unto this nation and the nations of the Earth and warned them of the judgments which are to come as you have been moved upon by the power of the Holy Ghost and the inspiration of the Lord? You have done this year by year for a whole generation as men count time. Therefore your garments are clean of the blood of this generation and especially of this nation.

Therefore as I have said in a former commandment so I the Lord say again unto mine apostles go ye alone by yourselves whether in heat or in cold and cleanse your feet with water pure water. It matters not whether it be by the running stream or in our closets but bear their testimonies before the Lord and the heavenly hosts.

And when you have all done this then gather yourselves together in your holy places and cloth yourselves in the robes of the Holy Priesthood and there offer up your prayers according to my holy law. Let him who Presides be mouth and kneel upon the holy altar and there let mine apostles bring all there testimonies before my face and before the heavenly hosts and before the justified spirits made perfect.

And thus saith the Lord unto you mine apostles when you bring these testimonies before me let them be presented by name as far as the spirit shall present them unto you, The Presidents of the United States, The Supreme Court, The Cabinet, The Senate & House of Congress of the United States, The Governors of the States and Territories, The Judges & Officers sent unto you and all men & persons who have taken part in persecuting you or bringing distress upon you or your families or have sought your lives or sought to hinder you from keeping my commandments or from enjoying the rights which the Constitutional laws of the land guarantee unto you.

And what I the Lord say unto you mine apostles I say unto my servants the seventies, The high priests, the elders and The priests and all my servants who are pure in heart and who have born testimony unto this nation. Let them go forth & Cleanse their feet in pure water and bear testimony of it unto your Father who is in heaven.

And thus saith the Lord unto mine apostles and mine elders when ye do these things with purity of heart, I the Lord will hear your prayers and am bound by oath and covenant to defend you and fight your battles as I have said in a former commandment it is not my will that mine elders should fight the battles of Zion for I will fight your battles. Nevertheless, <u>let no Man be afraid to lay down his life for my sake for he that layeth down his life for my sake shall find it again and have eternal life.</u>

The nation is ripened in iniquity and the cup of the wrath of mine indignation is full, and I will not stay my hand in judgment upon this nation or the nations of the Earth. I have **decreed wars** and **judgments upon the wicked** and my wrath and indignation are about to be poured out upon them. And the wicked and rebellious shall know that I am God. As I the Lord have spoken so will I the Lord fulfill. **<u>I will spare none who remain in Babylon but I will burn them up</u>** Saith the Lord of Hosts. As I the Lord have suffered so will I put all enemies under my feet, for I the Lord utter my word, and it shall be obeyed and the day of wrath and indignation shall come upon the wicked.

And I say again wo unto that nation or house or people, who seek to hinder my people from obeying the Patriarchal Law of Abraham which leadeth to a celestial glory which has been revealed unto my saints through the mouth of my servant Joseph for whosoever doeth these things shall be damned saith the Lord of Hosts and shall be broken up & washed away from under heaven by the judgments which I have sent forth and shall not return unto me void.

. And thus **with the sword and by bloodshed and with famine & plagues and earthquakes and the thunders of heavens and the vivid lightnings** shall this nation and the nations of the Earth be made to feel the chastening hand of an Almighty God **until they are broken up and destroyed**, and wasted away from under heaven, and no power can stay my hand. Therefore let the wicked tremble. Let them that blaspheme my name hold their lips, for **destruction will swiftly over take them**.

All that I the Lord have spoken through the mouth of my prophets and apostles since the world began concerning the last dispensation and fullness of times, concerning my church which has been called out of the wilderness of darkness and Error, and concerning the Zion and Kingdom of God and concerning Babylon the Great, And what I have spoken through the mouth of my servant Joseph shall all be fulfilled. And though heaven and Earth pass away my words shall not pass away, but shall all be fulfilled saith the Lord.

These revelations and testimonies you have before you. Let my saints search the word of the Lord and treasure up wisdom and be prepared for that which is to come. As I have decreed so shall **my judgments begin at the House of God.** There are those in my church who have a name among you who are adulterers and adulteresses and those who blaspheme my name and those who love and make a lie, and those who revel and drink with the drunken. If they do not speedily repent of their wickedness and abominations, they shall be severed from the ordinances of my house Saith the Lord.

There are many who have need to repent whose hearts are set upon the things of this world, who aspire to the honors of men, and do not honor the Priesthood, nor seek to build up the Kingdom of God as they should. Neither do they learn or comprehend that the rights of the Priesthood are inseparably connected with the powers of heaven and that the powers of heaven cannot be controlled nor handled only upon the principles of righteousness. Such should repent and turn unto the Lord and seek for the Holy Spirit to guide them. **Judgments will begin at my House,** and from thence will they go forth unto the wicked, and the wicked cannot escape. Blessed are the pure in heart, for my blessings await them in this life and eternal Life in the world to come.

Thus Saith the Lord unto you my servants the apostles who dwell in the flesh fear ye not your enemies. Let not your hearts be troubled. I am in your midst. I am your advocate with the Father. I have given mine angels charge concerning you. Mine eyes are upon you. And the eyes of your Heavenly Father and the heavenly hosts, and all justified spirits made perfect are a watching over you.

Your works are manifest before the face of my servants who have sealed their testimony with their blood and before all of my servants of the Twelve Apostles whom I have taken unto myself. The veil is taken from off their faces and they know your works. They await your coming when you have finished your testimony in the flesh.

Therefore be ye faithful until I come. My coming is at the door. Call upon the Lord in mighty prayer. Ask and you shall receive whatever you agree as touching any thing and ask the Father in my name it shall be given unto you. Seek diligently to build Up Zion and magnify your high calling and your enemies shall not prevail over you. Zion shall not be moved out of her place. Zion shall prevail against her enemies. My people shall not be hindered in the building of my temples unto my holy name if they will harken to my voice and do as I command them.

The blood of my servant Joseph & Hyrum and of mine apostles and elders which have been shed for the word of God & testimony of Jesus Christ cries from the ground for vengeance upon the nation who have shed their blood but the blood shall speedily be avenged and shall cease to cry unto me for the hour of God's judgment is fully come and shall be poured out without measure upon the wicked.

But harken & hear O ye apostles elders & people of my church to the word of the Lord concerning you that for all the blessings that I will pour out upon you and the inhabitants of Zion, and the judgments and destructions upon the wicked that I will be inquired of by you to ask the Father in my name to do and to perform these things for you, As I told all the House of Israel by my servant Moses that they should ask at my hand for all those blessing which I the Lord had promised unto Israel in the **Latter Days**, And as I the Lord ordained mine apostles who were with me in my ministry, and promised them that they should sit upon twelve thrones judging the Twelve Tribes of Israel, wo I say unto you mine apostles whom I have raised up in these last days that I have ordained you to bear record of my name and of the Gospel of Jesus Christ **to the Gentiles** first and then to the House of Israel. I have also ordained you to set upon thrones **and judge the Gentiles** and all of the inhabitants of the Earth unto whom you have borne testimony of my name in the day and generation in which you live.

Therefore how great is your calling and responsibility before me. Therefore gird up the loins of your minds and magnify your callings in the fear of God and prepare ye for the coming of the Son of Man which is nigh at the door. No man knoweth the day nor the hour but the Signs of Both Heaven and Earth indicate his Coming as promised by the Mouth of my disciples. The fig trees are leaving and the hour is nigh. Therefore prepare yourselves O ye saints of the Most High God with oil in your lamps, for blessed is he that watcheth for the coming of the Son of Man Again hear ye the word of the Lord O ye mine apostles whom I have chosen in these last days to bear record of my name and to lead my people Israel until the coming of the Son of Man.

I the Lord have raised up unto you my **servant John Taylor to preside over you and to be a Law Giver unto my Church.** He has mingled his blood with that of the martyred prophets. Nevertheless while I have taken my servants Joseph & Hyrum Smith unto myself I have preserved my servant John Taylor for a wise purpose in me. I have also taken many others of the apostles unto myself for I take whom I will take and preserve in life them whom I will preserve according to the council of my own will.

And while my servant **John Taylor is your President I wish to ask the rest of my servants of the apostles** the question

Although you have one to preside over your Quorum and over the Church which is the order of God in all generations, do you not all of you hold the Apostleship which is the highest authority ever given to man on Earth? You do.

Therefore you hold in common the keys of the Kingdom of God in all the world. You each of you have power to unlock the veil of Eternity and hold conversation with God the Father and his Son Jesus Christ, and to have the administration of angels. It is your right privilege & duty to inquire of the Lord his mind & will concerning yourselves the inhabitants of Zion and their interest. **And whenever any one of you receive the word of the Lord, let it be written and presented in your councils and whatever by a united consent you deem wisdom to be presented unto the people let it be presented by the President my servant John Taylor as the word of the Lord.** In this way you will uphold him & strengthen his hands as all the burthen should not rest upon one man. For thus Saith the Lord all of mine Apostles should be full of the Holy Ghost of inspiration and revelation and know the mind & will of God and be prepared for that which is to come. Therefore let mine apostles keep my commandments and obey my laws and the gates of Hell shall not prevail against you. Fear not for lo I am with you until I come. I come quickly, even so Amen."

"George Washington`s Vision" by Anthony Sherman

I originally believed this vision when first read many years ago. It has a familiar ring to America's real history. However, this account has been proven false by many sources including Snoops.com seen here:
http://www.snopes.com/history/american/vision.asp

However, it is important that you, the reader, know that this is a false vision. Because, many Latter-Day Saints still circulate this vision as truth. If you, the reader, know more information about this vision than the documented sources above, please contact me. It has a "low rating"

Anthony Sherman wrote:

You doubtless heard the story of Washington's going to the thicket to pray in secret for aid and comfort from God, the interposition of whose Divine Providence brought us safely through the darkest days of tribulation. One day, I remember it well, when the chilly winds whistled through the leafless trees, though the sky was cloudless and the sun shown brightly, he remained in his quarters nearly all the afternoon alone. When he came out, I noticed that his face was a shade paler than usual. There seemed to be something on his mind of more than ordinary importance. Returning just after dusk, he dispatched an orderly to the quarters who was presently in attendance. After a preliminary conversation of about an hour, Washington, gazing upon his companion with that strange look of dignity which he alone commanded, related the event that occurred that day.

"George Washington's Vision"

This afternoon, as I was sitting at this table engaged in preparing a dispatch, something seemed to disturb me. Looking up, I beheld standing opposite me a singularly beautiful female. So astonished was I, for I had given strict orders not to be disturbed, that it was some moments before I found language to inquire the cause of her presence. A second, a third and even a fourth time did I repeat my question, but received no answer from my mysterious visitor except a slight raising of her eyes.

By this time I felt strange sensations spreading through me. I would have risen but the riveted gaze of the being before me rendered volition impossible. I assayed once more to address her, but my tongue had become useless, as though it had become paralyzed.

A new influence, mysterious, potent, irresistible, took possession of me. All I could do was to gaze steadily, vacantly at my unknown visitor. Gradually the surrounding atmosphere seemed as if it had become filled with sensations, and luminous. Everything about me seemed to rarefy, the mysterious visitor herself becoming more airy and yet more distinct to my sight than before. I now began to feel as one dying, or rather to experience the sensations which I have sometimes imagined accompany dissolution. I did not think, I did not reason, I did not move; all were alike impossible. I was only conscious of gazing fixedly, vacantly at my companion.

Presently I heard a voice saying, "Son of the Republic, look and learn," while at the same time my visitor extended her arm eastwardly, I now beheld a heavy white vapor at some distance rising fold upon fold. This gradually dissipated, and I looked upon a stranger scene. Before me lay spread out in one vast plain all the countries of the world — Europe, Asia, Africa and America. I saw rolling and tossing between Europe and America the billows of the Atlantic, and between Asia and America lay the Pacific.

"Son of the Republic," said the same mysterious voice as before, "look and learn." At that moment I beheld a dark, shadowy being, like an angel, standing or rather floating in mid-air, between Europe and America. Dipping water out of the ocean in the hollow of each hand, he sprinkled some upon America with his right hand, while with his left hand he cast some on Europe. Immediately a cloud raised from these countries, and joined in mid-ocean. For a while it remained stationary, and then moved slowly westward, until it enveloped America in its murky folds. Sharp flashes of lightning gleamed through it at intervals, and I heard the smothered groans and cries of the American people.

A second time the angel dipped water from the ocean, and sprinkled it out as before. The dark cloud was then drawn back to the ocean, in whose heaving billows in sank from view. A third time I heard the mysterious voice saying, "Son of the Republic, look and learn," I cast my eyes upon America and beheld villages and towns and cities springing up one after another until the whole land from the Atlantic to the Pacific was dotted with them.

Again, I heard the mysterious voice say, "Son of the Republic, the end of the century cometh, look and learn." At this the dark shadowy angel turned his face southward, and from Africa I saw an ill omened specter approach our land. It flitted slowly over every town and city of the latter. The inhabitants presently set themselves in battle array against each other. As I continued looking I saw a bright angel, on whose brow rested a crown of light, on which was traced the word "Union," bearing the American flag which he placed between the divided nation, and said, "Remember ye are brethren." Instantly, the inhabitants, casting from them their weapons became friends once more, and united around the National Standard.

"And again I heard the mysterious voice saying "Son of the Republic, look and learn." At this the dark, shadowy angel placed a trumpet to his mouth, and blew three distinct blasts; and taking water from the ocean, he sprinkled it upon Europe, Asia and Africa. Then my eyes beheld a fearful scene: From each of these countries arose thick, black clouds that were soon joined into one. Throughout this mass there gleamed a dark red light by which I saw hordes of armed men, who, moving with the cloud, marched by land and sailed by sea to America. Our country was enveloped in this volume of cloud, and I saw these vast armies devastate the whole county and burn the villages, towns and cities that I beheld springing up. As my ears listened to the thundering of the cannon, clashing of sword, and the shouts and cries of millions in mortal combat, I heard again the mysterious voice saying, "Son of the Republic, look and learn" When the voice had ceased, the dark shadowy angel placed his trumpet once more to his mouth, and blew a long and fearful blast. "Instantly a light as of a thousand suns shone down from above me, and pierced and broke into fragments the dark cloud which enveloped America. At the same moment the angel upon whose head still shone the word Union, and who bore our national flag in one hand and a sword in the other, descended from the heavens attended by legions of white spirits. These immediately joined the inhabitants of America, who I perceived were will nigh overcome, but who immediately taking courage again, closed up their broken ranks and renewed the battle.

Again, amid the fearful noise of the conflict, I heard the mysterious voice saying, "Son of the Republic, look and learn." As the voice ceased, the shadowy angel for the last time dipped water from the ocean and sprinkled it upon America. Instantly the dark cloud rolled back, together with the armies it had brought, leaving the inhabitants of the land victorious!

Then once more I beheld the villages, towns and cities springing up where I had seen them before, while the bright angel, planting the azure standard he had brought in the midst of them, cried with a loud voice: "While the stars remain, and the heavens send down dew upon the earth, so long shall the Union last." And taking from his brow the crown on which blazoned the word "Union," he placed it upon the Standard while the people, kneeling down, said, "Amen."

The scene instantly began to fade and dissolve, and I at last saw nothing but the rising, curling vapor I at first beheld. This also disappearing, I found myself once more gazing upon the mysterious visitor, who, in the same voice I had heard before, said, "Son of the Republic, what you have seen is thus interpreted: Three great perils will come upon the Republic. The most fearful is the third, but in this greatest conflict the whole world united shall not prevail against her. Let every child of the Republic learn to live for his God, his land and the Union." With these words the vision vanished, and I started from my seat and felt that I had seen a vision wherein had been shown to me the birth, progress, and destiny of the United States.

"Moroni`s Prophetic Message to Joseph" by Joseph Smith

This particular statement by Moroni to Joseph Smith was recorded in the Journal of Discourses by Joseph himself. Notice how the order of events flow through this piece. It includes the early church from before 1830, through when Christ will come to the New Jerusalem. (Rating: High)

(Journal of Discourses, 5:339)
"Behold, notwithstanding you have seen this great display of power, by which you may ever be able to detect the evil one, yet I give unto you another sign, and when it comes to pass then know that the Lord is God, and that he will fulfil his purposes, and that the knowledge which this record contains will go to every nation, and kindred, and tongue, and people under the whole heaven.

This is the sign: when these things begin to be known, that is, when it is known that the Lord has shown you these things, the workers of iniquity will seek your overthrow. They will circulate false hoods to destroy your reputation; and also will seek to take your life; but remember this, if you are faithful, and shall hereafter continue to keep the commandments of the Lord, you shall be preserved to bring these things forth; for in due time he will give you a commandment to come and take them. When they are interpreted, the Lord will give the holy priesthood to some, and they shall begin to proclaim this gospel and baptize by water, and after that, they shall have power to give the Holy Ghost by the laying on of their hands.

Then will **persecution rage more and more**; for the iniquities of men shall be revealed, and those who are not built upon the Rock will **seek to overthrow the church**; but it will increase the more opposed, and spread farther and farther, increasing in knowledge till they shall be sanctified, and receive an inheritance where the glory of God will rest upon them; and **when** this takes place, and all things are prepared, **the ten tribes of Israel will be revealed in the north country, whither they have been for a long season**; and **when** this is fulfilled will be brought to pass that saying of the prophet,—'And the **Redeemer shall come to Zion**, and unto them that turn from transgression in Jacob, saith the Lord.'

But, notwithstanding the workers of iniquity shall seek your destruction, the arm of the Lord will be extended, and you will be borne off conqueror if you keep all his commandments. Your name shall be known among the nations, for the work which the Lord will perform by your hands shall cause the righteous to rejoice and the wicked to rage; with the one it shall be had in honor, and with the other in reproach; yet, with these it shall be a terror, **because of the great and marvelous work which shall follow the coming forth of this fullness of the gospel.** Now, go thy way, remembering what the Lord has done for thee, and be diligent in keeping his commandments, and he will deliver thee from temptations and all the arts and devices of the wicked one. Forget not to pray, that thy mind may become strong, that when he shall manifest unto thee, thou mayest have power to escape the evil, and obtain these precious things."

Learning Points:
A.   There is a lot here, but the main portion for the TIMELINE is that WHEN the Great Persecution takes place and glory of God rests upon the Saints of God, then the Lost 10 Tribes return from their Northern retreat. Then Jesus will come to Zion. ....In that order.

Alphabetical Index